SOme SLAVES OF VIRGINIA

THE COHABITATION REGISTERS OF 27 FEBRUARY 1866 FROM THE LOST RECORDS LOCALITIES DIGITAL COLLECTION OF THE LIBRARY OF VIRGINIA

VOLUME III:

Montgomery County,
Prince Edward County,
Richmond County, Roanoke County,
Scott County

COMPILED BY

Sandra Barlau

HERITAGE BOOKS
2019

HERITAGE BOOKS

AN IMPRINT OF HERITAGE BOOKS, INC.

Books, CDs, and more—Worldwide

For our listing of thousands of titles see our website
at
www.HeritageBooks.com

Published 2019 by
HERITAGE BOOKS, INC.
Publishing Division
5810 Ruatan Street
Berwyn Heights, Md. 20740

Cover portraits: Mary Timbers Harrison, her son Scott R. Harrison, Sr.
and grandson Scott R. Harrison, Jr.

International Standard Book Numbers
Paperbound: 978-0-7884-3408-2

Table of Contents

PREFACE

The Library of Virginia's Lost Records Localities Digital Collection is a gold mine of slave information. The following is the Library's description of the Cohabitation Registers:

> "A cohabitation register, or as it is properly titled, Register of Colored Persons...cohabiting together as Husband and Wife on 27 February 1866, was the legal vehicle by which former slaves legitimized both their marriages and their children. The information about an individual person contained in a cohabitation register is literally priceless as it is often the first time that a former slave appeared officially in the public record and because of the extensive kinds of information that the register recorded."

One of the most time-consuming aspects of researching ancestors is reading the handwritten documents. A majority of the writing is hard to decipher and indexes for enslaved and free people of color are rare. Every page of every document needs to be read to determine if a slave is mentioned.

I accessed the Cohabitation Records of the Library of Virginia's Lost Records Localities Digital Collection and put the information in book form. I included an index of the surnames, first names, states, and counties. There are 32 tables comprised of 28 counties.

ABBREVIATIONS

Co – County

dec'd - deceased

est - estimated

f – father

fr wf – first wife

hus - husband

m - mother

mos – months

occ – occupation

off – offspring

pob - place of birth

res – residence

w – wife

wks - weeks

VA - Virginia

INTRODUCTION

These cohabitation records may help you put families together and aid in forming extended family members. The original documents have been transcribed into a database by the Library of Virginia and are on the library's website. (See the Lost Records Localities Digital Collection, Cohabitation Records.) The individual tables in each database can be queried for a name or a place. The original documents are included on the site. The database lists the page and line number for each row of data. The original documents may or may not be numbered.

The tables are comprised of two different types of information: *A Register of Children of Colored Persons Whose Parents Had Ceased to Cohabit Which the Father Recognizes to be His* and *A Register of Colored Persons Cohabiting Together as Husband and Wife.*

The Register of Children usually gives the child's name, age, place of birth, residence, and the last owner. Also included are the parent's names, ages, residences, and last owner.

The Cohabiting Records generally include the husband's and wife's names and ages, their residence, their last owner with his/her residence, and a list of their children and ages plus a date of the start of their cohabitation or the number of years together.

Although the information in each table is similar it may be arranged in different sequences. The place of birth is usually the county and the residence is usually the town. Ages are given and can aid in estimating a birth year. The same applies to estimating a death year. Some registers indicate children by a first wife. Names can be repeated more than once on a page with different owners, wives, and ages.

I indexed the states and counties in order to facilitate searching. Counties are indexed under *County* and include counties not in a titled Table. States other than Virginia are indexed under *State* and include Washington, D.C. (indexed as D.C.). Some cities outside of Virginia did not indicate a state. I put the assumed state in [ ] so it could be indexed.

Some handwriting is difficult to read. In some cases the name has an underscore between letters (e.g. Mi_n_a). Names beginning with an underscore are indexed first (e.g. __mia). Some letters can be mistaken for others: "L" and "S", "T" and "F", J" and "I". The letter "n" can look like "u", "nn" could be "rr".

There are question marks next to some of the names and places in this transcription in which the handwriting is too faint or difficult to read. Be sure to peruse the entire index and the original document to make your own decision regarding the spelling of the name, county or town. You may discover a name that has a similar spelling to the one you are researching.

Good luck in your research.

Table 17 Montgomery County

Register of Colored Persons cohabiting together as Husband and Wife, 1866 Feb 1866

(pg/ln; hus/age; hus pob; hus res; occ; last owner; res; w/age; pob; res; last owner; res; children/ages; date cohab)

1/1: Arnold Merritt 65; Montgomery; Christiansburg; Laborer; David WADE; Montgomery; Rebecca Hughes 63; Buckingham; Christiansburg; John J. WADE; Montgomery; Ø; 10 Dec 1851

1/2: Daniel Jones 25; Campbell; Christiansburg; Carpenter; George COX; Wythe; Ellen Jackson 25; Powhatan; Christiansburg; John MILLER; Montgomery; Ø; 1 Dec 1865

1/3: Mattison Cox 50; Campbell; Christiansburg; Tanner; William COX; Campbell; Mary Jones 55; Campbell; Christiansburg; George COX; Wythe; Ø; 15 Jan 1846

1/4: Benjamin W. Stuart 66; Augusta; Christiansburg; Blacksmith; Daniel LANGHORN; Campbell; Sarah Campbell 52; Montgomery; Christiansburg; Daniel MONTAGUE; Montgomery; Ø; 30 Jan 1857

1/5: Lewis Pate 49; Montgomery; Christiansburg; Farmer; William DAVIS; Montgomery; Elizabeth Anderson 50; Bedford; Christiansburg; James SHIELDS; Montgomery; William J. 9, Sarah J. 21, Emeline 20, Ann 19, Henrietta 17; 20 July 1841

1/6: Granville Saunders 28; Montgomery; Christiansburg; Waiter; George ANDERSON; Montgomery; Maria Brown 25; Montgomery; Christiansburg; Agness INGRAM; Montgomery; Allen 8; 28 Dec 1858

1/7: Dandridge Brown 21; Montgomery; Christiansburg; Waiter; Free; Ø; Mary Curtis 20; Montgomery; Christiansburg; Susan WADE; Montgomery; Ø; 15 Apr 1865

1/8: Epperson Harston 31; Franklin; Christiansburg; Waiter; Elizabeth HARSTON; Franklin; Lucy Ann Turner 29; Bedford; Christiansburg; Joseph SIGMOND; Franklin; Ø; 11 Dec 1856

1

1/9: Albert Johnson 26; Henrico; Christiansburg; Farmer; Augustus HOBSON; Christiansburg; Matilda Morrison 26; Pittsylvania; Christiansburg; James GARDER; Christiansburg; Ellen 8 mos; 1 July 1863

1/10: Richard Willis 45; Culpeper; Christiansburg; Farmer; Benjamin CURTIS; Christiansburg; Chaney Thompson 28; Bedford; Christiansburg; John BIRCHFIELD; Roanoke; Ø; 15 Mar 1861

1/11: Germon Baker 40; Patrick; Christiansburg; Farmer; Thomas WILSON; Christiansburg; Barbara Ann Smith 25; Norfolk; Christiansburg; Russell CARPER; Montgomery; Ø; 7 Dec 1864

1/12: Thomas Preston 31; Bedford; Christiansburg; Farmer; Anna PRESTON; Campbell; Lythia Jane Watson 32; Giles; Christiansburg; John J. WADE; Montgomery; ~~William 3, Mary Jane 7 mos~~; 15 Aug 1856

1/13: Henry Saunders 27; Winchester, Frederick Co. W. Virginia; Christiansburg; Farmer; Arthur McKORKLE; Floyd; Ellen Webster 21; Montgomery; Christiansburg; A.S. WOOLWINE; Montgomery; Jennie 1 mo; 15 Oct 1861

1/14: Spencer Curtis 27; Montgomery; Christiansburg; Farmer; Henry WADE; Montgomery; Emily Scott 30; Rockbridge; Christiansburg; Crockett PIERCE; Montgomery; Kate 4, Emma 1; 12 Mar 1859

1/15: Alfred Walker 33; Mecklenburg; Christiansburg; Blacksmith; Thomas WALLTHAN; Montgomery; Malinda E. Holly 36; Montgomery; Christiansburg; Catharine HARMER; Montgomery; Maria Jane 9, Henry Thomas 5; 10 Nov 1855

1/16: Spencer Haden 65; Montgomery; Christiansburg; Barber; William WADE; Montgomery; Filice Johnson 74; Montgomery; Christiansburg; William B. CHARLTON; Montgomery; Samuel 30; 1 Nov 1829

1/17: Elijah Rawlings 28; Montgomery; Christiansburg; Laborer; Agnes ENGLES; Montgomery; Matilda Curtis 18; Montgomery; Christiansburg; Susanna WADE; Montgomery; Ø; 18 Aug 1865

1/18: Osborn Wilson 28; Mecklenburg; Christiansburg; Blacksmith; Edward CRATICK; Montgomery; Mary Jane Watts 19; Rockbridge; Christiansburg; Thomas D. WOOD; Montgomery; Ø; 15 Nov 1866

1/19: Mitchell Fortner 22; Montgomery; Christiansburg; Farmer; Mary WADE; Montgomery; Nellie Fowler 20; Knox Co., Tennessee; Christiansburg; Henry BUFINGTON; Cabell Co., W. Virginia; Charles L. 2 mos; 10 June 1865

1/20: Gabel Forrow 29; Bath; Christiansburg; Farmer; Margaret MORRISON; Bath; Charlota Carter 36; Rockbridge; Christiansburg; Thomas WOOD; Montgomery; Catherine 1; 1 Aug 1861

1/21: Siras Hobson 60; Cumberland; Christiansburg; Farmer; Rice D. MONTAGUE; Montgomery; Jemimah Beavers 59; Montgomery; Christiansburg; John COOPER; Fayette Co, W. Virginia; Ø; 2 Oct 183_

1/22: Isaac Hogans 42; Pulaski; Christiansburg; Farmer; Elizabeth KENT; Pulaski; Martha Dean 33; Pulaski; Christiansburg; William TRULLINGER?; Pulaski; Fanny 12, William 10, Ellen 8, Gilbert 6, Humphrey 5, Cornelia 2, Jacob 1; 29 Oct 1853

1/23: James Melton 30; Franklin; Christiansburg; Ann FLIGGER; Montgomery; Mary Niece 34; Montgomery; Christiansburg; William DAVIS; Montgomery; Herrietta 6, Carrie 3, George M. 5 mos; 1 Jan 1858

1/24: William Wilburn 29; Pulaski; Christiansburg; Sheffield BAYERS; Pulaski; Catharine Odes 21; Kanawha Co. W. Virginia; Christiansburg; William BUSTRE; Kanawha Co., W. Virginia; Ø; 10 July 1865

1/25: Paten Tyens 40; Campbell; Christiansburg; Farmer; James W. KERBY; Montgomery; Eliza Batton 46; Montgomery; Christiansburg; James W. KERBY; Montgomery; Martha S. 19, Thomas A. 16, George W. 14, Truelove 10; 4 Oct 1847

1/26: Squire Fordice 60; Montgomery; Christiansburg; Farmer; John BIRCHFIELD; Montgomery; Ann Thompson 45; Bedford; Christiansburg; Abraham BIRCHFIELD; Montgtomery; James 25, Serena 19, Peter 10, Charles 9, Kent 6; 1 Dec 1836

1/27: Minnis Headen 34; Bedford; Christiansburg; Blacksmith; Elizabeth HEADEN; Montgomery; Fannie Carey 26; Montgomery; Christiansburg; Mary WADE; Montgomery; Minnis 5, John H. 2; 23 June 1860

1/28: Thomas James 23; Mecklenburg; Christiansburg; Farmer; Robert R. LIPSCOME; Montgomery; Mary Frances Morgan 1_; Montgomery; Christiansburg; Henry FOLTZ; Montgomery; Ø; 18 June 1864

1/29: James Carr 26; Albemarle; Christiansburg; Farmer; Egbert WATSON; Albemarle; Harriet Souders 2_; Montgomery; Christiansburg; Michael SOUDERS; Montgomery; Ø; 30 Mar 1864

1/30: Harrison King 41; Giles; Christiansburg; Farmer; Jame? HOGE; Montgomery; Eliza Campbell 28; Washington (D.C.); Christiansburg; Giles THOMAS; Montgomery; George 4, Nancy 2; 25 Dec 1861

1/31: Anderson Carter 48; Bedford; Christiansburg; Farmer; Elizabeth CARTER; Franklin; Fanny Feather 23; Bedford; Christiansburg; William FEATHER; Roanoke; John 5, Ann B. 3; 10 Feb 1859

1/32: John Lawson 45; Montgomery; Christiansburg; Farmer; Jacob ZULL; Montgomery; Sarah Brown 46; Franklin; Christiansburg; William SMITH; Montgomery; Rhoda E. 16, Maria J. 13, Samuel W. 11, Mary J. 8, Cager Monroe 5, John T. 1; 18 Apr 1848

1/33: Richard Saunders 82; Amelia; Christiansburg; Farmer; William HENDERSON; Botetourt; Margaret Dandridge 65; Montgomery; Christiansburg; James PRESTON; Montgomery; Robert 38, Edward 37, Edmonia 35, David 33, Amanda 25; 12 May 1825

1/34: Daniel Smith 24; Montgomery; Christiansburg; Engineer; Charles H. BARNETT; Montgomery; Salinda Barbason 24; Campbell; Christiansburg; Free Born; Ø; Maranda Kirk? 1; 30 Oct 1864

1/35: Othello Fraction 21; Montgomery; Christiansburg; Farmer; Robert PRESTON; Montgomery; Mary Carr 27; Henry; Christiansburg; Ballard PRESTON; Montgomery; Ø; 10 May 1864

1/36: Mattison Beverly 54; Appomattox; Christiansburg; Farmer; Free Born; Ø; Elizabeth Beverly 38; Buckingham; Christiansburg; Free Born; Ø; Rasmus 24, Silvestus 23, William 22, Samuel 19, Lurany? 17, Mary 13; 6 Aug 1848

1/37: Jacob Ease 36; Montgomery; Christiansburg; Farmer; James KENT; Montgomery; Catharine Page 27; Montgomery; Christiansburg; James KENT; Montgomery; Amanda J. 12, James 6, Sanders C. 5, Emma J. 1; 1 Jan 1854

1/38: ___ille Sherman 3_; Montgomery; Christiansburg; Farmer; James KENT; Montgomery; Maria __kins 22; Montgomery; Christiansburg; James KENT; Montgomery; Henry 1; 24 Dec

1/39:____ 39; Montgomery; Christiansburg; Farmer; Ø; Ø; Millie Ann Henderson; Montgomery; Christiansburg; James KENT; Montgomery; Lewis 17, Alice 8, Richard 3, Eliza 6, ___ 1; Mar

2/1: Henry Washington 60; James City; Montgomery; Shoemaker; Alexander ESKRIDGE; Montgomery; Elizabeth Johnson 38; Montgomery; Montgomery; Lloyd LAGER; Montgomery; Rhoda 15, Clara 14, Henry 12, Charles 9, Walter 8, Cecelia A. 6, Ellen 4, Kate E. 1; 10 Dec 1850

2/2: David Carey 22; Montgomery; Montgomery; Farmer; Mary WADE; Montgomery; Angeline Johnson 19; Cabell Co., W. Virgina; Montgomery; Robert HOLBEE; Cabell Co., W. Virginia; Ø; 16 July 1865

2/3: Jeremiah Preston 42; Bedford; Montgomery; Laborer; John DYE; Roanoke; Louisa Wright 39; Roanoke; Montgomery; James HUFF: Roanoke; Ø; 14 Nov 1853

2/4: George Fortner 27; Montgomery; Montgomery; Farmer; Hamilton WADE; Montgomery; Julia Davis 34; Montgomery; Montgomery; Robert LATIMER; Montgomery; Andrew 3, Eliza 2, Linda 9 mos; 15 Nov 1861

2/5: Robert Smith 49; Caroline; Montgomery; Farmer; Daniel HOGE; Montgomery; Nancy Williams 34; Pulaski; Montgomery; James HOGE; Montgomery; John 11, Henry 6, Robert 3, Thomas 1; 5 Mar 1847

2/6: William Campbell 26; Montgomery; Montgomery; Farmer; Hamilton SHIELDS; Montgomery; Josephine Campbell 23; Montgomery; Montgomery; Rice D. MONTAGUE; Montgomery; McClellan 6, Sarah 4, Mary 3, Samuel 1; 2 Jan 1860

2/7: Norbern Banks 48; Roanoke; Montgomery; Miller; Nathaniel HARVEY; Montgomery; Rachel Burk 48; Roanoke; Montgomery; Nathaniel HARVEY; Latitia A. 26, Mariah L. 20, Ellen S. 18, Bessie 15, William G. 14, Mary R. 10; 25 Dec 1840

2/8: Robert McQua 55; Mecklenburg; Montgomery; Farmer; Edward CRATICK; Montgomery; Clarisa Legan 45; Montgomery; Montgomery; Millie WADE; Ø; 1 May 1857

2/9: Benjamin Dill 37; Montgomery; Montgomery; Farmer; John J. WADE; Montgomery; Matilda Wang__ 37; Montgomery; Montgomery; Wadde CURRAN; Nelson 13, Ester 11, Shiptan 9, John 6; 25 Dec 1853

2/10: John Alexander 27; Montgomery; Montgomery; Farmer; Caper GRANT; Roane Co, Tennessee; Sarah J. Carter 24; Roane Co, Tennessee; Montgomery; Caper GRANT; Ø; 15 Oct 1863

2/11: Alexander Dawson 40; Lunenburg; Montgomery; Farmer; William A. STONE; Montgomery; Grace Paters 40; Lunenburg; Montgomery; William A. STONE; Montgomery; Ø; 1 Sept 1846

2/12: Allen Lewis 49; Montgomery; Montgomery; Farmer; Hiram HORNBERGER; Montgomery; Charlotta Palmer 46; Pulaski; Montgomery; Margaret TAYLOR; Pulaski; Henry 22, Ann 20, Easter 19, Lewis 17, Julia 14, Flemming 12, John 10, Sarah 10, Isabel 6, Crockett 5, Lucy 2; 20 June 1840

2/13: Joseph Robinson 38; Gloucester; Montgomery; Farmer; John B. RADFORD; Montgomery; Margaret Forge 29; Pulaski; Montgomery; Margaret TAYLOR; Polaski; Ø; 25 Nov 1860

2/14: George Sermon 24; Montgomery; Montgomery; Laborer; Charles H. LYNCH; Campbell; Laticia Campbell; Montgomery; Montgomery; Rice D. MONTAGUE; Montgomery; Clay 9, George 7, Sarah 5, Ida B. 2, Charles 10 mos; 15 May 1856

2/14: Scotland Stokes 43; Lunenburg; Montgomery; Farmer; William A. STONE; Montgomery; Parhena/Zarhena Bragg 30; Lunenburg; Montgomery; William A. STONE; Montgomery; Cesar 15, Permelia 13, Richard 11, Mary S. 8, Millie 6, Harriet V. 4, Robert D. 2; 15 Jan 1852

2/15: William Jones 81; King William; Montgomery; Farmer; Alexander ESKRIDGE; Montgomery; Millie Akens 70; Henrico; Montgomery; Alexander ESKRIDGE; Montgomery; Richard 41, Charles 38, Daniel 35, Gabel 32, Moses 28, William 23; 1 Oct 1824

2/16: Robert Jones 28; Lunenburg; Montgomery; Farmer; White COLEMAN; Halifax; Margaret Hancock 27; Kanawha Co, W. Virginia; Montgomery; William BUSTON; Kanawha Co W. Virginia; Ø; 25 Oct 1863

2/17: Barnet Brown 24; Montgomery; Montgomery; Farmer; David HALL; Montgomery; Josephine Barrett 24; Montgomery; Montgomery; Charles MILLER; Montgomery; William P. 3; 15 Nov 1862

2/18: Robert Wilbern 70; Halifax; Montgomery; Farmer; Wadde CURRAN; Montgomery; Angeline Barrett; 59; Pulaski; Montgomery; Jacob SHUFFLEBARGER; Pulaski; William 32; 1 Oct 1825

2/19: Hamilton Brown 26; Montgomery; Montgomery; Farmer; William MARTIN; Pulaski; Ruth Finley 23; Montgomery; Montgomery; John COMPTON; Bland; Ø; 25 Dec 18_5

2/20: Samuel Smith 37; Russell; Montgomery; Farmer; Creed TAYLOR; Montgomery; Julia Frow 28; Russell; Montgomery; Creed TAYLOR; Montgomery; Gilbert 10, Sarah 8, Margaret 5, Robert 4, Joseph 3, Mary 1; 1 Jan 1854

2/21: William D. Street 55; Wythe; Montgomery; Farmer; John B. RADFORD; Montgomery; Nancy Parmer 41; Pulaski; Montgomery; John B. RADFORD; Montgomery; Millie 22, John 19, William 16, Edmond 14, Pocahontas 12, Lydia A. 9, Buford 6, James 4, Julia 1; 10 July 1841

2/22: William Burton 30; Bedford; Montgomery; Montgomery; Edward CHRISTIAN; Campbell; Rachel Anderson 37; Bath; Montgomery; Alexander ESKRIDGE; Montgomery; John P. 1; 25 Dec 1863

2/23: George Clark 30; Patrick; Montgomery; Farmer; Mary STAPLES;; Greenboro, No. Carolina; Biddie Barrett 21; Montgomery; Montgomery; Mary TAYLOR; Montgomery; Walla 5, Nancy 3, Mary N. 1; 10 Dec 1860

2/24: Isaac Glenn 46; Montgomery; Montgomery; Farmer; John D. HOWE; Pulaski; Maria J. Hunter 35; Pulaski; Montgomery; Crockett BROWN; Pulaski; Eliza 21, Millie 17, Harvey 14, Anderson 11, Arminta 8, Harry 6; 25 Dec 1845

2/25: Booker Sefted 43; Bedford; Montgomery; Farmer; John GOOD; Montgomery; Martha A. SHAW 24; Franklin; Montgomery; Griffith D. BUSH; Montgomery; Priscilla 1; 20 Dec 1864

2/26: Harry A. Trueheart 69; Bath; Montgomery; Farmer; Alexander ESKRIDGE; Montgomery; Jane Merritt 38; Bedford; Montgomery; Thomas CHRISTIAN; Montgomery; Caroline 9, Easter 5; 15 Mar 1855

2/27: Felix Johnson 30; Knox Co, Tennessee; Montgomery; Brick Layer; John N. LYLE; Montgomery; Mary Carr 21; Prince Edward; Montgomery; Egbert WATSON; Prince Edward; John W. 1; 14 Apr 1865

2/28: Ferry Fields 60; Campbell; Montgomery; Farmer; Eli FLIGGER; Montgomery; Mary Tinsley 33; Buchanan; Montgomery; Alexander ESKRIDGE; Montgomery; Ø; 22 May 1854

2/29: Gordon Mills 30; Pulaski; Montgomery; Farmer; Daniel HOGE; Montgomery; Ellen Reed 33; Caroline; Montgomery; Daniel HOGE; Montgomery; James 8, Walter 2, Gorden 8 mos; 15 Oct 1856

2/30: Mills Black 36; Pulaski; Montgomery; Farmer; John D. HOWE; Pulaski; Hannah Ripper 30; Pulaski; Montgomery; William HOGE; Pulaski; John 14, Stuart 12, Nancy 10, Lucinda 8, James 7, Andrew 6, Elizabeth 4, Olivia _. 1; 8 Apr 1850

2/31: Joseph Jemison 58; Roanoke; Montgomery; Farmer; John SLUSER; Montgomery; Frances Hardee 39; Augusta; Montgomery; John SLUSHER; Montgomery; Catherine 17; 18 Feb 1846

2/32: Benjamin Anderson 48; Cumberland; Montgomery; Farmer; John MILLER; Pulaski; Julia Granville 27; Montgomery; Montgomery; William SMITH; Montgomery; Ø; 15 Oct 1859

2/33: Wesley Wagner 24; Pulaski; Montgomery; Farmer; Daniel HOGE; Montgomery; Sarah Coleman 19; Montgomery; Montgomery; Daniel HOGE; Montgomery; Alice 3, Margaret J. 1; 25 Dec 1862

2/34: Peter Anderson 47; Montgomery; Montgomery; Farmer; William DOBBINS; Pulaski; Nancy Jones 39; Montgomery; Montgomery; Mary TAYLOR; Montgomery; Sidney 17; 10 Feb 1848

2/35: Robert Clark 27; Patrick; Montgomery; Farmer; Mary STAPLES; Greenboro Co, No. Carolina; Sarah A. Woodfock 24; Caroline; Montgomery; Samuel STAPLES; Patrick; Robert 4, David 1; 7 Sept 1860?

2/36: Daniel White 50; Bedford; Montgomery; Richard P. JONES; Montgomery; Catharine Ingram 43; Pulaski; Montgomery; Richard P. JONES; Montgomery; Thomas R. 8, James B. 5, Julia A. 3; 26 Dec 1854

2/37: ___ Phillips 33; Floyd; Montgomery; Laborer; Edward HAMMITT; Montgomery; Clementine Jones 37; Montgomery; Montgomery; Edward HAMMITT; Montgomery; William R. 7, Nancy R. 3; 21 Oct 1855

2/38: ___ ___ 39; Floyd; Montgomery; Farmer; John LUCAS; Montgomery; C__cia Lewis 38; Ø; Montgomery; Nathaniel HAR__; Montgomery; Harriet R. 11, James 7, Carter 4, Floyd; 15 Dec 185_

3/1: ___ Scott 45; Roanoke; Montgomery; Farmer; William THOMAS; Montgomery; Margaret Snyder 29; Montgomery; Montgomery; Blair COOK; Montgomery; William 12, Charlotta 10, Lucy C. 8, Charles E. 6, Robert 3, Tobias 6 wks; 10 Oct 1853

3/2: Thomas Dill 31; Montgomery; Montgomery; Farmer; David WADE; Montgomery; Elizabeth Greer 28; Nottoway; Montgomery; Henry FOLTZ; Montgomery; Virginia 12, Joseph 8, Eliza 5, Spencer 2; 8 May 1854

3/3: Monroe Baily 34; Roanoke; Montgomery; Farmer; Henry EDMONSON; Montgomery; Susan Boyd _7; Montgomery; Montgomery; John GARDNER; Montgomery; Ø; 12 Apr 1852

3/4: Joseph Dill 34; Montgomery; Montgomery; Farmer; John WADE; Montgomery; Adaline Brooks 23; Montgomery; Montgomery; Harvey BLACK; Montgomery; Ø; 10 Sept 1862

3/5: Taylor McNorton 45; Montgomery; Montgomery; Farmer; Sarah A. PRESTON; Montgomery; Syrena Montague 42; Montgomery; Montgomery; Sarah A. PRESTON; Montgomery; Mary C. 12, Edward P. 10, Hugh F. 7, James W. 3, Charles M. 1; 26 Oct 1850

3/6: Frank McNorton 29; Montgomery; Montgomery; Laborer; George GILMORE; Pittsylvania; Lucy Dabney 24; Albemarle; Montgomery; George WILMER; Pittsylvania; Emily 4, Mildred 2; 15 Dec 1862

3/7: Peter Nowlen 30; Goochland; Montgomery; Laborer; Mary MOORE; Henrico; Eliza Aplen 31; Washington; Montgomery; Nancy APLEN; Goochland; Ø; 5 July 1863

3/8: Henry Johnson 36; Pulaski; Montgomery; Farmer; Walter PRESTON; Montgomery; Louisa Boone 24; Pulaski; Montgomery; Preston PUGH; Montgomery; Eviline 7 mos; 25 Dec 1864

3/9: William Pondexter 28; Henry; Montgomery; Blacksmith; Balard PRESTON; Montgomery; Elizabeth Burks 22; Montgomery; Montgomery; Sarah PRESTON; Montgomery; Ø; 26 Dec 1861

3/10: Abraham Carter 22; Henrico; Montgomery; Farmer; Lerod BOWLER; Henrico; Charlotta Fisher 20; Northampton; Montgomery; George FERGUSON; Bowling Green Co, Kentucky; Samuel 3, Millie? 6 wks; 1 June 1862

3/11: Joshua Lawton 28; Buford Dist, So. Carolina; Montgomery; Farmer; Free Born; Ø; Rebecca Stewart 30; Greenbrier; Montgomery; Daniel LANGHORN; Campbell; Isabella 1; 1 Jan 1863

3/12: Charles Williams 25; Montgomery; Montgomery; Farmer; Henry FOLTZ; Montgomery; Charity Clark 18; Pittsylvania; Montgomery; Henry FOLTZ; Montgomery; Mary Lucy 11 mos; 1 Aug 1864

3/13: Henry Lewis 32; Spotsylvania; Montgomery; Laborer; Ann E. DANGERFIELD; Spotsylvania; Mary Johnson 36; Montgomery; Montgomery; Hiram HORNBERGER; Montgomery; Germinia? 9, James 7, Isabella 5, William R. 2; 1 Jan1856

3/14: James Harvey 23; Campbell; Montgomery; Farmer; George CALAHAN; Montgomery; Emma Taylor 21; Montgomery; Montgomery; Free Born; Ø; Charles 3, Lucy 1; 15 Aug 1862

3/15: __h Gray 42; Prince Edward; Montgomery; Farmer; James GARNETT; Montgomery; Elizabeth Taylor 35; Roanoke; Montgomery; Joseph DELWEILER; Roanoke; William M. 5; 25? Dec 186_

3/16: __ny Stratton 40; St. Louis, Missouri; Montgomery; Farmer; Ferdinard ROWER; Pulaski; Ersie Calvin 30; Jackson, Mississippi; Montgomery; Ferdinand ROWER; Pulaski; Sophia 6, Moses 1; 25 Dec 18_5

3/17: ___ Smith 26; Henry; Montgomery; Farmer; Henry BERNET; Henry; Charlotte Barkes 24; Montgomery; Montgomery; Sarah PRESTON; Montgomery; Reuben 3, Caroline 1; 28 Dec 1863

3/18: __nk Moon 28; Montgomery; Montgomery; Farmer; George GILMER; Pittsylvania; Lucy Carter 21; James City; Montgomery; George WILMER; Pittsylvania; Daniel 3, William 4 mos; 1 Jan 1862

3/19: __nas Baker 69; Spotsylvania; Montgomery; Laborer; Ann E. DANGERFIELD; Spotsylvania; Martha Jones 63; Bedford; Montgomery; Francis HENDERSON; Montgomery; Emily 16, John H. 13, Jane A. 11, Margaret 8, Minerva 4; 10 Feb 1848

3/20: __ham Edmonson 28; Montgomery; Montgomery; Farmer; Thomas M. BARNET; Montgomery; Lucy Jeffers 38; Montgomery; Montgomery; Sarah DUDLEY; Montgomery; Laticia M. 4, Virginia F. 2, Ratleth W. 9 mos; 1 Sept 1861

3/21: Abraham Crawford 27; Buckingham; Montgomery; Farmer; Alexander FERGUSON; Franklin; Willie Talliaffero 38; Montgomery; Montgomery; Sarah TALLIAFFERO; Franklin; Ø; 22 Dec 1885

3/22: John Tollowell 36; Franklin; Montgomery; Farmer; James CALOWAY; Franklin; Mary Kent 34; Franklin; Montgomery; James CALOWAY; Franklin; Frances 6, Eliza A. 4, Lucy J. 1; 10 Mar 1859

3/23: David Williams 21; Franklin; Montgomery; Farmer; Mary ALDRIDGE; Floyd; Rebecca Kent 18; Franklin; Montgomery; Charles REYNOLDS; Franklin; Mary 1; Dec

3/24: William Kyles 54; Montgomery; Montgomery; Farmer; James OTEY; Montgomery; Julia Ann SHERMAN 39; Wythe; Montgomery; James OTEY; Montgomery; Calvin 24, Edie 22, Margaret 20, Floyd 19, Marie 17, Mary 16, Edward 14, Granville 13, Sarah 8, Caroline 7; Aug

3/25: James Summons 46; Botetourt; Montgomery; Farmer; Ferdinand ROSS; Montgomery; Amanda Brown 29; Bedford; Montgomery; John STONER; Bedford; Emiline 8, Abraham 10 mos; Dec

3/26: William Green 37; Montgomery; Montgomery; Farmer; William GARNET; Montgomery; Nancy Price 28; Floyd; Montgomery; Pleasant PRICE; Franklin; Susanna 13, Sarah J. 12, Elizabeth 11, Philice A. 6; 10 June 1851

3/27: Samuel Saunders 57; Montgomery; Montgomery; Farmer; Charles Peck; Montgomery; Lucy 52; Montgomery; Montgomery; Charles PECK; Montgomery; James H. 20; 20 July 1846

3/28: Robert H. Robertson 21; Lancaster; Montgomery; Farmer; James OTEY; Montgomery; Caroline M. Otey 20; Bedford; Montgomery; James OTEY; Montgomery; Ø; 25 Dec 1865

3/29: John Turner 40; Loudoun; Montgomery; Farmer; John JONES; Loudoun; Malinda Lustra 25; Floyd; Montgomery; William LUSTRA; Floyd; Ø; 1 Jan 1864

3/30: Jefferson Hardee 23; Pulaski; Montgomery; Farmer; Floyd WALL; Montgomery; Sophia James 20; Franklin; Montgomery; Floyd WALL; Montgomery; Henrietta 3, Sheridan 9 mos; 14 June 1862

3/31: Henry Guerrant 38; Franklin; Montgomery; Farmer; William GUERRANT; Montgomery; Ann Brown 27; Montgomery; Montgomery; William GUERRANT; Montgomery; Giles 8; 25 Nov 1852

3/32: Albert Pattison 43; Montgomery; Montgomery; Farmer; Hugh CROCKETT; Montgomery; Charlotte Taylor 25; Roanoke; Montgomery; Charles T. BARNETT; Montgomery; George 4, John 2; 25 Dec 1861

3/33: Moses Hopkins 64; Pulaski; Montgomery; Farmer; James R. KENT; Montgomery; Leanna Lehm? 49; Pulaski; Montgomery; James R. KENT; Montgomery; Ø; 25 Dec 185_

3/34: Alexander Hopkins 24; Montgomery; Montgomery; Farmer; James R. KENT; Montgomery; Edie Kyle 25; Wythe; Montgomery; James OTEY; Montgomery; Washington 3; 25 Jan 1861

3/35: Silas Melvine 30; Montgomery; Montgomery; Waiter; Jackson LUCAS; Montgomery; Martha Brooks 26; Franklin; Montgomery; Daniel BROWN; Montgomery; Eliza M. 3; 10 Nov 1862

3/36: Lewis Whitting 65; Albemarle; Montgomery; Farmer; William WHITTING; Roanoke; Silvia Gray 21; Montgomery; Montgomery; James BARNETT; Montgomery; Emiline 23; Mary 19, Ellen 18; __ Sept 1835

3/37: Wyatt Price 37; Henrico; Montgomery; Farmer; Robert CHRISTIAN; New Kent; Rose Johnson 36; Charles City; Montgomery; Abraham CHRISTIAN; New Kent; Ø; 12 Apr 1855

3/38: __ge Brooks; ___; Montgomery; Farmer; Thomas SHANNON; Giles; Rhoda Thompson 3_; Giles; Montgomery; Samuel CHARLTON; Giles; Charles W. 12; 20 Nov 1852

3/39: ___; ___; Montgomery; Farmer; James OTEY; Montgomery; Christian Jackson; Montgomery; Montgomery; James OTEY; Montgomery; Ø; 10 Sept 18_4

4/1: Noah Saunders 37; Roanoke; Montgomery; Farmer; Free Born; Ø; Maria Griffin 37; Montgomery; Montgomery; John PEPPER; Montgomery; George A. 8, Louisa 6, Charles E. 2, Ellie 9 mos; Dec

4/2: Jacob Henry 46; Charlotte; Montgomery; Farmer; Robert A. MOULTON; Bland; Julia Smith 21; Middlesex; Montgomery; Stillman SNOW; Pulaski; Frances 2; 10 June 1863

4/3: Frank Dean 40; Cumberland; Montgomery; Farmer; James HAMMIT; Montgomery; Mary Taylor 34; Montgomery; Montgomery; James HAMMIT; Montgomery; Henry 9, Josephine 7, Jennie 4, Frank 1; 25 Dec 1856

4/4: James? Johnson 35; Montgomery; Montgomery; Farmer; Charles BOYER; Montgomery; Dicia Sephas 25; Wythe; Montgomery; Charles BOYER; Montgomery; Joseph 8, Philice 7, James 5, Flora 1; 16 Sept 1856

4/5: Archer Boon 48; Pulaski; Montgomery; Farmer; Gordon CLOYD; Pulaski; Emma Brand 28; Amelia; Montgomery; Austin SEAY?; Amelia; Elvira 4 mos; 1 Jan 1855

4/6: Thomas Griffin 48; Botetourt; Montgomery; Farmer; John D. BARNETT; Montgomery; Sarah Legans 37; Montgomery; Montgomery; Free Born; Ø; Giles 22, John 19; 28 July 1839

4/7: John Fraction 60; Montgomery; Montgomery; Farmer; Robert PRESTON; Montgomery; Fanny Johnson 57; Floyd; Montgomery; Ballard PRESTON; Montgomery; Ø; 25 Dec 1859

4/8: Calvin Saunders 37; Franklin; Montgomery; Farmer; James CALOWAY; Franklin; Amanda Reynolds 25; Floyd; Montgomery; James CALOWAY; Franklin; Sarah 8, Benjamin 7, Minerva 3, David 2; 25 Dec 1856

4/9: Armstead Raglin 38; Albemarle; Montgomery; Farmer; George GILMER; Albemarle; Ellen Fraction 37; Montgomery; Montgomery; George GILMER; Albemarle; Ø; 18 Dec 1856

4/10: George Williams 39; Alabama; Montgomery; Farmer; Jacob KENT; Montgomery; Julia Bratton 40; Montgomery; Montgomery; Jacob KENT; Montgomery; Virginia 17, Washington 13, Morris A. 7, Henry 2, Robert 2 mos; 10 Sept 1847

4/11: Orville McNorton 25; Montgomery; Montgomery; Farmer; William B. PRESTON; Montgomery; Easter Jane Fraction 21; Montgomery; Montgomery; James PRESTON; Montgomery; Ethel 1; 28 Dec 1863

4/12: George W. Russell 37; Wythe; Montgomery; Shoemaker; Gordon KENT; Wythe; Lavinia Green 18; Baltimore Co., Maryland; Montgomery; Zediah WILSON; Montgomery; Ø; 10 Dec 1865

4/13: James Hickman 37; Giles; Montgomery; Farmer; Gordon CLOYD; Pulaski; Louisa Anderson 38; Montgomery; Montgomery; Floyd McDANIEL; Montgomery; Floyd H. 6, Jerry 4 mos; 1 Apr 1858

4/14: Henry Jackson 33; Roanoke; Montgomery; Farmer; Jonas HENDERSON; Montgomery; Almeta Williams 25; Montgomery; Montgomery; James HOGE; Montgomery; Margaret A. 3, Henrietta 1; 18 Dec 1861

4/15: Henry Boles 64; Campbell; Montgomery; Farmer; Frank HENDERSON; Montgomery; Nancy Winfer 51; Montgomery; Montgomery; Jonas HENDERSON; Montgomery; Charles C. 19, James N. 19, Samuel A. 16; 10 Feb

4/16: Caswell Edmonson 43; Montgomery; Montgomery; Farmer; Maria EDMONSON; Montgomery; Martha Reb 45; Montgomery; Montgomery; Howard PAYTON; Montgomery; Cornelius 27, Ann 21; 10 Nov

4/17: Lewis Edmonson 75; Montgomery; Montgomery; Farmer; Maria EDMONSON; Montgomery; Rebeca Shavers 53?; Cumberland; Montgomery; Free Born; Ø; Ø; 20 Oct

4/18: Matthew Page 30; Montgomery; Montgomery; Farmer; James KENT; Montgomery; Frances P. Hatcher 21; Montgomery; Montgomery; Parris? WALL; Montgomery; John Page 2; 1 Apr

4/19: Isaac Rees? 57; Montgomery; Montgomery; Farmer; Howard PATON; Montgomery; Lucy Garitson 46; Montgomery; Montgomery; Charles BARNETT; Montgomery; Martha 35, Clary 22, Caswell 17, George 10, Margaret 5; 4 Sept

4/20: Gibson Brooks 20; Fauquier; Montgomery; Farmer; Frank SMITH; Fauquier; Adaline Brooks 30; Montgomery; Montgomery; Jacob KEISTER; Montgomery; Ø; 10 June

4/21: Jeremiah Burrell 51; Surry; Montgomery; Farmer; Nancy BURK; Monroe; Sarah Ann Lee 44; Montgomery; Montgomery; Elizabeth AMOS; Montgomery; Lidia J. 2, Nancy _. 30, Robert 27, Nathaniel 24, Elva 22, Elizabeth 20, Thomas 12, John 8; 14 Feb 1833

4/22: Adam Parmer 55; Pulaski; Montgomery; Farmer; John B. RADFORD; Montgomery; Mary Middleton 55; Bedford; Montgomery; John B. RADFORD; Montgomery; Harriet 19, Margaret 17, Albert 11, Samuel 9; 1 Oct 1832

4/23: _ratton 35; Montgomery; Montgomery; Farmer; Archbald WHITE; Montgomery; Susan Williamson 39; Albemarle; Montgomery; Egbert WATSON; Albemarle; Reuben 11, Nancy 9, Thomas 7, Gilbert 5, Agness 4, Mary 2; 2 Oct 1854

4/24: _verly 48; Montgomery; Montgomery; Farmer; Floyd McDONALD; Montgomery; Lucinda Brown 45; Pulaski; Montgomery; William THOMAS; Montgomery; Ø; 30 July 1846

4/25: __adley 63; Montgomery; Montgomery; Farmer; Archbald WHITE; Montgomery; Leanna Smith 55; Bedford; Montgomery; Archbald WHITE; Montgomery; Gilbert 35; 15 Dec 1830

4/26: William Caloway 25; Amherst; Montgomery; Farmer; James KENT; Montgomery; Elizabeth Campbell 19; Montgomery; Montgomery; James KENT; Montgomery; Ellen 5, Anna 3, Rebecca 1; 19 July 1861

4/27: John Lestre 31; Lunenburg; Montgomery; Farmer; Free Born; Ø; Anna Pate 22; Montgomery; Montgomery; James SIMPKINS; Montgomery; William H. 2, Isaac J. 1; 11 Apr 1863

4/28: William Lewis 39; Montgomery; Montgomery; Farmer; Gabel WHORTON; Montgomery; Emily L. Pate 23; Montgomery; Montgomery; Gabel WHORTON; Montgomery; Ø; 25 Dec 1858

4/29: Anderson Stone 26; Prince Edward; Montgomery; Farmer; James STONE; Montgomery; Harriet Parmer 28; Montgomery; Montgomery; John B. RADFORD; Montgomery; Jacob 5 mos; 1 Jan 1865

4/30: Harvey Gun 58; Montgomery; Montgomery; Farmer; Mary TAYLOR; Montgomery; Fannie Brown 57; Montgomery; Montgomery; David P. HALL; Montgomery; Ø; 1 Feb 1860

4/31: Albert Day 45; Worchester Co. Maryland; Montgomery; Farmer; Henry RIPPLE; Montgomery; Martha Peck 32; Franklin; Montgomery; John McDONALD; Montgomery; Hugh 5; 10 Sept 1858

4/32: Thomas Morris 66; Henry; Montgomery; Blacksmith; Berin NORMEN; Henry; Phebe Finney 65; Franklin; Montgomery; James SIMPKINS; Montgomery; Eliza 27, Isam 25, Ann 19; 15 Dec 1831

4/33: John Campbell 51; Cumberland; Montgomery; Farmer; Ann KENT; Montgomery; Nancy King 47; Montgomery; Montgomery; Ann KENT; Montgomery; William 29, Jacob 25, Elizabeth 21, Laura 18, John 13, Champ 10; 10 Oct 1835

4/34: William Jones 31; Pulaski; Montgomery; Farmer; Jane PETERMAN; Montgomery; Lucy Dandridge 30; Montgomery; Montgomery; William PECK; Montgomery; Charles 6, L. Norvell 8 mos; 20 Jan 1855

4/35: Simon Rice 22; Wayne; Montgomery; Farmer; James B. HARLEY; Montgomery; Ann Madders 23?; Montgomery; Montgomery; Gordon HALL; Montgomery; Mary 11 mos; 25 Dec 1864

4/36: Spencer Johnson 27; Montgomery; Montgomery; Farmer; Amanda HENDERSON; Montgomery; Martha Henderson 2_; Pulaski; Montgomery; Amanda HENDERSON; Montgomery; Ø; 10 Feb 1865

4/37: Andrew Hopkins 35; Caroline; Montgomery; Farmer; Daniel HOGE; Montgomery; Harriet Boyd 19; Lunenburg; Montgomery; Hugh GIBSON; Montgomery; James E. 1 mo; 27 Dec 1864

4/38: Samuel Bai_ 27; Augusta; Montgomery; Farmer; William JOHNSON; Montgomery; Rosanna Myers? 2_; Montgomery; Montgomery; Giles HENDERSON; Samuel 3, Ellen 4; 2 Jan

4/39: ___ Wha__ 40; Montgomery; Montgomery; Farmer; Edward? BARNETT; Montgomery; Louisa __ 4_; Pulaski?; Montgomery; David WADE; Montgomery; Henderson 11, Nancy 9

5/1: Peter Morgan 49; Nottoway; Montgomery; Farmer; Henry FOLTZ; Montgomery; Millie Foltz 39; Lunenburg; Montgomery; Henry FOLTZ; Thadeous 24, Taylor 18, Mary F. 17, Emily T. 15, Margaret 13, Peter 11, Alice 10, Samuel 8, Henry 7, Mollie 4, William 3; 10 Apr 1840

5/2: Nathanel Wright 38; Pittsylvania; Montgomery; Farmer; James T. MILLER; Montgomery; Elsey James 24; Franklin; Montgomery; Thomas CHILDREE; Montgomery; Andrew 5, Amanda 1; 10 Aug1859

5/3: Scipton Good 32; Montgomery; Montgomery; Farmer; Mary T. WALLHALL; Montgomery; Priscilla A. Taylor 26; Montgomery; Montgomery; James BROWN; Montgomery; Mary E. 7, Lucynthia 5, James N. 3, Francis 1; 4 July 1857

5/4: Allen Wright 27; Pittsylvania; Montgomery; Farmer; Nathaniel HARVEY; Montgomery; Nancy James 24; Franklin; Montgomery; Thomas CHILDREE; Montgomery; Margaret 8, Lewis 7, Harriet 1; 25 Dec 1857

5/5: Charles Taylor 42; Montgomery; Montgomery; Farmer; Garner BENNET; Montgomery; Arminia Edmonson 21; Roanoke; Montgomery; James KENT; Roanoke; Ø; 18 Jan 1866

5/6: Reuben Bluens 24; Montgomery; Montgomery; Farmer; James EVANS; Roanoke; Nancy A. Fraction 18; Montgomery; Montgomery; Harrison BENNET; Roanoke; Ø; 1 Jan 1866

5/7: Pleasant Mays 34; Montgomery; Montgomery; Farmer; James BROWN; Montgomery; Ellen Saunders 36; Montgomery; Montgomery; Henry BROWN; Montgomery; Ø; 10 Oct 1857

5/8: Richard Jones 27; Spotsylvania; Montgomery; Farmer; Uriah SOUTHERN; Pulaski; Caroline Wright 26; Pittsylvania; Montgomery; James MILLER; Montgomery; Lavinia 7 mos; 1 May 1863

5/9: Robert Watson 27; Pittsylvania; Montgomery; Farmer; Robert K. LIPSCOME; Montgomery; Martha Daniel 29; Mecklenburg; Montgomery; Robert I. LIPSCOME; Montgomery; General Warren 7, Virginia 4, Mary J. 6 mos; 4 Jan 1856

5/10: Joseph Blaney 25; Roanoke; Montgomery; Farmer; Charles BARNETT; Montgomery; Charlotta Taylor 21; Montgomery; Montgomery; Charles BARNETT; Montgomery; John 2, Maria 5 mos; 5 Jan 1852

5/11: Samuel Maze 42; Montgomery; Montgomery; Farmer; Thomas BROWN; Montgomery; Catharine Hu_de 41; Lunenburg; Montgomery; Thomas BROWN; Montgomery; James B. 14, Joseph 12, Rosanna 10, Maria 9, Virginia C. 7, Charles T. 5; 1 Sept 1850

5/12: Lewis Glasville 33; Lunenburg; Montgomery; Farmer; William STONE; Montgomery; Maria Boswell 38; Lunenburg; Montgomery; William STONE; Montgomery; Ø; 10 Mar 1857

5/13: Robert Payne 42; Amherst; Montgomery; Farmer; Free Born; Ø; Dilcy Flagens 27; Montgomery; Montgomery; Charles RONALD; Montgomery; Ø; 28 Dec 1862

5/14: Jefferson Johnson 48; Montgomery; Montgomery; Farmer; James H. HOGE; Montgomery; Maria Moulton 33; Montgomery; Montgomery; Edward J. AMOS; Montgomery; Sarah 8, Andrew J. 2 mos; 10 Dec 1855

5/15: Archambald Coleman 45; Caroline; Montgomery; Farmer; Daniel H. HOGE; Montgomery; Hannah Johnson 60; Henrico; Montgomery; James H. HOGE; Montgomery; Ø; 12 Sept 1852

5/16: Franklin Barber 30; Orange; Montgomery; Farmer; Andrew J. CAMP; Campbell; Ellen Snyder 24; Montgomery; Montgomery; Andrew J. CAMP; Campbell; James 1; 30 Aug 1864

5/17: Peter Williams 54; Gloucester; Montgomery; Farmer; James H. HOGE; Montgomery; Catharine Mosely 51; Chesterfield; Montgomery; James H. HOGE; Montgomery; Nancy 34, Silvian 33, Preston 21, Nathaniel 20, George 16, Ellen 13, Amelia 23; 10 Nov 1830

5/18: Major Liggens 71; Roanoke; Montgomery; Farmer; William RUTLIDGE; Montgomery; Dilsey McCray 66; Henrico; Montgomery; Charles RONALD; Montgomery; Taylor 29, Dilsey 27; 14 Dec 1825

5/19: Mark Anthony 72; Nottoway; Montgomery; Farmer; Henry FOLTZ; Montgomery; Fanny Yearant 55; Montgomery; Montgomery; Henry FOLTZ; Montgomery; Sophia 16, Caroline 13; 2 Sept 1836

5/20: James Gray 52; Lunenburg; Montgomery; Carpenter; Priscilla WINN; Lunenburg; Jane Foltz 45; Lunenburg; Montgomery; Henry FOLTZ; Montgomery; Emeline G. 22, Pad? 20, Rosetta 17, Daniel 16, John 14, Hoyl 13, Mary E. 11, Matilda 9, Catharine 7, Nellie 3; 15 Nov 1838

5/21: Preston Jackson 26; Roanoke; Montgomery; Farmer; Jonas ANDERSON; Montgomery; Catharine Jenison 18; Montgomery; Montgomery; John SLUSHER; Montgomery; Olie Frances 2, John A. 5 mos; 10 Sept 1861

5/22: Edward Armstrong 46; Rockbridge; Montgomery; Boatman; Free Born; Ø; Henrietta Owens 21; Montgomery; Montgomery; John B. RADFORD; Montgomery; Ø; 10 May 1863

5/23: Oscar Johnson 53; Giles; Montgomery; Farmer; William SMITH; Montgomery; Nancy Duke 47; Montgomery; Montgomery; Charles H. MILLER; Montgomery; Ø ; 1 Sept 1865

5/24: Andrew Young 28; Franklin; Montgomery; Waiter; Free Born; Ø; Eliza Hendrick 35; Montgomery; Montgomery; Hugh KENT; Montgomery; William N. 2; 3 Mar 18__

5/25: Richard Baily 60; Fauquier; Montgomery; Farmer; William JOHNSON; Montgomery; Asley Glosper 40; Franklin; Montgomery; Abraham SMITH; Montgomery; Ø; 1 Jan 1865

5/26: Tobias Smith 44; Montgomery; Montgomery; Farmer; Giles J. HENDERSON; Montgomery; Eveline Melvine 47; Montgomery; Montgomery; Hugh KENT; Montgomery; Louisa J. 18, Cecelia 18, Abraham 16, Millie C. 15, Mary L. 13, Elsie 12, Moses 8, Eliza M. 4; 2 May 1843

5/27: William Paterson 40; Buckingham; Montgomery; Farmer; Edward JAMES; Montgomery; Clara Owens 40; Floyd; Montgomery; Edward JAMES; Montgomery; Ø; 1 Mar 1852

5/28: Thomas Banks 40; Floyd; Montgomery; Farmer; William B. PRESTON; Montgomery; Maria Lewis 25; Montgomery; Montgomery; William B. PRESTON; Montgomery; Ø; 25 Dec 1863

5/29: Robert Thompson 40; Giles; Montgomery; Farmer; Thomas SHANNON; Giles; Rhoda A. Austin 33; Pulaski; Montgomery; James CLOYD; Pulaski; Ø; 10 Nov 1846

5/30: Andrew Taylor 29; Roanoke; Montgomery; Farmer; James THOMAS; Montgomery; Margaret Goldston 26; Roanoke; Montgomery; David THOMAS; Montgomery; Sarah J. 7, George W. 4, Vina Elizabeth 1; 26 Dec 1857

5/31: Joseph Burton 53; Botetourt; Montgomery; Farmer; William DAVIS; Montgomery; Hannah Taylor 45; Montgomery; Montgomery; William DAVIS; Montgomery; Charles L. 22, Joseph 20, Sarah 12, Lewellen 4; 11 Sept 184_

5/32: Sampson Gleeves 37; Wythe; Montgomery; Farmer; John P. MATHEWS; Washington Co, Tennessee; Harriet Engle 31; Pulaski; Montgomery; John P. MATHEWS; Washington Co, Tennessee; Emily I. 11, Rufus M. 9, George A. 4; 1 Sept 185_

5/33: George W. Russell 26; Montgomery; Montgomery; Farmer; Isaac DUDLEY; Montgomery; Agnes Williamson 32; Albemarle; Montgomery; Isaac WHITE; Montgomery; Ø; 20 Mar186_

5/34: Hugh Crockett 25; Montgomery; Montgomery; Farmer; Floyd SMITH; Montgomery; Caroline Curtis 29; Montgomery; Montgomery; Susanna WADE; Montgomery; Norvell 2, Samuel S. 1; 24 July 1863

5/35: David Knight 60; Lunenburg; Montgomery; Farmer; Henry FOLTZ; Montgomery; Crecia Ann Morgan _0; Charlotte; Montgomery; Robert LIPSCONE; Montgomery; Agnes 4, Dean 2; 2 Nov 185_

5/36: Granville H. Glieves/Gliever 49; Wythe; Montgomery; Farmer; James P. HAMMIT; Montgomery; Emily Ross; Ø; Montgomery; James P. HAMMIT; Montgomery; Saunders 13, Stephen 8, Pierre 3, Granville 4 mos; 15 May 185_

5/37: Josiah Day 43; Pittsylvania; Montgomery; Farmer; Free Born; Ø; Charlotta Gilber__; Ø; Montgomery; Nathaniel HARVEY; Montgomery; Sarah 21, Josiah 17, Mary E. 14, Chester 10, America 8, Anderson 6, Granville 4, John 2, Mollie 1 wk; 10 Aug 184_

5/38: ___ Cheese 50; Nottoway; Montgomery; Farmer; William T. WOODEN; Prince Edward; Emma Day; Ø; Montgomery; James STONE; Pulaski; Samuel 5, Nancy 3, Ida I. 3 mos; 4 Oct 18__

5/39: ___ J__; Montgomery; Montgomery; Farmer; Walter PRESTON; Montgomery; Susan __; Ø; Montgomery; Walter PRESTON; Montgomery; Alice 2

6/1: Alfred Davis 37; Montgomery; Montgomery; Farmer; William DAVIS; Montgomery; Julia Hitson 33; Bedford; Montgomery; William DAVIS; Montgomery; Ø; 25 Dec 1857

6/2: Rola Dykes 53; Montgomery; Montgomery; Farmer; Howard PATEN; Montgomery; Rachel Twine 54; Montgomery; Montgomery; David SHANKS; Roanoke; David 22, Patrick 15, Rola 14, Thomas 11; 30 Dec 1843

6/3: Richard Harris 60; Spotsylvania; Montgomery; Laborer; Ann E. DANGERFIELD; Spotsylvania; Mary Owens 48; Botetourt; Montgomery; Charles THOMAS; Roanoke; Ø; 21 Jan 1855

6/4: David Burks 54; Roanoke; Montgomery; Farmer; Henry TAYLOR; Montgomery; Priscilla Owens 42; Botetourt; Montgomery; Charles THOMAS; Roanoke; Rachel 20, Ann E. 14, Sarah J. 12, Joseph W. 9, Lucy 4, Mary F. 8 mos; 17 Apr 1840

6/5: Washington Chancellor 40; Madison; Montgomery; Farmer; James THOMAS; Montgomery; Eliza Stewart 24; Montgomery; Montgomery; William DAVIS; Montgomery; Harriet 5, Thomas 3; 9 Mar 1861

6/6: John Jackson 33; Montgomery; Montgomery; Farmer; Howard PATEN; Montgomery; Emeline Buford 245; Bedford; Montgomery; Hugh CROCKETT; Montgomery; Rose 1; 25 Dec 1863

6/7: Crockett Barrett 27; Pulaski; Montgomery; Farmer; Jesse PEPPER; Pulaski; Sarah J. Neeten 22; Roanoke; Montgomery; Flemming LUVENCE; Montgomery; Charles E. 2, Louiada 1; 15 Apr 1861

6/8: Caleb Deaton 26; Roanoke; Montgomery; Farmer; William DAVIS; Montgomery; Eliza Ann Warrick 30; Amherst; Montgomery; William DAVIS; Montgomery; Ø; 10 Mar 1861

6/9: William Clark 27; Campbell; Montgomery; Farmer; Charles D. LUCAS; Montgomery; Maria Ross 19; Pittsylvania; Montgomery; Robert LIPSCOME; Montgomery; Ø; 20 Nov 1865

6/10: Andrew Hicks 54; Roanoke; Montgomery; Farmer; Collin BASS; Roanoke; Malinda Edmonson 47; Montgomery; Montgomery; Collin BASS; Roanoke; Fanny 25, Ann 23, Hannah 19, Elizabeth 13, Florence 11, Lucinda 6, Martha 4; 5 Oct 1833

6/11: Andrew Oliver 29; Montgomery; Montgomery; Farmer; John BLACK; Blacksburg; Fanny Vaugn 25; Montgomery; Montgomery; Edward J. AMOS; Montgomery; Robert 3, Andrew 5; 1 Sept 1859

6/12: Nelson Steptoe 32; Roanoke; Montgomery; Farmer; John H. SMITH; Roanoke; Elvira Gray 24; Montgomery; Montgomery; David EDMONSON; Montgomery; Lucinda 10, Julia 8, George 4, Robert 3; 12 Oct 1854

6/13: Jeremiah Hickman 26; Giles; Montgomery; Farmer; Gorden CLOYD; Pulaski; Martha Smith 22; Pulaski; Montgomery; Gorden CLOYD; Pulaski; James D. 7 mos; 28 July 1852

6/14: Richard Smith 79; Pulaski; Montgomery; Farmer; Gorden CLOYD; Pulaski; Uriah S. Butler 67; Pulaski; Montgomery; Gorden CLOYD; Pulaski; Jeremiah 34, Hale 31, Rosanna 24, Margaret 23, Cynthia 22, Martha 21, Harrison 16, Isaac 14, Emily 12; 20 Aug 1828

6/15: Robert Austin 38; Pulaski; Montgomery; Farmer; Gorden CLOYD; Pulaski; Lucinda Henderson 30; Montgomery; Montgomery; James R. KENT; Montgomery; George 10, Robert 8, Rhoda 5, James 2, Lettie 4 mos; 22 Mar 1853

6/16: Daniel Crawford 31; Montgomery; Montgomery; John BLACK; Montgomery; Ann Crawford 26; Logan Co, W. Virginia; Montgomery; Floyd McDONALD; Montgomery; Mary E. 3; 10 Feb 1861

6/17: Walter McNaughton 28; Montgomery; Montgomery; Carpenter; George GILMER; Pittsylvania; Eliza A. Perry 27; Albemarle; Montgomery; George GILMER; Pittsylvania; Nancy K. 1; 15 May 1859

6/18: Joseph Jones 31; Montgomery; Montgomery; Farmer; John CRAIG; Montgomery; Patience Page 25?; Pulaski; Montgomery; John CRAIG; Montgomery; Ø; 14 Sept 1864

6/19: General Hawkins 42; Nottoway; Montgomery; Farmer; William HOGE; Bland; Eliza Jones 25; Ambers (Amherst?); Montgomery; Richard P. JONES; Montgomery; Harriet 2, Johnson 1; 15 Mar 1862

6/20: Hampton? McDaniel 29; Ambers (Amherst?); Montgomery; Blacksmith; Richard P. JONES; Montgomery; Ann Jones 25; Montgomery; Montgomery; Jacob ZULL; Montgomery; Maria 1; 15 Dec 1862

6/21: Edward? Brown 64; Montgomery; Montgomery; Gardener; Hugh KENT; Montgomery; Amanda Follis 59; Bedford; Montgomery; George W. ANDERSON; Montgomery; Ø; 1 Nov 1850

6/22: Lewis Phillips 36; Floyd; Montgomery; Farmer; Jackson LUCAS; Montgomery; Ame Sparks 29; Montgomery; Montgomery; William CHILDREE; Montgomery; Samuel 11, John 10, David 8, Mary 6, Jane? 4, Catharine 2, Peter 1; 1 Jan 1852

6/23: Spencer Alexander 58; Montgomery; Montgomery; Farmer; Arthur McCORCKLE; Montgomery; Eliza Pepper 35; Montgomery; Montgomery; Arthur McCORCKLE; Montgomery; Mary 34, Jane 33, John 32, Caroline 31, Charles 21, Susan 16, Sarah 16, Smith 15, Fanny 12; 25 Dec 1831

6/24: David C. Alexander 36; Montgomery; Montgomery; Farmer; Thomas CHILDREE; Montgomery; Margaret A. Brooks 24; Pulaski; Montgomery; John LUCAS; Montgomery; Hannah 10, Floyd 8, Emeline 5, Crockett 3, John 1; 1 Dec 1855

6/25: Nelson Russell 56; Montgomery; Montgomery; Farmer; Isaac DUDLEY; Montgomery; Teressa Jeffeson 50; Mecklenburg; Montgomery; Isaac DUDLEY; Montgomery; Sidney 26, George 24, Montgomery 17; 15 Nov 1851

6/26: _oshua Brown 21; Roanoke; Montgomery; Farmer; Sarah LANAHAN; Roanoke; Fanny Anthony 18; Prince George; Montgomery; Miles WILSON; Montgomery; Laura 1; 15 July 1865

6/27: _ewis Fairfax 46; Culpeper; Montgomery; Farmer; James MILLER; Montgomery; Bettie Paterson 25; Buckingham; Montgomery; James MILLER; Montgomery; Isabella 1; 15 Dec 1863

6/28: William Johnson 53; Montgomery; Montgomery; Farmer; Charles GARDNER; Montgomery; Mary Johnson 38; Pulaski; Montgomery; Stephen KERBY; Pulaski; Sarah 16, William W. 7, Ellen 2, James 7 mos; 1 Dec 1847

6/29: ___ Lawrence 38; Montgomery; Montgomery; Farmer; Free Born; Ø; Emeline Alexander 26; Montgomery; Montgomery; William TAYLOR; Montgomery; Elizabeth 8, John 6, Euzitta? 2, Mary 9 mos; 25 Feb 1858

6/30: _eorge Hosburn 47; Campbell; Montgomery; Farmer; Eli FLIGER; Montgomery; Eliza Black 25; Pulaski; Montgomery; Boston WAGLE; Montgomery; Grace A. 4, Floyd 2; 6 July 1861

6/31: __wis Brown 38; Augusta; Montgomery; Farmer; Samuel DOBBINS; Floyd; Millie Howard 39; Floyd; Montgomery; Ira HOWARD; Floyd; Ø; 15 Aug 1861

6/32: _n_as Kee 48; Lunenburg; Farmer; Free Born; Ø; Martha A. Lestre 47; Lunenburg; Montgomery; Free Born; Ø; William 19; 15 Nov 1845

6/33: Reuben? Bluens 60; Augusta; Montgomery; Shoemaker; William JOHNSON; Montgomery; Anacha Flemmings 50; Montgomery; Montgomery; John STEPHENS; Montgomery; Reuben 25, Jackson 20, George 19, Henry 17, Richard 14, David 12, John 9; 10 Nov 1838

6/34: __niel Jones 39; Botetourt; Montgomery; Farmer; John B. RADFORD; Montgomery; Eden Brown 21; Bedford; Montgomery; John B. RADFORD; Montgomery; Nancy 8, Sarah 7, Richard 5, Elizabeth 4, Moses 8 mos; 1 Sept 1858

6/35: _enry Wiser 40; Montgomery; Montgomery; Farmer; Jeremiah KYLE?; Montgomery; Susan Vice 43; Botetourt; Montgomery; Free Born; Ø; Ø; 10 Apr 1851

6/36: __anuel Toler 70; Pittsylvania; Montgomery; Farmer; Robert LIPSCONE; Montgomery; Rosanna Lipscone 3_; ___; Montgomery; Robert LIPSCONE; Montgomery; Rafe 11, Eliza 8, Ira 6, Doretha? 3, Anne B. 3 mos; 12 Dec 185_

6/37: __rles Fortner 24; Montgomery; Montgomery; Blacksmith; Mary WADE; Montgomery; Maria Pend__; ___; Montgomery; Elizabeth MILLER; Montgomery; Edward 3, William 11 mos; 4 July 1861

6/38: ___ Morgan 24; Luenenburg; Montgomery; Farmer; Henry FOLTZ; Montgomery; Amanda M__; ___; Montgomery; Walla STAPLES; Montgomery; Ø; 25 Dec 1865

6/39: ___ ___; 22; Bedford; Montgomery; Farmer; Allison JEDDER; Bedford; Mary _. ___; ___; Montgomery; John GORDEN; Roanoke; Mary E. 2 mos; 1865

7/1: Samuel Stuart 29; Patrick; Montgomery; Laborer; John LYBROOK; Montgomery; Virginia Johnson 20; Patrick; Montgomery; Free Born; Ø; Ø David 3, Hamilton 1; 15 Sept 186_

7/2: Nelson Moulten 45; Bedford; Montgomery; Farmer; William SUBLETT; Montgomery; Tenie Coleman 50; Baltimore Co, Maryland; John PETERMAN; Montgomery; Ø; 15 Sept 1858

7/3: Allen Norrill 27; Montgomery; Montgomery; Farmer; Howard PATEN; Montgomery; Jane Charlton 24; Montgomery; Montgomery; David EDMONSON; Montgomery; Allen 6, Sarah 2; 10 Sept 1855

7/4: John Day 31; Roanoke; Montgomery; Farmer; Free Born; Ø; Caroline Taylor 30; Roanoke; Montgomery; Henry EDMONSON; Montgomery; Milton H. 8, Mary E. 7, Sarah A. 5, Zurah H. 2, Elizabeth 6 mos; 2 Aug 1856

7/5: Gilbert Vaugn 46; Montgomery; Montgomery; Farmer; Mary WADE; Montgomery; Charlotta I. Campbell 39; Montgomery; Montgomery; Robert MILLER; Montgomery; Henry C. 18, James W. 16, Rosa Bella 10, Anne E. 6; 3 Apr 1846

7/6: Abraham Vaugn 48; Montgomery; Montgomery; Laborer; Mary WADE; Montgomery; Rachel Armstrong 51; Montgomery; Montgomery; Edmond J. AMOS; Montgomery; Fanny 24, Richard 22, Daniel 17, Elfine 15, Joseph 14, Rose 12; 15 Sept 1841

7/7: George W. Randolph 37; Roanoke; Montgomery; Farmer; Walter DIALLY; Montgomery; Harriet Morris 40; Kanawha Co., W. Virginia; Montgomery; George HOLIBY; Cabell Co., W. Virginia; Ø; 15 Nov 1862

7/8: Lewis Truss 62; Augusta; Montgomery; Farmer; William BRUFFY; Giles; Addoway Black 50; Frederick; Montgomery; John LYBROOK; Montgomery; Ø; 12 Nov 1861

7/9: Floyd Dobbins 30; Montgomery; Montgomery; Farmer; Free Born; Ø; Lurana Phillips 32; Floyd; Montgomery; Christopher H. WILLIS; Montgomery; Mary 11, Drusilla 8, Amisity 8, Melvina 5, Louisa 2; 1_ Sept 1854

7/10: John Lewis 34; Montgomery; Montgomery; Farmer; Wadda CURRAN; Montgomery; Caroline Hall 27; Montgomery; Montgomery; Asa HALL; Montgomery; Richard 12, Andrew 10, Cynthia 8, Maria 6, Mazarine? 2; 25 Oct 1855

7/11: Frederic Clark 60; Patrick; Montgomery; Farmer; Mary STAPLES; Greensboro Co, No. Carolina; Sarah Fortner 30; Halifax; Montgomery; William FORTNER; Montgomery; Buchanan 12, Julia 6, Mary 3; 8 Sept 1853

7/12: Alexander Edmonson 25; Montgomery; Montgomery; Farmer; Rice D. MONTAGUE; Montgomery; Mary McGee 21; Montgomery; Montgomery; William MONTAGUE; Montgomery; William 2, Henry 5 mos; 10 June 1862

7/13: Jacob S. Cox 68; Stokes Co, No. Carolina; Montgomery; Farmer; Walla STAPLES; Montgomery; Hannah Staples 70; Patrick; Montgomery; Walla STAPLES; Montgomery; Ø; 1 Apr 1836

7/14: Washington Morrison 57; Montgomery; Montgomery; Farmer; Henry C. WADE; Montgomery; Roxanna Sheler 42; Lunenburg; Montgomery; William DOBBINS; Pulaski; Amelia A. 7; 1 Jan 1850

7/15: William Jones 30; Montgomery; Montgomery; Farmer; Jacob ZULL; Montgomery; Eliza Rose 19; Montgomery; Montgomery; Free Born; Ø; Hulda Ann 2; 10 Dec 1862

7/16: Stephen Walker 44; Lunenburg; Montgomery; Farmer; William STONE; Montgomery; Frances Williams 30; Lunenburg; Montgomery; William STONE; Montgomery; Mary F. 5 mos; 1 Apr 1862

7/17: Armsted Rollins 62; Montgomery; Montgomery; Farmer; Jacob ZULL; Montgomery; Sarah Bragg 33; Lunenburg; Montgomery; William STONE; Montgomery; Samuel 7, Eliza 4, Willa 2; 5 Apr 1858

7/18: Abraham Jones 69; Montgomery; Montgomery; Farmer; Jacob ZULL; Montgomery; Amelia Milton 53; Prince Edward; Montgomery; Jacob ZULL; Montgomery; William 32, Charles 30, Ann 26, Julia 22, Henry 21, Mary 18; 16 Apr 1832

7/19: Archambald Coleman 39; Montgomery; Montgomery; Farmer; William PECK; Montgomery; Charlotte Weathers 43; Caroline; Montgomery; Daniel HOGE; Montgomery; Mary 20, Sarah 16, Matilda 15, Caroline 14, Leah 3; 7 Feb 1844

7/20: Thomas Morrison 24; Montgomery; Montgomery; Laborer; James BARNETT; Montgomery; Fanny Jones 23; Bedford; Montgomery; Isabella JONES; Bedford; Luanna 1; 25 Dec 1864

7/21: William Raford 40; Montgomery; Montgomery; Cabinet Maker; John BARNETT; Montgomery; Patza? Gaiter 27; Rockbridge; Montgomery; Samuel BARNETT; Montgomery; Ø; 25 Oct 1858

7/22: Samuel Ford 38; Pulaski; Montgomery; Farmer; Margaret B. TAYLOR; Pulaski; Lucy Parmer 36; Pulaski; Montgomery; Margaret B. TAYLOR; Pulaski; Jabes D. 12, Hiram 7, Taylor 2; 25 Dec 1848

7/23: Anderson Stiff 29; Montgomery; Montgomery; Farmer; Floyd SMITH; Montgomery; Philice Brown 20; Montgomery; Montgomery; Floyd SMITH; Montgomery; Teressa G. 1; 25 Dec 1863

7/24: Michael Jordan 42; Albemarle; Montgomery; Laborer; Thomas MITCHELL; Bedford; Caroline Spinner 31; Albemarle; Montgomery; Thomas MITCHELL; Bedford; Mary A. 25, William D. 15, Wilhelmina 13, Socrates 11, John A. 5, Tandy J. 4; 1 Aug 1841

7/25: Joseph Nelson 22; Montgomery; Montgomery; Farmer; Mary EDMONSON; Montgomery; Margaret J. Taylor 18; Montgomery; Montgomery; Samuel BARNETT; Montgomery; Josephine 4 mos; 10 Jan 1864

7/26: Lewis Jenkins 24; Charleston, So. Carolina; Montgomery; Laborer; John BURGESS; Montgomery; Catharine Momen 22; Campbell; Montgomery; John PURCELL; Campbell; Ø; 25 Dec 1864

7/27: Andrew Alexander 25; Campbell; Montgomery; Laborer; William BURROWS; Campbell; Plina Johnson 20; Campbell; Montgomery; William H. MOMEN; Campbell; Ø; Ø 20 Jan 1864

7/28: James Mattison Bush 24; Franklin; Montgomery; Farmer; Griffin BUSH; Montgomery; Ida Fennall 23; Montgomery; Montgomery; Edward HAMMITT; Montgomery; Craig 1; 25 Dec 1864

7/29: Peter Campbell 36; Montgomery; Montgomery; Farmer; James CURRAN; Montgomery; Eveline __phas 22; Wythe; Montgomery; Charles BOWYER; Montgomery; Sarah 7, Laura 1; 10 Mar 1859

7/30: Samuel Hayden 33; Montgomery; Montgomery; Farmer; James CURRAN; Montgomery; Maria Rollins 27; Montgomery; Montgomery; William R. PEPPER; Montgomery; Sarah F. 9, Charles H. 7, Spencer 5, Harriet 1; 1 Aug 1852

7/31: Harrison Jones 32; Buckingham; Montgomery; Laborer; Lynch JONES; Campbell; Mary Cox 40; Campbell; Montgomery; Michael CLARK; Campbell; Martha A. 18, Joseph 16, Louisa 13, Allen 9, Eliza F. 6, Matilda A. 2; 10 Feb 1849

7/32: William Lucas 26; Spotsylvania; Montgomery; Farmer; Frank FIPS; Smyth; Lucy Morris 18; Montgomery; Montgomery; Henry FULTZ; Montgomery; Ø; 2_ Dec 1865

7/33: Granville Nichols 23; Bedford; Montgomery; Farmer; Benjamin TINSLEY; Roanoke; Maria Paterson 21; Montgomery; Montgomery; Lucy B. FRANKLIN; Roanoke; Ellen A. 4, James 1; 1 Dec

7/34: Charles Jones 26; Montgomery; Montgomery; Farmer; Thomas WALLTHRAL; Washington; Fanny Calloway 31; Roanoke; Montgomery; David DOUGHTERTY; Montgomery; Harriet 7, Charles B. 5, Ida B. 3, Thomas S. 3 mos; 1 Oct 1859

7/35: Samuel Brown 35; Roanoke; Montgomery; Farmer; Ferdinand RORER/ROVER; Pulaski; Emeline Noell 23; Patrick; Montgomery; Florintine ROBINSON; Roanoke; Flora 5, Henry 3, Grant 1; 25 Dec 1857

7/36: Wyatt Lagran 25; Appomattox; Montgomery; Farmer; Josiah LAGRAN; Montgomery; Jane Abbott 24; Appomattox; Montgomery; Josiah LAGRAN; Montgomery; James E. 1; May 1865

7/37: James Jones 25; Montgomery; Montgomery; Farmer; David BARNETT; Montgomery; Sarah Harris 24; Albemarle; Montgomery; David BARNETT; Montgomery; Henry 11, Joseph 9, Frank P. 5, __ella 4, Alice

7/38: ____ ____ 5_; Bedford; ___; Waiter; William LAGRAN; Botetourt; Mary Roberts 5_; Roanoke; Montgomery; Pitt__ W___; Montgomery

7/39: ___ ____; ___; ___; Farmer; Sarah SWEAT___; Win__ ___; Franklin?; Montgomery; Par__;

8/1: __milton Shields 23; Montgomery; Montgomery; Farmer; Adam EARHEART; Montgomery; Mary Coleman 20; Montgomery; Montgomery; Daniel H. HOGE; Montgomery; Ø; 1 Apr 1862

8/2: John Henderson 37; Campbell; Montgomery; Blacksmith; Andrew J. LUCAS; Montgomery; Ruth Rollins 30; Montgomery; Montgomery; Edward EVANS; Montgomery; Ø; 1 May 1865

8/3: Brooks Howard 23; Floyd; Montgomery; Farmer; Ira HOWARD; Floyd; Leticia Kennedy 22; Floyd; Montgomery; Giles KENNEDY; Franklin; Douglas G. 1; 15 May 1864

8/4: Charles Abbott 22; Appomattox; Montgomery; Farmer; Josiah GRANT; Montgomery; Patience Abbott 44; Appomattox; Montgomery; Josiah GRANT; Montgomery; Ø; 1 Nov 1863

8/5: Lewis Hawkins 28; Roanoke; Montgomery; Laborer; James KENT; Roanoke; Sarah Stokes 45; Campbell; Montgomery; William COX; Campbell; Ø; 25 Dec 1865

8/6: Thomas Brown 56; Henrico; Montgomery; Farmer; Samuel PAGE; Montgomery; Mary Johnson 47; Montgomery; Montgomery; Floyd SMITH; Montgomery; Eunice 8, Ellen 5; 1 Sept 1853

8/7: Samuel Givens 39; Augusta; Montgomery; Miller; William JOHNSON; Montgomery; Julia Barnett 32; Botetourt; Montgomery; Henry SMITH; Montgomery; Ø; 5 Mar 1853

8/8: John Wilkerson 28; Albemarle; Montgomery; Farmer; Archambald WHITE; Montgomery; Fannie Norwell 22; Montgomery; Montgomery; Archambald WHITE; Montgomery; William 2, Charles 1; 21 Apr 1863

8/9: Giles Johnson 43; Montgomery; Montgomery; Laborer; John A. LANG; Montgomery; Maria Anderson 24; Montgomery; Montgomery; Robert RYAN; Montgomery; Caleb 1, Mary P. 6 mos; 1 Sept 1864

8/10: John Bratten 42; Montgomery; Montgomery; Farmer; George W. ANDERSON; Montgomery; Millie Johnson 35; Pulaski; Montgomery; Hugh CROCKETT; Montgomery; William 17, Bertha 14, Sarah 10, Nancy 8, Amanda 5, Millie 3; 25 Dec 1848

8/11: Alfred Johnson 49; Montgomery; Montgomery; Farmer; Joseph KENT; Montgomery; Marenda Brown 40; Giles; Montgomery; Sarah EDMONSON; Montgomery; David 23, Alfred 21, Andrew 20, Caswell 18, James 16, Rilla 14, Ellen 12, Leanna 9, Maria 5, Mary 2; 20 Dec 1841

8/12: Absalom Johnson 68; Amelia; Montgomery; Farmer; John BEAN; Montgomery; Susan Ogle 45; Henrico; Montgomery; Adam EARHEART; Montgomery; Andrew 1; 1 May 1864

8/13: Charles Taylor 23; Montgomery; Montgomery; Farmer; George EARHEART; Montgomery; Ellen Pearman 20; Pulaski; Montgomery; Montgomery THOMAS; Montgomery; Ø; 1 Nov 1861

8/14: Lewis Sheffy 46; Roanoke; Montgomery; Farmer; William MONTAGUE; Montgomery; Mary Lewis 33; Montgomery; Montgomery; George W. CURRAN; Montgomery; Ø; 15 Sept 1858

8/15: Charles Bell 32; Summersett; Montgomery; Farmer; Fannie McCUE; Montgomery; Hannah E. Kyle 33; Montgomery; Montgomery; William MONTAGUE; Montgomery; Ø; 25 Nov 1862

8/16: Lawrence Gibbs 40; Norfolk; Montgomery; Farmer; Abraham WOOLDRIDGE; Chesterfield; Ellen Paterson 26; Campbell; Montgomery; John PAYNE; Campbell; Ø; 1 Sept 1861

8/17: George W. Russell 36; Botetourt; Montgomery; Farmer; Alex P. ESKRIDGE; Montgomery; Sarah Webster 37; Montgomery; Montgomery; Wesley FRIZZELL; Montgomery; Ø; 25 Nov 1851

8/18: Aaron Morgan 35; Campbell; Montgomery; Farmer; Richard MORGAN; Floyd; Frances Taylor 25; Campbell; Montgomery; Edmond H. CALLAHAN; Montgomery; William A. 4, John H. 2, George W. 1; 25 Sept 1851

8/19: Randall Langhorn 41; Montgomery; Montgomery; Farmer; Daniel LANGHORN; Campbell; Mary Green 32; Pittsylvania; Montgomery; Free Born; Ø; Ø; 15 Oct 1863

8/20: Lewis Briggs 24; Roanoke; Montgomery; Farmer; Free Born; Ø; Hariet Jennings 24; Campbell; Montgomery; William M. CANNAHAN; Montgomery; William W. 4, Nancy 2; 1 May 1861

8/21: Richard Taylor 65; Montgomery; Montgomery; Farmer; George EARHEART; Montgomery; Nancy Holms 51; Montgomery; Montgomery; Gorden CHRISTMAN; Montgomery; Ø; 20 July 1862

8/22: Lewis Fortner 65; Giles; Montgomery; Laborer; Rice D. MONTAGUE; Montgomery; Elizabeth Robinson 27; Bedford; Montgomery; Florintine ROBINSON; Roanoke; Scott 2; 21 July 1861

8/23: Floyd Melvin 33; Montgomery; Montgomery; Farmer; William TAYLOR; Montgomery; Amy Cox 28; Floyd; Montgomery; Jackson LUCAS; Montgomery; Ø; 15 Oct 1860

8/24: Moses Bean 63; Roanoke; Montgomery; Farmer; Richard Jones; Montgomery; Eliza Fisher 44; Montgomery; Montgomery; Mary WADE; Montgomery; Kate C. 12, Isabella 11, Eldred 9, Edward 6, Ma_et F. 4, George D. 2; 10 Sept 1852

8/25: Alfred Hergens 25; Alabush Co. Mississippi; Montgomery; Farmer; Calvin SAUNDERS; Pulaski; Elizabeth Jones 19; Lunenburg; Montgomery; White COLEMAN; Charlotte; Bettie 9 mos; 1 May 1865

8/26: Benjamin Wilson 35; Lunenburg; Montgomery; Farmer; William STONE; Montgomery; Lucy Jones 34; Lunenburg; Montgomery; White COLEMAN; Charlotte; Vinnie 5, Jane 2, Isabella 4 mos; 25 Dec 1860

8/27: Philip Walker 37; Lunenburg; Montgomery; Farmer; Musgrove STONE; Montgomery; Jat ___ 20; Greene; Montgomery; Musgrove STONE; Montgomery; Giles 3, Angeline 2; 15 Mar 1862

8/28: Harvey G__ns 25; Montgomery; Montgomery; Farmer; John GRAYSON; Montgomery; Margaret Burks 31; Pulaski; Montgomery; Elizabeth CLOYD; Pulaski; James 2; 15 Mar 1863

8/29: Daniel Hopkins 43; Montgomery; Montgomery; Farmer; John GRAYSON; Montgomery; Jane Washington 25; Washington; Montgomery; Joseph K. SHANKLEY; Montgomery; Edward 1; 10 Nov 1864

8/30: Allen _olman 54; Pulaski; Montgomery; Farmer; Elizabeth CLOYD; Pulaski; Julia Chester 40; Chowan Co., No. Carolina; Montgomery; Frances JONES; Montgomery; Ø; 25 Dec 1862

8/31: Joseph Parmer 43; Montgomery; Montgomery; Farmer; John B. RADFORD; Montgomery; Mary Owens 26; Montgomery; Montgomery; John B. RADFORD; Montgomery; Malcolm 3; 25 Dec 1859

8/32: James? Bracket 61; Roanoke; Montgomery; Farmer; Joseph SHANKLIN; Montgomery; Elsee Arnold 61; Roanoke; Montgomery; Joseph SHANKLIN; Montgomery; Isabella 27, Margaret 22, Fanny 20; 1 May 1826

8/33: ___ Wade 55; Montgomery; Montgomery; Farmer; John B. RADFORD; Montgomery; Lucy Bouser? 31; Bedford; Montgomery; John B. RADFORD; Montgomery; Anderson 15, Washington 11, Henrietta 9, Julia 6, Hamilton 5, Mary 3, John 5 mos, William 5 mos; 28 Feb 1848

8/34: William Liverpool 48; Amherst; Montgomery; Farmer; John B. RADFORD; Montgomery; Nicey Penalton 25; Bedford; Montgomery; John B. RADFORD; Montgomery; Malinda 10, Irene 7, Martin 2, Robert 2 wks; 3 Mar 1857

8/35: Robert Apson 47; Campbell; Montgomery; Laborer; Charles Henry LYNCH; Campbell; Mary Coleman 30; Montgomery; Montgomery; George EARHEART; Montgomery; Emma 17; 16 Mar 1860

8/36: ___ ___; 36; Tazewell; Montgomery; Farmer; Giles THOMAS; Montgomery; Hannah Sauls 35; Washington; Montgomery; Giles THOMAS; Montgomery; Ø; 28 Aug 1852

8/37: ___ ___; _0; Henrico; Montgomery; Farmer; Giles THOMAS; Montgomery; Carey Hogans 46; Frederick Co. Maryland; Montgomery; Phillip B. SNAP; Washington; Charles 20, Amanda? 26, Sarah 14, Caroline 12, Alexander? 9; 15 Sept 182_

8/38: ___ ___; _; ___; ___; Farmer; Giles THOMAS; Montgomery; Amanda F. Snidon 26; Montgomery; Montgomery; Charles D. PECK; Montgomery; __ land 3, Levi 11 mos; 15 May

8/39: ___ ___; _; ___; ___; Jo__ __d; Montgomery; Ann Mills 20; Pulaski; Montgomery; John B. RADFORD; Montgomery

Table 18 Prince Edward

Register of Children of Colored Persons in P. Edward County, State of Virginia whose Parent had ceased to cohabit on 27 February 1866 which the Father recognizes to be his

(pg/ln; child age; pob; res; last owner; res; f/res; f/age; f last owner; res; m/age; res; m last owner; res; f)

1/1: H. Robinson 15; Prince Edward; Missouri; C. BALDWIN; Prince Edward; Prince Edward; 59; Mrs. W. WILSEY; Farmville; Lina Robinson; Deceasd; C. BALDWIN; Prince Edward

1/2: R. Robinson 12; Prince Edward; City Point; C. BALDWIN; Prince Edward; Prince Edward; 59; Mrs W. WILSEY; Farmville; Lina Robinson; Deceased; C. BALDWIN; Prince Edward

1/3: C. Robinson 18; Cumberland; Missouri?; A. SHIELDS; Missouri; Prince Edward; 59; Mrs. W. WILSEY; Farmville; Sukey Robinson; Deceased; A. SHIELDS

1/4: Celia Robinson 14; Cumberland; Missouri?; A. SHIELDS; Missouri; Prince Edward; 59; Mrs. W. WILSEY; Farmville; Sukey Robinson; Deceased; A. SHIELDS

1/5: Nancy Robinson 11; Prince Edward; Missouri?; A. SHIELDS; Missouri; Prince Edward; 59; Mrs. W. WILSEY; Farmville; Sukey Robinson; Deceased; A. SHIELDS; Va?; Peter Robinson

1/7: Washington Cousin 16; Prince Edward; Unknown; Unknown; Unknown; Prince Edward; 59; Born Free; Ø; L. Robinson 40; Farmville; J. McGLEASAN; Prince Edward; Henry Cousin

1/10: Henry Cook 18; Charlotte; Farmville; B. WOOD; Farmville; Unknown; Col. J. RICE; Farmville; Mary Ellis 34; Farmville; Baber? WOOD; Farmville

1/11: Sarah Cook 16; Charlotte; Farmville; B. WOOD; Farmville; Unknown; Col. J. RICE; Farmville; Mary Ellis 34; Farmville; Baber? WOOD; Farmville

1/13: Napoleon Cox 12; Prince Edward; Liberia; John WATSON; Prince Edward; Prince Edward; 36; Mrs. Mary COX; Lunenburg; Queen Cox; Deceased; John WATSON; Prince Edward; Washington Cox

1/14: William W. Cox 10; Prince Edward; Liberia; John WATSON; Prince Edward; Prince Edward; 36; Mrs. Mary COX; Lunenburg; Queen Cox; Deceased; John WATSON; Prince Edward

1/16: Madora Jackson 16; Prince Edward; Prince Edward; Mrs. Asa DUPUY; Prince Edward; Prince Edward; 30; Pat JACKSON; Farmville; Lina Cox 32; Prince Edward; Mrs. Asa DUPUY; Prince Edward

1/19: Sophy Berkeley 30; Cumberland; Unknown; B. HARRISON; Buckingham; Prince Edward; 80; Baker SCOTT; Prince Edward; Laura Berkeley 46; Unknown; B. HARRISON; Cumberland

1/20: Phebe Berkeley 28; Cumberland; Unknown; B. HARRISON; Buckingham; Prince Edward; 80; Baker SCOTT; Prince Edward; Laura Berkeley 46; Unknown; B. HARRISON

1/21: Stephen Berkeley 26; Cumberland; Unknown; B. HARRISON; Buckingham; Prince Edward; 80; Baker SCOTT; Prince Edward; Laura Berkeley 46; Unknown; B. HARRISON

1/22: Patrick Berkeley 24; Cumberland; Unknown; B. HARRISON; Buckingham; Prince Edward; 80; Baker SCOTT; Prince Edward; Laura Berkeley 46; Unknown; B. HARRISON; Peyton Berkeley

1/23: Patsey Berkeley 29; Cumberland; Unknown; B. HARRISON; Buckingham; Prince Edward; 80; Baker SCOTT; Prince Edward; Laura Berkeley 46; Unknown; B. HARRISON; Cumberland

1/25: Easther Cole 13; Prince Edward; Unknown; Charles MORTON; Prince Edward; Prince Edward; 50; George SAUNDERS; Buckingham; Isabel Hicks 26; Prince Edward; Charles MORTON; Prince Edward; Henry Cole

1/27: Catherine Thomas 12; Prince Edward; Prince Edward; H. WOOTTEN; Prince Edward; Prince Edward; 40; F.T. WOOTTEN; Prince Edward; Emily Wootten 34; Prince Edward; H. WOOTTEN

1/28: Julia Thomas 11; Prince Edward; Prince Edward; H. WOOTTEN; Prince Edward; Prince Edward

1/29: Martha Thomas 9; Prince Edward; Prince Edward; H. WOOTTEN; Prince Edward; Prince Edward

1/30: Jenny Thomas 7; Prince Edward; Prince Edward; H. WOOTTEN; Prince Edward; Prince Edward

1/31: Robert Thomas 6; Prince Edward; Prince Edward; H. WOOTTEN; Prince Edward; Prince Edward; Ø; Ø; Ø; Ø; Ø; Ø; Ø; Ruben Thomas

1/33: Spencer Wootten 20; Prince Edward; Prince Edward; H. WOOTTEN; Prince Edward; Prince Edward; 40; Richard MILLER; Prince Edward; Katy Wootten 34; Prince Edward; F.T. WOOTTEN; Prince Edward; George Miller

1/34: Doctor W. Wootten 8; Prince Edward; Prince Edward; H. WOOTTEN; Prince Edward; Prince Edward; 40; Richard MILLER; Prince Edward

2/1: Robert Wootten 13; Prince Edward; Prince Edward; F.T. WOOTTEN; Prince Edward; Prince Edward; 51; Pat JACKSON; Prince Edward; Matilda Wootten; Deceased; F.T. WOOTTEN; Ø; Dan Williams

2/3: Sally Ann Washington 10; Prince Edward; Prince Edward; Mr. A. LIGAN; Prince Edward; Prince Edward; 38; Mr. A. LIGAN; Prince Edward; Susan Wade 28; Prince Edward; Mr. A. LIGAN; Ø; George Washington

2/5: Herod Evans 20; Halifax; Unknown; William CARRINGTON; Charlotte; Prince Edward; 45; William CARRINGTON; Prince Edward; Polly Alesey; Deceased; William CARRINGTON; Prince Edward; Herod Evans

2/7: Fayette Morton 18; Prince Edward; Prince Edward; H. VAUGHAN; Prince Edward; Prince Edward; 46; F.T. WOOTTEN; Prince Edward; Eliza Vaughan; Deceased; Henry VAUGHAN; Prince Edward

2/8: Armstead Morton 16; Prince Edward; Prince Edward; H. VAUGHAN; Prince Edward; Ø; Ø; Ø; Ø; Ø; Ø; Ø; William Morton

2/10: Sarah Abernathy 12; Lunenburg; Prince Edward; John COUCH; Lunenburg; Lunenburg; 35; ABERNATHY; Lunenburg; Mary Couch 42; Prince Edward; Johnathan COUCH; Lunenburg; Edward Abernathy

2/11: Lucy J. Abernathy 9; Lunenburg; Prince Edward; John COUCH; Lunenburg; Lunenburg; 35; ABERNATHY; Lunenburg

2/13: Sarah Boswell 8; Mecklenburg; Mecklenburg; J.F. PETTIS; Mecklenburg; Prince Edward; 29; G. POINDEXTER; Mecklenburg; Maria Pettis 28; Mecklenburg; John L. PETTIS; Mecklenburgh; Shepperd Bosley

2/16: Patty Branch 12; Prince Edward; Petersburg; Archy WARNACK; Prince Edward; Prince Edward; 38; John WARNACK; Prince Edward; Frances Warnack 33; Prince Edward; L.D. WARNACK; Prince Edward; Joel Branch

2/19: Baker Pegrain 5; Prince Edward; Prince Edward; H. STOKES; Prince Edward; Prince Edward; 40; H. STOKES; Prince Edward; Sally Ann Stokes 36; Prince Edward; H. STOKES; Prince Edward; Jack Pegrain

2/20: Ellen Pegrain 1; Prince Edward; Prince Edward

2/22: Ella

2/23: Salina Venable 13; Prince Edward; Prince Edward; G. HARDY; Lunenburg; Prince Edward; 48; F.N. WATKINS; Prince Edward; Rosetta Venable; Deceased; George HARDY

2/24: Agnes Venable 12; Prince Edward; Prince Edward; G. HARDY; Lunenburg; Prince Edward; 48; F.N. WATKINS; Prince Edward; Rosetta Venable; Deceased; George HARDY; Lunenburg; Armstead Venable

2/26: William Rice 18; Prince Edward; Prince Edward; William HUNT; Prince Edward; Prince Edward; 40; William J. RICE; Prince Edward; Jenilla; Deceased; William BENCH; Prince Edward; William Rice

2/27: Eliza Rice 16; Prince Edward; Prince Edward; William HUNT; Prince Edward; Prince Edward; 40; William J. RICE; Prince Edward

2/29: George Steger 24; Prince Edward; Boston?, (Massachusetts); Born Free; Ø; Petersburg; 70; Born Free; Ø; Sally Holmes 44; Prince Edward; Born Free; Ø; G_ate Steger

2/30: Frank Steger 23; Prince Edward; Boston?, (Massachusetts); Born Free; Ø; Petersburg; 70; Born Free; Ø; Sally Holmes 44; Prince Edward; Born Free

2/32: Charles Crawley 10; Lunenburg; Petersburg; Maj. R. ALLEN; Lunenburg; Prince Edward; 34; Alex CRAWLEY; Prince Edward; Sarah Allen 32; Petersburg; R. ALLEN; Lunenburg; Alex Crawley

2/33: Sally Crawley 8; Lunenburg; Petersburg; Maj. R. ALLEN; Lunenburg; Prince Edward; 34; Alex CRAWLEY; Prince Edward; Sarah Allen 32

2/34: Alex Horace 12 mos; Prince Edward; Prince Edward; Born Free; Ø; Prince Edward; 32; H. THWEATT; Prince Edward; Jenny Holmes 30; Farmville; Born Free; Ø; Sam Horace

3/1: _ancy Redd 8; Prince Edward; Prince Edward; Mrs. Parmela WATSON; Prince Edward; Prince Edward; 32; John W. REDD; Prince Edward; Nancy Watson 29; Prince Edward; Mrs. Amelia WATSON; Ø; Benjamin Redd

4/1: William McCall 18; Amelia; Amelia; James JOHNS; Amelia; Prince Edward; 54; William FRETWELL; Amelia; Cilia Johns 60; Ø; James JOHNS; Amelia; Anderson McCall

4/3: Sally Evans 7; Prince Edward; Unknown; J. TODD; Pittsylvania; Prince Edward; 32; Born Free; Ø; Mary Brown 30; Unknown; J. TODD; Pittsylvania; Isham Evans

4/5: Patsey Grigg

4/6: Clem Watkins 8; Prince Edward; Prince Edward; Dr. W. CARRINGTON; Halifax; Prince Edward; 36; Dr. William CARRINGTON; Halifax; Laurey Watkins; Deceased; Dr. William CARRINGTON; Halifax; Thomas Watkins

5/1: Margaret Rennsalaes 8; Christian Co., Kentucky; Prince Edward; William JONES; Farmville; Prince Edward; 32; William B. JONES; Prince Edward; Sally Jones 30; Farmville; William B. JONES; Farmville; Van Rennsalaes

5/2: Nannie Rennsalaes 5; Christian Co., Kentucky; Prince Edward; William JONES; Farmville; Prince Edward; 32; William B. JONES; Prince Edward; Sally Jones 30; Farmville

5/4: Harry Wootten 6; Prince Edward; Prince Edward; H. WOOTTEN; Prince Edward; Prince Edward; 30; H. WOOTTEN; Prince Edward; Lucy Pollard 23; Prince Edward; H. WOOTTEN; Prince Edward; Jack Wootten

5/6: Lizzie Walker 6; Prince Edward; Prince Edward; Thomas BELL; Prince Edward; Prince Edward; 23; Stephen FUQUA; Prince Edward; Molly Bell 29; Buckingham; Thomas BELL; Prince Edward; Marshal Walker

5/8: Molly Booker 8; Farmville; Prince Edward; Mrs. F. SMITH; Cumberland; Greensborough (Greensboro?), No. Carolina; 30; G.W. DANIEL; Farmville; Frances James 40; Prince Edward; Mrs. F. SMITH; Ø; Israel Booker

5/9: Patsy Booker

5/10: Sarah Winston 6; Spotsylvania; Prince Edward; Born Free; Ø; Prince Edward; 36; Janah/Jonah BRENT; Spotsylvania; Jane King 30; Spotsylvania; Born Free; Ø; John Winston

5/12: Newman Jefferson 10; Pa__ville; Washington; Born Free; Ø; Prince Edward; 36; G.W. DANIEL; Prince Edward; Chloe King 36; Washington; Born Free

5/13: Sarah Jefferson 13; Pa__ville; Washington; Born Free; Ø; Prince Edward; 36; G.W. DANIEL; Prince Edward; Chloe King 36; Washington; Born Free; Ø; Thomas Jefferson

5/15: Rose S. Winn 15; Cumberland; Cumberland; Ben WILSON; Cumberland; Cumberland; 38; Ben WILSON; Cumberland; Amy Booker 36; Cumberland; Benjamin WILSON; Cumberland; Sevian? Winn

5/18: Phebe Cabell 17; Prince Edward; Prince Edward; R.C. ANDERSON; Prince Edward; Prince Edward; 56; R.C. ANDERSON; Prince Edward; Eda Ann Cabell; Deceased; R.C. ANDERSON; Prince Edward

5/20: Patrick Cabell 15; Prince Edward; Prince Edward; R.C. ANDERSON; Prince Edward; Prince Edward; 56; R.C. ANDERSON; Prince Edward; Eda Ann Cabell; Deceased; R.C. ANDERSON; Prince Edward

5/: Gilbert Cabell 14; Prince Edward; Prince Edward; R.C. ANDERSON; Prince Edward; Prince Edward; 56; R.C. ANDERSON; Prince Edward; Eda Ann Cabell; Deceased

5/21: Harriet Cabell 13; Prince Edward; Prince Edward; R.C. ANDERSON; Prince Edward; Prince Edward; 56; R.C. ANDERSON; Prince Edward; Eda Ann Cabell; Deceased; R.C. ANDERSON; Prince Edward

5/22: Grace Cabell 12; Prince Edward; Prince Edward; R.C. ANDERSON; Prince Edward; Prince Edward; 56; R.C. ANDERSON; Prince Edward; Eda Ann Cabell; Deceased; R.C. ANDERSON; Prince Edward

5/23: Charlotte Cabell; 9; Prince Edward; Prince Edward; R.C. ANDERSON; Prince Edward; Prince Edward; 56; R.C. ANDERSON; Prince Edward; Eda Ann Cabell; Deceased; R.C. ANDERSON; Prince Edward

5/24: Landon Cabell 4; Prince Edward; Prince Edward; R.C. ANDERSON; Prince Edward; Prince Edward; 56; R.C. ANDERSON; Prince Edward; Eda Ann Cabell; Deceased; R.C. ANDERSON; Prince Edward; C__h Cabell

5/26: Lucy Miller 10; Amherst; Prince Edward; James WILLIAMS; Amherst; Amherst; 50; FLETCHER; Amherst; Sallie Miller 28; Prince Edward James WILLIAMS; Amherst

5/27: Buck Miller 6; Amherst; Prince Edward; James WILLIAMS; Amherst; Amherst; 50; FLETCHER; Amherst; Sallie Miller 28; Prince Edward James WILLIAMS; Amherst; Henry Miller

5/29: Buck Austin 10; Buckingham; Prince Edward; William SHAW; Buckingham; Buckingham; 29; Cal FORBES; Buckingham; Patty Shaw 30; Buckingham; William SHAW; Buckingham; Henry Austin

5/31: Gallon Washington 5; Buckingham; Prince Edward; George COX; Buckingham; Prince Edward; 24; George COX; Buckingham; Catherine Venable 24; Buckingham; George COX Buckingham; George Washington

5/34: Charles Pigot Rainout/Rumont 18; Buckingham; Prince Edward; T.F. WOMACK; Farmville; Buckingham; 50; Matthew COX; Buckingham; Caroline Pigot 54; Prince Edward; Thomas WOMACK; Prince Edward; Lewis Rainout/Rumont?

6/1: William Johnson 13; Nottoway; Prince Edward; Isaac EPPES; Dinwiddie; Prince Edward; 40; Ransom? CHUMMY; Prince Edward; Sallie Eppes 36; Dinwiddie; Isaac EPPES; Dinwiddie; Israel Johnson

6/3: Archy Branch 19; Prince Edward; Amelia; Benjamin FLIPPEN; Amelia; Prince Edward; 42; Miss Alice AMES; Amelia; Martha Fippen 40; Amelia; Benjamin FLIPPEN; Amelia; Henry Branch

6/5: James Phillips 5; Prince Edward; Prince Edward; Joseph PHILLIPS; Prince Edward; Prince Edward; 30; Joseph PHILLIPS; Prince Edward; Mary J. Phillips 29; Prince Edward; Joseph PHILLIPS; Prince Edward

6/6: Nannie Phillips 6; Prince Edward; Prince Edward; Joseph PHILLIPS; Prince Edward; Prince Edward; 30; Joseph PHILLIPS; Prince Edward; Mary J. Phillips 29; Prince Edward; Joseph PHILLIPS; Prince Edward; Joseph Phillips

6/8: Alice Phillips 12; Prince Edward; Prince Edward; Davy OWENS; Powhatan; Prince Edward; 30; Joseph PHILLIPS; Prince Edward; Mahala Phillips 30; Prince Edward; David OWENS; Prince Edward; Joseph Phillips

6/10: Amanda Elliott 17; Prince Edward; Prince Edward; Born Free; Ø; Prince Edward; 62; Willis ELLIOTT; Prince Edward; Fanny Valentine 65; Lunenburg; Born Free; Ø; Daniel Elliott

6/12: Sarah Gilham 13; Nottoway; Petersburg; Born Free; Ø; Prince Edward; 58; Mrs. Katy JONES; Nottoway; Mary Gilham; Deceased Born Free; Ø; William Gilham

6/13: James A. Gilham 20; Nottoway; Prince Edward; Born Free; Ø; Prince Edward; 58; Mrs. Katy JONES; Nottoway; Mary Gilham; Deceased Born Free; Ø; William Gilham

6/15: William Wiley 6; Prince Edward; Amelia; Benjamin FLIPPEN; Amelia; Prince Edward; 38; Mrs. BRADSHAW; Prince Edward; Pernilla Flippen 30; Prince Edward; Benjamin FLIPPEN; Prince Edward; James Robert Wiley

6/17: Robert Alexander 18; Prince Edward; Prince Edward; Sarah FLIPPEN; Prince Edward; Lunenburg; 39; Born Free; Ø; Jane Wiley 34; Prince Edward; Sarah FLIPPEN; Ø; Alex Alexander

6/18: Amelia Ann Alexander 14; Prince Edward; Prince Edward; Sarah FLIPPEN; Prince Edward; Lunenburg; 39; Born Free; Ø; Jane Wiley 34; Prince Edward; Sarah FLIPPEN

6/20: William Jones 3; Prince Edward; Prince Edward; Joseph LIGAN; Prince Edward; Prince Edward; 24; T. POINDEXTER; Prince Edward; Cara Ligan 22; Prince Edward; Joseph LIGAN; Ø; William Jones

6/22: Catherine Branch 13; Prince Edward; Prince Edward; Mrs. M. MOTTLEY; Prince Edward; Prince Edward; 36; Mrs. M. MOTTLEY; Prince Edward; Laura? Bowman 28; Prince Edward; Mrs. M. MOTTLEY; Ø; Beverly Branch

6/24: Madison Anderson 15; Nottoway; Prince Edward; William JONES; Nottoway; Prince Edward; 56; George ANDERSON; Prince Edward; Dicey Jones; Deceased; William JONES; Nottoway; Griffin Anderson

6/27: William Johnson 16; Mecklenburg; Mecklenburg; Thomas CRATE; Mecklenburg; Prince Edward; 50; Unknown; Prince Edward; Diana Johnson 54; Prince Edward; Joseph CRATE; Buckingham; Henry Foster

6/30: Robert Paulett 11; Campbell; Prince Edward; Charles HUNTER; Campbell; Prince Edward; 48; R.S. PAULETT; Prince Edward; Polly Hunter; Deceased; Charles M. HUNTER; Campbell; George Paulett

6/31: V_etta A. Paulett 14; Prince Edward; Prince Edward; Charles HUNTER; Campbell; Prince Edward; 48; R.S. PAULETT; Prince Edward; Polly Hunter; Deceased; Charles M. HUNTER; Campbell

6/33: William Cunningham 17; Cumberland; Cumberland; O. SANDERSON; Cumberland; Prince Edward; 44; H.P. TAYLOR; Prince Edward; Frances Cunningham 36; Cumberland; O. SANDERSON; Cumberland; Edward Cunningham

6/34: Frank Cunningham 15; Cumberland; Cumberland; O. SANDERSON; Cumberland; Prince Edward; 44; H.P. TAYLOR; Prince Edward; Frances Cunningham 36; Cumberland; O. SANDERSON; Cumberland

7/1: Emily Byassy 8; Prince Edward; Prince Edward; H. STOKES; Prince Edward; Prince Edward; 36; H. STOKES; Prince Edward; Susan Stokes 35; Prince Edward; H. STOKES; Prince Edward

7/2: Eliza Byassy 6; Prince Edward; Prince Edward; H. STOKES; Prince Edward; Prince Edward; 36; H. STOKES; Prince Edward; Susan Stokes 35; Prince Edward; H. STOKES; Prince Edward

7/3: Pinkey Byassy 2; Prince Edward; Prince Edward; H. STOKES; Prince Edward; Prince Edward; 36; H. STOKES; Prince Edward; Susan Stokes 35; Prince Edward; H. STOKES; Prince Edward

7/4: Betty Byassy 9 mos; Prince Edward; Prince Edward; H. STOKES; Prince Edward; Prince Edward; 36; H. STOKES; Prince Edward; Susan Stokes 35; Prince Edward; H. STOKES; Prince Edward; Clem Byassy

7/6: Francis Stokes 5; Prince Edward; Prince Edward; R. STOKES; Prince Edward; Prince Edward; 40; R. STOKES; Prince Edward; Ellen Stokes 24; Prince Edward; Richard STOKES; Prince Edward; John Stokes

7/8: Sylvia Scott 6; Prince Edward; Prince Edward; S.B. SCOTT; Prince Edward; Prince Edward; 34; Richard SCOTT; Prince Edward; Ester Rowlett 34; Prince Edward; S.B. SCOTT; Prince Edward; Henry Scott

7/10: Samuel Wise 13; Prince Edward; Prince Edward; E. EDWARDS; Prince Edward; Lunenburg; 36; Richard STOKES; Lunenburg; Catherine Edmunds 50; Prince Edward; E. EDMUNDS; Prince Edward; Richard Stokes

7/12: __ex Randan 15; Prince Edward; Prince Edward; J. BONDURANT; Prince Edward; Prince Edward; 40; John BONDURANT; Prince Edward; Mary A. Anderson 24; Deceased; J. BONDURANT; Prince Edward; Beverly Randan

7/13: John Randan 20; Prince Edward; Texas; J. BONDURANT; Prince Edward; Prince Edward; 40; John BONDURANT; Prince Edward; Ø; Deceased; J. BONDURANT; Prince Edward;

7/15: James Waddell 21; Prince Edward; Prince Edward; George SCOTT; Cumberland; Prince Edward; 40; James SCOTT; Prince Edward; Jenny Crawley 45; Prince Edward; James T. GRAY; Prince Edward

7/16: Emily Jane Waddell 22; Prince Edward; Prince Edward; Dr. OWEN; Prince Edward;; Prince Edward; 40; James SCOTT; Prince Edward; Jenny Crawley 45; Prince Edward; James T. GRAY; Prince Edward

7/17: Milly Waddell 18; Prince Edward; Prince Edward; George SCOTT; Cumberland; Prince Edward; 40; James SCOTT; Prince Edward; Jenny Crawley 45; Prince Edward; James T. GRAY; Prince Edward

7/18: Maria Waddell 12; Prince Edward; Prince Edward; George SCOTT; Cumberland; Prince Edward; 40; James SCOTT; Prince Edward; Jenny Crawley 45; Prince Edward; James T. GRAY; Prince Edward; James Waddell

7/20: Clem Wilson 18; Prince Edward; Prince Edward; H. THAXTON; Prince Edward; Prince Edward; 40; H. THAXTON; Prince Edward; Violet Thaxton 54; Prince Edward; H. THAXTON; Prince Edward; Wilson Thaxton

7/23: Benjamin Vaughan 18; Prince Edward; Prince Edward; G. VAUGHAN; Prince Edward; Prince Edward; 50; George VAUGHAN; Prince Edward; C. Burton 36; Prince Edward; George VAUGHAN; Prince Edward; George Vaughan

7/25: Lucy Peters 4; Prince Edward; Prince Edward; John WYGLE?; Unknown; Prince Edward; 42; Dr. SPENCER; Farmville; Abbey Peters 30; Unknown; John WYGLE?; Unknown; Ben Peters

7/27: Francis Baker 15; Cumberland; Florida; J.M. OBERTON/OVERTON?; Florida; Farmville; 38; H. RICHARDSON; Prince Edward; Betsey Baker 28; Deceased; Johnathan OBERTON/OVERTON?; Deceased; Pleasant Baker

7/29: John Booker 9; Cumberland; Cumberland; Mrs. PAGE; Cumberland; Farmville; 74; William ARMSTEAD; Richmond; Judy Booker 24; Cumberland; Mrs. PAGE; Cumberland; Major Booker

7/30: James Miller

7/31: Clem Brown 11; Cumberland; Pa__ville; C. ANDERSON; Prince Edward; Charlotte; 60; T. ANDERSON; Cumberland; Susan Venable 34; Farmville; C. ANDERSON; Ø; Harrison Brown

7/33: Wilson Jackson 15; Buckingham; Prince Edward; C. ANDERSON; C.? (Prince?) Edward; Buckingham; T. ANDERSON; Cumberland; Susan Venable 34; Farmville; C. ANDERSON; Ø; Jack Jackson

8/1: James A. Cobb 20; Prince Edward; Buckingham; H. TUCKER; Buckingham; Prince Edward; 48; James T. LIGAN; Prince Edward; Melinda Cobb 50; Not Known; Henry TUCKER; Buckingham

8/2: Huston Cobb 17; Prince Edward; Buckingham; H. TUCKER; Buckingham; Prince Edward; 48; James T. LIGAN; Prince Edward

8/3: Agnes Cobb 15; Prince Edward; Buckingham; H. TUCKER; Buckingham; Prince Edward; 48; James T. LIGAN; Prince Edward

8/4: Francis Cobb 12; Prince Edward; Buckingham; H. TUCKER; Buckingham; Prince Edward; 48; James T. LIGAN; Prince Edward; Ø; Ø; Ø; Ø ; Benjamin Cobb

8/5: Benjamin Booker 16; Prince Edward; Prince Edward; James WOOTTEN; Prince Edward; Prince Edward; 42; James T. LIGAN; Prince Edward; Betsey Booker 30; Deceased; James WOOTTEN; Prince Edward

8/6: Edwin Booker 13; Prince Edward; Prince Edward; James WOOTTEN; Prince Edward; Prince Edward; 42; James T. LIGAN; Prince Edward

8/7: Fanny Booker 11; Prince Edward; Prince Edward; James WOOTTEN; Prince Edward; Prince Edward; 42; James T. LIGAN; Prince Edward

8/8: Page Booker 9; Prince Edward; Prince Edward; James WOOTTEN; Prince Edward; Prince Edward; 42; James T. LIGAN; Prince Edward

8/9: Amelia Booker 5; Prince Edward; Prince Edward; James WOOTTEN; Prince Edward; Prince Edward; 42; James T. LIGAN; Prince Edward; Ø; Ø; Ø; Ø; Edward Booker

8/10: Thomas Jones 14; Pittsylvania; Pittsylvania; Dr. LEFTRIDGE; Pittsylvania; Prince Edward; 38; James C. HUNT; Prince Edward; Maria Jones 28; Not Known; Dr. LEFTRIDGE; Pittsylvania

8/11: David G. Jones 12; Pittsylvania; Pittsylvania; Dr. LEFTRIDGE; Pittsylvania; Prince Edward; 38; Ø; Ø; Ø; Ø; George Jones

8/12: Mary Branch 15; Cumberland; Prince Edward; Pat JACKSON; Prince Edward; Prince Edward; 63; James D. LIGAN; Prince Edward; Lucella Branch 38; Deceased; Patrick JACKSON; Prince Edward

8/13: Davy Branch 17; Cumberland; Prince Edward; Frank CARTER; Prince Edward; Prince Edward; 63; Ø; Prince Edward

8/14: Lucy Branch 14; Cumberland; Petersburg; Pat JACKSON; Prince Edward; Prince Edward; 63; Ø; Prince Edward

8/15: Branch Branch 10; Cumberland; Petersburg; Pat JACKSON; Prince Edward; Prince Edward; 63; Ø; Prince Edward; Ø; Ø; Ø; Ø; Jiggem Branch

8/16: Harriet Miller 21; Prince Edward; Prince Edward; B. RODGERS; Halifax; Prince Edward; 50; Ed MILLER; Prince Edward; Lizzie Miller 40; Prince Edward; Richard MILLER; Prince Edward

8/17: Francis Miller; Prince Edward; Prince Edward; Ed WITT; Prince Edward; Prince Edward; Ø; Ø; Prince Edward; Ø; Ø; Ø; Ø; Herbert Miller

8/18: Miller 15; Prince Edward; Prince Edward; Ed WITT; Prince Edward; Prince Edward; 60; Richard MILLER; Prince Edward; Eliza Miller 35; Deceased; Ed WITT; Prince Edward

8/19: Catherine Miller 17; Prince Edward; Prince Edward; Ed WITT; Prince Edward; Prince Edward; Ø; Ø; Prince Edward

8/20: Adeline Miller 12; Prince Edward; Prince Edward; Ed WITT; Prince Edward; Prince Edward; Ø; Ø; Prince Edward

8/21: Louisa Miller 10; Prince Edward; Prince Edward; Ed WITT; Prince Edward; Prince Edward; Ø; Ø; Prince Edward

8/22: Ellen Miller 8; Prince Edward; Prince Edward; Ed WITT; Prince Edward; Prince Edward; 60; Ø; Prince Edward; Ø; Ø; Ø; Ø; David Miller

8/23: Griffin Williams 21; Prince Edward; Charlotte; Charles HUNLEY; Charlotte; Prince Edward; 70; Eda EDMONDS; Prince Edward; Dicey Williams 50; Not Known; Matt RICHARDS; Prince Edward; Anderson Williams

8/25: William Ligan 10; Prince Edward; Prince Edward; Mrs. Ag LIGAN; Prince Edward; Prince Edward; 44; Mrs. Ag LIGAN; Prince Edward; Betsey Ligan 39; Farmville; Mrs. Ag LIGAN; Prince Edward; Solomon Ligan

8/27: William Young 22; Lunenburg; Prince Edward; L. IRVING; Prince Edward; Prince Edward; 50; Richard STOKES; Prince Edward; Mary Dazzle 19; Deceased; Born Free; Ø; Phillip Stokes

8/29: Phillis Crawley 13; Lunenburg; Prince Edward; Richard STOKES; Prince Edward; Prince Edward; 36; Alex CRAWLEY; Prince Edward; Eda Stokes 44; Prince Edward; Richard STOKES; Prince Edward; Solomon Crawley

8/32: Ann Stokes 10; Prince Edward; Prince Edward; Richard STOKES; Prince Edward; Prince Edward; 60; Richard STOKES; Prince Edward; Eda Stokes 44; Prince Edward; Richard Stokes; Prince Edward; Henry Stokes

8/34: Nancy Terry 12; Halifax; Prince Edward; B.J. ROGERS; Halifax; Prince Edward; 32; Thomas POWELL; Halifax; Ann Jones 26; Prince Edward; B.J. ROGERS; Halifax; Terry Powell

Table 19 Prince Edward

Register of Colored Persons cohabiting together as Husband and Wife

pg/ln; h/age; pob; h res; occ; last owner; res; w/age; pob; last owner; res; children/age; date cohabitation

1/1: Robert Lacey 66; Prince Edward; Prince Edward; Laborer; Dr. J. LACEY; Prince Edward; Harriet Lacy 68; Prince Edward; Prince Edward; Nathan HARVEY; Charlotte; Ø; 25 Dec 1830

1/2: Emanuel Lee 46; Prince Edward; Prince Edward; Laborer; Sam CARTER; Prince Edward; Jane Lee 24; Prince Edward; Prince Edward; Mrs. J. RICE; Prince Edward; Ø; 15 Sept 1865

1/3: Wesley Hill 22; Prince Edward; Prince Edward; Laborer; Born Free; Ø; Lucy J. Hill 19; Lunenburg; Prince Edward; John RICE; Prince Edward; Mary E. Hill infant; 25 Dec 1863

1/4: George Redd 44; Prince Edward; Prince Edward; Laborer; Truman REDD; Prince Edward; Rose Redd 36; Prince Edward; Prince Edward; Alex FAULKNER; Prince Edward; Amanda Redd 3; 12 May 1862

1/5: Sidney Smith 26; Nottoway; Prince Edward; Laborer; Mrs. M. FARRELL; Prince Edward; Lucy Smith 18; Prince Edward; Prince Edward; Mrs. S. PERKINSON; Prince Edward; Ø; 20 Dec 1865

1/6: William Jeter 24; Nottoway; Prince Edward; Laborer; Mrs. S. PERKINSON; Prince Edward; Alice Jeter 20; Prince Edward; Prince Edward; Mrs. A. WATKINS; Prince Edward; Sydney Jeter 2; 1 Apr 1863

1/7: Spencer Watson 60; Prince Edward; Prince Edward; Laborer; Samuel WATSON; Prince Edward; Lesea Watson 45; Halifax; Prince Edward; Alex FAULKNER; Prince Edward; 16; 1 Jan 1863

1/8: Spot Saunders 29; Bedford; Prince Edward; Laborer; Jacob OBERLEY; Prince Edward; Dilsey Saunders 30; Prince Edward; Prince Edward; Syrus ALLEN; Prince Edward; Ø; 1 Apr 1858

1/9: Peter Allen 38; Prince Edward; Prince Edward; Laborer; John J. RIGGEN; Prince Edward; Peggie Allen 26; Prince Edward; Prince Edward; John J. RIGGEN; Prince Edward; Samuel T. Allen 10, Martha Allen 3; 1 Jan 1856

1/11: Pat Anderson 50; Prince Edward; Prince Edward; Laborer; Leach ANDERSON; Prince Edward; Sallie Anderson 48; Cumberland; Prince Edward; Thomas DAVIS; Prince Edward; Ø; 30 Jan? 1863

1/12: William Austin 38; Prince Edward; Prince Edward; Laborer; Samuel WATSON; Prince Edward; Hannah Austin 34; Prince Edward; Prince Edward; A.A. ALLEN; Charlotte; Henry F. Austin 15, Spencer B. Austin 13, C. Francis Austin 12, Mary L. Austin 10, Sarah Jane Austin 1; 25 Dec 1848

1/17: Asa Frinnell 50; Cumberland; Prince Edward; Laborer; Dr. MATTAN__; Prince Edward; Rhoda Frinnell; Cumberland; Prince Edward; Robert PAGE; Cumberland; Beverly Fralan 16, Nancy Fralan 14, Asher Fralan 11; 1 Jan 1836

1/20: Berry Watson 28; Prince Edward; Prince Edward; Laborer; Mr. A. WATSON; Prince Edward; Martha Watson 23; Prince Edward; Prince Edward; Richard CARTER; Prince Edward; Betty Watson 3; 1 May 1860

1/21: Daniel Fralan 28; Cumberland; Prince Edward; Laborer; Robert PAGE; Cumberland; Frances Fralan 26; Cumberland; Prince Edward; James D. JENKINS; Cumberland; John D. Fralan 5; 19 Jan 1860

1/22: Adam Watson 66; Prince Edward; Prince Edward; Laborer; Mrs. A. WATSON; Prince Edward; __lby Watson 56; Prince Edward; Prince Edward; John REDD; Prince Edward; Ø; 15 May 1850

1/23: Lee Redd 32; Prince Edward; Prince Edward; Laborer; John REDD; Prince Edward; Martha Redd 28; Prince Edward; Prince Edward; George REDD; Prince Edward; Frank Redd 4, Abram Redd infant; 1 Mar 1860

1/24: Taylor Page 22; Prince Edward; Prince Edward; Laborer; Dr. BERKELEY; Prince Edward; Anna Page 20; Nottoway; Prince Edward; _.W. FITZGERALD; Prince Edward; Ø; 20 Jan 1866

1/26: Jack Top 68; Prince Edward; Prince Edward; Laborer; B.J. WANHAM; Prince Edward; Selpha Top 27; Prince Edward; Prince Edward; James WATSON; Prince Edward; Aggie Tap 8, Lucy Top 6, Benjamin Top 7, Jackson Top 2, Ellen infant; 20 Apr 1851?

1/31: Isham Woodson 60; Prince Edward; Prince Edward; Laborer; Richard WOODSON; Prince Edward; Betsy Woodson 52; Prince Edward; Prince Edward; Charles MORTON; Prince Edward; Ø; 1 Jan 1846

1/32: Claiborne Baker 38; Prince Edward; Prince Edward; Laborer; N. HAINEY?; Charlotte; Milly Baker 30; Prince Edward; Prince Edward; Richard WOODSON; Prince Edward; Mariah W. Baker 7, Willis 3; 10 June 1854

1/34: Pitt Baulden 32; Prince Edward; Prince Edward; Laborer; Mr. H. WATKINS; Prince Edward; M.A. Baulden 23; Nottoway; Prince Edward; Asa DICKINSON; Prince Edward; Ø; 6 Aug 1862

1/35: Edward Jackson 52; Prince Edward; Prince Edward; Laborer; Mr. M. FAWLER; Prince Edward; Sally Jackson 38; Prince Edward; Prince Edward; Mrs. WATSON; Prince Edward; Ø; 12 Aug 1852

1/36: Madison Baulden 58; Prince Edward; Prince Edward; Laborer; Mr. WATKINS; Prince Edward; Elsey Baulden 46; Prince Edward; Prince Edward; Miss C.A. WOOD; Prince Edward; Amanda Baulden 17, Mary Baulden 13, Edward Baulden 20, Sterling Baulden 18; 12 Sept 1839

2/1: Thomas Coleman 23; Prince Edward; Prince Edward; Laborer; Thomas EWING; Prince Edward; Susan Coleman 23; Lunenburg; Prince Edward; Alex CRAWLEY; Prince Edward; Ø; 25 Dec 1862

2/2: Alpheus Smithers 22; Albemarle; Prince Edward; Laborer; G. HARPER; Prince Edward; Betsy Smithers 20; Prince Edward; Prince Edward; Lill ELLIOTT; Prince Edward; William Smithers infant; 20 Oct 1865

2/3: Armstead Crawley 60; Lunenburg; Prince Edward; Laborer; Alex CRAWLEY; Prince Edward; Emily Crawley 54; Bedford; Prince Edward; Richard STOKES; Prince Edward; Ø; 25 Dec 1828

2/4: John Wesley 32; Prince Edward; Prince Edward; Laborer; Frank REDD; Prince Edward; Mary Redd 28; Prince Edward; Prince Edward; Louann? REDD 28; Prince Edward; Lucy Jane Wesley 3; 25 Dec 1860

2/5: Isaac Redd 28; Prince Edward; Prince Edward; Laborer; Truman REDD; Prince Edward; Lucy A. Redd 36; Nottoway; Prince Edward; Asa DICKINSON; Prince Edward; John Redd 3, Isaac Redd infant; 25 Dec 1862

2/7: Anderson Redd 36; Prince Edward; Prince Edward; Laborer; Truman REDD; Prince Edward; Elvira Redd 34; Prince Edward; Prince Edward; Ed REDD; Prince Edward; Frank Redd 10, Henry Redd 8, Samuel? Redd 7, John Redd 2; 25 Dec 1853

2/11: Syndey Jeffries 30; Prince Edward; Prince Edward; Laborer; Ed JEFFRIES; Prince Edward; Abby Jeffries 26; Prince Edward; Prince Edward; William H. CARY; Prince Edward; Fanny Jeffries _; 31 Dec 1861

2/12: Henry Redd 35; Prince Edward; Prince Edward; Laborer; T. REDD; Prince Edward; Polly S. Redd _4; Lunenburg; Prince Edward; Alex CRAWLEY; Prince Edward; Albert Redd 4, Elizabeth Redd 1; 25 Dec 1860

2/14: Thomas Foster 22; Prince Edward; Prince Edward; Laborer; James FOSTER; Prince Edward; Sarah Foster 20; Prince Edward; Prince Edward; Hiram? REDD; Prince Edward; Perlinna Foster infant; 1 Dec 1864

2/15: Patrick Ewing 46; Prince Edward; Prince Edward; Laborer; Thomas EWING; Prince Edward; Jane Ewing 44; Prince Edward; Prince Edward; Mrs. B. FAWLKES; Prince Edward; Emma Ewing 16, Susan Ewing 13, Martha Ewing 12, Doctor Ewing 8, Spencer Ewing 4; 15 Aug 1842

2/20: Booker Foster 48; Cumberland; Prince Edward; Laborer; F.D. REDD; Prince Edward; Ann Foster 54; Cumberland; Prince Edward; F.D. REDD; Prince Edward; Samuel B. Foster 19, Emma Foster 16, Anderson Foster 13, Nulty Foster 10; 1 Jan 1830

2/24: Anderson Childs 32; Prince Edward; Prince Edward; Laborer; F.D. REDD; Prince Edward; Mary Childs 28; Prince Edward; Prince Edward; R. STOKES; Prince Edward; Booker Childs 1; 1 Jan 1861

2/25: Charles Early 24; Prince Edward; Prince Edward; Laborer; F.D. REDD; Prince Edward; Sarah Early 20; Prince Edward; Prince Edward; Miss C.H. REDD; Prince Edward; Charles Early 1; 25 Jan 1865

2/26: Abram Morgan 32; Prince Edward; Prince Edward; Laborer; F.D. REDD; Prince Edward; Jane Morgan 32; Prince Edward; Prince Edward; J.T. REDD; Prince Edward; May Susan Morgan 8, Alice Morgan 6, Patrick Morgan 4, infant; Jan 1857

2/30: Nelson Naylor 59; Prince Edward; Prince Edward; Laborer; John W. REDD; Prince Edward; Amy Naylor 54; Buckingham; Prince Edward; J.W. REDD; Prince Edward; Maria Naylor 17, Nelson Naylor 15, Melvin Naylor 12; 1 Jan 1846

2/33: Henry Thweatt 28; Prince Edward; Prince Edward; Laborer; Luther JEFFRIES; Prince Edward; Mary A. Jeffries 23; Albemarle; Prince Edward; William WOODSON; Prince Edward; James Jeffries infant; 12 Nov 1860

2/34: Benjamin Redd 60; Prince Edward; Prince Edward; Laborer; Truman REDD; Prince Edward; Maria Redd 41; Prince Edward; Prince Edward; James FOSTER; Prince Edward; Ø; 20 June 1860

2/35: Peter Watkins 46; Charlotte; Prince Edward; Laborer; Lee REDD; Prince Edward; Lina Watkins 34; Pittsylvania; Prince Edward; Dr. H. WATKINS; Prince Edward; John Watkins 5; 25 Dec 1854

2/36: J.W. Randolph 32; Prince Edward; Prince Edward; Laborer; George FAWLKES; Prince Edward; M.E. Randolph 24; Prince Edward; Prince Edward; Frank RICE; Prince Edward; Ø; 1 Apr 1864

2/37: William Scott 36; Prince Edward; Prince Edward; Laborer; W.F. SCOTT; Prince Edward; Betsy Scott 26; Prince Edward; Prince Edward; Daniel ALLEN; Prince Edward; Maria Scott 4; 27 Dec 1858

2/38: Mack Cardwell 28; Prince Edward; Prince Edward; Laborer; James WHITEHEAD; Prince Edward; Lina Cardwell 27; Prince Edward; Prince Edward; Samuel CARTER; Prince Edward; Jacob Cardwell 5, Jeff Cardwell 4, Stonewall Cardwell 3, Andrew Cardwell infant; 1 Sept 1858

3/1: Jeff Brown 36; Prince Edward; Prince Edward; Laborer; Mrs. MICHAUX; Prince Edward; Lucinda? 36; Prince Edward; Prince Edward; Mrs. HILL; Prince Edward; George P. Brown, infant; 10 Nov 1865

3/2: Hampton Wade 49; Lunenburg; Prince Edward; Laborer; Philip SNEED; Prince Edward; Sarah Wade 36; Lunenburg; Prince Edward; P. SNEED; Prince Edward; Andrew J. Wade infant; 18 Mar 1865

3/3: Clem Carrington 54; Prince Edward; Prince Edward; Laborer; Mrs. P. DUPUY; Prince Edward; Martha Carrington 45; Prince Edward; Prince Edward; Mrs. P. DUPUY; Prince Edward; John Carrington 18, Mary J. Carrington 17, George W. Carrington 16, Randal W. Carrington 15, Celia Carrington 10, Clem Carrington 9, Thomas G. Carrington 8, Abram Carrington 5, Archy Carrington 2, Rachel C. Carrington 1; 1 Nov 1846

3/14: Nace Butler 54; Maryland; Prince Edward; Laborer; Numan TUCKER; Charlotte; Sukey Butler 23; Charlotte; Prince Edward; R. CHUBB__; Bedford; George Butler 1, Milly Butler 3; 25 Dec 1860

3/15: Lewis Gilharn 56; Bedford; Prince Edward; Laborer; Rice GILHAM; Prince Edward; Louisa Gilham 45; Prince Edward; Prince Edward; Rice GILHAM; Prince Edward; William Gilham 19; 4 July 1836

3/16: James Watson 28; Prince Edward; Prince Edward; Laborer; Miss. M. JEFFRIES; Prince Edward; Elsey Watson 22; Prince Edward; Prince Edward; William F. SCOTT; Prince Edward; infant; 25 Dec 1865

3/17: Peter Davenport 28; Prince Edward; Prince Edward; Laborer; Samuel B. DAVENPORT; Prince Edward; Margaret Davenport 25; Prince Edward; Prince Edward; James N. GILHAM; Prince Edward; Rachel Davenport infant; 25 Dec 1860

3/18: Henry Clay 36; Charlotte; Prince Edward; Laborer; Dr. James? DUPUY; Prince Edward; Rachel Clay 38; Charlotte; Prince Edward; Mrs. P. DUPUY; Prince Edward; Ø; 15 Mar 1864

3/19: Richard Branch 54; Prince Edward; Prince Edward; Laborer; E.L. WOMACK; Prince Edward; Chaney Branch 44; Charlotte; Prince Edward; D.F. WOMACK; Prince Edward; Catherine Branch infant; 30 Oct 1856

3/20: William Hall 62; Balderlotte?; Prince Edward; Laborer; James BELL; Prince Edward; Lousia Hall 40; Prince Edward; Prince Edward; Dr. H. LACEY; Prince Edward; Whitfield Hall 12, Lydia Hall 9, Brittania Hall 7, Isaac Hall 4, James Hall 1; 25 Dec 1846

3/25: Daniel Casey 48; Cumberland; Prince Edward; Laborer; George W. BELL; Prince Edward; Betsey Casey 46; Prince Edward; Prince Edward; Lazarus P__INCH?; Cumberland; Benjamin Casey 16, Jenny Casey 8, Gaskill Casey 5; 25 Dec 1843

3/28: Thomas Jefferson _4; Prince Edward; Prince Edward; Laborer; Archy WOMACK; Prince Edward; Charlotte Jefferson 64; Powhatan; Prince Edward; Jessee MICHAUX; Prince Edward; Ø; 25 Dec 1830

3/29: Peyton Dillan 60; Prince Edward; Prince Edward; Laborer; John DILLON; Prince Edward; Nancy Dillon 44; Prince Edward; Prince Edward; Eliza BAKER; Prince Edward; Ø; 28 Dec 1854

3/30: Lewis Johnson 48; Amelia; Prince Edward; Laborer; F. ANDERSON; Prince Edward; Susan Johnson 23; Prince Edward; Prince Edward; H.C. GUTHRIE; Prince Edward; Ø; 10 Jan 1853

3/31: James Woodson 42; Tennessee; Prince Edward; Laborer; Richard WOODSON; Prince Edward; Betsey Woodson 46; Prince Edward; Prince Edward; Mrs. E. BAKER; Prince Edward; Ø; 1 Mar 1850

3/32: Branch Dillon 44; Prince Edward; Prince Edward; Laborer; John DILLON; Prince Edward; Violet Dillon 32; Prince Edward; Prince Edward; James WHITEHEAD; Prince Edward; 25 Dec 1853

3/33: James Elkin 38; Prince Edward; Prince Edward; Laborer; C. ELKIN; Prince Edward; Matilda Elkin 28; Prince Edward; Prince Edward; James PIGG; Prince Edward; Ø; 25 Dec 1862

3/34: Anthony Harvey 76; Charlotte; Prince Edward; Laborer; Charles C. HARVEY; Prince Edward; Christian Harvey 64; Charlotte; Prince Edward; Mr. P. THORNTON; Charlotte; Ø; 1 Jan 1816

3/35: Maguhate? Rice 36; Prince Edward; Prince Edward; Laborer; Mrs. M. RICE; Prince Edward; Elila Rice 32; Prince Edward; Prince Edward; Mr. S. BALDWIN; Prince Edward; Washington Rice 6, Lucy Jane Rice 2; 18 Oct 1854

3/38: Lignus Harvey 48; Charlotte; Prince Edward; Laborer; William THORNTON; Prince Edward; Peggy Harvey 41; Charlotte; Prince Edward; Allen BAKER; Prince Edward; Betsey Harvey 16; 1 Jan 1849

3/39: Robert Corcoran 28; Prince Edward; Prince Edward; Laborer; J. COCHRAN; Prince Edward; Harriett Corcoran 2_; Prince Edward; Prince Edward; Mrs. Eliza BAKER; Prince Edward; William Corcoran 5, Harvey? Corcoran 4; 1 Jan 1860

4/1: James Harvey 44; Charlotte; Prince Edward; Laborer; Thomas HARVEY; Charlotte; Jane Harvey 34; Charlotte; Prince Edward; Thomas HARVEY; Prince Edward; Alice Harvey 13, Lizzie Harvey 10, Sarah Harvey 9, Clem Harvey 5, Jenny Harvey infant; 1 Jan 1850

4/6: Peter Elliott 44; Prince Edward; Prince Edward; Laborer; Allan ELLIOTT; Pittsylvania Co., (No Carolina); Nancy Elliott 34; Prince Edward; Prince Edward; Allan ELLIOTT; No. Carolina; William Elliott 18, Sarah Elliott 14, Felix Elliott, Fanny Elliott 8, Mary Elliott 7, Albert Elliott 10, Julia Elliott infant; 1 Jan 1848

4/13: _ist_l Carter 55; Prince Edward; Prince Edward; Laborer; William A. WOMACK; Prince Edward; America Carter 39; Prince Edward; Prince Edward; German GILHAM; Prince Edward; Jhas. Carter 16, Fanny Carter 12, Olivia Carter 5, Burrell Carter 3; 1 Jan 18__

4/17: John Baker 38; Prince Edward; Prince Edward; Laborer; Mrs. E. BAKER; Prince Edward; Judy Baker 36; Appomattox; Prince Edward; R. WYATT; Prince Edward; Frederick Baker 16, Ed Baker 12, John Baker 11, Rose Baker 8, Ida Baker 7, David Baker 4, Violet Baker 2; 15 Feb 1848

4/24: Dr. Walker 38; Appomattox; Prince Edward; Laborer; G. GILHAM; Prince Edward; Tina Walker 28; Appomattox; Prince Edward; Mrs. B.A. MATTLEY; Prince Edward; John Walker 10, Elizah Walker 7; 25 Dec 1859

4/26: Archy Davenport 36; Prince Edward; Prince Edward; Laborer; S.B. DAVENPORT; Prince Edward; Fanny Davenport 34; Appomattox; Prince Edward; H. PA_PHIN; Appomattox; Ø; 15 July 1848

4/27: Zach Gaines 56; Bedford; Prince Edward; Laborer; B.F. WOMACK; Prince Edward; Sukey Gaines 44; Charlotte; Prince Edward; D.F. WOMACK; Prince Edward; Rachel Gaines 6, Henry Gaines 9, Richard Gaines 8, R. Ann Gaines 6, Gaines infant; 25 Dec 1858

4/32: Thomas Baker 26; Prince Edward; Prince Edward; Laborer; Eliza BAKER; Prince Edward; Lucy Baker 22; Appomattox; Prince Edward; Thomas HICKS; Prince Edward; Mary _. Baker, Sarah E. Baker (twins) infants; 25 Dec 1864

4/34: Aaron Dodson 40; Prince Edward; Prince Edward; Laborer; D.F. WOMACK; Prince Edward; Mary J. Dodson 36; Charlotte; Prince Edward; D.F. WOMACK; Prince Edward; Judith Dodson 16, Spencer Dodson 13, Frank Dodson 12, Betsey Ann Dodson 6, Stanhope Dodson 4, Robert L. Dodson infant; 25 Dec 1864

5/1: William Smith 46; Charlotte; Prince Edward; Laborer; Nathan PRICE; Charlotte; Rachel Smith 40; Prince Edward; Prince Edward; Nathan PRICE; Charlotte; Hannah Smith 16, May Smith 3, Panetta? 5; 1 Jan 1846

5/4: Tim Scott 28; Cumberland; Prince Edward; Laborer; John OVERTON; Cumberland; Nancy Scott 22; Prince Edward; Prince Edward; R. MARSHAL; Prince Edward; James Scott 2; 2 Dec 1859

5/5: Jerry Johnson 48; Prince Edward; Prince Edward; Laborer; John JENKINS; Prince Edward; M.A. Johnson 42; Charlotte; Prince Edward; Dr. DICKINSON; Prince Edward; Lucy Johnson 8, Clem Johnson 8. William Johnson 6, Peter Johnson 2; 1 Jan 1855

5/9: Samuel Richardson 28; Prince Edward; Prince Edward; Laborer; Born Free; Ø; Margaret Richardson 28; Prince Edward; Prince Edward; Dr. TERRY; Prince Edward; Maithat? Richardson 12, Louisa Richardson 10, Samuel Richardson 9, Nancy Richardson 7, Norman Richardson 5, Sallie Richardson 3; 26 Dec 1852

5/15: Archer Scott 24; Prince Edward; Prince Edward; Laborer; W. WHITEHEAD; Prince Edward; Maria Scott 18; Prince Edward; Prince Edward; John DILLON; Prince Edward; Ø; 25 Dec 1865

5/16: George Miller 50; Prince Edward; Prince Edward; Laborer; William CHUMMY; Lunenburg; Rosetta Miller 46; Lunenburg; Prince Edward; William CHUMMY; Lunenburg; Patrick Miller 16, Lucinda Miller 13, Martha Miller 10, Anderson Miller 5, Missouri Miller infant; 1 Jan 1850

5/21: John Chafin 53; Cumberland; Prince Edward; Laborer; Isham GILLAM; Buckingham; Mary Chafin 22; Pennsylvania; Prince Edward; Born Free; Ø; 25 Dec 1865

5/22: Abram Brown 56; Prince Edward; Prince Edward; Laborer; James B. ELY; Prince Edward; Nicey Brown 50; Ø; Prince Edward; H.E. WATKINS; Prince Edward; Stokes Brown 15, Marshal Brown 12, Albert Brown 9; 1 Jan 1830

5/25: William Anderson 38; Amelia; Prince Edward; Laborer; H. ANDERSON; Prince Edward; Hannah And 28; Prince Edward; Prince Edward; Thomas PERKINSON; Prince Edward; Lucinda Anderson 2; 25 Dec 1864

5/26: Luke Johnson 28; Fredericksburg; Prince Edward; Laborer; William D. PRICE; Prince Edward; Mary Johnson 28; Cumberland; Prince Edward; B.A. WILSON; Cumberland; Charles Johnson 15; 1 Jan 1852

5/27: Thomas Anderson 36; Prince Edward; Prince Edward; Laborer; R.H. WATKINS; Prince Edward; America Johnson 38; Prince Edward; Prince Edward; Mrs. H. FOWLKES; Prince Edward; Daniel Anderson 9, Priscila Anderson 8, Parthena Anderson 6, Thomas Anderson 2; 25 Dec 185_

5/31: Daniel Cheatham 30; Lunenburg; Prince Edward; Laborer; B. CHEATHAM; Prince Edward; Cornelia C. 30; Lunenburg; Prince Edward; Adam McKINNEY; Prince Edward; Minnie Cheatham 6, John Cheatham 4, Lewis Cheatham 1; 20 Aug 186_

5/34: William Mitchell 64; Charlotte; Prince Edward; Laborer; Charles DANIEL; Prince Edward; Anna Mitchell 60; Buckingham; Prince Edward; _. SHEPHERD; Richmond; Ø; 20 Aug 1852

5/35: Armstead Wootten 28; Prince Edward; Prince Edward; Laborer; Taylor WOOTTEN; Prince Edward; Susan Wootten 32; Prince Edward; Prince Edward; Dr. L.T. WOOTTEN; Prince Edward; Pathe? Wootten 4, Mayat Wootten 2, Wootten infant; 19 July 1852

5/38: Branch Booker 24; Prince Edward; Prince Edward; Laborer; J.T. LOCKETT; Prince Edward; Mary Booker 20; Prince Edward; Prince Edward; Edmund WOODS; Amelia; Ø; 25 Dec 1866

6/1: Isham Evans 32; Prince Edward; Prince Edward; Carpenter; Born Free; Ø; Sarah Evans 30; Prince Edward; Prince Edward; J. OVERBY; Prince Edward; Palmer Evans 11, Eliza Evans 6, Cornelia Evans 1; 20 Feb 1854

6/4: Daniel King 44; Granville Co., So. Carolina; Prince Edward; Laborer; Dr. William CARRINGTON; Halifax; Katy King 44; Charlotte; Prince Edward; Dr. William CARRINGTON; Halifax; Paul King 18, Hampton King 16, Lewis King 14, Scylla? King 11, Washington King 8, Meschack Washington 6, John Washington 4, Elizabeth Washington 1; 25 Dec 1846

6/12: Jeremy Ross 30; Cumberland; Prince Edward; Laborer; James AMOS; Cumberland; Rosina Ross 21; Prince Edward; Prince Edward; S. SHEPHERD; Prince Edward; James Ross infant; 1 Oct 1865

6/13: Booker Glenn 54; Charlotte; Prince Edward; Laborer; C.C. LUCKET; Prince Edward; Dolly Glenn 55; Prince Edward; Prince Edward; Mrs.? M.A. WANHAM; Prince Edward; Ø; 25 Dec 1843

6/14: Robert Eppes 50; No. Carolina; Prince Edward; Laborer; Phil BOLLING; Buckingham; Sally Eppes 45; No. Carolina; Prince Edward; Phillip BOLLING; Buckingham; Phillip Eppes 13, Washington (Eppes?) 15; 25 Dec 1839

7/1: G.H. Mason 29; Surry; Prince Edward; Laborer; H.E. WARREN; Prince Edward; Frances Mason 21; Gloucester; Prince Edward; P.H. JACKSON; Prince Edward; Robert L. Mason 2; 27 Dec 1862

7/2: Dennis Clark 58; Prince Edward; Prince Edward; Laborer; Mrs. P. CLARK; Prince Edward; Sallie Clark 50; Prince Edward; Prince Edward; Charles WADE; Prince Edward; Minerva Clark 10, Dennis Clark 8; 25 Dec 1836

7/4: Walker Johnson 48; Prince Edward; Prince Edward; Laborer; Sylvanius JOHNSON; Petersburg; Julia Johnson 48; Prince Edward; Prince Edward; Mr. N. _OTTLEY; Prince Edward; Ø; 25 Dec 1852

7/5: Lewis Green 47; Mecklenburg; Prince Edward; Laborer; Dr. Thomas OWEN; Prince Edward; Mary Green 47; Prince Edward; Prince Edward; Dr. Thomas OWEN; Prince Edward; Cobin Green 10, Ranison? Green 8; 25 Dec 1851

7/6: H.B. Thompson 26; Prince Edward; Prince Edward; Laborer; John H. BOYD; Jefferson, Tennessee; M.E. Thompson 23; Petersburg; Prince Edward; John H. BOYD; Jefferson, Tennessee; Ø; 1 Feb 1863

7/8: Dennis Wootten 28; Prince Edward; Prince Edward; Laborer; W.T. WOOTTEN; Prince Edward; Nelly Wootten 23; Prince Edward; Prince Edward; Charles WADE; Prince Edward; Sarah Wootten 3, Felix infant; 18 25 Dec 51

7/10: Anderson Harper 75; Nottoway; Prince Edward; Laborer; Mrs. Sarah HARPER; Nottoway; Catherine Harper 60; Prince Edward; Prince Edward; Samuel BRADSHAW; Prince Edward; Ø; 1 Jan 1863

7/11: Isaac Johnson 40; Chesterfield; Prince Edward; Laborer; Ransom CHUMMY; Prince Edward; E. Jane Johnson 27; Amelia; Prince Edward; Mrs. Mary MILLER; Nottoway; Ø; 25 Dec 1851

7/13: Peter Reed 35; Prince Edward; Prince Edward; Laborer; William S. MORTON; Cumberland; Emily Reed 28; Greensboro, Georgia; Prince Edward; Miss Anne MORTON; Cumberland; Philip Reed 4, Janius? Reed 2; 15 May 1851

7/15: James Reed 48; Prince Edward; Prince Edward; Laborer; J.G. SMITH; Prince Edward; Jane Reed 37; Amelia; Prince Edward; James OVERTON; Prince Edward; Meyers Reed 16, Nelson Reed 12, Adolphus Reed 10, Sydney Reed, 8, Samuel Reed 6, Lulu Reed 4; 25 Dec 1846

7/21: Hercules Booker 32; Amelia; Prince Edward; Laborer; Mr. B. HURT; Prince Edward; Maria Booker 24; Prince Edward; Prince Edward; B.A. FARLEY; Prince Edward; Ø; 25 Dec 1862

7/22: Henry Branch 42; Prince Edward; Prince Edward; Laborer; Miss Alice AMES; Amelia; M. Ann Branch 38; Prince Edward; Prince Edward; P.A. ELLINGTON; Prince Edward; Washington Branch 18, Maria Branch 16, Sarah Branch 14, M. Cath Branch 12, Creed Branch 10, Cassandra Branch 6, Math Branch 2; 15 Apr 1846

7/29: James Phillips 28; Prince Edward; Prince Edward; Laborer; James PHILLIPS; Prince Edward; Caroline Phillips 21; Prince Edward; Prince Edward; James VAUGHAN; Amelia; Ø; 25 Dec 1855

7/30: Robert Scott 26; Prince Edward; Prince Edward; Laborer; Mrs. Lou LIGAN; Prince Edward; Patty Scott 21; Prince Edward; Prince Edward; James A. WATSON; Prince Edward; Ø ; 28 Dec 1864

7/31: Edwin Miller 56; Prince Edward; Prince Edward; Laborer; Geles. A. MILLER; Amelia; Milly Miller 35; Nottoway; Prince Edward; Charles A. CRUMP; Nottoway; Taylor Miller 18, Emma Miller 13, Alice Miller 7, Bettey Miller 12; 1 Jan 1847

7/35: Benjamin Miller 60; Amelia; Prince Edward; Laborer; P. MILLER; Nottoway; Phebe Miller 32; Nottoway; Prince Edward; W.D. WILDINSON; Prince Edward; Laura A. Miller 8, Benjamin Miller 6, Jackson Miller 3, William Miller 2; 20 Sept 1854

7/39:Nim Robinson 40; Prince Edward; Prince Edward; Laborer; John OVERTON; Cumberland; Sarah Robinson 23; Prince Edward; Prince Edward; James WATHAL; Prince Edward; Ø; 25 Dec 1863

8/1: Stephen Patterson 56; Prince Edward; Prince Edward; Laborer; Samuel HUNT; Prince Edward; Lucinda Patterson 30; Prince Edward; Prince Edward; Samuel HUNT; Prince Edward; Sophia Patterson 11, Brice Patterson 9; 1 Jan 185_

8/3: Baker Scott 28; Prince Edward; Prince Edward; Laborer; Samuel HUNT; Prince Edward; Pattie Scott 24; Prince Edward; Prince Edward; W. WILSON; Prince Edward; Abner Scott 2; 25 Dec 1863

8/4: Madison Eames 48; Cumberland; Prince Edward; Laborer; S.D. SPENCER; Prince Edward; Caroline Eames 54; Prince Edward; Prince Edward; Thomas WOMACK; Prince Edward; Ø; 1 Jan 1850

8/5: Robert Bee 41; Richmond; Prince Edward; Laborer; Born Free; Ø; Martha Bee 36; Prince Edward; Prince Edward; Born Free; Ø; Willie Bee 3, Samuel Bee 7; 25 Dec 1851

8/6: James Knight 38; Prince Edward; Prince Edward; Laborer; William T. RICE; Prince Edward; Prudence Rice 32; Prince Edward; Prince Edward; Henry MOTLEY; Prince Edward; Betty Rice 16, John Rice 8, Mary Rice infant; 25 Dec 1850

8/10: John Johnson 48; Prince Edward; Prince Edward; Laborer; Born Free; Ø; Mary Johnson 40; Buckingham; Prince Edward; Born Free; Ø; 15 Oct 1853

8/11: James Trent 24; Buckingham; Prince Edward; Laborer; James COLEMAN; Buckingham; Fanny Trent 18; Prince Edward; Prince Edward; Dr. T. VENABLE; Prince Edward; Ø; 20 Feb 1866

8/12: Samuel Bartlett 53; Prince Edward; Prince Edward; Laborer; born Free; Ø; Mary Bartlett 48; Cumberland; Prince Edward; George W. DANIEL; Prince Edward; Samuel Bartlett 19, Woodson Bartlett 17, Paul Bartlett 15, James Bartlett 7, Fred Bartlett 5, George Bartlett 3, Catherine Bartlett 17, Ella Bartlett 12, Jenny Bartlett 8, Margaret Bartlett; 15 Mar 1836

8/22: Noah H. Blue 28; Dumfries; Prince Edward; Laborer; N. MATTHEWS; Lunenburg; H. Ann Blue 26; Lunenburg; Prince Edward; Robert DICKERSON; Prince Edward; Alice L. Blue 3, Thomas F. Blue infant; 15 Nov 1862

8/24: Fred Land 34; Buckingham; Prince Edward; Laborer; William LAND; Warren, Kentucky; Hannah C. Land 38; Prince Edward; Prince Edward; Born Free; Ø; Ø; 25 Dec 1864

8/25: Mose Haskins 36; Farmville; Prince Edward; Laborer; Albert BALDWIN; Buckingham; Mary Haskins 28; Buckingham; Prince Edward; C. ELKIN; Buckingham; John Haskins 13, Phil Haskins 10, Guil? Haskins 6, Haskins infant; 25 Dec 1852

8/29: Ben Bartlett 54; Buckingham; Prince Edward; Laborer; Born Free; Ø; Jane Bartlett 46; Pittsylvania; Prince Edward; Born Free; Ø; Ø; 1 Jan 1858

8/30: Sam Rain 22; Prince Edward; Prince Edward; Laborer; William WEAVER; Prince Edward; Eliza Rain 21; Prince Edward; Prince Edward; John FOSTER; Prince Edward; infant; 25 Dec 1863

8/31: Spencer Griffin 56; Nottoway; Prince Edward; Laborer; B. MARSHAL; Lunenburg; Maria Griffin 44; Prince Edward; Prince Edward; Mrs. HARPER; Nottoway; Ø; 25 Dec 1844

8/32: Fred Miller 61; Prince Edward; Prince Edward; Laborer; E.F. MILLER; Prince Edward; Charity Miller 52; Nottoway; Prince Edward; E.F. MILLER; Prince Edward; Anderson Miller 20, Armstead Miller 17, Sam Miller 13, Jeter Miller 9; 1 Feb 1825

8/36: Peter Booker? 24; Nottoway; Prince Edward; Laborer; Mrs. Sallie HARPER; Nottoway; Louisa Booker 24; Nottoway; Prince Edward; T.J. OSBORN; Nottoway; Carlethn/Carlether? Booker 2; 1 Jan 1864

8/37: Ephraim Taylor 70; Lunenburg; Prince Edward; Laborer; William CLEMENTS; Prince Edward; Margaret Taylor 60; Prince Edward; Prince Edward; Ed MILLER; Prince Edward; Ø; 15 Sept 1860

8/38: Beverly Branch 44; Prince Edward; Prince Edward; Laborer; Daniel WITT; Prince Edward; Polly Branch 36; Cumberland; Prince Edward; Daniel WITT; Prince Edward; Fanny Branch 12, Eliza Branch 11, Alice Branch 5, infant; 25 Dec 1853

9/1: Robert White 46; Prince Edward; Farmville; Laborer; Dr. SPENCER; Farmville; Susan White 40; Prince Edward; Farmville; S.W. VENABLE; Petersburg; Isaac White 16, Hopson White 14; 25 Dec 1846

9/3: Samuel Bradley 38; Prince Edward; Farmville; Laborer; William DUNNINGTON; Charlotte; Martha Bradley 38; Prince Edward; Farmville; Sam WHEELER; Appomattox; Sarah Bradley 17, Jenny Bradley 12, Emily Bradley 10, George Bradley 8, Isiah Bradley 4, James Bradley 4; 15 Oct 1845

9/9: Abram Taylor 26; Prince Edward; Farmville; Laborer; George R. DAVIS; Prince Edward; Betsey Taylor 24; Prince Edward; Farmville; George R. DAVIS; Prince Edward; Julia A. Taylor 8, Robert Taylor 4 mos; 26 Dec 1860

9/11: Charles Allen 52; Buckingham; Farmville; Laborer; William ANDERSON; Cumberland; Avy? Allen 36; Cumberland; Farmville; Benjamin WILSON; Cumberland; Ø; 1 Jan 1858

9/12: John Randal 50; Prince Edward; Farmville; Laborer; Dr. P. SOUTHALL; Cumberland; Clarissa Randal 70; Prince Edward; Farmville; Dr. P. SOUTHALL; Cumberland; Ø; 25 Dec 1859

9/13: John Armstead 26; Prince Edward; Prince Edward; Laborer; Mr. S. WILSON; Prince Edward; Susan Armstead 26; Prince Edward; Farmville; Mrs. B. WILSON; Prince Edward; Ann Armstead 3, Cornelia Armstead 5; 25 Dec 1859

9/15: William Wootten 34; Charlotte; Prince Edward; Laborer; Frank WOOTTEN; Prince Edward; Martha Wootten 30; Prince Edward; Prince Edward; Mrs. P. CLARK; Prince Edward; May Wootten 6, John Wootten 4, Rose Wootten 12 mos; 20 Nov 1858

9/18: William D. Evans 35; Prince Edward; Prince Edward; Painter; Born Free; Ø; Margaret Evans 36; Prince Edward; Prince Edward; Born Free; Ø; Nancy Evans 10, Robert Evans 9, William D. Evans 6; 20 Aug 1858

9/19: Nelson Wootten 56; Prince Edward; Prince Edward; Laborer; F.T. WOOTTEN; Prince Edward; Eda Wootten 39; Prince Edward; Prince Edward; F.T. WOOTTEN; Prince Edward; Camilla Wootten 18, Calvin Wootten 9; 1 Jan 1846

9/21: Peyton Hilton 44; Prince Edward; Prince Edward; Laborer; R.C. ANDERSON; Prince Edward; Agnes Hilton 36; Prince Edward; Prince Edward; R.C. ANDERSON; Prince Edward; Henry Hilton 20, Betty Hilton 18, Hampton Hilton 9, Peyton Hilton 4, Pelina Hilton 7, Calvin Hilton 3; 1 Dec 1845

9/27: Nick Cabell 54; Prince Edward; Prince Edward; Laborer; Hugh MOSTON?; Prince Edward; Sinai Cabell; Charlotte; Prince Edward; R.C. ANDERSON; Prince Edward; Sam Cabell 4 mos; 1 Aug 1865

9/28: Beverly Booker 28; Prince Edward; Prince Edward; Laborer; Hugh MOSTON; Prince Edward; Rachel Booker 27; Prince Edward; Prince Edward; R.C. ANDERSON; Prince Edward; William H. Booker 2; _ Apr 1862

9/29: William Hinton 28; Prince Edward; Prince Edward; Laborer; R.C. ANDERSON; Prince Edward; Sally Hinton 26; Prince Edward; Prince Edward; James WILLIAMS; Amherst; Ø; 20 Feb 1866

9/30: Charles Lyman 28; Buckingham; Prince Edward; Laborer; Thomas H. GARNETT; Prince Edward; Patty Lyman 30; Buckingham; Prince Edward; William SHAW; Buckingham; Becky Lyman 7, Rose Lyman 6, Martha Lyman 3, infant; 1 Apr 1859

9/34: J_v_ Hill 24; Prince Edward; Prince Edward; Laborer; Born Free; Ø; Joanna Hill 26; Appomattox; Prince Edward; F. SAMPSON; Prince Edward; Bitty Hill 3; 25? Dec 1861

9/35: William Scott 30; Prince Edward; Prince Edward; Laborer; Beverly SCOTT; Prince Edward; Harriet Scott 26; Prince Edward; Prince Edward; Beverly SCOTT; Prince Edward; Archy Scott 8, Creed Scott infant; 1 Jan 1858

9/37: George Washington 24; Buckingham; Prince Edward; Laborer; George COX; Buckingham; Lucy A. Washington 22; Buckingham; Prince Edward; J. C__TE; Buckingham; Carnie Washington 4, George Washington 1; 1 Jan 1860

10/1: Spencer Anderson 46; Buckingham; Prince Edward; Laborer; Archy GILLS; Buckingham; Mary Anderson 28; Buckingham; Prince Edward; Mrs. E. FORBES; Buckingham; Ø; 1 Oct 1864

10/2: Anderson Brown 39; Prince Edward; Prince Edward; Laborer; A.W. WOMACK; Prince Edward; Fanny Brown 24; Prince Edward; Prince Edward; David WOMACK; Prince Edward; Ø; 25 Dec 1863

10/3: Albert Williams 36; Prince Edward; Prince Edward; Laborer; Joe ALLEN; Prince Edward; Julia Williams 26; Prince Edward; Prince Edward; A. VENABLE; Prince Edward; James E. Williams 2; 18 Dec 1858

10/4: Robert Taylor 48; Prince Edward; Prince Edward; Laborer; Mrs. N. DAVIS; Prince Edward; Winnie Taylor 34; Prince Edward; Prince Edward; William RICE; Prince Edward; Henry Taylor 15, Robert W. Taylor 13, Mary E. Taylor 11, Nancy H. Taylor 10; 25 Dec 1846

10/8: Van Rennsalaes 32; Louisiana; Prince Edward; Laborer; J.N?. JONES; Prince Edward; Rhoda Rennsalaes 24; Prince Edward; Prince Edward; William E. BEUFORD; Prince Edward; Tom Rennsalaes 1 mo; 12 Oct 1862

10/10: John T. Beasley 26; Prince Edward; Prince Edward; Laborer; Jack BEASLEY; Prince Edward; Elvira Beasley 34; Prince Edward; Prince Edward; William JONES; Farmville; Thompson Beasley 2, infant; 1 Jan. 1863

10/12: Curtis Pollard 29; Charlotte; Prince Edward; Laborer; Thomas S. POLLARD; Charlotte; Lucy Pollard 23; Prince Edward; Prince Edward; H. WOOTTEN; Prince Edward; Ø; 1 Aug 1865

10/13: Ben Moseley 38; Prince Edward; Prince Edward; Laborer; William WILBURN; Cumberland; Judy Moseley 40; Cumberland; Prince Edward; H. WILBURN; Cumberland; Jane Moseley 6, Maria Moseley 2; 1 Jan 1859

10/15: Amos Carter 60; Prince Edward; Prince Edward; Laborer; Thomas TREADWAY; Prince Edward; Rachel Carter 50; Prince Edward; Prince Edward; Thomas TREADWAY; Prince Edward; Ø; 25 Dec 1836

10/17: Marshal Walker 28; Buckingham; Prince Edward; Laborer; Stephen FUQUA; Prince Edward; Maria Walker 22; Prince Edward; Prince Edward; Jack BEASLEY; Prince Edward; Ø; 10 Oct 1855

10/18: Watt Redd 56; Charlotte; Prince Edward; Laborer; Albert REDD; Prince Edward; Katie Redd 30; Prince Edward; Prince Edward; Numan REDD; Prince Edward; Eghun? Redd 16, Peyton Redd 13, Asa Redd 9, Watts Redd 8, Elizabeth Redd 5, Anne Redd 3; 30 June 1836

10/24: Branch Faulkes 24; Prince Edward; Prince Edward; Laborer; Mrs. M. FAULKES; Prince Edward; Louisa Faulkes 26; Cumberland; Prince Edward; James PRICE; Prince Edward; Ø; 20 Nov 1863

10/25: John Ross 40; Albemarle; Prince Edward; Laborer; Gabriel HOPPER; Prince Edward; Eliza Ross 34; Prince Edward; Prince Edward; John P. HUGHES; Prince Edward; Mary Ross 1; 30 Sept 1863

10/26: Thomas Jefferson 36; Cumberland; Prince Edward; Laborer; G.W. DANIEL; Prince Edward; Frances Jefferson 40; Prince Edward; Prince Edward; Mrs. F. SMITH; Cumberland; Ø; 1 June 1861

10/27: Pleasant Miles 56; Amelia; Prince Edward; Wheelwright; Dr. CHAPPELL; Buckingham; Martha Miles 44; Amelia; Prince Edward; John MEADOW; Amelia; Joseph Miles 16; 15 Oct 1838

10/28: John Winston 36; Hanover; Prince Edward; Hackman; Josiah BRENT; Spotsylvania; Indiana Winston 34; Buckingham; Prince Edward; Miss Lee? LAND; Buckingham; Robert Winston infant; 12 Aug 1864

10/29: Isham Scott 28; Prince Edward; Prince Edward; Laborer; Mrs. M.J. SCOTT; Prince Edward; Susan Scott 21; Prince Edward; Prince Edward; Mrs. P. FOWLKES; Prince Edward; Laura Scott 6, Mary Scott 5, Isham Scott 2; 1 Jan 1859

10/32: Emmanuel Price 28; Prince Edward; Prince Edward; Laborer; John H. ARMSTEAD; Prince Edward; Sarah Price 24; Prince Edward; Prince Edward; Mrs. Ann WEST; Prince Edward; Susan Price 5, John Price 2; 1 May 1860

10/34: Robert Jackson 30; Prince Edward; Prince Edward; Laborer; Mrs. Betty WOODSON; Prince Edward; Julia A. Jackson 30; Charlotte; Prince Edward; Isham GILLAM; Buckingham; Ø; 1 Aug 1865

10/35: Ed Lee 48; Prince Edward; Prince Edward; Laborer; Dr. THAXTON; Prince Edward; Ann Lee 49; Prince Edward; Prince Edward; J.W. MORTON; Prince Edward; Ø; 1 Jan 1866

10/36: Nick Cabell 70; Prince Edward; Prince Edward; Laborer; Dr. W.S. MORTON; Cumberland; Isabell Cabell 80; Nottoway; Prince Edward; Joseph WILLIAMS; Prince Edward; Ø; 25 Dec 1820

10/37: George Deem 54; Prince Edward; Prince Edward; Laborer; Erastus DAVIS; Prince Edward; Eliza Deem 47; Prince Edward; Prince Edward; Erastus DAVIS; Prince Edward; William Deem 19, George Deem 15, James Deem 13, Booker Deem 11, Lucy Deem 9, Judy Deem 3; 25 Dec 1840

11/1: Carter Stratton 28; Cumberland; Prince Edward; Laborer; V. PARRISH; Cumberland; Lucy Stratton 24; Cumberland; Prince Edward; Sam GLOVER; Cumberland; Thomas Stratton 9 (1st husband), David Stratton 7 (1st husband), Mary Stratton 3 (1st husband), 12 Aug 1856; Martha Stratton 1; 20 Aug 1865

11/5: James Pheasant 42; Prince Edward; Farmville; Laborer; William BARRETT; Richmond; Mary Pheasant 40; Prince Edward; Farmville; Born Free; Ø; Lavinia Pheasant 18, John Pheasant 16, James Pheasant 14, William C. Pheasant 9, Robert D. Pheasant 2; 20 Dec 1848

11/10: Clem Fountain 38; Charlotte; Farmville; Laborer; Clem REED; Farmville; Jane Fountain 26; Surry; Farmville; H.E. WARREN; Prince Edward; Maria Fountain 3, Richard Fountain 2; 18 Oct 1859

11/12: Joseph Morris 29; Lunenburg; Farmville; Laborer; George W. CLAYBORN; Prince Edward; Nelly Morris 24; Prince Edward; Farmville; H.E. WATKINS; Prince Edward; Cornelia Morris 4, Mary Morris 2; 19 Oct 1860

11/14: Joseph Madison 28; Prince Edward; Farmville; Laborer; R.W. PRICE; Prince Edward; Ellen Madison 18; Prince Edward; Farmville; John DOLBY; Prince Edward; Ø; 14 Oct 1863

11/15: Zach Ellis 60; Prince Edward; Farmville; Laborer; John D. SMITH; Prince Edward; Rosetta Ellis 36; Cumberland; Farmville; Dr. SPENCER; Farmville; Celina Ellis 16, Ellis Ellis 10, Margaret Ellis 8, Zach Ellis 4, Elizabeth Ellis 1; 20 Oct 1849

11/20: George Lyman 23; Buckingham; Prince Edward; Laborer; John DOLBY; Farmville; Mary Lyman 36; Prince Edward; Farmville; John DOLBY; Farmville; Ellen Lyman 17 (1st husband), William Lyman 19 (1st husband); 1st marriage 1846; 2nd marriage 1 Sept 1862

11/23: William H. Neal 28; Lunenburg; Prince Edward; Laborer; H. RICHARDSON; Prince Edward; Martha Neal 28; Prince Edward; Prince Edward; H. RICHARDSON; Prince Edward; Emma Neal 6, Mary Neal 10; 1st marriage 1855; 2nd marriage 12 Oct 1863

11/25: Isham Woods 64; Charlotte; Farmville; Laborer; William T. WOOD; Farmville; Nancy Wood 44; Charlotte; Farmville; Mrs. WHEELER; Farmville; Jeff Wood 26; 8 Jan 1836

11/27: James Hobson 36; Cumberland; Prince Edward; Laborer; F. LIPSCOMB; Cumberland; Frances Hobson 31; Prince Edward; Prince Edward; H. RICHARDSON; Prince Edward; Daniel 12 (1st husband), Margaret 8 (1st husband), Theodore 6 (2nd husband), Margaret 4 (2nd husband); 2 Apr 1861

11/31: William Bates 48; Prince Edward; Prince Edward; Laborer; James McNULT; Prince Edward; Nancy Bates 40; Cumberland; Prince Edward; James McNULT; Prince Edward; Ø; 25 Dec 1843

11/32: Patrick Henry 36; Cumberland; Prince Edward; Laborer; George W. DANIEL; Prince Edward; Rosetta Henry 32; Prince Edward; Prince Edward; William ELVIN; Prince Edward; Henry Henry 18, Thomas Henry 14, Edmonia Henry 12, Dora Henry 5, Samuel Henry 12 mos; 18 Oct 1843

11/37: Allen Robinson 50; Cumberland; Prince Edward; Mason; Ed ROBINSON; Appomattox; Celia Robinson 56; Washington, D.C.; Prince Edward; N. DAVIS; Farmville; Ø; 12 Oct 1858

11/38: H. Williams 29; Washington, D.C.; Prince Edward; Laborer; Mrs. K. ANDERSON; Washington, D.C.; Agnes Williams 26; Charlotte; Prince Edward; Charles MORTON; Prince Edward; Ø; 6 Feb 1866

12/1: Henry Hudson 57; Prince Edward; Prince Edward; Laborer; Mrs. Charles WOODS; Farmville; Julia Hudson 42; Prince Edward; Prince Edward; Jack MILLS; Prince Edward; Louisa Hudson 19, Branch Hudson 18, Betty Hudson 13, J__ H. Hudson 15, Alice Hudson 4, Ella Hudson 6, Frank Hudson 8; 15 Aug 1845

12/8: Edmund Giles 50; Amelia; Farmville; Blacksmith; William PORTER; Farmville; Lavinia Giles 28; Amelia; Farmville; William FRETWELL; Amelia; Ø; 11 Oct 1865

12/9: Isaac Morris 51; Lunenburg; Prince Edward; Laborer; James McNULT; Prince Edward; Laura Morris 30; Charlotte; Prince Edward; James McNULT; Prince Edward; Betty Morris 17, Corine? Morris 5; 25 Dec 1845

12/10: Thomas Brown 42; Buckingham; Prince Edward; Mason; J__ W. EPPES; Buckingham; Betty Brown 32; Buckingham; Prince Edward; William EVANS; Buckingham; Nannie Brown 13, William Brown 11, Emma Brown 8, Louis Brown 10, Elizabeth Brown 7, Keziah Brown 5; 17 Sept 1853

12/17: James Bartlett 65; Prince Edward; Farmville; Boatman; Born Free; Ø; Maria Bartlett 35; Prince Edward; Prince Edward; Born Free; Ø; Augustus Bartlett 23 (1st husband), James Bartlett 22 (1st husband), William Bartlett 18 (1st husband), Ennis Bartlett 12, Catherine Bartlett 8, Emily Bartlett 4; 14 Oct 1851

12/23: Thomas Scott 30; Prince Edward; Farmville; Carptenter; Dr. PETERS; Farmville; Sally Scott 40; Mecklenburg; Farmville; William WARDIN; Farmville; Mary Scott 10, Elvira Scott 8, Fanny Scott 2; 14 Sept 1856

12/26: George Diggs 28; Mathews; Farmville; Hackman; Dr. THAXTON; Farmville; Martha Diggs 26; Prince Edward; Farmville; Born Free; Ø; 14 Feb 1866

12/27: William Dawson 64; Richmond; Farmville; Gardener; Clem REED; Farmville; Cooper Dawson 56; Prince Edward; Farmville; Clem REED; Farmville; Robert Dawson 12; 25 Dec 1836

12/28: George Hendrick 25; Buckingham; Farmville; Laborer; William DUNNINGTON; Prince Edward; Mary Hendrick 20; Prince Edward; Farmville; William RICE; Farmville; Mary A. Hendrick 2; 14 Mar 1864

12/29: A. Jackson 30; Cumberland; Farmville; Laborer; George W. DANIEL; Prince Edward; Joanna Jackson 25; Cumberland; Farmville; William PLUME; Cumberland; Ø; 10 Apr1863

12/30: William Carter 52; Farmville; Farmville; Laborer; Born Free; Ø; Mary Carter 43; Petersburg; Farmville; Born Free; Ø; Ø; 24 Dec 1842

12/31: John Jackson 36; Cumberland; Farmville; Laborer; George W. DANIEL; Farmville; Rose Jackson 25; Cumberland; Farmville; John RANDOLPH; Cumberland; Ø; 15 Apr1864

12/32: Phineas Cole 30; Prince Edward; Farmville; Laborer; Mrs. M.E. VENABLE; Prince Edward; Eliza Cole 23; Buckingham; Farmville; Charles BLANTON; Prince Edward; Ada Cole 6, Emma Cole 2, Virgie Cole infanat; 20 Apr 1862

12/35: Henry Watkins 48; Prince Edward; Farmville; Laborer; Patrick JACKSON; Farmville; Patty Watkins 38; Cumberland; Farmville; James FLIPPIN; Nottoway; Ø; 30 Dec 1858

12/36: Daman Trent 32; Buckingham; Farmville; Laborer; Samuel DRUIN; Buckingham; Sally Trent 28; Cumberland; Farmville; V. PARRISH; Cumberland; Easter Trent 13, Margaret Trent 11, Julia Trent 7; 20 Mar 1852

12/39: James Marshal 45; Prince Edward; Farmville; Laborer; Mrs. Sally OWEN; Prince Edward; Jane Marshal 22; Lunenburg; Farmville; Mrs. Polly COX; Lunenburg; Jacob Marshal 5, John Marshal 1; 14 July1860

13/1: Thornton Rowlett 26; Cumberland; Farmville; Laborer; John R. WILSON; Cumberland; Ella Rowlett 19; Cumberland; Farmville; Mrs. Nancy BOOKER; Cumberland; Ø; 1 Jan 1866

13/2: Lewis Brown 25; Prince Edward; Prince Edward; Laborer; Frank WATKINS; Prince Edward; Frances Brown 2_; Prince Edward; Prince Edward; Mrs. P. Ligan SCOTT; Prince Edward; Rose Brown 9, Abbe Brown 8, Henry Brown 6, Abram Brown 5, Stephan Brown 12 mos; 25 Dec 1854

13/7: James Stokes 47; Prince Edward; Prince Edward; Farmer; Henry STOKES; Prince Edward; Eltsey Stokes 53; Prince Edward; Prince Edward; Ogden J. CLARK; Prince Edward; Alexander 30; 1st marriage 1836; 2nd marriage 25 Dec 1865

13/9: Edward Clark 57; Prince Edward; Prince Edward; Farmer; Mrs. Phebe CLARK; Prince Edward; Mary Clark 48; Charlotte; Prince Edward; William WEAVER; Prince Edward; Ellen 16; 28 Oct 1836

13/10: Stephen Brown 40; Prince Edward; Prince Edward; Farmer; Frank WALKINS/WATKINS; Prince Edward; Eliza Brown 32; Prince Edward; Prince Edward; Mrs. SMITH; Prince Edward; Lewis Brown 9, Hattie Brown 7, Harriet Brown 4, William Brown 1; 25 Dec 1855

13/15: William Nelson; Lunenburg; Prince Edward; Farmer; Henry STOKES; Prince Edward; Lucinda Nelson 28; Prince Edward; Prince Edward; John FOSTER; Prince Edward; Richard Nelson 9, William Nelson 7, Rosetta Nelson 1; 25 Dec 1856

13/18: Richard Goode 43; Goochland; Prince Edward; Laborer; Frank WALKINS/WATKINS; Prince Edward; Betsey Goode 39; Mecklenburg; Prince Edward; Henry WALKINS/WATKINS; Prince Edward; Jesse Goode 22, Maria Goode 18, Jennie Goode 16, Aleck Goode 14, Frank Goode 12, Laura Goode 10, George Goode 8, Philip Goode 2; 25 Dec 1840

13/26: George Scott 44; Prince Edward; Prince Edward; Laborer; Robert HOLLIDAY; Prince Edward; Fanny Scott 45; King William; Prince Edward; Robert HOLLIDAY; Prince Edward; Holly Scott 17, Henry Scott 16, James Scott 13, George Scott 12, Charles Scott 6, Edward Scott 4; 20 Oct 1841

13/32: Joseph Walker 54; Buckingham; Farmville; Laborer; Joseph D. WICK; Prince Edward; Judy Walker 74; Prince Edward; Prince Edward;

Harmen CLARK; Prince Edward; Millie 22; 1st marriage 1841; 2nd marriage 14 Oct 1853

13/34: Edward Ellis 41; Cumberland; Prince Edward; Laborer; Alex WEST; Prince Edward; Julia Ellis 36; Cumberland; Prince Edward; Born Free; Ø; Mary Ellis 18, John Ellis 15, Emma Ellis 12; 28 Dec 1846

13/37: James Stokes 43; Prince Edward; Prince Edward; Laborer; Collins STOKES; Prince Edward; Ellen Stokes 30; Prince Edward; Prince Edward; Sam B. SCOTT; Prince Edward; Mary Stokes 19, Ella Jane Stokes 16, Champrey Stokes 14, Eliza Stokes 12; 24 Dec 1846

14/1: Carter Braxton 40; Richmond; Prince Edward; Laborer; Dr. Thomas OWENS; Prince Edward; E. Jane Braxton 40; Prince Edward; Prince Edward; Dr. T. OWENS; Prince Edward; Pleasant Braxton 11; 25 Dec 1846

14/2: Vans Neal 48; Cumberland; Prince Edward; Laborer; William A. COCK; Cumberland; E. Ann Neal 40; Prince Edward; Prince Edward; William MUNDY; Prince Edward; Catherine Neal 20, Peter Neal 19, Peggy Neal 17, Abbie Neal 15, Lee Neal 13, Edward Neal 8, Cornelius Neal 6, Camilla Neal 4, Judith Neal 1; 28 Dec 1842

14/11: Patrick Clark 56; Prince Edward; Prince Edward; Laborer; H.A. CLARK; Prince Edward; Sophy Clark 35; Cumberland; Prince Edward; H.A. CLARK; Prince Edward; Ø; 24 Dec 1846

14/12: Caesar Wootten 52; Gloucester; Prince Edward; Laborer; H. WOOTTEN; Prince Edward; Vina Wootten 50; Prince Edward; Prince Edward; William YORKER; Prince Edward; Ø; 20 July 1866

14/13: Archy B. McGhee 77; Prince Edward; Prince Edward; Laborer; William McGHEE; Prince Edward; Judy McGhee 70; Prince Edward; Prince Edward; Farnk CARTER; Prince Edward; Caesar McGhee 13, Mary McGhee 11, Maria McGhee 9, Edward McGhee 6, Sally McGhee 4, James McGhee 1; 1st marriage 1850; 2nd marriage 14 Oct 1864

14/19: Booker Watkins 40; Prince Edward; Prince Edward; Laborer; Drury SMITH; Lunenburg; Nancy Watkins 35; Prince Edward; Prince Edward; Edmund SCOTT; Prince Edward; Archer Scott Watkins 7, Scott Archer Watkins 7, Mary Watkins 3, Amy Watkins 4; 25 Dec 1851

14/23: Scipio Lang 54; Prince Edward; Prince Edward; Laborer; Mrs. M.C. WOMACK; Prince Edward; Mary Ann Lang 65; Prince Edward; Prince Edward; Mrs. M.C. WOMACK; Prince Edward; Jenny Lang 14, Abram Lang 6, George Lang 4, Henrietta Lang 3; 25 Dec 1846

14/27: Felix Miller 26; Prince Edward; Prince Edward; Carpenter; B.T. MILLER; Prince Edward; Emma Miller? 24; Prince Edward; Prince Edward; Mrs. Benjamin CLARK; Prince Edward; Betsy Ann Miller 2; 20 Dec 1861

14/28: Ed Pincher 30; Prince Edward; Prince Edward; Farmer; Phil SOUTHALL; Prince Edward; Hannah Pincher 30; Prince Edward; Prince Edward; Legget LOCKET; Prince Edward; Phil Pincher 7, Wallace Pincher 5, Nannie Pincher 4, Byrd Pincher 9 mos; 20 Aug 1857

14/32: Robert Dennis 36; Prince Edward; Prince Edward; Laborer; Thomas CLARK; Prince Edward; Caroline Dennis 36; Charlotte; Prince Edward; Joseph HINES; Charlotte; Samuel Dennis 20; 25 Dec 1846

14/33: Nathan Rideout 55; Prince Edward; Prince Edward; Laborer; Mrs. Patsey ROWLETT; Charlotte; Docia Rideout 60; Prince Edward; Prince Edward; Mrs. P. ROWLETT; Charlotte; Ø; 24 Dec 1846

14/34: Richard Warren 40; King & Queen; Prince Edward; Laborer; Mrs. __ny TOTTY?; Prince Edward; Rachel Warren 26; Buckingham; Prince Edward; John LANCASTER; Cumberland; Aleck Warren 4; 20 Aug1861

14/35: Doc Smith 36; Cumberland; Prince Edward; Laborer; James BLANTON; Cumberland; Parmelia Smith 30; Charlotte; Prince Edward; J. MADISON; Cumberland; Jane Smith 13; 20 Aug 1853

14/36: Abbet? Burrell 35; Prince Edward; Prince Edward; Laborer; Nat VENABLE; Prince Edward; Caroline Burrell 55; Warrenton, No. Carolina; Prince Edward; Ed RICE; Farmville; Ø; 14 Dec 1862

14/37: Robert Chester 32; Charlotte; Prince Edward; Blacksmith; Beverly SCOTT; Prince Edward; Milly Ann Chester 21; Prince Edward; Prince Edward; B. SCOTT; Prince Edward; Peyton Chester 3, Susan Chester 2 mos; 12 Dec 1862

14/39: Samuel Jones 50; Buckingham; Farmville; Laborer; James LAVEN; Hanover; Arabella Jones 50; Cumberland; Farmville; Mrs. C. ARMSTEAD; Cumberland; Emma Jones 10 (1st husband); 20 Feb 1861

71

15/1: Pat Johnson 52; Prince Edward; Farmville; Farmer; Dr. PETERS; Farmville; Jenny Johnson 34; Prince Edward; Farmville; William WOMACK; Prince Edward; Katie Johnson 12; 16 July 1854

15/2: Abram Miles 36; Prince Edward; Farmville; Farmer; William WOMACK; Prince Edward; Lydia Miles 33; Buckingham; Farmville; William BOLLING; Buckingham; Ø; 25 Dec 1854

15/3: James Madison 54; Campbell; Farmville; Farmer; F.N. WATKINS; Prince Edward; M. Madison 53; Campbell; Farmville; F.N. WATKINS; Prince Edward; Ø; 15 May 1833

15/4: James Evans 32; Prince Edward; Farmville; Farmer; Mrs. Jane MORTON; Prince Edward; Amy Evans 31; Prince Edward; Farmville; George PLUME; Cumberland; Amanda Evans 7; 15 Nov 1857

15/5: James Evans 33; Prince Edward; Farmville; Farmer; J.B. ELY; Prince Edward; Sarah Evans 20; Prince Edward; Farmville; J.B. ELY; Prince Edward; James Evans 2; 25 Dec 1853

15/6: John Watkins 26; Halifax; Farmville; Farmer; P. LEACH; Cumberland; Julia Watkins 18; Cumberland; Farmville; Ben WILSON; Cumberland; Mary Watkins 2, Martha Watkins 3 mos, 1 Apr 1864

15/7: Isham Smith 50; Cumberland; Farmville; Farmer; Pat JACKSON; Prince Edward; Fany? Smith 28; Cumberland; Farmville; Mrs. A. WOODFIN; Cumberland; Albert Smith 3 mos; 19 Oct 1865

15/8: M. Nevison 28; Sussex; Farmville; Blacksmith; S.W. DANIEL; Farmville; Ann Nevison 22; Cumberland; Farmville; Mrs. A. BOOKER; Cumberland; Ø; 25 Dec 1864

15/10: Sam Horace 31; Prince Edward; Farmville; Laborer; J.B. ELY; Prince Edward; Betsey Horace 25; Prince Edward; Farmville; J.B. ELY; Prince Edward; Randal Horace 7, Ella Horace 6, Susan Horace 4, Johnny Horace 1; 25 Dec 1858

15/14: Randal Scott 76; Prince Edward; Farmville; Laborer; J.A. SCOTT; Prince Edward; Lucy Scott 58; Prince Edward; Farmville; J.A. SCOTT; Prince Edward; Ø; 15 Jan 1861

15/15: Henry Fuller 60; Prince Edward; Farmville; Laborer; J.T. GRAY; Prince Edward; Ann Fuller 41; Prince Edward; Farmville; J.R. THOMPSON; Farmville; Pryor Fuller 15, William Fuller 12, Jane Fuller 10, Patience Fuller 5, Lucy Fuller 1: 15 Oct 1843

15/20: Aaron Swater 24; Amherst; Farmville; Laborer; J.H. IRVING; Amherst; Louisa Swater 25; Amherst; Farmville; William VENABLE; Farmville; Fanny Swater 4, Anne S. Swater 2; 1 Mar 1861

15/22: Alex Clemms 34; Cumberland; Farmville; Laborer; C. HOBSON; Cumberland; C. Clemms 26; Cumberland; Farmville; Jenny BOOKER; Cumberland; Betty Clemms 7; 1 Mar 1857

15/23: Ellis Bland 33; Nottoway; Prince Edward; Laborer; John H. KNIGHT; Prince Edward; C. Bland 21; Prince Edward; Farmville; John H. KNIGHT; Prince Edward; Ellen Bland 5, William Bland 2 mos; 1 June 1860

15/25: Samuel Branch 30; Prince Edward; Prince Edward; Laborer; William P. ELAM; Cumberland; Sally Branch 25; Prince Edward; Farmville; Mrs. Mary WOOD; Farmville; Ø; 1 Sept 1862

15/26: ?. Williamson 38; Rockingham; Farmville; Laborer; Born Free; Ø; Mary Williamson 40; No. Carolina; Farmville; Joseph BRIDWELL; Farmville; Ø; 1 Mar 1864

15/27: R. Patterson 48; Prince Edward; Prince Edward; Laborer; William L. RICE; Farmville; Julia Patterson 48; Prince Edward; Prince Edward; T.E. SCOTT; Prince Edward; Claiborne Patterson 7, Louis Patterson 9, Molly Patterson 14; 15 Oct 18_1

15/30: Mercer Sanders 30; Buckingham; Farmville; Laborer; John DUPUY; Cumberland; Nancy Sanders 32; Prince Edward; Farmville; John DUPUY; Cumberland; Lavin__ Sanders 13, Pinkey Sanders 7, Robert Sanders 5, Mollie Sanders 3, infant; 10 Aug 1851

15/35: Nathan Harvey 49; Prince Edward; Farmville; Laborer; F. WATKINS; Prince Edward; M. Harvey 38; Lynchburg; Farmville; F. WATKINS; Prince Edward; Clem Harvey 19, Nathan Harvey 16, Puss Harvey 17, Agnes Harvey 15, Mattie Harvey 13, Lucy Harvey 10, Sterling Harvey 8, Buddy Harvey 6; 15 Oct 1843

16/1: William Hill 34; Petersburg; Prince Edward; Laborer; Born Free; Ø; Martha Hill 43; Prince Edward; Prince Edward; E. BRUCE; Prince Edward; Ø; 25 Dec 1856

16/2: Sam Spraggans 50; Charlotte; Prince Edward; Laborer; Dr. PETERS; Farmville; Matilda Spraggans 45; Charlotte; Prince Edward; C. ANDERSON; Prince Edward; Ø; 4 Apr 1861

16/3: Richard Batts/Botts 59; Cumberland; Prince Edward; Laborer; Martha? ANDERSON; Cumberland; Clara Batts/Botts 50; Cumberland; Prince Edward; John RANDOLPH; Prince Edward; Paul; 16 Jan 1826

16/4: Simon Venable 46; Cumberland; Prince Edward; Laborer; Ann WILSON; Cumberland; Dina Venable 45; Cumberland; Prince Edward; Mary HOBSON; Cumberland; John Venable 10, Benjamin Venable 5; 20 Aug 1854

16/6: Madison Mottley 38; Amelia; Prince Edward; Laborer; Joseph PHILLIPS; Prince Edward; M.J. Mottley 28; Prince Edward; Prince Edward; Mr. MOTTLEY; Prince Edward; Harriet Mottley 9 mos; 1 Jan 1862

16/7: A. Langhorn 44; Buckingham; Prince Edward; Laborer; G.W. DANIEL; Prince Edward; Char. Langhorn 47; Cumberland; Prince Edward; G.W. DANIEL; Prince Edward; Sam S. Langhorn 21; 25 Dec 1842

16/8: Sam? Horace 32; Prince Edward; Prince Edward; Laborer; H. THWEATT; Prince Edward; Sally Horace 34; Appomattox; Prince Edward; R. PAULETT; Prince Edward; Willie Horace 2 mos; 25 Dec 1859

16/9: Rob Strang 24; Cumberland; Prince Edward; Laborer; Alden SMITH; Cumberland; Sarah Strang 22; Cumberland; Prince Edward; O. SMITH; Cumberland; Ø; 1 Aug 1861

16/10: George Miller 50; Prince Edward; Prince Edward; Laborer; Bard CHUMMY; Lunenburg; Rose C. Miller 48; Nottoway; Prince Edward; R. CHUMMY; Lunenburg; Patrick Henry 16, Lucinda Henry 12, Martha Henry 10, Anderson Henry 5, Missouri Henry 12 mos; 1 Jan 1848

16/15: Peter Minnis 56; Prince Edward; Prince Edward; Laborer; Lain VENABLE; Prince Edward; Katy Minnis 44; Prince Edward; Prince Edward; Th. VENABLE; Prince Edward; Robert Minnis 16, Charles Minnis 13, Nathan Minnis 12, Henry Minnis 8, David Minnis 6; 25 Dec 1846

16/20: H. Harrison 78; Brunswick; Prince Edward; Laborer; Jeff WILLIAMS; Prince Edward; Aggy Harrison 50; Sussex; Prince Edward; Joseph WILLIAMS; Prince Edward; Jenny Harrison 20, Henrietta Harrison 16; 15 Oct 1836

16/22: Kit Harvey 48; Charlotte; Prince Edward; Laborer; Sam WHEELER; Appomattox; Sarah Harvey 36; Campbell; Prince Edward; Sam WHEELER; Appomattox; Lee Harvey 14; 25 Dec 1849

16/23: Jessee Evans 58; Buckingham; Farmville; Laborer; William EVANS; Buckingham; Melinda Evans 50; Campbell; Farmville; William EVANS; Buckingham; Ada Evans 16; 1 Mar 1836

16/24: H. Watkins 36; Buckingham; Farmville; Laborer; John DUPUY; Cumberland; Frances Watkins 42; Powhatan; Farmville; John DUPUY; Cumberland; Ø; 1 Mar 1851

16/25: Allen Goodman 50; Amelia; Farmville; Laborer; Zach GOODMAN; Cumberland; Clara Goodman 40; Cumberland; Farmville; Mrs. C. BOOKER; Farmville; Calvin Goodman 18, Margaret Goodman 17, Sarah Goodman 15, Merritt Goodman 2; 20 June 1846

16/29: Isham Powell 60; Goochland; Farmville; Laborer; Demas BLAKE; Cumberland; Nancy Powell 40; Buckingham; Farmville; Pat JACKSON; Farmville; Jenny Powell 18, Nelson Powell 8, Catherine Powell 4; 15 May 1836

16/32: Moses Coles 58; Prince Edward; Farmville; Laborer; Sam VENABLE; Prince Edward; Melinda Coles 40; Halifax; Farmville; M. McSLOCUM?; Farmville; Ø; 15 Oct 1862

16/33: Joseph Booker 35; Charlotte; Farmville; Laborer; Joseph GOFFREY; Richmond; Eliza Booker 20; Prince Edward; Farmville; T. VENABLE; Prince Edward; Ø; 1 Jan 1866

16/34: Kit Eggleston 56; Cumberland; Farmville; Laborer; G.W. DANIEL; Farmville; Violet Eggleston 26; Cumberland; Farmville; G.W. DANIEL; Prince Edward; Martha Jane Eggleston 9, William Henry Eggleston 8; 25 Dec 1853

16/36: Ben Anderson 48; Cumberland; Farmville; Laborer; D.W. CHAPPELL; Buckingham; Nancy Anderson 40; Prince Edward; Farmville; J.B. HILLARD; Farmville; Alice Anderson 19, Jenny Anderson 17, Billy Anderson 10, Charley Anderson 7, Nelly Anderson 5, Jimmy Anderson 3 wks; 7 Mar 1841

17/1: James Sanders 26; Buckingham; Prince Edward; Farmer; CLARK & LIGAN; Prince Edward; Becky Sanders 28; Prince Edward; Prince Edward; Pat CHAMBERS; Prince Edward; Ø; 20 Feb 1866

17/2: Joseph Chambers 50; Prince Edward; Prince Edward; Farmer; Dr. CHAMBERS; Prince Edward; Sally Chambers 38; Prince Edward; Prince Edward; John OVERTON; Cumberland; Henderson Chambers 9, Dennis Chambers 8, Margaret Chambers 6, Lesser Chambers 4, Rachel Chambers 2; 25 Dec 1846

17/7: George Grigg 28; Prince Edward; Prince Edward; Farmer; Dr. CARRINGTON; Prince Edward; Eliza Grigg 28; Prince Edward; Prince Edward; Agee LYON; Prince Edward; Ø; 4 Aug 1865

17/8: Ed Moseby 56; Prince Edward; Prince Edward; Farmer; James McNULT; Prince Edward; Jenny Moseby 50; Cumberland; Prince Edward; Mrs. Ann JOHNS; Buckingham; Ø; 2 Mar 1848

17/9: Harry Lee 50; Charlotte; Prince Edward; Farmer; Charles BRUCE; Charlotte; Peggy Lee 42; Charlotte; Prince Edward; Andrew VENABLE; Prince Edward; Uretta Lee 22, Maria Lee 18, Ellen Lee 16, Sylas Lee 13, Rufus Lee 6, Catherine Lee 4, Pleasant Lee 2; 16 May 1842

17/16: Calvin? Hays 44; Prince Edward; Prince Edward; Laborer; Louisa LIGAN; Prince Edward; Nancy Hays 50; Prince Edward; Prince Edward; P. LIGAN; Charlotte; Ø; 20 June 1846

17/17: James Booker 40; Prince Edward; Prince Edward; Laborer; John DILLON; Prince Edward; Fanny Booker 36; Prince Edward; Prince Edward; H.E. WATKINS; Prince Edward; Mary Ann Booker 15; 25 Dec 1844

17/18: Winder Stokes 50; Lunenburg; Prince Edward; Laborer; Henry STOKES; Prince Edward; Citty Stokes 50; Lunenburg; Prince Edward; H. STOKES; Prince Edward; Mary Jane Stokes 12; 24 June 1846

17/19: Hal Chambers 60; Lunenburg; Prince Edward; Laborer; Thomas HAMBLIN; Lunenburg; Hannah Chambers 50; Lunenburg; Prince Edward; John AUGIN?; Lunenburg; Hal Chambers 8, William F. Chambers 15; 28 June 1830

17/23: Jessee Logan 28; Prince Edward; Prince Edward; Laborer; David WOMACK; Prince Edward; Julia Logan 24; Prince Edward; Prince Edward; William WOMACK; Prince Edward; George Logan 9, Betty Logan 7 mos; 25 Dec 1856

17/25: Shad Daniel 38; Prince Edward; Prince Edward; Laborer; T.T. TATLY?; Prince Edward; Martha Daniel 26; Prince Edward; Prince Edward; Charles WEED; Prince Edward; Sally Daniel 6 mos; 24 June 1860

17/26: Peter Lindsay 54; Prince Edward; Prince Edward; Laborer; R.C. ANDERSON; Prince Edward; Mary Lindsay 44; Prince Edward; Prince Edward; R.C. ANDERSON; Prince Edward; Patty Lindsay 14; 24 Aug 1836

17/27: Willis Pegram 39; Brunswick; Prince Edward; Laborer; E. EVANS; Prince Edward; Celia Pegram 26; Lunenburg; Prince Edward; H.E. STOKES; Prince Edward; Ø; 30 Aug 1858

17/28: Anderson Watkins 50; Charlotte; Prince Edward; Laborer; Samuel CLARK; Prince Edward; Polly Watkins 40; Prince Edward; Prince Edward; B.J. WORSHAM; Prince Edward; Jackson Watkins 3; 24 July 1846

17/29: Sam White 45; Prince Edward; Prince Edward; Laborer; R.W. PRICE?; Prince Edward; Lucy WHITE 38; Prince Edward; Prince Edward; Mrs. N. WOODSON; Prince Edward; Myra White 5, Martha White 3; 26 Dec 1847

17/31: John Pay_y 28; Prince Edward; Prince Edward; Laborer; Mrs. M. WHITEHEAD; Prince Edward; Puss Pay_y 20; Prince Edward; Prince Edward; John DILLON; Prince Edward; Milly Pay_y 5 mos; 24 June 1856

17/32: Ed Walker 74; Lunenburg; Prince Edward; Laborer; R. STOKES; Prince Edward; Betty Walker 48; Lunenburg; Prince Edward; Alex CRAWLEY (dead); Lunenburg; Ø ; 26 Dec 1826

17/33: Daniel Hicks 26; Prince Edward; Prince Edward; Laborer; James D. LIGAN; Prince Edward; Maria Hicks 22; Prince Edward; Prince Edward; James WOOTTEN; Prince Edward; Lilybeth Hicks 2, Henry Hicks 6 mos; 20 Apr 1864

17/35: Benjamin Cobb 48; Prince Edward; Prince Edward; Laborer; James D. LIGAN; Prince Edward; Eliza Cobb 35; Prince Edward; Prince Edward; William WEAVER; Prince Edward; Jeta Cobb 6, Alice 2; 29 Oct 1850

17/37: Cyrus Fox 28; Prince Edward; Prince Edward; Laborer; Ed EDMUNDS; Prince Edward; Docia A. Fox 24; Prince Edward; Prince Edward; Ed EDMUNDS; Prince Edward; Fanny Jane Fox 1; 24 Dec 1863

17/38: Richard Scott 29; Prince Edward; Prince Edward; Laborer; Louisa LIGAN; Prince Edward; Lucy Jane Scott 26; Prince Edward; Prince Edward; Joseph LIGAN; Prince Edward; Alexander Scott 7, Fanny Scott 4, Ida Scott 2, John Scott; 20 Oct 1858

18/1: Bing/Burg Munford 41; Halifax; Farmville; Mason; Mrs. M.B. EPPES; Buckingham; Martha Munford 30; Charlotte; Farmville; James MADISON; Cumberland; Landaina? Munford 11, John Henry Munford 9, Bing/Burg Munford 7, Wiley Munford 4, Harriet Munford 2; 4 Jan 1854

18/6: Albert Johns 40 Cumberland; Farmville; Cook; Mrs. Nancy BLANTON; Cumberland; Amelia Johns 38; Cumberland; Farmville; C. COLEMAN; Cumberland; America Johns 12, Albert Johns 3, Armstead Johns 15 (1st husband); 15 Oct 1851

18/9: Patrick Johns 36; Cumberland; Farmville; Laborer; Mrs. N.E. BLANTON; Cumberland; Martha Johns 36; Cumberland; Farmville; W. BLANTON; Cumberland; Martha Johns 12 mos; 20 Sept 1864

18/10: Wyatt Horace 49; Buckingham; Farmville; Laborer; Patrick JACKSON; Farmville; Margaret Horace 46; Prince Edward; Farmville; H. THWEATT; Prince Edward; Sam Horace 28, Nat Horace 21, Patty Horace 20; 20 Dec 1838

18/13: Edmund Johnson 46; Prince Edward; Farmville; Shoemaker; G.B. WRIGHT; Prince Edward; Betsy Johnson 46; Prince Edward; Farmville; Eliza A. MORTON; Prince Edward; Ø; 24 Dec 1843

18/14: Edmund Logan 48; Clement, Tennessee; Farmville; Laborer; H. RICHARDSON; Prince Edward; Amy Logan 60; Prince Edward; Farmville; H. RICHARDSON; Prince Edward; Ø; 19 Oct 1862

18/15: George Watkins 28; Danville; Farmville; Laborer; H.E. WATKINS; Prince Edward; Lucy Watkins 28; Prince Edward; Farmville; D. WOMACK; Prince Edward; Jenny Watkins 2; 30 Nov 1862

18/16: William Duinin 30; Prince Edward; Prince Edward; Teamster; John DALBY; Prince Edward; Cleia? Duinin 24; Prince Edward; Farmville; John DALBY; Prince Edward; Henry Duinin 4, Mary Duinin 2, Emma Duinin 3 mos; 25 Dec 1861

18/19: Charles Ely 60; Appomattox; Prince Edward; Laborer; James B. ELY; Farmville; Tabby Ely 56; Appomattox; Prince Edward; William WILBURN; Cumberland; Ø; 4 July 1856

18/20: Decker Ayres 30; Buckingham; Prince Edward; Laborer; E.L. WORSHAM; Dinwiddie; Hannah Ayres 26; Prince Edward; Prince Edward; James LIGAN; Prince Edward; Thomas Ayres 10 (1st husband), Betty Ayres 8 (1st husband), Powell Ayres 8 mos; 1st marriage July 1856; 2nd marriage 25 Dec 1861

18/23: Edmund Watkins 30; Prince Edward; Prince Edward; Laborer; John DUPUY; Cumberland; Sarah Watkins 26; Prince Edward; Prince Edward; William BRADSHAW; Cumberland; Eura? Watkins 14 (1st husband), Caroline 8, Creasey 3; 4 Feb 18_5

18/26: John Hunley 54; Halifax; Prince Edward; Laborer; H. RICHARDSON; Prince Edward; Harriet Hunley 44; Prince Edward; Prince Edward; H. RICHARDSON; Prince Edward; Ellis Hunley 16, Remus Hunley 10; 25 Dec 1847

18/28: Nat Walton 46; Prince Edward; Prince Edward; Laborer; William WALTON; Prince Edward; Julia Walton 32; Nottoway; Prince Edward; William WALTON; Prince Edward; Henry C. Walton 11, Martha Walton 10, Mary Walton 8, Lucius Walton 5, Leana Walton 3, Thomas Walton infant; 25 Dec 1853

18/34: Richard Palmer 36; Prince Edward; Prince Edward; Laborer; H.L. BRANSON; Washington; Ann Palmer 40; Farmville; Prince Edward; Terry LOTTY; Prince Edward; James R. Palmer 12 (1st husband), Frank Palmer 6; 25 Dec 1854

18/36: Henry Goode 24; Prince Edward; Prince Edward; Laborer; Frank WATKINS; Prince Edward; Betty Goode 23; Prince Edward; Prince Edward; Dr. CARRINGTON; Prince Edward; Caroline Goode 8 mos; 4 Aug 1865

18/37: Harry Nash 48; Prince Edward; Prince Edward; Laborer; Ed CLARK; Prince Edward; Lizzie Nash 34; Prince Edward; Prince Edward; J.L. LIGAN; Prince Edward; Polly Nash 5, David Nash 2, Fann Nash 1; 1 Aug 1846

19/1: Jack Jones 55; Buckingham, Farmville; Laborer; William B. JONES; Buckingham; Susan Jones 35; Prince Edward; Farmville; Thomas VENABLE; Prince Edward; Monroe Jones 14, Alice Jones 12, Alpheus Jones 10, Archer Jones 6, Irene Jones 2; 20 Nov 1851

19/6: Benjamin Winston 42; Goochland; Farmville; Laborer; Mrs. Ann WINSTON; Cumberland; Ann Winston 22; Prince Edward; Farmville; Fred SMITH; Cumberland; Emeline 7 (by fr wf dead), Clara 3 (by fr wf dead); 20 Mar 1854

19/8: Henry Rowlett 28; Prince Edward; Prince Edward; Laborer; Thomas ROWLETT; Prince Edward; Jane Rowlett 29; Prince Edward; Prince Edward; Dr. Thomas OWEN; Prince Edward; Jacob Rowlett 11, Nancy Rowlett 9, Tara Rowlett 7, Sarah Rowlett 5, Mary Rowlett infant; 20 Jan 1865

19/14: Jack Reed 30; Prince Edward; Prince Edward; Laborer; H. WOOTTEN; Prince Edward; Elizabeth Reed 30; Prince Edward; Prince Edward; Pleasant FOWLER; Prince Edward; Henry Reed 12, Stephen Reed 10, Sarah Reed 8, Nancy Reed 6, Ellen Reed 5; 30 Nov 1852

19/19: James Wootten 21; Prince Edward; Prince Edward; Laborer; H. WOOTTEN; Prince Edward; Matilda Wootten 30; Prince Edward; Prince Edward; Pleasant FOWLER; Prince Edward; Fannie Fowler 15, James Fowler 13, Samuel Fowler 11, Calvin Fowler 9, Ellen Fowler 7, Edmund Fowler 5 (all by former husband now dec'd); 20 Dec 1865

19/25: Joseph Spencer 35; Charlotte; Farmville; Laborer; Judah SPENCER; Charlotte; Jenny Spencer 27; Charlotte; Farmville; Thomas W. SPENCER; Charlotte; James Spencer infant; 25 Dec 1859

19/26: James Wootten 25; Prince Edward; Prince Edward; Laborer; H. WOOTTEN; Prince Edward; Millie Wootten 20; Prince Edward; Prince Edward; Sam B. SCOTT; Prince Edward; Ø; 10 Jan 1864

19/27: Edward Branch 34; Prince Edward; Prince Edward; Blacksmith; Mrs. Alice ALINS; Prince Edward; Nancy Branch 25; Petersburg; Prince Edward; William McGHEE; Prince Edward; Robert Branch 11, William E. Branch 9, Richard Branch 7, Sydney Branch 5 (all by former wife now dec'd); 1st marriage 25 Dec 1854; 2nd marriage 25 Dec 1864

19/31: Daniel Wootten 46; Prince Edward; Prince Edward; Laborer; H. WOOTTEN; Prince Edward; Fannie Wootten 48; Prince Edward; Prince Edward; H. WOOTTEN; Prince Edward; Jack Wootten 25, Emley Wootten 24, James Wootten 20 (all by former hus of Fannie); 25 Dec 1855

19/34: Ed Rowlett 28; Prince Edward; Farmville; Laborer; Mrs. Mary ROWLETT; Prince Edward; Ann Rowlett 20; Nottoway; Farmville; Dr. JARNETT; Prince Edward; Patty Rowlett 5, James Rowlett infant; 20 Jan 1860 (There are DeJARNETTEs in Caroline County.)

19/36: Paschal Shideler 41; Lunenburg; Prince Edward; Laborer; Thomas SHACKLETON; Lunenburg; Mary Shideler 37; Prince Edward; Prince Edward; Hamlin STOKES; Lunenburg; Andy Shideler 16, Eliza Shideler 14, Tampa Shideler 8; 20 Sept 1846

19/39: Anthony Stokes 24; Lunenburg; Prince Edward; Laborer; Susan STOKES; Lunenburg; Judah Stokes 22; Lunenburg; Prince Edward; Jarman STOKES; Lunenburg; Ø; 20 Mar 1864

19/40: Anthony Morning 25; Nottoway; Prince Edward; Laborer; Billy MORNING; Halifax; Bettey Morning 16; Halifax; Prince Edward; Harriet DUNCAN; Prince Edward; Ø; 25 Dec 1865

20/1: Richard Rowlett 40; Lunenburg; Prince Edward; Laborer; William B. ROWLETT; Prince Edward; Catherine Rowlett 37; Lunenburg; Prince Edward; Mrs. Betty STOKES; Prince Edward; Delia Rowlett 13, Mary 11, Harriet 9, Nancy 7, Edward 5, Jane infant; 25 Dec 1854

20/4: Albert Stokes 31; Lunenburg; Prince Edward; Laborer; Mrs. Betty STOKES; Prince Edward; Polly Stokes 32; Prince Edward; Prince Edward; Hamilton STOKES; Lunenburg; Gertrude 12, Ann Jane 10, Depha 6, Eda 3, Albert 2; 20 Dec 1854

20/6: James Powell 21; Halifax; Prince Edward; Laborer; Thomas POWELL; Halifax; Mary Powell 22; Lunenburg; Prince Edward; Mumford HURT; Prince Edward; Lucinda 8, Norah 4, 20 Aug 1865

20/7: William Stokes 26; Lunenburg; Prince Edward; Laborer; Susan STOKES; Lunenburg; Harriet Stokes 24; Mecklenburg; Prince Edward; P. RUSSELL; Lunenburg; Adeline 6, Joseph 2; 18 June 1860

20/8: E. Rowlett 57; Prince Edward; Prince Edward; Laborer; Thomas ROWLETT; Prince Edward; Nancy Rowlett 58; Charles City; Prince Edward; Thomas O. ROWLETT; Prince Edward; Henry 28, Jerry 18; 25 June 1828

20/9: Henry Watkins 60; Prince Edward; Prince Edward; Laborer; Dr. PETERS; Prince Edward; Harriet Watkins 53; Prince Edward; Prince Edward; Mrs. WALTON; Prince Edward; Henry 30, Albert 20, Doctor 15; 26 June 1829

20/10: Griffin Braggs 50; Prince Edward; Prince Edward; Laborer; Mrs. Patsey CHAMBERS; Prince Edward; Mary A. Braggs 35; Prince Edward; Prince Edward; John H. KNIGHT; Prince Edward; Catherine 23, Joseph 19, Henry 18, Allen 17, Abner 12, William 8; 28 Nov 1836

20/11: Isaac Reed 26; Prince Edward; Prince Edward; Laborer; James ALLEN; Prince Edward; Louisa Reed 27; Charlotte; Prince Edward; Thomas C. SPENCER; Prince Edward; Betty 10, Patrick 7, Barbery 4, James Henry 3 mos; 25 June 1862

20/13: Henry Smith 45; Prince Edward; Prince Edward; Laborer; Louis JONES; Buckingham; Martha Smith 25; Prince Edward; Prince Edward; Mrs. Mary C. WOMACK; Prince Edward; Delia 12, Frederick 8; 14 Sept 1851

20/14: Elisha Lipscomb 70; King William; Farmville; Laborer; John DUPUY; Cumberland; Betsey Lipscomb 56; Prince Edward; Prince Edward; Born Free; Ø; Ø; 15 Sept 1851

20/15: John Anderson 65; Amelia; Farmville; Laborer; Alex B. WEST; Prince Edward; Lucinda Anderson 50; Cumberland; Prince Edward; Dr. Thomas HICKSON; Prince Edward; Monroe? 15; 14 Oct 1836

20/16: Daniel Bruce 66; Charlotte; Farmville; Laborer; Pat JACKSON; Farmville; Jane Bruce 50; Charlotte; Farmville; David BELL; Charlotte; Christian 30, John 14, Jenny 6, Ellen 2; 24 Dec 1827

20/18: William Smith 53; Farmville; Farmville; Laborer; Born Free; Ø; Martha Smith 46; Farmville; Farmville; F.B. WRIGHT; Farmville; Edmonia 18, Flora 16, Daniel 14, Robert 7, Emily infant; 25 Dec 1840

20/20: Sampson Taylor 26; Cumberland; Farmville; Laborer; Dr. LEACH; Cumberland; Martha Taylor 23; Prince Edward; Farmville; ALLMAN; Prince Edward; William infant; 28 Feb 1863

20/21: Alex Bates 39; Halifax; Farmville; Shoemaker; Thomas NOBLE; Farmville; Elvira Bates 35; Amelia; Farmville; Egbert WOMACK; Prince Edward; John 11, Stepney 7, Ida 1 1/2, Preston 4; 20 Oct 1850

20/23: John Page 25, Powhatan; Farmville; Grocer; Albertas SAUNDERS; Buckingham; Isabella Page 20; Buckingham; Farmville; Weaver DRUIN; Buckingham; Ø; 28 Dec 1862

20/24: George Pickett 24; Buckingham; Farmville; Butcher; Thomas F. WOMACK; Buckingham; Agnes Pickett 18; Buckingham; Farmville; Eliza EPPES; Buckingham; Matt 12 mos; 4 Sept 1864

20/25: William Johnson 33; Prince Edward; Prince Edward; Laborer; Mrs. M.C. WOMACK; Prince Edward; Amanda Johnson 25; Prince Edward; Prince Edward; Mrs. Jerusha HARVEY; Prince Edward; Alice 8, Andrew 5, Phillis 2; 25 Dec 1856

20/26: Matt Johnson 31; Prince Edward; Prince Edward; Laborer; Mrs. M.C. WOMACK; Prince Edward; Nancy Johnson 25; Prince Edward; Prince Edward; T.F. VENABLE; Prince Edward; Daniel 9, __ans 4, Douglass 7; 24 Oct 1856

20/27: Edward Matthews 28; Prince Edward; Farmville; Laborer; Thomas WOMACK; Buckingham; Betty Matthews 19; Prince Edward; Farmville; Dr. BERKELEY; Prince Edward; Josephine 13 mos; George 3; 25 Dec 1860

20/28: Henry Brier 60; Prince Edward; Prince Edward; Carpenter; T.L. MORTON; Prince Edward; Betsey Brier 50; Prince Edward; Prince Edward; Jack GUNTER; Appomattox; Patrick 24, Lucy 20, Sophy 18, Rachel 16; 20 June 1830

20/30: Hercules Smith 54; Prince Edward; Prince Edward; Carpenter; Mrs. Nancy BLANTON; Cumberland; Amanda Smith 44; Prince Edward; Prince Edward; Wilson WOODRUFF; Cumberland; Dolly 13, Minna 12, Dinah 10, Hannah 2, (stepchildren); 20 Feb 1865

20/32: Clem Reed 59; Charlotte; Farmville; Carpenter; Dr. PETERS; Farmville; Louisa Reed 35; Prince Edward; Farmville; Born Free; Ø; Isaac 21, Emma 15, Nannie 8; 25 Dec 1836

20/34: Nathan Butler 37; Prince Edward; Farmville; Grocer; Pat JACKSON; Farmville; Matilda Butler 35; Prince Edward; Farmville; Pat JACKSON; Farmville; Pattie 17, Elworth 12, Adeline 10, Fayette 8, Sydney 5, Anne 9 mos; 1st marriage 1 Jan 1850

20/37: James Smith 36; Cumberland; Farmville; Laborer; G.W. DANIEL; Farmville; Ann Smith 42; Cumberland; Farmville; William PORTER; Farmville; Louisa; 1st marriage 1848, 2nd marriage 25 Dec 1859

21/1: Henry Green 23; Nelson; Prince Edward; Laborer; T.W. ROBERTS; Nelson; Betty Green 20; Prince Edward; Prince Edward; T.W. ROBERTS; Nelson; Paul Green 1, Silas Green 1 (twins); 1 Apr 1853

21/3: Benjamin Perkinson 40; Prince Edward; Prince Edward; Laborer; Dan PERGUSON; Prince Edward; Tena Perkinson 34; Lunenburg; Prince Edward; H. STOKES; Lunenburg; Patience Perkinson 6, Thomas Perkinson 7, Sallie Perkinson 16; 25 Dec 1840

21/6: Daniel Johnson 50; Prince Edward; Prince Edward; Laborer; J. CUNNINGHAM; Prince Edward; Anan Johnson 44; Prince Edward; Prince Edward; J. CUNNINGHAM; Prince Edward; John Johnson 18, Martha Johnson 16, Mary Johnson 14, Eliza Johnson 12, Edward Johnson 4; 1 Mar 1843

21/11: Sterling Bolling 60; Prince Edward; Prince Edward; Laborer; Mrs. A. WATKINS; Prince Edward; Lucy Bolling 48; Prince Edward; Prince Edward; Mrs. A. WATKINS; Prince Edward; Pitt Bolling, Patrick Bolling 18, Phebe Bolling 17, Martha Bolling 13; 10 Oct 1827

21/15: William J. Rice 40; Prince Edward; Prince Edward; Laborer; William J. RICE; Prince Edward; Harriet Rice 29; Prince Edward; Prince Edward; P. COCHRAN; Prince Edward; Jenny Rice 6; 15 Sept 1854

21/16: Samuel Baulden 40; Prince Edward; Prince Edward; Laborer; Mrs. DUPUY; Prince Edward; Betsey Baulden 34; Prince Edward; Prince Edward; William BEACH; Prince Edward; Peter Baulden 14, Hannah Baulden 12, Sam Baulden 6, Emaline Baulden 3; 1 Jan 1848

21/20: Wilson Carter 64; Prince Edward; Prince Edward; Laborer; R. RANDALL; Prince Edward; Sena Carter 43; Prince Edward; Prince Edward; R. RANDALL; Prince Edward; Betsey Carter 20, Louisa Carter 19; 1 Jan 1840

21/22: Abram Gibbs 30; Prince Edward; Prince Edward; Laborer; Born Free; Ø; Ann Gibbs 28; Prince Edward; Prince Edward; Born Free; Ø; Queen Gibbs 2; 1 Nov 1859

21/23: Charles Badley 48; Prince Edward; Prince Edward; Laborer; Born Free; Ø; Sally Badley 44; Prince Edward; Prince Edward; Born Free; Ø; Emrick/Eunick? Badley 19, H.L. Badley 17, William D. Badley 15, Lucy J. Badley 13, Lizzie Badley 11, Sally Badley 1; Oct 1845

21/29: A. Crawley 34; Lunenburg; Prince Edward; Laborer; Alex CRAWLEY; Prince Edward; Katy Crawley 34; Richmond; Prince Edward; John H. KNIGHT; Prince Edward; Ø; 25 Dec 1863

21/30: Thomas Bench 34; Prince Edward; Prince Edward; Laborer; Elisha BENCH; Prince Edward; Martha Bench 40; Prince Edward; Prince Edward; H.E. WATKINS; Prince Edward; Sam Bench 6; 25 Dec 1856

21/31: R. Pegram 66; Cumberland; Prince Edward; Laborer; F. ANDERSON; Cumberland; Maria Pegram 50; Prince Edward; Prince Edward; Dr. DILLON; Prince Edward; Hannah Pegram 16, Sally Pegram 13; 25 Dec 1834

21/33: Samuel Burton 34; Prince Edward; Prince Edward; Laborer; Mrs. M. CHAMBERS; Prince Edward; Susan Burton 28; Prince Edward; Prince Edward; L. CARY; Prince Edward; Sarah C. Burton 7, Rachel Burton 6, Milly Burton 3, Lucy Burton 2, infant; 25 Dec 1854

21/39: Isaac Perkins 30; Prince Edward; Prince Edward; Laborer; Sam BONDURANT; Prince Edward; Susan Perkins 23; Prince Edward; Prince Edward; S. BONDURANT; Prince Edward; William Perkins 5, Jackson Perkins 4, James Perkins 6 mos; 20 June 1859

22/1: William T. Clark 32; Prince Edward; Prince Edward; Farmer; Sam L. CLARK; Prince Edward; Judy Clark 26; Prince Edward; Prince Edward; S.T. CLARK; Prince Edward; Patrick H. Clark 10, John Clark 8, Anderson Clark 6, M. Ann Clark 4; 15 May 1855

22/5: Taylor Clark 40; Prince Edward; Prince Edward; Laborer; Sam L. CLARK; Prince Edward; Mary J. Clark 35; Prince Edward; Prince Edward; H. SAUNDERS; Prince Edward; Ø; 15 Mar 1859

22/6: Robert Mitchell 24; Appomattox; Prince Edward; Laborer; Samuel MITCHELL; Appomattox; Pat Mitchell 17; Prince Edward; Prince Edward; P. HUBBARD; Prince Edward; 5 mos; 1 Sept 1865

22/7: Joel Branch 38; Prince Edward; Prince Edward; Laborer; John WOMACK; Prince Edward; Pat Branch 28; Prince Edward; Prince Edward; L.D. WOMACK; Prince Edward; Elizabeth Branch 6; 25 Dec 1858

22/8: Sawney Watson 52; Prince Edward; Prince Edward; Laborer; James DUPUY; Prince Edward; Catherine Watson 46; Prince Edward; Prince Edward; Albert REDD; Prince Edward; Sawney Watson 19, Timothy Watson 20, Laura Watson 18, J.B. Watson 12, Catherine Watson 10, Porter Watson 8; Mar 1836

22/14: John Baxter 31; Prince Edward; Prince Edward; Laborer; Hugh MORTON; Prince Edward; Lucy Baxter 46; Prince Edward; Prince Edward; Frank REDD; Prince Edward; Rachel Baxter 5, Osborne Baxter 3, Daniel Baxter 3 wks; 25 Dec 1859

22/17: Jacob Bridewell 48; Prince Edward; Prince Edward; Laborer; J. BRIDEWELL; Prince Edward; Annes? Bridewell 48; Prince Edward; Prince Edward; William BRIDEWELL; Prince Edward; John Bridewell 17, Aaron Bridewell 15, Peter Bridewell 11, Alex Bridewell 9, Henry Bridewell 6, Patsy Bridewell 5, Harriet Bridewell 4; 30 Dec 1848

22/24: Jack Pegram 40; Brunswick; Prince Edward; Farmer; Col. H. STOKES; Prince Edward; Jemina Pegram 30; Lunenburg; Prince Edward; H. STOKES; Prince Edward; Milly Pegram 4, John Pegram 1; 20 Dec 1856

22/26: Anthony Perkinson 66; Nottoway; Prince Edward; Laborer; Maj. WARHAM; Nottoway; R. Perkinson 60; Prince Edward; Prince Edward; R. PERKINSON; Prince Edward; Ø; 1 Jan 1824

22/27: Shadrack Branch 66; Prince Edward; Prince Edward; Farmer; R.C. ANDERSON; Prince Edward; Elsy Branch 52; Prince Edward; Prince Edward; Hugh MORTON; Prince Edward; Ø; 15 May 1865

22/28: Edwin Brown 36; Prince Edward; Prince Edward; Farmer; Mrs. A. WATKINS; Prince Edward; Susan Brown 35; Prince Edward; Prince Edward; Hugh MORTON; Prince Edward; Bethe Brown 18, Stokes Brown 16, Webster Brown 13, Alice Brown 11, Lavinia Brown 7, Edwin Brown 3, Rosa Brown 1; 2 Jan 1846

22/35: George Washington 28; Prince Edward; Prince Edward; Laborer; John FOSTER; Prince Edward; Nancy Washington 28; Prince Edward; Prince Edward; Charles WADE; Prince Edward; James Washington 4, George Washington 2; 25 Dec 1861

22/37: Armstead Venable 48; Prince Edward; Prince Edward; Laborer; F.N. WATKINS; Prince Edward; Isabella Venable 28; Prince Edward; Prince Edward; F.N. WATKINS; Prince Edward; Pat Venable 6, Sam Venable 5 mos; 15 Oct 1860

22/39: Peter Venable 26; Amelia; Prince Edward; Laborer; Joseph OVERTON; Prince Edward; L.A. Venable 24; Prince Edward; Prince Edward; Joseph PHILLIPS; Prince Edward; Walter J. Venable 2, Maggie Venable 1; 1 Feb 1860

23/1: John Thomas 36; Prince Edward; Prince Edward; Farmer; Ed MILLER; Prince Edward; Harriet Thomas 29; Prince Edward; Prince Edward; John FOSTER; Prince Edward; Wilson Thomas 7, Patty Thomas 5, Ruth Thomas 10 mos; 30 Nov 1858

23/4: H. Richardson 54; Prince Edward; Prince Edward; Farmer; Charles REED; Prince Edward; Judy Richardson 38; Prince Edward; Prince Edward; Charles REED; Prince Edward; Sam Richardson 8, Thomas Richardson 7, Betty Richardson 5, Emma Richardson 4, Nannie Richardson 3; 24 Dec 1853

23/9: Charles Johnson 38; Prince Edward; Prince Edward; Farmer; Ed EDMUNDS; Prince Edward; Clarissa Johnson 28; Prince Edward; Prince Edward; Ed EDMUNDS; Prince Edward; Mary V. Johnson 8, Ann T. Johnson 4, Eddie Johnson 1; 25 Dec 1857

23/12: Phillip Stokes 50; Lunenburg; Prince Edward; Farmer; Richard STOKES; Prince Edward; Ada Stokes 44; Lunenburg; Prince Edward; Richard STOKES; Prince Edward; Ø; 20 June 18160

23/13: Benjamin Jones 28; Prince Edward; Prince Edward; Farmer; B.I. ROGERS; Halifax; Ann Jones 26; Halifax; Prince Edward; B.I. ROGERS; Halifax; Ellis Jones 6, Caroline Jones 4, Thomas Jones 3, Evan Jones 2; 30 Oct 1858

23/17: Clem Byassy 36; Lunenburg; Prince Edward; Farmer; Henry STOKES; Prince Edward; Elvira Byassy 30; Lunenburg; Prince Edward; Henry STOKES; Prince Edward; Summers Byassy 15, Puss Byassy 12, Andrew Byassy 10, Ashley Byassy 8, Dodson Byassy 6; 25 Dec 1850

23/22: Scipio Stokes 29; Lunenburg; Prince Edward; Farmer; Richard STOKES; Prince Edward; Adeline Stokes 29; Lunenburg; Prince Edward; Richard STOKES; Prince Edward; Sarah Stokes 9, Patty Stokes 4, Amelia Stokes 3, Jane Stokes 2; 13 Oct 1856

23/26: Nelson Stokes 32; Lunenburg; Prince Edward; Laborer; Richard STOKES; Prince Edward; Car. Stokes 25; Lunenburg; Prince Edward; Richard STOKES; Prince Edward; Freeman Stokes 10, Eliza Stokes 9, Betty Stokes 7, Waddie Stokes 6; 28 Dec 1854

23/31: David Stokes 29; Lunenburg; Prince Edward; Laborer; Richard STOKES; Prince Edward; Ellen Stokes 24; Lunenburg; Prince Edward; Richard STOKES; Prince Edward; Emma Stokes 14 mos; George Stokes 10, Francis Stokes 5, John Stokes 1; 26 Dec 1855

23/34: Richard Miller 35; Prince Edward; Prince Edward; Laborer; B.R. ROGERS; Halifax; Eliza Miller 29; Halifax; Prince Edward; B.R. ROGERS; Halifax; William Miller 6, Louisa Miller 5, George Miller 3; 20 Dec 1857

23/37: Branch Miller 38; Prince Edward; Prince Edward; Laborer; R.A. MILLER; Prince Edward; Emily Miller 29; Prince Edward; Prince Edward; R.A. MILLER; Prince Edward; Mattie Miller 7, Carrie Miller 5, Charity Miller 3, Betsey Miller 1; 25 Dec 1857

24/1: William Redd 66; Cumberland; Prince Edward; Laborer; Mrs. F. REDD; Prince Edward; Fanny Redd 56; Prince Edward; Prince Edward; Born Free; Ø; Judah Redd 18, John William Redd 17, Susan Redd 13, Nelson Redd 12, Emily W. Redd 11, Jackson Redd 9, Daniel J. Redd 6, Becky J. Redd 5; 25 Dec 1830

24/9: Matt Miller 35; Prince Edward; Prince Edward; Laborer; Ed MILLER; Prince Edward; Jenny Miller 20; Cumberland; Prince Edward; Dr. BLANTON; Cumberland; Ø; 25 Dec 1865

24/10: ~~Wilson Gills 32; Amelia; Prince Edward; Laborer; Miles GILLS; Amelia~~

24/11: Daniel Forest 78; Prince Edward; Prince Edward; Laborer; Matt FALSE; Prince Edward; Hannah Forest 80; Prince Edward; Prince Edward; Drury SMITH; Prince Edward; Ø; 20 June 1834

24/12: Robert James 40; Prince Edward; Prince Edward; Laborer; L. ROWLETT; Prince Edward; Easter Rowlett 34; Prince Edward; Prince Edward; Samuel B. SCOTT; Prince Edward; Giles B. James 8 mos; 20 Oct 1861

24/13: Beverly Jeffries 56; Prince Edward; Prince Edward; Laborer; Dr. PETERS; Farmville; Eliza Jeffries 35; Prince Edward; Prince Edward; Allen CHAMBERS; Prince Edward; Ø; 20 June 1829

24/14: Paul Watson 32; Prince Edward; Prince Edward; Laborer; Daniel WATSON; Prince Edward; Judah Watson 30; Prince Edward; Prince Edward; John A. SCOTT; Prince Edward; Emma Watson 8, Jennie Ann Watson 6, John A. Watson 4, Fannie Watson 2, Stokes Watson 2 mos; 25 Dec 1856

24/19: George Dallas 22; Prince Edward; Prince Edward; Laborer; Henry BUDD; Cumberland; Mary Dallas 18; Cumberland; Prince Edward; Joseph MORROW; Cumberland; Robert Dallas 1; 18 May 1864

24/20: John H. Edmonds 51; Charlotte; Prince Edward; Laborer; E. EDMONDS; Prince Edward; Cath Edmonds 50; Prince Edward; Prince Edward; E. EDMONDS; Prince Edward; Ø; 25 Dec 1854

24/21: Dennis Hamlin 24; Charlotte; Prince Edward; Laborer; Dr. SPENCER; Farmville; Jenny Hamlin 18; Prince Edward; Prince Edward; John BONDURANT; Prince Edward; Ø; 20 Apr 1865

24/22: Bev Randon 40; Prince Edward; Prince Edward; Laborer; H. STOKES; Prince Edward; Ann Randon 34; Lunenburg; Prince Edward; H. STOKES; Prince Edward; Beverly Randon 10, Minnie Randon 8, George Randon 6, Booker Randon 4, Stokes Randon 2; 20 Jan 1855

24/27: Africa Crawley 74; Nottoway; Prince Edward; Laborer; James T. GRAY; Prince Edward; Jenny Crawley 45; Prince Edward; Prince Edward; James T. GRAY; Prince Edward; Stephen Crowley 9; James Crawley 7; 1 Jan 1856

24/29: Hercules Price 72; Prince Edward; Prince Edward; Laborer; P. JACKSON; Farmville; Milly Price 70; Prince Edward; Prince Edward; P. JACKSON; Farmville; Ø; 19 Jan 1826

24/30: Jim Tucker 75; Prince Edward; Prince Edward; Laborer; George BOOKER; Prince Edward; Patsey Tucker 74; Prince Edward; Prince Edward; Mrs. MICHAUX; Prince Edward; Ø; 25 Dec 1836

24/31: Robert Womack 56; Lunenburg; Prince Edward; Laborer; H. THAXTON; Prince Edward; Violet Womack 54; Bedford; Prince Edward; H. THAXTON; Prince Edward; Polly Womack 12, Melinda Womack 14; 25 Dec 1844

24/33: Richmond Rice 30; Prince Edward; Prince Edward; Laborer; Mrs. Martha CLARK; Prince Edward; Mary E. Rice 26; Prince Edward; Prince Edward; James L. LIGAN; Prince Edward; Elizabeth Rice 7, Edmund Rice 4, Annie Rice 5 mos; 2 Dec 1854

24/36: Matt Griggs 56; Prince Edward; Prince Edward; Laborer; William BEATTEY; Prince Edward; Eliza Griggs 48; Charlotte; Prince Edward; James B. ELY; Prince Edward; Isaac Griggs 7, Matt Griggs 8; Nannie Griggs 1, Fanny Griggs 12; 25 Dec 1851

25/1: Saul Berkeley 54; Prince Edward; Prince Edward; Laborer; James VENABLE; Prince Edward; Margaret Berkeley _2; Charlotte; Prince Edward; James VENABLE; Prince Edward; Edward Berkeley 13, Emma Berkeley 6, Early Berkeley 5, Bruce Berkeley 1; 28 Dec 1853

25/5: James A. Scott 36; Cumberland; Ø; Carpenter; V. PARRISH; Cumberland; Martha Scott 27; Buckingham; Farmville; E.H. DAVIS; Buckingham; Ø; 7 May 1863

25/6: Robert Wheeler 24; Charlotte; Prince Edward; Laborer; Samuel WHEELER; Prince Edward; Lydia Wheeler 26; Appomattox; Prince Edward; Thomas VENABLE; Appomattox; Charles Wheeler 1, Birdie Wheeler 8; 15 Mar 1850

25/8: Willis Johnson 70; Amelia; Prince Edward; Laborer; Newton HARPER; Nottoway; Patsey Johnson 66; Prince Edward; Prince Edward; F. ELLERTON; Prince Edward; Ø; 25 Dec 1820

25/9: Lanta Johnson 60; Prince Edward; Prince Edward; Laborer; Nat MATLEY; Prince Edward; Lucy Johnson 24; Cumberland; Prince Edward; Jim O__TOW; Cumberland; Salle Johnson 6 mos; 20 Apr 1865

25/10: B. Queensbury 60; Prince Edward; Prince Edward; Laborer; Jim QUEENSBURY; Prince Edward; Lina Queensbury 40; Prince Edward; Prince Edward; Taylor WOOTTEN; Prince Edward; Ø; 1 Jan 1856

25/11: Booker Johnson 46; Amelia; Prince Edward; Laborer; Richard MILLER; Prince Edward; Sally Johnson 36; Nottoway; Prince Edward; Marg. WOOD; Prince Edward; Mary Johnson 14, Jane Johnson 10; 25 Dec 1826

25/12: Henry Miller 71; Prince Edward; Prince Edward; Laborer; Edward MILLER; Prince Edward; Vina Miller 62; Prince Edward; Prince Edward; James MADISON; Cumberland; Eliza Miller 16, Maria Miller; Ø; 1 Jan 1840

25/14: Effert Jones 28; Amelia; Prince Edward; Laborer; Richard MILLER; Prince Edward; Mary Jones 26; Prince Edward; Prince Edward; Thomas WOOTTEN; Prince Edward; Josephine Jones 1; 25 Dec 1864

25/16: Anthony Oliver 62; Caswell, No. Carolina; Prince Edward; Laborer; W. HATCHETT; Prince Edward; Julia Oliver 42; Prince Edward; Prince Edward; William HATCHETT; Prince Edward; Jim Oliver 14, Lill Oliver 12, Allen Oliver 7, Sam Oliver 6, Norah Oliver 2; 1 Jan 1824

25/21: Pat Henry 50; Prince Edward; Prince Edward; Laborer; Alice ALMS; Prince Edward; Elvira Henry 34; Prince Edward; Prince Edward; J.T. BRANCH; Prince Edward; Isabella Henry 13, Eliza Ann 12, Oora? J. 10, Mi__ie 8, P.H. 26 days; 25 Dec 1851

25/26: Floyd Miller 24; Prince Edward; Prince Edward; Laborer; R.A. MILLER; Prince Edward; Lizzie Miller 24; Prince Edward; Prince Edward; B. WITT; Prince Edward; Sydney Miller 4, Nannie Miller 2, Molly Miller 1; 15 Mar 1861

25/29: Aaron Miller 45; Prince Edward; Prince Edward; Laborer; R.A. MILLER; Prince Edward; Martha Miller 41; Prince Edward; Prince Edward; R.A. MILLER; Prince Edward; Ø; 1 Jan 1826

25/30: Sydney Miller 26; Prince Edward; Prince Edward; Laborer; R.A. MILLER; Prince Edward; Amanda Miller 26; Cumberland; Prince Edward; R.A. MILLER; Prince Edward; Willie J. Miller 3; 25 Dec 1860

25/31: William Armstead 42; Prince Edward; Prince Edward; Laborer; R.A. MILLER; Prince Edward; Lizzie Miller 22; Prince Edward; Prince Edward; R.A. MILLER; Prince Edward; Harriet Miller 2; 1 Jan 1864

25/32: Joseph Ewing 24; Prince Edward; Prince Edward; Laborer; Thomas EWING; Prince Edward; Pattie Ewing 22; Prince Edward; Prince Edward; William L. WOOTTEN; Prince Edward; Joseph A. Ewing 4, J.T. Ewing 2; 1 Apr 1861

25/33: Giles Miller 40; Prince Edward; Prince Edward; Laborer; B.R. RODGERS; Halifax; Amelia Miller 34; Prince Edward; Prince Edward; B.R. ROGERS; Prince Edward; Margaret A. Miller 18, Paulina Miller 16, Amanda Miller 14, Robert Miller 12, Lewis Miller 9, Giles Miller 5, Alpheus Miller 1; 25 Dec 1844

26/1: Cary Branch 44; Cumberland; Prince Edward; Laborer; N. WOMACK; Cumberland; Nancy Branch 33; Prince Edward; Prince Edward; Born Free; Ø; Ø; 25 Dec 1861

26/2: William Jackson 30; Prince Edward; Prince Edward; Laborer; Pat JACKSON; Farmville; Ann Jackson 30; Cumberland; Prince Edward; Ben WILSON; Cumberland; Ø; 1 July 1862

26/3: O. Lipscomb 43; Cumberland; Farmville; Laborer; Born Free; Ø; Mary Ann Lipscomb 36; Fluvanna; Farmville; Born Free; Ø; William Lipscomb 16; 25 Dec 1848

26/4: Hampton Booker 56; Charlotte; Farmville; Laborer; William DUNNINGTON; Charlotte; Mary Booker 46; Nottoway; Farmville; Asa DICKINSON; Prince Edward; Ø; 25 Dec 1865

26/5: Douglass? Dennis 36; Prince Edward; Prince Edward; Laborer; Thomas GARDNER; Prince Edward; Harriet Dennis 29; Charlotte; Prince Edward; Born Free; Ø; Ø; 1 Jan 1861

26/6: Thomas Smith 26; Prince Edward; Prince Edward; Laborer; Mrs. M. MOTLEY; Prince Edward; Martha Smith 24; Amelia; Prince Edward; Thomas BLANTON; Prince Edward; Julia Smith 5, Thomas Smith 4, George Smith 2; 15 May 1860

26/9: Emmanuel Marshal 38; Charlotte; Prince Edward; Laborer; John DANIEL; Prince Edward; Salina Marshal 40; Prince Edward; Prince Edward; James VENABLE; Prince Edward; Cornelia Marshal 2; 15 Nov 1853

26/10: Benjamin Smith 24; Charlotte; Prince Edward; Laborer; H. VENABLE; Prince Edward; Hester M. Smith 24; Kanawha; Prince Edward; Watt GETTS; Prince Edward; Willie Smith 1; 15 Oct 1863

26/11: Benjamin Allen 23; Charlotte; Prince Edward; Laborer; James CRAWLEY; Prince Edward; M.J. ALLEN 18; Prince Edward; Prince Edward; H. VENABLE; Prince Edward; Ø; 15 Aug 1865

26/12: Claiborne Allen 40; Charlotte; Prince Edward; Laborer; Addison BRIDEWELL; Prince Edward; La__ Allen 40; Charlotte; Prince Edward; Nat WILSON; Prince Edward; Wyatt Allen 15, Ch_tina Allen 8, Jessie Allen 6; 25 Dec 1826

26/15: Adam Gaines 38; Charlotte; Prince Edward; Laborer; James CRAWLEY; Prince Edward; Jane Gaines 40; Richmond; Prince Edward; James CRAWLEY; Prince Edward; Ø; 15 Nov 1849

26/16: Henry Woodson 52; Prince Edward; Prince Edward; Laborer; James VENABLE; Prince Edward; Amanda Woodson 54; Charlotte; Prince Edward; James VENABLE; Prince Edward; Charles Woodson 19, Loudon Woodson 18; 1 Jan 1862

26/17: Gen Washington 60; Buckingham; Prince Edward; Laborer; Henry DAVIS; Prince Edward; Martha Washington 4_; Prince Edward; Prince Edward; Sam WHEELER; Prince Edward; Jane Washington 13, Jeff Washington 10, Eliza Washington 5, Lucy Washington 4; 15 Jan 1826

26/22: Richard Woodson 23; Prince Edward; Prince Edward; Laborer; James VENABLE; Prince Edward; Agnes Woodson 20; Prince Edward; Prince Edward; P. COLEMAN; Cumberland; Sarah Woodson 8 mos; 15 Apr 1865

26/23: Booker Foster 37; Nottoway; Prince Edward; Laborer; J.T. BRANCH; Prince Edward; Mariah Foster 32; Nottoway; Prince Edward; Buck RUDD; Nottoway; Ed Foster 9, Martha Foster 6, Callahan Foster 4, Henrietta Foster 15; 25 Dec 1853

26/27: Isaac Brown 34; Charlotte; Prince Edward; Laborer; James VENABLE; Prince Edward; Elvira Brown 26; Prince Edward; Prince Edward; Dr. GLENN; Prince Edward; Marshal Brown 5, Julia A. Brown 3, Jenny Brown 9 mos; 1 Jan 1859

26/30: Albert Short 46; Prince Edward; Prince Edward; Laborer; William BEUFORD; Prince Edward; Amy F. Short 38; Prince Edward; Prince Edward; B. MORSE; Prince Edward; James Short 18, Mary Short 16, Anna Short 14, Amelia Short 12, Edney Short 10, Sally Short 8, Sydney Short 6, William Short 4

26/38: John A. Stokes 28; Campbell; Prince Edward; Laborer; H.? SHACKLETON; Lunenburg; Bertina Stokes 22; Prince Edward; Prince Edward; Ridley FULSE; Lunenburg; Thomas Stokes 4, Johnny Stokes 4

27/1: Teacher Singleton 44; Campbell; Farmville; Laborer; Patrick JACKSON; Farmville; Pamalia Singleton 35; Prince Edward; Farmville; Patrick JACKSON; Farmville; Watt Singleton 20, Margaret Singleton 18, Betty Singleton 16, Richard Singleton 14, Robert Singleton 12, Page Singleton 10, Rosa Singleton 1; 24 Mar 1866

27/8: Albert Green 45; Cumberland; Farmville; Laborer; S.G. SPENCER; Cumberland; Maria Green 35; Louisa; Farmville; James PIERSON; Farmville; Benjamin Green 13, Leo Green 12, Mary Green 8; 4 July 1851

27/11: Henry Bartlett 45; Farmville; Farmville; Laborer; Born Free; Ø; Rhoda Bartlett 44; Prince Edward; Farmville; Born Free; Ø; John Bartlett 25, George Bartlett 22, Mary J. Barlett 20, Caledonia Bartlett 14, Betsy Bartlett 12, Mamranth? J. Bartlett 6, James W. Bartlett 7, A.L. Bartlett 6, Simuel? Bartlett 18; 20 May 1840

27/20: Samuel Cook 68; Prince Edward; Prince Edward; Farmer; H.E. WATKINS; Prince Edward; Fanny Cook 55; Prince Edward; Prince Edward; James D. WOODS; Prince Edward; Samuel Cook 30, Cornelius Cook 29, Drucilla Cook 25; 20 June 1835

27/23: Jacob Eppes 30; Charlotte; Farmville; Laborer; Miss Lina REED; Charlotte; Virginia Eppes 25; Buckingham; Farmville; William DUNNINGTON; Charlotte; Louisa Ann Eppes 8; 20 May 1853

27/24: Matt Harris 46; Prince Edward; Prince Edward; Farmer; S.H. WOOTTEN; Prince Edward; Lucy Harris 43; Charlotte; Prince Edward; Richard STOKES; Prince Edward; Joseph Harris 13, Ed Harris 10; 20 Nov; 1853

27/25: Charles Taylor 44; Prince Edward; Farmville; Laborer; Mrs. Martha WILSEY; Farmville; Parthenia Taylor 30; Buckingham; Farmville; Charles ANSON; Farmville; Susan Taylor 10, Robert Taylor 5, Patsey Taylor 3; 26 Nov 1855

27/29: Richard Booker 24; Cumberland; Farmville; Laborer; George W. DANIEL; Farmville; Sarah Booker 23; Prince Edward; Farmville; George W. DANIEL; Farmville; Ø; 20 Nov 1862

27/30: Patrick Carter 53; Prince Edward; Farmville; Laborer; James D. LIGAN; Prince Edward; Bettie Carter 21; Prince Edward; Farmville; Mrs. Betsy HICKSON; Prince Edward; Patrick Carter 2, Katie Carter 16 (by 1st wife dec'd), Sarah Carter 10 (by 1st wife dec'd); 1st marriage 10 July 1848, 2nd marriage 1 Oct 1864

27/33: William Jones 33; Prince Edward; Farmville; Laborer; Dr. Benjamin PETERSON; Farmville; Martha Jones 33; Cumberland; Farmville; Rosa THAXTON; Cumberland; Rosa Jones 14, Frank Jones 12, Jane Jones 7; 11 Mar 1851

27/36: Jacob Booker 53; Prince Edward; Farmville; Laborer; Dr. William S. MORTON; Cumberland; Lucy Booker 39; Prince Edward; Farmville; John DUPUY; Cumberland; Betty Booker 18, Alice Booker 14, Moses Booker 17, Agnes Booker 10, Nicholas Booker 5; 20 Mar 1834

28/1: John Edwards 30; Prince Edward; Farmville; Laborer; Mrs. Lucy ALLEN; Prince Edward

28/2: Andrew Scott 30; Charlotte; Farmville; Laborer; Mrs. Louisa REED; Charlotte; Margaret Scott 20; Amelia; Farmville; Miss Willis STEGER; Cumberland; Willie Scott 2; 1 Mar 1864

28/3: Edward Evans 37; Prince Edward; Farmville; Laborer; Thomas TREADWAY; Prince Edward; Rosetta Evans 30; Prince Edward; Farmville; Martha GUTHRIE; Prince Edward; Cabell Evans 8; 4 July 185_

28/4:Richard Taylor 54; Prince Edward; Farmville; Shoemaker; Thomas VENABLE; Prince Edward; Mary Taylor 35; Buckingham; Farmville; William L. THORNTON; Charlotte; Ø; 1 Dec 1836

28/5: Archy Thweatt 38; Prince Edward; Farmville; Laborer; G.W. DANIEL; Prince Edward; Ellen Thweatt 31; Cumberland; Farmville; William L. THORNTON; Charlotte; Titus Thweatt 12, George Thweatt 9, David Thweatt 7 mos; 1 Apr 1861

28/8: James Holcomb 25; Charlotte; Farmville; Laborer; Patrick JACKSON; Farmville; Ella Holcomb 19; Lynchburg; Farmville; Hez. FORD; Lynchburg; Ø; 29 Aug 1865

28/9: Stokes Brown 65; Prince Edward; Farmville; Laborer; H.E. WATKINS; Prince Edward; Sukey Brown 35; Prince Edward; Farmville; Dr. THAXTON; Farmville; Caroline Brown 15, Stephen Brown 12, Oscar Brown 8, (stepchild), Robert Brown 10, (stepchild) Staunton Brown 12 (stepchild); 20 Aug 1840

28/14: Samuel Jackson 24; Prince Edward; Farmville; Laborer; Born Free; Ø; Rosa Jackson 20; Prince Edward; Farmville; born Free; Ø; Ø; 8 June 1865

28/15: Caesar Watson 76; Prince Edward; Farmville; Laborer; John PRICE; Cumberland; Sally Watson 32; Prince Edward; Farmville; Mrs. Polly WOMACK; Prince Edward; Phil Brooks 15 (stepchild); 20 Aug 1859

28/16: Elijah Anderson 65; Amelia; Farmville; Laborer; Robert DUVALL; Keysville; Scylla Anderson 50; Cumberland; Farmville; John D. SMITH; Prince Edward; Ø; 20 June 1841

28/17: Thomas Armstead 51; Charlotte; Farmville; Shoemaker; Patrick JACKSON; Farmville; Mildred Armstead 45; Charlotte; Farmville; James VENABLE; Prince Edward; Ella Armstead 18, Leroy Armstead 16, William Armstead 14, Ida Armstead 12, Hezekiah Armstead 8, Robertta Armstead 6; 20 Dec 1839

28/22: Tazewell Branch 36; Prince Edward; Farmville; Shoemaker; Dr. W.H. THAXTON; Farmville; Harriet Branch 26; Prince Edward; Farmville; Alex CARRINGTON; Charlotte; Richard Branch 15 (2nd wife's son); 19 June 1858

28/23: David Bagby 27; Lunenburg; Prince Edward; Laborer; John B. GAULIN; Lunenburg; Louisa Bagby 20; Lunenburg; Prince Edward; Joel JOHNS; Lunenburg; Ø; 18 July 1860

28/24: Lewis Alms 29; Prince Edward; Prince Edward; Laborer; Walter ALMS; Prince Edward; Nancy Alms 30; Prince Edward; Prince Edward; John FOSTER; Prince Edward; Ø; 25 Dec 1861

28/25: Scipio Bentley 56; Cumberland; Farmville; Laborer; Peter FOSTER; Cumberland; America Bentley 40; Cumberland; Prince Edward; William BOOKER; Cumberland; Julia Bentley 16, Jane Bentley 14; 20 Jan 1850

28/27: Solomon Crawley 26; Lunenburg; Prince Edward; Laborer; Alex B. CRAWLEY; Prince Edward; Eda Crawley 21; Lunenburg; Prince Edward; Edward CRAWLEY; Lunenburg; Robert Crawley 13, Sarah Crawley 11, Jaime? Crawley 9, Martha Crawley 1; 26 Dec 1860

28/31: George Willis 40; Brunswick; Prince Edward; Farmer; John EDWARD; Charlotte; Betsy Willis 38; Charlotte; Prince Edward; Mrs. Jenny EDWARDS; Charlotte; Sterling Willis 18, Betty Willis 16, Celia Willis 14, Milly Willis 12, Ellen Willis 10, Littleton Willis 8, Anne Willis 6, Louisa Willis 1; 1 Jan 1856

29/1: Winston Spraggins 46; Charlotte; Prince Edward; Laborer; B.S. SCOTT; Prince Edward; Holly Spraggins 51; Prince Edward; Prince Edward; B.S. SCOTT; Prince Edward; Lina Spraggins 13; Dec 1846

29/2: Nelson Page 49; Prince Edward; Prince Edward; Laborer; Joseph WHITEHEAD; Prince Edward; Rosella Page 32; Prince Edward; Prince Edward; William ELLIOTT; Prince Edward; William Page 13, Amanda Page 10, Mary Page 6, Becky Page 4, Gabriella Page 3, Birdie Page 1; Dec 1851

29/8: Horace Burke 37; Charlotte; Prince Edward; Laborer; Benjamin BURKE; Prince Edward; Agnes Burke 50; Prince Edward; Prince Edward; Joseph WATSON; Prince Edward; Drusilla Burke 14, Horace Burke 3; Dec 1851

29/10: Paul Reed 34; Cumberland; Prince Edward; Laborer; John RANDOLPH; Prince Edward; Louisa Reed 29; Prince Edward; Prince Edward; Dr. Alex DILLON; Prince Edward; Richard Reed 9; Dec 1856

29/11: Thomas Clark 45; Prince Edward; Prince Edward; Laborer; Born Free; Ø; Lydia Clark 30; Richmond; Born Free; Ø; Ø; Dec 1846

29/12: Nash Hanlon 64; Charlotte; Prince Edward; Laborer; Miss F. HANLON; Prince Edward; Rhoda Hanlon 48; Prince Edward; Prince Edward; Thomas VENABLE; Prince Edward; Stephen Hanlon 18; Jan 1834

29/13: Julius Johnson 60; Prince Edward; Prince Edward; Laborer; Andrew VENABLE; Prince Edward; Docia Johnson 48; Prince Edward; Prince Edward; Joseph WATSON; Prince Edward; Jacob Johnson 18, Elvira; Johnson 16, Florida Johnson 14, Archer Johnson 12, Julius Johnson 9, Isham Johnson 6, Maria Johnson 2, Marshal Johnson 11; July 1840

29/21: Daniel Coleman 69; Cumberland; Prince Edward; Laborer; John VENABLE; Prince Edward; Agnes Coleman 52; Prince Edward; Prince Edward; John VENABLE; Prince Edward; Collin Coleman 19, Paul Coleman 17, Silas Coleman 15, Buck Coleman 9; Dec 1828

29/25: Nic Reed 48; Prince Edward; Prince Edward; Laborer; Frank WOOD; Prince Edward; Sukey Reed 30; Prince Edward; Prince Edward; Richard VENABLE; Prince Edward; Nick Reed 9, Benjamin Reed 7, Isham Reed 5, Lewis Reed 1; Dec 1851

29/29: George Watson 30; Prince Edward; Prince Edward; Laborer; Mrs. Emily DUPUY; Prince Edward; Agnes Watson 25; Prince Edward; Prince Edward; George DUPUY; Prince Edward; Ø; Dec 1860

29/30: Daniel Parnnell 76; Prince Edward; Prince Edward; Laborer; Mrs. Emily DUPUY; Prince Edward; Nicey Parnnell 50; Prince Edward; Prince Edward; Samuel McGHEE; Prince Edward; Ø; Dec 1835

29/31: Hawkins Lucas 53; Rockbridge; Prince Edward; Laborer; Jane MORTON; Prince Edward; Nancy Lucas; Prince Edward; Prince Edward; Andrew VENABLE; Prince Edward; Hawkins Lucas 19, Duke Lucas 12, Hannah Lucas 10, Jane Lucas 8, Agnes Lucas 4; Dec 1844

29/36: Nathan Wootten 50; Prince Edward; Prince Edward; Laborer; S.H. WOOTTEN; Prince Edward; Matilda Wootten 44; Prince Edward; Prince Edward; B. ROWLETT; Prince Edward; Isa Wootten 17, Jane Wootten 4, Harriet Wootten 6; Mar 1849

30/1: David Bates 33; Prince Edward; Prince Edward; Laborer; William OWEN; Prince Edward; Nancy Bates 33; Prince Edward; Prince Edward; John D. SPENCER; Charlotte; Letty E. Bates 12, Elvira Bates. Anderson M. Bates 9, Jane V. Bates 6, Travann Bates 3, Julia infant; Dec 1850

30/7: Somerville Anderson 64; Powhatan; Prince Edward; Laborer; G.? TRUEHEART; Prince Edward; Parthenia Anderson 39; Prince Edward; Prince Edward; Dr. METLAINER; Prince Edward; Ø; Oct 1861

30/8: Lewis Dupuy 61; Prince Edward; Prince Edward; Laborer; Joseph DUPUY; Prince Edward; Lydia Dupuy 50; Prince Edward; Prince Edward; Joseph DUPUY; Prince Edward; Ø; Dec 1835

30/9: Spencer Daniel 51; Cumberland; Prince Edward; Laborer; R.P. DANIEL; Prince Edward; Sally Daniel 36; Bedford; Prince Edward; R. Lee REDD; Prince Edward; James Daniel 19, John Daniel 15, Samuel Daniel 11, Spencer Daniel 4, Elizabeth Daniel 2; Oct 1846

30/14: Benjamin Redd 32; Prince Edward; Prince Edward; Laborer; John W. REDD; Prince Edward; Harriet Redd 25; Prince Edward; Prince Edward; Mrs. Patsy ALMS; Prince Edward; Ø; Nov 1868

30/15: Creed Scott 40; Prince Edward; Prince Edward; Laborer; J.B. McGEE; Mississippi; Elvira Scott 39; Prince Edward; Prince Edward; J.B. McGEE; Prince Edward; George Scott 12, Jessee Scott 7, Robert Scott 2; Dec 1844

30/16: H.R. Allen 55; Prince Edward; Prince Edward; Laborer; James B. ALLEN; Prince Edward; Temperance Allen 68; Prince Edward; Prince Edward; John W. REDD; Prince Edward; Samuel Allen 20, Betty Allen 8, David Allen 7; Dec 1851?

30/21: Armstead Wynn 25; Nottoway; Prince Edward; Laborer; Albert HOBBS; Dinwiddie; Maria Wynne 22; Nottoway; Prince Edward; Lee HAWKS; Dinwiddle; Ø; Dec 1864

30/22: Pack Miller 21; Nottoway; Prince Edward; Laborer; Peter MILLER; Nottoway; Mary Miller 22; Nottoway; Prince Edward; William WORSHAM; Nottoway; Louis Miller 2; Dec 1863

30/23: Benjamin Miller 58; Nottoway; Prince Edward; Laborer; A.P. MILLER; Nottoway; Martha Miller 46; Nottoway; Prince Edward; A.P. MILLER; Nottoway; Ø; Dec 1831

30/24: Ed Miller 24; Nottoway; Prince Edward; Laborer; A.P. MILLER; Nottoway; Harriet Miller 22; Nottoway; Prince Edward; William WORSHAM; Nottoway; Lucy B. Miller 4; Dec 1857

30/25: Henry Miller 29; Amelia; Prince Edward; Laborer; A.P. MILLER; Nottoway; Louisa Miller 21; Amelia; Prince Edward; A.P. MILLER; Nottoway; Laura A. Miller infant, Samuel Miller 4, Armstead Miller infant; Jan 1851

30/28: William H. Jackson 33; Caroline; Prince Edward; Laborer; R.W. SCOTT; Prince Edward; Betty Jackson 26; Prince Edward; Prince Edward; Thomas EWING; Prince Edward; Ø; Dec 1859

30/29: Isham Johnson 35; Caroline; Prince Edward; Laborer; R.W. SCOTT; Prince Edward; Elizabeth Johnson 35; Prince Edward; Prince Edward; Charles S. OWEN; Prince Edward; Ø; Jan 1856

31/1: Kit Smith 61; Prince Edward; Prince Edward; Farmer; Alf CHILDERS; Amelia; Fanny Smith 50; Prince Edward; Prince Edward; Alf CHILDERS; Amelia; Ø; 4 July 1836

31/2: William Pride 26; Amelia; Prince Edward; Farmer; Mrs. M. OVERTON; Prince Edward; Dica Pride 38; Prince Edward; Prince Edward; Mrs. M. FOWLER; Prince Edward; Ø; 30 Mar 1865

31/3: Limey? Overton 28; Nottoway; Prince Edward; Farmer; Mrs. M. OVERTON; Prince Edward; Elvira Overton 26; Amelia; Prince Edward; T. FARLEY; Prince Edward; Major Overton 1; 20 June 1865

31/4: Richard Lawson 80; Halifax; Prince Edward; Farmer; William RICE; Farmville; Isabel Lawson 70; Halifax; Prince Edward; William RICE; Farmville; Ø; 13 Jan 1820

31/5: Thomas Morgan 35; Nottoway; Prince Edward; Shoemaker; Joseph PHILLIPS; Prince Edward; Phebe Morgana 40; Prince Edward; Prince Edward; Mrs. P. BRADSHAW; Prince Edward; Ella Morgan 8, Sydney Morgan 6; 15 Oct 1859

31/7: David Lewis 26; Prince Edward; Prince Edward; Farmer; William WEAVER; Prince Edward; Betty Lewis 19; Prince Edward; Prince Edward; Mrs. M. BRADSHAW; Prince Edward; Ø; 1 Mar 1865

31/8: Robert Morgan 28; Nottoway; Prince Edward; Farmer; Joseph PHILLIPS; Prince Edward; Indiana Morgan 25; Prince Edward; Prince Edward; Mrs. M. BRADSHAW; Prince Edward; Eliza Morgan 6, Robert Morgan 5, Sallie Morgan 2; 4 Mar 1857

31/11: Jack Walton 35; Prince Edward; Prince Edward; Farmer; Joseph FARLEY; Prince Edward; M.A. Walton 21; Prince Edward; Prince Edward; Joseph PHILLIPS; Prince Edward; Mary E. Walton 1; 25 Dec 1864

31/12: George Symms 32; Lunenburg; Prince Edward; Farmer; Joseph HARDY; Lunenburg; Elvira; Symms 21; Lunenburg; Prince Edward; Joseph HARDY; Lunenburgh; Hannah Symms 2; 25 Dec 1863

31/13: H. Knuckles 54; Cumberland; Prince Edward; Farmer; Joseph WATSON; Prince Edward; Laura Knuckles 35; Prince Edward; Prince Edward; Mrs. M. MOTLEY; Prince Edward; Eliza Knuckles 10; 25 Dec 1862

31/14: Thomas Shedrick 42; Prince Edward; Prince Edward; Farmer; Mrs. M. BRADSHAW; Prince Edward; S.E. Shedrick 30; Prince Edward; Prince Edward; Thomas OVERTON; Prince Edward; William Shedrick 21, Edward Shedrick 18, Lucy Shedrick 16, Sarah E. Shedrick 9, John Thomas Shedrick 4, David Shedrick 1; 25 Dec 1843

31/20: Joseph Williams 29; Prince Edward; Prince Edward; Farmer; Mrs. M. BRADSHAW; Prince Edward; Julia Williams 26; Prince Edward; Prince Edward; Joseph PHILLIPS; Prince Edward; Lee Williams 3, infant; 14 Oct 1863

31/22: Cullen Stokes 36; Prince Edward; Prince Edward; Blacksmith; Mrs. M. BRADSHAW; Prince Edward; Martha Stokes 33; Nottoway; Prince Edward; Benjamin OVERTON; Nottoway; Alice Stokes 12, Winni Stokes 4, Robert Stokes 3; Nov 1853

31/25: Peter Witt 34; Prince Edward; Prince Edward; Laborer; E.B. WITT; Prince Edward; Elvira Witt 24; Cumberland; Prince Edward; E.B. WITT; Prince Edward; Ø; 25 Dec 1860

31/26: William Clark 38; Prince Edward; Prince Edward; Laborer; Thomas CLARK; Prince Edward; Mary S. Clark 29; Prince Edward; Prince Edward; John M. CLARKSTON; Kanawha; Ann Clark 7, Molly Clark; 25 Dec 1853

31/28: Asa Clark 35; Prince Edward; Prince Edward; Farmer; Dr. CLARK; Prince Edward; Sally Clark 29; Prince Edward; Prince Edward; Dr. CLARK; Prince Edward; Archy Clark 10, Jane Clark 13; 1st marriage 25 Dec 1849; 2nd marriage 25 Dec 1853?

31/30: Nick Morgan 49; Prince Edward; Prince Edward; Farmer; William McGHEE; Prince Edward; Hannah Morgan 48; Prince Edward; Prince Edward; Drury CALHOUN; Prince Edward; Mac Morgan 13, Molly Morgan 11, Henry Morgan 6; 25 Dec 1836

31/33: Cale__n Rojas 50; Prince Edward; Prince Edward; Farmer; John RODGAS; Halifax; Mary P. Rogas 48; Prince Edward; Prince Edward; T. POLLARD; Nottoway; Ed Radgers 20, Henry Radgers 16

31/35: Shepherd Boswell 29; Mecklenburg; Prince Edward; Farmer; George POINDEXTER; Mecklenburg; Mary Boswell 40; Lunenburg; Prince Edward; John COUCH; Lunenburg; Ø; 12 Dec 1860

31/36: Thomas Brown 31; Prince Edward; Prince Edward; Farmer; F. WATKINS; Prince Edward; Fanny Brown 25; Prince Edward; Prince Edward; F. WATKINS; Prince Edward; Eliza Brown 4, Albert Brown 2; 25 Dec 1859

31/38: James Foster 24; Cumberland; Prince Edward; Farmer; Frank REDD; Prince Edward; Martha Foster 20; Lunenburg; Prince Edward; H. STOKES; Prince Edward; Booker Foster 2, Mary F. Foster 4 mos; 25 Dec 1862

32/1: Reuben Thomas 40; Prince Edward; Prince Edward; Laborer; William T. WOOTTEN; Prince Edward; Katy Thomas 34; Prince Edward; Prince Edward; F.T. WOOTTEN; Prince Edward; Edwin Thomas 5; 1 Dec 1861

32/2: Daniel Williams 51; Prince Edward; Prince Edward; Laborer; Pat JACKSON; Prince Edward; Susan Williams 36; Prince Edward; Prince Edward; James LIGAN; Prince Edward; Ellen Williams 10, Mary J. Williams 5, Daniel Williams 4, Lucy Williams 6 mos; 15 Mar 1846

32/6: Peyton Cango 78; Prince Edward; Prince Edward; Laborer; William McGHEE; Prince Edward; Fanny Cango 68; Prince Edward; Prince Edward; William BELL; Prince Edward; Ø; 20 Mar 1865

32/7: Robert Branch 26; Prince Edward; Prince Edward; Laborer; William MORTON; Prince Edward; Caroline Branch 20; Prince Edward; Prince Edward; F.T. WOOTTEN; Prince Edward; Patty Branch 1; 15 Oct 1863

32/8: Jacob Folse 24; Prince Edward; Prince Edward; Laborer; Sam CHUMMY; Prince Edward; Henrietta? Fulse; Prince Edward; Prince Edward; Mrs. E. JORDAN; Prince Edward; William Fulse 8 mos; 14 Aug 1865

32/9: James Farley 66; Prince Edward; Prince Edward; Laborer; John FOSTER; Prince Edward; Pa__lia Farley 43; Prince Edward; Prince Edward; John FOSTER; Prince Edward; Polly Farley 21, Oliver Farley 19, Daniel Farley 11, James Farley 7; 1 Jan 1844

32/13: Henry Scott 52; Prince Edward; Prince Edward; Carpenter; J. MADISON; Cumberland; Matilda Scott 52; Prince Edward; Prince Edward; Mrs. M. FOWLER; Prince Edward; Nat J. Scott 23, Laura Scott 20, Mary Scott 19; 25 Dec 1841

32/16: William Fowler 35; Prince Edward; Prince Edward; Farmer; Mrs. M. FOWLER; Prince Edward; M. Louisa Fowler 29; Prince Edward; Prince Edward; Mrs. E. DUPUY; Prince Edward; Henry A. Fowler 9; 25 Dec 1856

32/17: Sam Bailey 29; Charlotte; Prince Edward; Laborer; John BAILEY; Charlotte; Lucy J. Bailey 28; Prince Edward; Prince Edward; Dr. JARNETT; Prince Edward; Ø; 20 Dec 1865

32/18: Nathan Owen 54; Prince Edward; Prince Edward; Laborer; Mrs. S. OWENS; Prince Edward; Lucy J. Owens 37; Prince Edward; Prince Edward; B. SUBLICK; Prince Edward; C.F. Owens 18, Nathan Owens 14, Nancy Owens 11, Abbey Owens 8, Nelson Owens 6, George Owens 2, James Owens infant; 1 Jan 1846

32/25: Isham Bench 44; Prince Edward; Prince Edward; Farmer; Elisha BENCH; Prince Edward; Phillis Bench 29; Prince Edward; Prince Edward; William WOMACK; Prince Edward; Hack Bench 18 mos; 20 Oct 1865

32/26: Gilman? Jeter 56; Prince Edward; Prince Edward; Miller; William ELLERTON; Prince Edward; Clara Jeter 46; Prince Edward; Prince Edward; Joseph WALTHAL; Prince Edward; John Jeter 20, Henry Jeter 19, Robert Jeter 14, Linsey Jeter 13; 12 Oct 1831

32/30: Allen Booker 23; Prince Edward; Prince Edward; Farmer; Tarn? WEAVER; Prince Edward; Melinda Booker 23; Prince Edward; Prince Edward; Mrs. M. CLARK; Prince Edward; Richard Booker 8 mos; 10 July 1865

32/31: Anderson Pryor 38; Amelia; Prince Edward; Farmer; Thomas GOODE; Prince Edward; Lucinda Pryor 28; Amelia; Prince Edward; Mrs. B. MOTLEY; Amelia; Delia Pryor 9, Nannie Pryor 6; 1 Jan 1856

32/33: Aaron Weaver 40; Cumberland; Prince Edward; Farmer; William WEAVER; Prince Edward; Becky Weaver 30; Prince Edward; Prince Edward; Mrs. L. BRADSHAW; Prince Edward; Maria Weaver 1; 25 Dec 1856

32/34: Charles A. Wade 34; Prince Edward; Prince Edward; Farmer; Ed CLARK; Prince Edward; Susan Wade 28; Prince Edward; Prince Edward; A. LIGAN; Prince Edward; Daniel Wade 2; 30 Mar 1861

32/35: Thomas Blunt 52; Southampton; Prince Edward; Farmer; Louisa LIGAN; Prince Edward; Lucy A.? Blunt 36; Prince Edward; Prince Edward; John FOSTER; Prince Edward; Ø; 18 Oct 1854

32/36: Douglass Evans 45; Roanoke; Prince Edward; Farmer; William CARRINGTON; Prince Edward; Marg Evans 24; Cumberland; Prince Edward; Dr. LEACH; Cumberland; Ø; 28 Dec 1865

32/37: William Morton 46; Prince Edward; Prince Edward; Farmer; F.T. WOOTTEN; Prince Edward; Susan Morton 54; Prince Edward; Prince Edward; John QUINBERRY; Prince Edward; Ø; 16 Aug 1864

32/38: Peter Branch 36; Prince Edward; Prince Edward; Blacksmith; John F. BRANCH; Prince Edward; Eliza Branch 38; Prince Edward; Prince Edward; H. CRATE; Prince Edward; Elvira Branch 14, Anderson Branch 11, Betty Branch 4; 17 Oct 1850

33/1: Pat Weaver 21; Prince Edward; Prince Edward; Laborer; William WEAVER; Prince Edward; Julia A. Weaver 34; Prince Edward; Prince Edward; Mrs. E. FAWLKES; Prince Edward; Henry M. Weaver 6, Francis Weaver 1; 1 Jan 1851

33/3: Albert Fawlkes 26; Prince Edward; Prince Edward; Laborer; Mrs. E. FAWLKES; Prince Edward; Laura A. Fawlkes 22; Prince Edward; Prince Edward; J.T. BRANCH; Prince Edward; Harry T. Fawlkes 2, __ M. Fawlkes infant; 25 Dec 1862

33/5: Daniel Elliott 62; Prince Edward; Prince Edward; Laborer; Willis ELLIOTT; Prince Edward; Sarah Elliott 40; Prince Edward; Prince Edward; E.W. MOSING?; Prince Edward; Henrietta Elliott 6, Floyd Elliott infant; 15 Mar 1858

33/7: G.H.L. Jones 26; Nottoway; Prince Edward; Laborer; D.A. BEASLEY; Prince Edward; Elvira Jones 20; Amelia; Prince Edward; D.A. BEASLEY; Prince Edward; Ø; 25 Dec 1862

33/8: Walker Jackson 50; Amelia; Prince Edward; Laborer; Samuel VAUGHAN; Prince Edward; Mary Jackson 36; Prince Edward; Prince Edward; James WALTHALL; Prince Edward; Ø; 15 Oct 1841

33/9: Reuben Gillham 58; Nottoway; Prince Edward; Laborer; M. Katy JONES; Nottoway; Sarah Gillham 32; Prince Edward; Prince Edward; Edward WINGLE; Nottoway; William H. Gillham 14, Paschal Gillham 10, Charles R. Gillham 9, Jack B. Gillham 8, Reuben Gillham 5, Ann Gillham 3, Joseph L. Gillham 1; 1 Oct 1850

33/16: Adolphus Mattley 24; Amelia; Prince Edward; Laborer; Sydney NOBLE; Amelia; Starry? Mattley 24; Amelia; Prince Edward; Mrs. Little PAGE; Amelia; Ø; 1 July 1865

33/17: Joseph Brown 42; Prince Edward; Prince Edward; Laborer; Ed LOCKET/LUCKET; Prince Edward; Grace A. Brown 34; Prince Edward; Prince Edward; Daniel WITT; Prince Edward; Daniel Brown 4, Julia Ann Brown; 12 Mar 1860

33/19: Reuben Simmes? 24; Prince Edward; Prince Edward; Laborer; Daniel WITT; Prince Edward; Martha Simmes? 20; Prince Edward; Prince Edward; H.M. VAUGHAN; Prince Edward; John S. Simmes? infant; 25 Dec 1863

33/20: Beverly Jeter 23; Prince Edward; Prince Edward; Laborer; S.F. FARLEY; Prince Edward; Mariah Jeter 21; Prince Edward; Prince Edward; Mrs. M. MOTTLEY; Prince Edward; Melinda Jeter 2, George D. Jeter infant; 12 June 1863

33/22: Ed Bland 40; Nottoway; Prince Edward; Laborer; George VAUGHAN; Prince Edward; Charity Bland 28; Nottoway; Prince Edward; George VAUGHAN; Prince Edward; Ø; 10 June 1859

33/23: James Roberts Wiley 38; Prince Edward; Prince Edward; Laborer; Mrs. M. BRADSHAW; Prince Edward; Jane Roberts Wiley 34; Prince Edward; Prince Edward; Sarah FLIPPEN; Prince Edward; Mary C. Wiley 12, Isabella Wiley 9, Betty Wiley 6, Fernando Wiley 4, Sallie Wiley infant; 1 Jan 1851

33/28: Sterling Atkins 28; Prince Edward; Prince Edward; Laborer; T.E. PERKINSON; Prince Edward; Jane Atkins 20; Prince Edward; Prince Edward; Watt RICHIE; Prince Edward; Ø; 1 Oct 1865

33/29: William Jones 24; Prince Edward; Prince Edward; Laborer; Thomas POINDEXTER; Pittsylvania; Victoria J. Jones 20; Pittsylvania; Prince Edward; Thomas POINDEXTER; Prince Edward; William Jones 2; 15 Mar 1862

33/30: Beverly Branch 36; Prince Edward; Prince Edward; Laborer; Mrs. M. MOTTLEY; Prince Edward; Ruth Branch 26; Cumberland; Prince Edward; Miss J. ATKINS; Prince Edward; Ann Branch 4, Francis Branch 3, John R. Branch 2, Mary Branch infant; 1 July 1859

33/34: Claiborne Wade 42; Nottoway; Prince Edward; Laborer; C. ROBINSON; Amelia; America Wade 43; Prince Edward; Prince Edward; Sarah FLIPPEN; Prince Edward; William Wade 18, Relay Wade 13, Sydney Wade 10, Joseph A. Wade 3; 20 Nov 1863

33/38: H. Smith 28; Lunenburg; Prince Edward; Laborer; Thomas BLANTON; Prince Edward; Laura Smith 20; Amelia; Prince Edward; Peyton JETER; Amelia; Ø; 30 Nov 1865

33/39: Daniel Booker 26; Prince Edward; Prince Edward; Laborer; Joseph R. GILLESPIE; Buckingham; Mary Booker 22; Prince Edward; Prince Edward; Edward GILLHAM; Cumberland; Daniel Booker 6; 25 Dec 1855

34/1: Phulding? Tibbs 24; Stafford; Prince Edward; Laborer; Joseph VAUGHAN; Nottoway; Louisa Tibbs 22; Prince Edward; Prince Edward; Giles MILLS?; Prince Edward; Joshua Tibbs 1; 10 May 1864

34/2: Scipio Lang 24; Prince Edward; Prince Edward; Laborer; Joseph W. WOMACK; Prince Edward; Eliza Lang 20; Buckingham; Prince Edward; John BONDURANT; Prince Edward; Henry Lang infant; 15 Aug 1864

34/3: Horace Langhorn 38; Prince Edward; Prince Edward; Laborer; Dr. DILLON; Prince Edward; Texianna Langham 22; Prince Edward; Prince Edward; Dr. DILLON; Prince Edward; Ø; 28 Dec 1865

34/4: William Banner 56; Brunswick; Prince Edward; Laborer; Dr. DILLON; Prince Edward; Mary Banner 28; Prince George; Prince Edward; H.E. WARREN; Prince Edward; Ø; 12 May 1858

34/5: Claiborne Hannah? (Harwah/Harmah?) 29; Appomattox; Prince Edward; Laborer; William M. HANNAH? (HARWAH/HARMAH?); Appomattox; Lizzie Hannah? 32; Petersburg; Prince Edward; Harry SWEET; Prince Edward; Ø; 26 Dec 1865

34/6: Daniel Woodson 22; Cumberland; Prince Edward; Laborer; Mrs. S. BRADSHAW; Prince Edward; Louisa Woodson 21; Prince Edward; Prince Edward; Richard MARSHAL; Prince Edward; Wilson Woodson infant; 1 Jan 1865

34/7: Richard Randal 46; Cumberland; Prince Edward; Laborer; Miss F. WILSON; Cumberland; Nancy Randal 36; Cumberland; Prince Edward; Dr. BATTLE; Tuscaloosa, Alabama; Minnie Randal 9; Dec 1855

34/8: Samuel Hines 40; Charlotte; Prince Edward; Laborer; Joseph F. HINES; Charlotte; Mary A. Hines 36; Prince Edward; Prince Edward; Joseph F. HINES; Charlotte; Palina Hines 12, Samuel Hines 10, Clark Hines 5, Lucy Hines 4, Tuta Hines infant; 1 Jan 185_

34/13: Henry Booker 38; Prince Edward; Prince Edward; Laborer; Mrs. V. PHILLIPS; Prince Edward; Melinda Booker 30; Prince Edward; Prince Edward; Mrs V. PHILLIPS; Prince Edward; Otilla Booker 6, Powell Booker infant; 25 Dec 1854

34/15: Griffin Anderson 56; Amelia; Prince Edward; Laborer; George ANDERSON; Nottoway; Quintanna Anderson48; Nottoway; Prince Edward; Paschal LIPSCOMB; Nottoway; Ø; 25 Dec 1865

34/16: Benjamin Ligan 59; Prince Edward; Prince Edward; Laborer; Joseph S. LIGAN; Prince Edward; Sukey Ligan 49; Prince Edward; Prince Edward; Joseph L. LIGAN; Prince Edward; Patrick Ligan 20; 25 Dec 1836

34/17: Daniel Johnson 60; Southampton; Prince Edward; Laborer; William ETHERIDGE; Amherst; Diana Johnson 54; Prince Edward; Prince Edward; Joseph CRATE; Buckingham; Ø; 28 Dec 1858

34/18: Joseph Foster 30; Prince Edward; Prince Edward; Laborer; Joseph CRATE; Buckingham; Mary Foster 22; Mecklenburg; Prince Edward; Joseph CRATE; Buckingham; Richard Foster 6, Anne Foster 2; 25 Dec 1859

34/20: Gaston Butler 32; Prince Edward; Prince Edward; Laborer; Thomas BELL; Prince Edward; Susan Butler 22; Prince Edward; Prince Edward; John ARMSTEAD; Prince Edward; William Butler 6, Sydney Butler 4, Sarah J. Butler 2, Carrie Butler infant

34/24: Henry Thweatt 40; Prince Edward; Prince Edward; Laborer; John A. DALBY; Farmville; Lucy J. Thweatt 36; Prince Edward; Prince Edward; Frank PINNACK; Prince Edward; Patsey Thweatt 12, Ann Thweatt infant; 1 Jan 1853?

34/26: Booker Bell 30; Prince Edward; Prince Edward; Laborer; George BELL; Prince Edward; Easter Bell 25; Prince Edward; Prince Edward; William BRADLEY; Prince Edward; Washington infant; 2 Jan 1864

34/27: Monroe Smith 26; Cumberland; Prince Edward; Laborer; Dr. C. RAINE; Cumberland; Patty Smith 20; Cumberland; Prince Edward; Mrs. S. SMITH; Cumberland; Ø; 25 Dec 1865

34/28: Joseph Washington 28; Cumberland; Prince Edward; Laborer; Joseph B. ELY; Prince Edward; Jane Washington 28; Rappahannock; Prince Edward; Joseph ARMSTEAD; Prince Edward; George Washington 4, J.B. Washington 2; 12 Mar 1860

34/30: Robert Freeler 28; Cumberland; Prince Edward; Laborer; Lyan AGEE; Prince Edward; Nancy Freeler 25; Cumberland; Prince Edward; Dr. Charles RAINS; Cumberland; Ø; 20 Oct 1860

34/31: Michael Patterson 78; Cumberland; Prince Edward; Laborer; Richard RANDOLPH; Prince Edward; Eliza Patterson 60; Buckingham; Prince Edward; Barnet HART; Appomattox; Ø; 25 Dec 1826

34/32: William Marshal 56; Campbell; Prince Edward; Laborer; James EVANS; Cumberland; Susan Marshal 44; Prince Edward; Prince Edward; John RANDOLPH; Prince Edward; George Marshal 12, Lockie Marshal 6, William Marshal 5; 12 Jan 1849

34/35: Robert Haskins 28; Prince Edward; Prince Edward; Laborer; Mrs. M. CHAMBERS; Prince Edward; Judah Haskins 22; Prince Edward; Prince Edward; Beverly SCOTT; Prince Edward; John H. Haskins 2; 15 Mar 1864

34/36: Edward Bagley 48; Lunenburg; Prince Edward; Laborer; Mrs. M.S. BAGLEY; Lunenburg; Louisa Bagley 42; Prince Edward; Prince Edward; George GAMFFREY; Richmond; Lucy Bagley 13, Griffin Bagley 12, Elvira Bagley 6, Mary J. Bagley 3; 4 May 1848

35/1: Alfred Ford 58; Sussex; Prince Edward; Laborer; Ben BELCHUS; Sussex; Ann Ford 44; Prince Edward; Prince Edward; J. Armstead; Prince Edward; Ø; 20 Aug 1865

35/2: Goliah Armstead 44; Prince Edward; Prince Edward; Laborer; John ARMSTEAD; Prince Edward; Jenny Armstead 28; Prince Edward; Prince Edward; B. MANE?; Prince Edward; Jeff Armstead infant; 25 Dec 1865

35/3: Len Richardson 50; Charlotte; Prince Edward; Laborer; Dr. SPENCER; Prince Edward; Katy Richardson 56; Prince Edward; Prince Edward; Dr. SPENCER; Ø; Ø; 1 Jan 1866

35/4: Joseph Bolling 60; Charlotte; Prince Edward; Laborer; William WATKINS; Charlotte; Aggie Bolling 44; Charlotte; Prince Edward; Isaac CAMDEN; Charlotte; Spencer Bolling 15; 1 Jan 1846

35/5: Peter Branch 51; Prince Edward; Prince Edward; Laborer; John J. SMITH; Prince Edward; Paula Branch 22; Prince Edward; Prince Edward; Mrs. M. MOTTLEY; Prince Edward; Ø; 20 Aug 1864

35/6: Andrew McCall 54; Williamsburg; Prince Edward; Laborer; William PRETTELL; Prince Edward; Judy F. McCall _0; Prince Edward; Prince Edward; S. SHEPHERD; Prince Edward; Adelaide McCall 17, Charlotte McCall 14, Boyd McCall 13, Mary McCall 12, John McCall 10, Lilly? McCall 4, Sally McCall 5, Abner McCall infant; 25 Dec 1846?

35/14: Frank Coleman; Albemarle; Prince Edward; Laborer; G. HARPER; Prince Edward; F. Coleman 31; Prince Edward; Prince Edward; Archy WOMACK; Prince Edward; Mary Coleman 7, Louisa Coleman 5, Beverly Coleman 4, Rose Coleman 3, Polly Coleman 1; 25 Dec 1855

35/19: Albert Burrell 45; Prince Edward; Prince Edward; Laborer; Branch WARSHAM; Prince Edward; Jane Burrell 25; Prince Edward; Prince Edward; __ Daniel ALLEN; Prince Edward; Agnes Burrell 4, Isaac Burrell 1; 25 Dec 1860

35/21: John Mickle 44; Cumberland; Prince Edward; Laborer; William L. WOMACK; Prince Edward; Maria Mickle 26; Prince Edward; Prince Edward; Joseph WHITEHEAD; Prince Edward; Cephas Mickle 4; 20 Sept 1859

35/22: Dennis Hicks 36; Charlotte; Prince Edward; Laborer; Dr. BERKELEY; Prince Edward; Celia Hicks 30; Prince Edward; Prince Edward; H. GUTHRIE; Prince Edward; Alex Hicks 4, Susan Hicks 3, Dennis Hicks infant; 25 Dec 1857

35/25: Robert Good 41; Prince Edward; Prince Edward; Laborer; Samuel BRUCE; Prince Edward; Elvira Good 30; Amelia; Prince Edward; R. WILLIAMS; Amelia; Eliza Good 13, John Good 12, Jessie Good 11, Martha Good 10, Augustus Good 7, Bettie Good 3, Sarah Good 3; 1 Jan 1848

35/32: Jordan Randolph 50; Prince Edward; Prince Edward; Laborer; James BERRY; Prince Edward; Betsey Randolph 24; Amelia; Prince Edward; William HARDWAY; Amelia; Louisa Good 4, Henry Good 3; 25 Dec 1859

35/34: Jack Randolph 50; Prince Edward; Prince Edward; Laborer; Jack JEFFRIES/JEFFINS; Prince Edward; Betty Randolph 50; Brunswick; Prince Edward; Milton EDWARDS; Charlotte; Ø; 20 Aug 1859

35/35: Sayler Booker _6; Albemarle; Prince Edward; Laborer; Charles SCOTT; Albemarle; Lizzie Booker 29; Prince Edward; Prince Edward; Dr. BERKELEY; Prince Edward; Louisa Booker 10, Molly Booker 6, Ellen Booker 1; 25 Dec 1851

35/38: Peter Witt 34; Prince Edward; Prince Edward; Laborer; Edward B. WITT; Prince Edward; Elvira Witt 20; Cumberland; Prince Edward; Edward B. WITT; Prince Edward; Ø; 20 August 1865

36/1: Johnson Redd 34; Prince Edward; Prince Edward; Laborer; John W. REDD; Prince Edward; Luc Redd 32; Prince Edward; Prince Edward; George REDD Prince Edward; Aggie Redd 12, Lucy Redd 11, Jessie Redd 9, Lewis Redd 4, Louisa Redd 5 mos; 25 Dec 1853

36/6: Ed Cunningham 44; Prince Edward; Prince Edward; Laborer; H.P. TAYLOR; Prince Edward; Letty A. Cunningham 23; Prince Edward; Prince Edward; Joseph MARTIN; Prince Edward; Ø; 20 Dec 1864

36/7: Edward Brown 32; Cumberland; Prince Edward; Laborer; Dr. LEACH; Cumberland; Louisa Brown 20; Cumberland; Prince Edward; Mrs. N. ALLEN; Cumberland; Betsy Brown 7, Thomas Brown 2; 1 June 1858

36/9: Lewis Parkey 63; Prince Edward; Prince Edward; Laborer; W.H. CHAPPELL; Buckingham; Celia Parker 60; Prince Edward; Prince Edward; John H. KNIGHT; Prince Edward; Ø; 1 Jan 1820

36/11: Harley Evans 56; Prince Edward; Prince Edward; Laborer; Born Free; Ø; Polly Evans 57; Prince Edward; Prince Edward; Born Free; Ø; John Evans 5, Eliza Evans 3; 25 Dec 1857

36/13: Wash Cavel 38; Prince Edward; Prince Edward; Laborer; John RANDOLPH; Prince Edward; Amanda Cavel 38; Prince Edward; Prince Edward; John RANDOLPH; Prince Edward; William Cavel 18, Robert Cavel 6; 25 Dec 1846

36/15: Lewis Booker 40; Prince Edward; Prince Edward; Laborer; John H. KNIGHT; Prince Edward; Martha Booker 26; Nottoway; Prince Edward; John H. KNIGHT; Prince Edward; Crecy Booker 3, Willie Booker 2; 1 Jan 1862

36/17: Cuff Moseley 60; Prince Edward; Prince Edward; Laborer; Col. T.H.T. CUAD?/T.H.THEAD?; Appomattox; Amelia Moseley 40; Prince Edward; Prince Edward; Thomas TREADWAY; Prince Edward; Ø; 25 Dec 1865

36/19: William Elam 56; Prince Edward; Prince Edward; Laborer; Joel ELAM; Prince Edward; Jenesta Elam 49; Prince Edward; Prince Edward; John O. ELAM; Prince Edward; Ø; 1 Jan 1841

36/20: Moses Mickle 36; Cumberland; Prince Edward; Laborer; William WOMACK; Prince Edward; Milly Mickle 29; Prince Edward; Prince Edward; William WOMACK; Prince Edward; Amanda Mickle 12, John Mickle 5, Silas Mickle 3; 1 Jan 1852

36/23: Alex Venable 65; Prince Edward; Prince Edward; Laborer; H.I. VENABLE; Prince Edward; Betsy Venable 54; Prince Edward; Prince Edward; Joseph VENABLE; Prince Edward; Fanny Venable 17, Mitty Venable 13; 1 May 1849

36/25: Emmanuel Lee 68; Campbell; Prince Edward; Laborer; John HARRIS; Prince Edward; Louisa Lee 36; Prince Edward; Prince Edward; Mrs. S. SMITH; Prince Edward; John C. Lee 5, Walter Lee 3, Lee Lee infant; 20 June 1855

36/28: Alex Scott 24; Prince Edward; Prince Edward; Laborer; Peyton GLENN; Prince Edward; Catherine Scott 21; Prince Edward; Prince Edward; William JONES; Prince Edward; Betty Scott infant; 12 June 1855

36/29: John Branch 28; Prince Edward; Prince Edward; Laborer; Bennett MAR_SE; Prince Edward; Mary Branch 28; Prince Edward; Prince Edward; John ARMSTEAD; Prince Edward; Edwin Branch 5; 20 June 1860

36/30: Thornton Evans 32; Cumberland; Prince Edward; Laborer; George O. SCOTT; Prince Edward; Elizabeth Evans 29; Buckingham; Prince Edward; William R. MEREDITH; Buckingham; Ø; 1 Dec 1858

36/31: Rolla Watkins 34; Charlotte; Prince Edward; Laborer; T.S. WATKINS; Prince Edward; Jane S. Watkins 31; Prince Edward; Prince Edward; Mrs. G. MAHAW?; Charlotte; Calloway Watkins 7, Louisa Watkins 5; 10 June 1859

36/33: York Carter 28; Prince Edward; Prince Edward; Laborer; Samuel CARTER; Prince Edward; Patience Carter 2_; Prince Edward; Prince Edward; Mrs. Ann RICE; Prince Edward; Sarah Carter 2, Ann Carter 6 mos; 26 Dec 1853

36/35: Washington Brown 48; Buckingham; Prince Edward; Laborer; P. BOLLING; Buckingham; Lilla Brown 36; Buckingham; Prince Edward; E.W. HUBBARD; Buckingham; Thomas Brown 20; 25 Dec 1846

36/36: Thomas Pennick 65; Henrico; Prince Edward; Laborer; James VENABLE; Prince Edward; Martha A. Pennick 38; Cumberland; Prince Edward; C.A. PRICE; Prince Edward; Ø; 15 Oct 1854

36/37: Page Armstead 28; Prince Edward; Prince Edward; Laborer; John ARMSTEAD; Prince Edward; Clem? Armstead 28; Prince Edward; Prince Edward; Mrs. M. PARTON; Prince Edward; John Armstead 7, Julia Armstead 4; 25 Dec 1858

36/39: William Bell

37/1: Richard Gaines 46; Prince Edward; Prince Edward; Carpenter; James LIGAN; Prince Edward; Clarissa Gaines 48; Prince Edward; Prince Edward; N.B. McGHEE; Prince Edward; Susan Gaines 15, Albert Thomas Gaines 15, Thomas Gaines 9, Collins Gaines 21; 25 Nov 1828

37/5: Simon Clark 34; Charlotte; Prince Edward; Farmer; Thomas WILBURN; Charlotte; Ann Clark 32; Charlotte; Prince Edward; Mrs. S. SMITH; Prince Edward; Emma Clark 1_ (1st husband), M.L. Clark 1_ (1st husband); 1st marriage 1852, 2nd marriage 20 Dec 1862

37/7: Charles Woodson 35; Prince Edward; Prince Edward; Laborer; William DUNNINGTON; Prince Edward; Tampa Woodson 28; Cumberland; Prince Edward; William DUNNINGTON; Prince Edward; Fanny Woodson 14, Charles Woodson 11, Becky Woodson 7 mos; 15 Mar 1851

37/10: Hal Scott 42; Prince Edward; Prince Edward; Laborer; Richard SCOTT; Prince Edward; Chaney Scott 30; Prince Edward; Prince Edward; B. ROWLETT; Prince Edward; Lewis Scott 10, William Scott 6, Alice Scott 4, Branch Scott 2; 24 Dec 1854

37/14: Austin Fowler 60; Charlotte; Prince Edward; Laborer; Pleasant FOWLER; Prince Edward; Eliza Fowler 40; Charlotte; Prince Edward; J.F. EDMUNDS; Charlotte; Albert Fowler 9; 2 Jan 1840

37/15: Robert Washington 46; Cumberland; Prince Edward; Laborer; Thomas CALDWELL; Cumberland; Mary Washington 36; Cumberland; Prince Edward; Born Free; Ø; John Washington 14, Sally Washington 10, Daniel Washington 8, Zachariah Washington 5; 20 Dec 1850

37/19: George Washington 35; Prince Edward; Prince Edward; Laborer; William A. COCK?; Cumberland; Tamar Washington 28; Cumberland; Prince Edward; William MUNDY; Prince Edward; Sarah Washington 11, Henry Washington 13, Cook Washington 7, Georgiana Washington 5, Nancy Washington 3 mos; 15 Aug 1850

37/24: Henry Booker 64; Prince Edward; Farmville; Laborer; William CHAPPELL; Buckingham; Vina Booker 48; Prince Edward; Prince Edward; C. ANDERSON; Charlotte; Moses Anderson 17 (1st husband), Lewis Booker 15, Henry Booker 21, Isabella Booker 18; 24 Dec 1852

37/28: Reuben Kinney 40; Hanover; Farmville; Porter; Dr. H. WOOD; Prince Edward; Ellen Kinney 30; Prince Edward; Farmville; Mrs. B. CARRINGTON; Prince Edward; Betsey Kinney 10, Harriet? Kinney 8, Reuben Kinney 4, Ida Kinney 1; 28 Dec 1855

37/32: Stephen Pankey 48; Prince Edward; Prince Edward; Laborer; Joseph McNULT; Prince Edward; Sarah Pankey 34; Augusta; Prince Edward; Joseph McNULT; Prince Edward; Thomas Pankey 12, Nat Pankey 8, Sarah Pankey 5, Harriet Pankey 2; 20 Sept 1862

37/36: Nelson Johnson 48; Prince Edward; Prince Edward; Laborer; Thomas L. MORTON; Prince Edward; Louisa Johnson 30; Prince Edward; Prince Edward; H.E. WATKINS; Prince Edward; Mary Johnson 15, Carrington Johnson 7, Betty Johnson 5, John Johnson 2; 25 Dec 1858

38/1: Robert Harvey 40; Campbell; Prince Edward; Farmer; Edward BARDMAN; Charlotte; Susan Harvey 40; Prince Edward; Prince Edward; Samuel BRUCE; Prince Edward; Rachel Harvey 19, Julius Harvey 12, Eliza Harvey 8; 1st marriage 1840, 2nd marriage 25 Dec 1860

38/4: Henry Staples 45; Lunenburg; Prince Edward; Farmer; Egbert STAPLES; Lunenburg; Maria Staples 40; Lunenburg; Prince Edward; Richard GRAFTON; Lunenburg; Amanda Staples 21, Elvira Staples 19, Eliza Staples 17, Henry Staples 15, Edmund Staples 13, Scott Staples 11, Mealy Staples 9, Emily Staples 7, Samuel Staples 5, Peggy Staples 1; 24 Dec 1844

38/14: Joseph Jenkins 38; Nottoway; Farmville; Farmer; Born Free; Ø; Suckey Jenkins 38; Cumberland; Prince Edward; Born Free; Ø; Catherine Smith 17, John Smith 13; 1st marriage 1 Jan 1846, 2nd marriage 31 Dec 1862

38/16: Jack Knight 68; Farmville; Farmville; Laborer; S.S. JOHNSON; Petersburg; Chaney Knight 66; Cumberland; Farmville; B.A. WILSON; Cumberland; Ø; 20 June 1846

38/17: William Fuqua 40; Charlotte; Farmville; Baker; P.H. JACKSON; Farmville; Patsey Fuqua 40; Prince Edward; Farmville; J.A. KOWADDIN/ROWADDIN, ROWADDIN/KOWADDIN; Richmond; Lucy Fuqua 10 (2nd wife), Ba_tanna Eppes 11 (1st husband), Edward Eppes 20 (1st husband), Margaret Eppes 18 (1st husband), Davy C. Fuqua 10 (1st wife); 24 Dec 1854

38/22: Pat Cummins 56; Prince Edward; Prince Edward; Laborer; Dr. A. DILLON; Farmville; Milly Cummins 31; Prince Edward; Prince Edward; Mr. E. MORTON; Prince Edward; Patrick Cummins 12, Ellis Cummins 7, Martha Cummins 6, Hannah Cummins 7, Austin Cummins 2; 12 May 1853

38/27: H. Hamilton 24; Prince Edward; Farmville; Blacksmith; Mrs. F. HAMILTON; Prince Edward; Violet Hamilton 21; Prince Edward; Farmville, B.J. WORSHAM; Prince Edward; Louisa M. Hamilton 6 mos; 10 Dec 1861

38/28: James Lee 50; Prince Edward; Prince Edward; Laborer; Dr. Thomas VENABLE; Prince Edward; Julia Lee 52; Prince Edward; Farmville; Dr. T. VENABLE; Prince Edward; Rose Lee 25, James Lee 20; 30 June 1836

38/30: William Jackson 58; Fredericksburg; Farmville; Laborer; Dr. James LYLE; Farmville; Clarissa Jackson 40; Cumberland; Farmville; Monroe JOHNS; Buckingham; Ø; 30 Aug 1830

38/31: Benjamin Foster 45; Prince Edward; Farmville; Cooper; Joseph G. WILLIAMS; Farmville; Gelina Foster 36; Prince Edward; Farmville; Mrs. Jacob MORTON; Prince Edward; Robert Foster 18, Archer Foster 16, Benjamin Foster 13, Judy Foster 11; 25 Dec 1847

38/35: Champion West 29; Prince Edward; Prince Edward; Laborer; Mrs. Ann HOLLIDAY; Prince Edward; Betty West 22; Prince Edward; Prince Edward; Beverly SCOTT; Prince Edward; Nat West 6, Sally West 3, Hal West 2; 20 Aug 1858

38/38: Doctor Jeffries 40; Prince Edward; Prince Edward; Baker; Marcus GLASSAN; Prince Edward; Car. Jeffries 38; Prince Edward; Prince Edward; J.B. ELY; Prince Edward; Sarah Jeffries 20 (1st husband); 20 Oct 1851

38/39: John Venable 22; Prince Edward; Prince Edward; Laborer; James LIGAN; Prince Edward; Jenny Venable 20; Prince Edward; Prince Edward; Mrs. P. BRADSHAW; Prince Edward; Lizzie 3 (1st husband); 25 Dec 1865

39/1: Joseph Brown 48; Cumberland; Prince Edward; Laborer; John A. SCOTT; Prince Edward; Lucy Brown 40; Charlotte; Prince Edward; Capt. H. RICHARDSON; Charlotte; Henry Brown 18, Betty Brown 16, Marg Brown 14, Alice Brown 12, Walter Brown 9, Lucy Brown 6, Nancy Brown 1, Mary Brown 1; 4 Jan 1842

39/9: Jack Hamilton 40; Charlotte; Prince Edward; Laborer; Ben SCOTT; Prince Edward; Mary Hamilton 34; Prince Edward; Prince Edward; Ben SCOTT; Prince Edward; Martha Hamilton 15, Minerva Hamilton 13, Glasscow Brown 12, Limby Brown 9, Jack Brown 4, Wyatt Brown 8, Eliza Brown 7, infant; 2 Dec 18_0

39/17: Joseph Watkins 60; Charlotte; Prince Edward; Laborer; Lee WATKINS; Charlotte; Martha Watkins 56; Charlotte; Prince Edward; Lee WATKINS; Charlotte; Ø; 29 Jan 1826

39/18: Alex Baste 29; Halifax; Prince Edward; Laborer; William CARRINGTON; Halifax; Ella Baste 24; Prince Edward; Prince Edward; F. WATKINS; Prince Edward; Ø; 12 Oct 1865

39/19: Wash Cox 36; Lunenburg; Prince Edward; Laborer; Mrs. Mary COX; Lunenburg; Lina Cox 32; Prince Edward; Prince Edward; Mrs. Asa DUPUY; Prince Edward; Nannie Cox 6, Jeff Cox 3, P_ea Cox 2; 12 Oct 1859

39/22: Peyton Berkeley 80; Prince Edward; Prince Edward; Laborer; Baker SCOTT; Prince Edward; Lydia Berkeley 76; Cumberland; Prince Edward; Thomas BELL; Prince Edward; Ø; 1 Jan 1855

39/23: C. Webber 44; Buckingham; Prince Edward; Carpenter; Born Free; Ø; Judy Webber 34; Prince Edward; Prince Edward; Born Free; Ø; Ø; 30 Oct 1856

39/24: Branch Lee 28; Cumberland; Prince Edward; Laborer; William H. McGHEE; Prince Edward; Nancy Lee 24; Cumberland; Prince Edward; William H. McGHEE; Prince Edward; Robert Lee 2, Howard Lee 2 mos; 6 Dec 1853

39/26: Daniel Hicks 48; Prince Edward; Prince Edward; Laborer; John H. KNIGHT; Prince Edward; Isabel Hicks 38; Prince Edward; Prince Edward; Charles MORTON; Prince Edward; Ø; 30 Aug 1855

39/27: Thomas Hannah 36; Charlotte; Prince Edward; Laborer; William HANNAH; Charlotte; Ann Hannah 38; Charlotte; Prince Edward; William HANNAH; Charlotte; Aaron Hannah 16, Letcher Hannah 8, James Hannah 6, John H. Hannah 3; 25 Dec 1840

39/29: Stephen Locket 54; Prince Edward; Prince Edward; Farmer; W.F. WOOTTEN; Prince Edward; Elvira Locket 40; Prince Edward; Prince Edward; Joel JOHNS; Lunenburg; Ellen Locket 17, Lucy Locket 15, Nannie Locke 13, Asa Locket 11, Andrew Locket 9, Amanda Locket 8, Rate Locket 12, Harriet Locket 4, William Locket 2; 25 Dec 1847

40/1: Archy Morton 34; Prince Edward; Prince Edward; Laborer; Joseph WILLIAMS; Prince Edward; Elizabeth Morton 23; Prince Edward; Prince Edward; Born Free; Ø; James Morton 2; 20 Oct 1863

40/2: Richard Burton 38; Prince Edward; Prince Edward; Hackman; Thomas M. NOBLE; Prince Edward; Cath Burton 36; Maryland; Prince Edward; George VAUGHAN; Prince Edward; Richard Burton 14, Cora Burton 11, Willie Burton 6; 15 Aug 1850

40/3: David Ellison 32; Prince Edward; Prince Edward; Laborer; Born Free; Ø; Nan Ellison 31; Prince Edward; Prince Edward; Born Free; Ø; William D. Ellison 3; 25 Dec 1858

40/5: Robert Booker 42; Cumberland; Prince Edward; Laborer; George W. DANIEL; Prince Edward; Ellen Booker 28; Buckingham; Farmville; James GLENN; Buckingham; Amanda Booker 7, Robert Booker 5, Martha A. Booker 3; 12 May 1855

40/9: Joseph Pride 46; Prince Edward; Farmville; Laborer; William H. DENNIS; Charlotte; Mary E. Pride 42; Charlotte; Farmville; William H. DENNIS; Charlotte; Catherine Pride 19, Clem Pride 17, Fanny Pride 15, James Pride 7 mos; 20 Mar 1846

40/13: Ed Logan 58; Halifax; Farmville; Laborer; H. RICHARDSON; Prince Edward; Judah Logan 70; Albemarle; Farmville; H. RICHARDSON; Prince Edward; Ø; 25 Dec 1857

40/14: N. Anderson 49; Buckingham; Farmville; Laborer; R.B. SHAW; Buckingham; Eliza Anderson 40; Buckingham; Farmville; R.B. SHAW; Buckingham; Robert Anderson 21, Pierce Anderson 15, Emma Anderson 10; 20 Aug 1840

40/17: Robert Lacey 42; Prince Edward; Farmville; Laborer; Mrs. M. WARSHAM; Prince Edward; Betsey Lacey 34; Prince Edward; Farmville; Mrs. M. FLOURNOY; Prince Edward; Daniel Lacey 7, Robert Lacey 5; 20 May 1849

40/19: Benjamin Peters 41; Prince Edward; Farmville; Laborer; Dr. SPENCER; Farmville; Ann Peters 25; Prince Edward; Farmville; H. VENABLE; Prince Edward; Ø; 20 Aug 1865

40/20: Pleasant Baker 38; Prince Edward; Farmville; Laborer; H. RICHARDSON; Prince Edward; Cora Baker 25; Prince Edward; Farmville; S. ANDERSON; Prince Edward; Ø; 18 Feb 1866

40/21: Major Booker 74; Powhatan; Farmville; Laborer; W. ARMSTEAD; Richmond; Mary Booker 56; Buckingham; Farmville; Mrs. Mary LAND; Buckingham; Ø; 30 aug 1859

40/22: R. Venable 50; Cumberland; Farmville; Laborer; T. ANDERSON; Cumberland; Susan Venable 34; Charlotte; Farmville; C. ANDERSON; Prince Edward; Buddy Venable 7; 13 Jan 18__

40/23: A Berkeley 44; Maryland; Farmville; Laborer; G.W. DANIEL; Prince Edward; L. Berkeley 36; Prince Edward; Farmville; S. FASE; Prince Edward; Monroe Berkeley 19, Eliza Berkeley 11, Elizabeth Berkeley 7; 25 Dec 18__

40/24: David Ross 36; Cumberland; Farmville; Laborer; G.W. DANIEL; Prince Edward; Margaret Ross 29; Prince Edward; Farmville; G.W. DANIEL Prince Edward; Letitia Ross 7, Mary Ann Ross 6; 5 Dec 1855

40/28: Peter Robinson 60; Buckingham; Farmville; Laborer; Mrs. M. WILSEY; Farmville; L. Robinson 40; Prince Edward; Farmville; I. McGLASSAN; Prince Edward; Peter Robinson 13, Elvira Robinson 11, Pleasant Robinson 8; 1 Jan 1852

40/31: Joseph Ward 50; Buckingham; Farmville; Laborer; G.W. DANIEL; Farmville; Mary Ward 36; Buckingham; Farmville; R. GORDON; Buckingham; Mary M. Ward 14, Eliza Ward 13, Nathan? Ward 4; 2 Jan 1851

40/34: Nelson Kyles 38; Cumberland; Farmville; Laborer; Dr. SPENCER; Farmville; Lucy Kyles 32; Prince Edward; Farmville; Dr. SPENCER; Farmville; Mary Kyles 12, Matilda Kyles 6, John Kyles 1; 1 Jan 1853

40/37: William Ellis 46; Farmville; Farmville; Laborer; Dr. PETERS; Farmville; Mary Ellis 34; Charlotte; Farmville; Baker WARD; Farmville; Ø; 9 Jan 1854

40/38: Alex Randall 46; Farmville; Farmville; Laborer; Pat JACKSON; Farmville; M. Randall 48; Cumberland; Farmville; P. JACKSON; Farmville; Alex Randall 17, James Randall 15, Claiborne Randall 10; 24 Dec 1848

41/1: Cooper Morton 50; Prince Edward; Prince Edward; Laborer; W.H. VENABLE; Prince Edward; Maria Morton 60; Prince Edward; Prince Edward; M.M. VENABLE; Prince Edward; Ø; 25 Dec 1846

41/2: Joseph Bedford 46; Prince Edward; Prince Edward; Laborer; A.B. VENABLE; Prince Edward; Rebecca Bedford 40; Prince Edward; Prince Edward; A.R. VENABLE; Prince Edward; Lucinda Bedford 16, Louisa Bedford 12, Albert Bedford 10; 1 Jan 1841

41/5: Branch Scott 30; Prince Edward; Prince Edward; Laborer; E.G. WALL; Prince Edward; Lizzie Scott 22; Charlotte; Prince Edward; A.R. VENABLE; Prince Edward; Scott 3, Scott infant; 1 Jan 1852

41/7: John Haskins 82; Prince Edward; Prince Edward; Laborer; John W. WEST; Prince Edward; Melinda Haskins 70; Prince Edward; Prince Edward; J.W. WEST; Prince Edward; Ø; 25 Dec 1831

41/8: Charles Redd 44; Prince Edward; Prince Edward; Laborer; Truman REDD; Prince Edward; Nancy Redd 42; Nottoway; Prince Edward; Mrs. P. FOWLKES; Prince Edward; Coleman Redd 18, Burrell Redd 8; 25 Dec 1826

41/10: Phineus Harvey 46; Prince Edward; Prince Edward; Laborer; Johann HARVEY; Prince Edward; Eliza Harvey 40; Prince Edward; Prince Edward; Johann HARVEY; Prince Edward; Albert Harvey 17, Mary Harvey 12, Martha Harvey 9, Samuel Harvey 6, Warsham Harvey 2, Taylor Harvey 14; 25 Dec 1844

41/16: Patrick Allen 52; Prince Edward; Prince Edward; Laborer; Syrus ALLEN; Prince Edward; Abby Allen 44; Prince Edward; Prince Edward; Syrus ALLEN; Prince Edward; Earlina Allen 17, Isiah Allen 15, Solomon Allen 13, Jackson Allen 10, Ellen Allen 8, Fanny Allen 6, Judith Allen 3; 25 Dec 1846

41/23: Stephen Brown 44; Prince Edward; Prince Edward; Laborer; Mrs. William CHAMBERS; Prince Edward; Mary Brown 34; Prince Edward; Prince Edward; Mrs. Mary BELL; Prince Edward; James Brown 18, Maria Brown 12, Fanny Brown 11, Martha Brown 9, Stephen Brown 2; 25 Dec 1846

41/28: ? Peters 76; Prince Edward; Prince Edward; Laborer; Dr. PETERS; Farmville; Sallie Peters 44; Prince Edward; Prince Edward; William R. TAYLOR; Prince Edward; Adolphus Peters 16, Abram Peters 10, John Peters 9, Patrick Peters 2; 20 Dec 1846

41/32: Jerry Womack 30; Prince Edward; Prince Edward; Laborer; Mrs. J. CARY; Prince Edward; L. Womack 20; Cumberland; Prince Edward; C. ANDERSON; Prince Edward; Barkas Womack 3; 25 Dec 1842

41/33: Jordan Redd 46; Prince Edward; Prince Edward; Laborer; Truman REDD; Prince Edward; Eggie Redd 30; Prince Edward; Prince Edward; Parson DANCE; Prince Edward; Ø; 25 Dec 1859

41/34: Jack Redd 48; Prince Edward; Prince Edward; Laborer; Truman REDD; Prince Edward; Judy Redd 26; Prince Edward; Prince Edward; Parson DANCE; Prince Edward; Ø; 25 Dec 1863

41/35: Richard Edmands 58; Charlotte; Prince Edward; Laborer; John EVANS; Charlotte; Julia Edmands 52; Charlotte; Prince Edward; William JOHNS; Prince Edward; Joseph Edmands 20, Ed Edmands 18, Violet Edmands 16, Louis Edmands 14, Richard Edmands 12, Sallie Edmands 11?, Frank Edmands 18, Mack Edmands 9; 28 Dec 1840

42/1: George Paulett 48; Prince Edward; Prince Edward; Laborer; R.S. PAULETT; Prince Edward; Milly Paulett 38; Amelia; Prince Edward; Jeff RICE; Farmville; Ø; 2 Jan 1860

42/2: Beverly Howard 56; Prince Edward; Prince Edward; Laborer; John RANDOLPH; Prince Edward; Harriet Howard 50; Prince Edward; Prince Edward; John RANDOLPH; Prince Edward; Ø; 25 Dec 1826

42/3: Sydney Howard 48; Prince Edward; Prince Edward; Laborer; John RANDOLPH; Prince Edward; Amanda Howard 24; Prince Edward; Prince Edward; Joseph VENABLE; Prince Edward; Sarah Howard 1; 2 Oct 1864

42/4: Thomas Jefferson 28; Buckingham; Prince Edward; Laborer; John V. CRATE; Buckingham; Ange Jefferson 22; Rappahannock; Prince Edward; Joseph GILLESPIE; Buckingham; Ø; 1 Feb 1862

42/5: Scipio Johnson 48; Prince Edward; Prince Edward; Laborer; F.J. WOOTTEN; Prince Edward; Frances Johnson 33; Nottoway; Prince Edward; J.L?. FLIPPEN; Prince Edward; Ø; 25 Dec 1853

42/6: George Miller 40; Prince Edward; Prince Edward; Laborer; B.R. RODGERS; Halifax; Caroline Miller 21; Halifax; Prince Edward; TURNER; Halifax; Richard Miller 3, Martha J. Miller 1 ½; 1 Jan 1862

42/7: Frank Brown 40; Prince Edward; Prince Edward; Laborer; S.D. BROWN; Lunenburg; Lousani Brown 34?; Prince Edward; Prince Edward; F.T. WOOTTEN; Prince Edward; Harriet Brown 12, Joseph Brown 5; 1 Jan 1854

42/10: Harry Miller 30; Prince Edward; Prince Edward; Laborer; Richard A. MILLER; Prince Edward; Lucy Miller 29; Prince Edward; Prince Edward; F.T. WOOTTEN; Prince Edward; Alice Miller 5, George Miller 3, Matty Miller infant; 25 Dec 1859

42/13: Josephus Wootten 28; Lunenburg; Prince Edward; Laborer; F.T. WOOTTEN; Prince Edward; Jane Wootten _4; Prince Edward; Prince Edward; Thomas I. OWEN; Prince Edward; Richard Wootten 3, Jane Wootten 2; 1 Jan 1861

42/15: David White 48; Amelia; Prince Edward; Laborer; H.M. VAUGHAN; Prince Edward; Betty White 32; Prince Edward; Prince Edward; F.T. WOOTTEN; Prince Edward; David White 5; 25 Dec 1859

42/16: Joseph Bartlett 50; Prince Edward; Prince Edward; Laborer; Nathan SPENCER; Prince Edward; Jane Bartlett 44; Lunenburg; Prince Edward; William D. WOMACK; Prince Edward; Ø; 1 Jan 1845

42/17: Chappell Smith 52; Halifax; Prince Edward; Laborer; J. OVERBY; Prince Edward; Martha Smith 55; Bedford; Prince Edward; J. OVERBY; Prince Edward; Ø; 1 Mar 1850

42/18: Syrus See 65; Cumberland; Prince Edward; Laborer; J. OVERBY; Prince Edward; Martha See 64; Prince Edward; Prince Edward; Joshua HINES; Prince Edward; Ø; 25 Dec 1850

42/19: Abram Scott 45; Prince Edward; Prince Edward; Laborer; W.F. SCOTT; Prince Edward; Easther Scott 40; Prince Edward; Prince Edward; J.H. LACY; Prince Edward; John Scott 6, Garrison Scott 3; 1 Jan 1859

42/21: John Scott 30; Prince Edward; Prince Edward; Laborer; W.F. SCOTT; Prince Edward; Marg Scott 28; Prince Edward; Prince Edward; Dr. CALHOUN; Lunenburg; Ø; 28 Dec 1859

42/22: J. Booker 40; Charlotte; Prince Edward; Laborer; J.M. BOOKER; Prince Edward; Jane Booker 32; Prince Edward; Prince Edward; J.M. BOOKER; Prince Edward; Ø; 25 Dec 1852

42/23: William Johns 36; Charlotte; Prince Edward; Laborer; ? DUPUY; Prince Edward; Nice Johns 26; Prince Edward; Prince Edward; J.M. BOOKER; Prince Edward; Betsy Johns 10; 25 Dec 1855

42/24: Africa Watson 60; Prince Edward; Prince Edward; Laborer; Samuel WATSON; Prince Edward; Milly Watson 46; Charlotte; Prince Edward; J.M. BOOKER; Prince Edward; Mary Watson 16, Julia Watson 14, Albert Watson 12, Alex Watson 11, Whes_y Watson 7, John M. Watson 5, Hatty Watson 2; 1 Jan 1842

42/31: Patrick Watson 50; Prince Edward; Prince Edward; Laborer; Samuel WATSON; Prince Edward; Cordella Watson 36; Prince Edward; Prince Edward; J.B. BELL; Prince Edward; Patrick Watson 16, Edward Watson 13, William Watson 6, Sarah Watson 1; 28 Dec 1846

42/35: Henry Bell 50; Prince Edward; Prince Edward; Laborer; J.B. BELL; Prince Edward; Julia Bell 40; Prince Edward; Prince Edward; Nat WILSON; Charlotte; Ø; 25 Dec 1841

42/36: William Bell 46; Richmond; Prince Edward; Laborer; J.B. BELL; Prince Edward; Biddy Bell 30; Prince Edward; Prince Edward; Samuel SCOTT; Prince Edward; Ø; 1 Jan 1864

42/37: Allen Bell 50; Prince Edward; Prince Edward; Laborer; G.W. BELL; Prince Edward; Cynthna Bell 54; Prince Edward; Prince Edward; John B. BELL; Prince Edward; Ø; 25 Dec 1859

42/38: Branch White 46; Prince Edward; Prince Edward; Laborer; Joseph WHITEHEAD; Prince Edward; Milly White 46; Prince Edward; Prince Edward; Phil SNEED; Prince Edward; Ø; 25 Dec 1860

42/39: Henry Thweatt 40; Prince Edward; Prince Edward; Laborer; Joseph WHITEHEAD; Prince Edward; Eda Thweatt 45; Prince Edward; Prince Edward; A.R. VENABLE; Prince Edward; Ø; 1 Jan 1860

43/1: Lewis Thompson 48; Nottoway; Prince Edward; Laborer; Ed MILLER; Prince Edward; Susan Thompson 49; Nottoway; Prince Edward; Miles GIBBS; Amelia; John Thompson 19, Page Thompson 14, Isabella Thompson 8, Catherine Thompson 10, Ella Thompson 12, Jenny Thompson 16; 24 Oct 1846

43/7: James Dickinson 84; Nottoway; Prince Edward; Laborer; John H. KNIGHT; Prince Edward; Juliet Dickinson 89; Nottoway; Prince Edward; John H. KNIGHT; Prince Edward; Dinah Dickinson 13, Jordan Dickinson 12, Betty Dickinson 11, Benjamin Dickinson 9, Landvina? Dickinson 7, Henry Dickinson 5, Junius Dickinson 3; 15 Mar 1851

43/14: Herbert Miller 50; Bedford Prince Edward; Laborer; Ed MILLER; Prince Edward; Eliza Miller 40; Prince Edward; Prince Edward; Richard MILLER; Prince Edward; Ø; 16 Dec 1851

43/15: Lewis Clark 66; Prince Edward; Prince Edward; Laborer; Mrs. Benjamin CLARK; Prince Edward; Elizabeth Clark 40; Prince Edward; Prince Edward; Martha AGNEW; Prince Edward; Alpheus Clark 20, Robert Clark 19, Edwin Clark 18, James Clark 15, Columbus Clark 14, Ann Maria Clark 13, Martha Clark 5, Faith Clark 4; 26 Dec 1841

43/23: David Miller 60; Prince Edward; Prince Edward; Laborer; Richard MILLER; Prince Edward; Phillis Miller 40; Cumberland; Prince Edward; Marshal CROWDER; Cumberland; Sally Ann Miller; 20 Oct 1861

43/24: Anderson Williams 70; Brunswick; Prince Edward; Laborer; Ed EDMUNDS; Prince Edward; Julia Williams 44; Prince Edward; Prince Edward; Ed EDMUNDS; Prince Edward; Educia Williams 21, Isaac Williams 17, Charles Williams 9, Almira Williams 13, Nicolas Williams 7, Taylor Williams 11, Washington Williams 6, Moses Williams 3, Mary Williams 4 mos; 25 Dec 1844

43/33: George Jackson 40; Nottoway; Prince Edward; Farmer; Sa_ JENNINGS; Prince Edward; Lucy Jackson 28; Prince Edward; Prince Edward; William NEAVES; Prince Edward; James A. Jackson 6 mos; 15 Apr 1864

43/34: Solomon Ligan 44; Prince Edward; Prince Edward; Farmer; Mrs. Ag LIGAN; Prince Edward; Martha Ligan 38; Prince Edward; Prince Edward; John FOSTER; Prince Edward; Celina Ligan 7 mos; 30 Nov 1854

43/35: Robert Gee 30; Lunenburg; Prince Edward; Farmer; Richard STOKES; Prince Edward; Rhoda Gee 28; Lunenburg; Prince Edward; Richard STOKES; Prince Edward; Fanny Gee 9, Jenny Gee 3, Robert Gee 2; 1 Jan 1856

43/38: John Reed 36; Cumberland; Prince Edward; Laborer; Frank REDD; Prince Edward; Anne Reed 22; Lunenburg; Prince Edward; Henry STOKES; Prince Edward; Lancaster Reed 4, Rhoda Reed 2; 1 Jan 1862

44/1: Alex Scott 38; Prince Edward; Prince Edward; Laborer; Mrs. Jane SCOTT; Prince Edward; Frances Scott 36; Prince Edward; Prince Edward; Col. VAUGHAN; Prince Edward; Agwood Scott 9, Judy Scott 4, Mary Scott infant; 20 Dec 1855

44/4: Beverley Jones 48; Prince Edward; Prince Edward; Gardener; T.F. VENABLE; Prince Edward; Parthenia Jones 28; Cumberland; Prince Edward; George GAUPHIN; Cumberland; Martha Jones 3 mos; 16 July 1858

44/5: Thomas Venable 52; Prince Edward; Prince Edward; Laborer; T.F. VENABLE; Prince Edward; Jenny Venable 48; Prince Edward; Prince Edward; Joseph L. LIGAN; Prince Edward; Rosetta Venable 15, Jenny Venable 9, Abraham Venable 8, Aggie Venable 13; 18 June 1836

44/9: Stephen Smith 38; Prince Edward; Prince Edward; Laborer; Joseph L. LIGAN; Prince Edward; Letty A. Smith 29; Prince Edward; Prince Edward; Joseph L. LIGAN; Prince Edward; Mary Smith 10; 15 Oct 1865

44/10: William Bailey 50; Cumberland; Prince Edward; Laborer; E. WOMACK; Prince Edward; Lizzie Bailey 40; Prince Edward; Prince Edward; David WOMACK; Prince Edward; Ø; 20 May 1865

44/11: Coleman Venable 38; Prince Edward; Prince Edward; Laborer; Joseph L. LIGAN; Prince Edward; Eliza Venable 40; Prince Edward; Prince Edward; Joseph T. LIGAN; Prince Edward; John Venable 5, Jack Venable 3; 14 Oct 1860

44/13: Ned Booker 42; Prince Edward; Prince Edward; Laborer; Joseph L. LIGAN; Prince Edward; Cora Ann Booker 28; Prince Edward; Prince Edward; Joseph LIGAN; Prince Edward; Ø; 1 May 1865

44/14: George Jones 38; Halifax; Prince Edward; Laborer; Joseph C. HUNT; Charlotte; Jane Jones 42; Pittsylvania; Prince Edward; Joseph C. HUNT; Charlotte; Ø; 19 Aug 1860

44/15: Dennis Scott 56; Prince Edward; Prince Edward; Laborer; Louisa LIGAN; Prince Edward; Violet A. Scott 55; Prince Edward; Prince Edward; William WALTON; Prince Edward; Betty Scott 14, Jack Scott 12, Spencer Scott 11, Agnes Scott 6, Louisa Scott 4; 20 Dec 1839

44/20: Charles Bell 65; Nottoway; Prince Edward; Laborer; Adam BELL; Lunenburg; Delia Bell 53; Lunenburg; Prince Edward; George HARDY; Lunenburg; Mitchell Bell 18, Frank Bell 15, Charles Bell 14, Baker Bell 12, Anderson Bell 10, Sylvia Bell 9, Martha Bell 5, Mary Bell 2 mos; 15 Nov 1838

44/28: Doctor Walker 25; Buckingham; Prince Edward; Laborer; William JONES/JANES; Prince Edward; Sarah Walker 28; Prince Edward; Prince Edward; William JONES/JANES; Prince Edward; Margaret Jones/Janes 6 (1st husband), Nannie Jones/Janes 4; 12 Mar 1865

44/30: William Ward 34; Prince Edward; Prince Edward; Laborer; Mrs. E. BLANTON; Prince Edward; M.E. Ward 30; Prince Edward; Prince Edward; John OVERTON; Prince Edward; Julia Ann Ward 14, Willie Ann Ward 12, Josephine Ward 10, Sarah Ward 8, James Ward 4; 29 Dec 1851

44/35: Jacob Branch 64; Prince Edward; Prince Edward; Laborer; Joseph D. LIGAN; Prince Edward; Lucy Branch 40; Prince Edward; Prince Edward; Mr. B. LIGAN; Prince Edward; Isaac Branch 18, Ben Branch 16, Milly Branch 6, Lilly Branch 3, Lucy Branch 2 mos; 18 Mar 1847

45/1: Jacob Hendrick 58; Prince Edward; Prince Edward; Laborer; William CARDWELL; Prince Edward; Lucinda Hendrick 44; Prince Edward; Prince Edward; James WHITEHEAD; Prince Edward; Francis Hendrick 15, Peter Hendrick 10, Amanda Hendrick 9; 1 Jan 1822

45/4: Lacey Haksins 42; Farmville; Farmville; Laborer; Pat JACKSON; Farmville; Juila Haskins 34; Prince Edward; Farmville; Pat JACKSON; Farmville; Doctor Haskins 5, Griffin Haskins 3, Raymond Haskins 3 mos, Hannah Haskins 6; 15 Oct 1858

45/8: Wash Bartlett 45 Farmville; Farmville; Laborer; William BARTLETT; Richmond Phillis Bartlett 36; Prince Edward; Farmville; Sm ANDERSON; Prince Edward; Frank Bartlett 2, Margaret Bertlett infant; 25 Dec 1849

45/10: Benjamin Baulden 36; Prince Edward; Prince Edward; Laborer; Mrs. A. HOLIDAY; Winchester; Esther Bauilden 37; Prince Edward; Prince Edward; Thomas MORTON; Prince Edward; Belinda Boulden 11, Charles Boulden 10, Mary Boulden 6, Dolly Boulden 3, infant; 16 June 1854

45/15: Collin Miller 36; Prince Edward; Prince Edward; Laborer; James LIGAN; Prince Edward; Polly Miller 35; Prince Edward; Prince Edward; Mrs. P. LIGAN; Prince Edward; Chinkpin Miller 2; 25 Dec 1858

45/16: George West 22; Prince Edward; Prince Edward; Laborer; Sam BRUCE; Prince Edward; Martha West 24; Prince Edward; Prince Edward; Sam BRUCE; Prince Edward; Abram West infant; 1 Jan 1855

45/17: James Wright 36; Prince Edward; Prince Edward; Laborer; James EVANS; Prince Edward; Laura Wright 28; Prince Edward; Prince Edward; H.H. BUDD; Cumberland; James Wright 7, George Wright 3, Victoria Wright 1; 25 Oct 1858

45/20: Lewis Eppes 25; Cumberland; Prince Edward; Laborer; A.S. ADAMS; Cumberland; M.A. Eppes 24; Prince Edward; Prince Edward; H.H. BUDD; Cumberland; Robert Eppes 2; 15 July 1863

45/21: Anthony Branch 48; Prince Edward; Prince Edward; Laborer; Samuel BRUCE; Prince Edward; Becky Branch 40; Cumberland; Prince Edward; Robert GARNETT; Cumberland; Edward Branch 11, Phillis Branch 9, Anthony Branch 6; 25 Dec 1854

45/24: Swain Moseley 36; Cumberland; Farmville; Laborer; Ben BOLLING; Prince Edward; Roseline Moseley 32; Cumberland; Farmville; John BLANTON; Cumberland; Georgia Moseley 10, Wylett Moseley 4, Susan Moseley 3, Morton Moseley infanat; 7 Aug 1952

45/28: Sampson Womack 32; Cumberland; Farmville; Laborer; John DALBY; Farmville; N. Womack 36; Charlotte; Farmville; BURENDINE; Prince Edward; Julia Ann Womack 3; 1 Jan 1860

45/29: Nelson Goodhopes 24; Prince Edward; Farmville; Laborer; Henry CRATE; Prince Edward; Amanda Goodhopes 19; Prince Edward; Farmville; Mrs. Susan TUGGLE; Prince Edward; Ø; 31 Jan 1866

45/30: James Royster 48; Cranberry, N. Carolina; Prince Edward; Laborer; Sylvanus JOHNSON; Petersburg; Dilsy Royster 34; Prince Edward; Prince Edward; George VAUGHAN; Prince Edward; Eddy Royster 7, Emma Royster 3, Bertie Royster 2; 28 Nov 1834

45/33: John Booker 40; Prince Edward; Prince Edward; Blacksmith; William ELLIOT; Prince Edward; Elvira Booker 32; Prince Edward; Prince Edward; M.S. CHILDERS; Prince Edward; Betsey Ann Booker 15, Beverley Booker 5, Matilda Bookeer 3, Sarah Booker infant; 25 Dec 1830

45/37: Washington Ross 39; Cumberland; Prince Edward; Cooper; Leach ANDERSON; Cumberland; Margaret Ross 25; Buckingham; Prince Edward; Miss H. WILHAN; Appomattox; Ø; 1 Jan 1862

45/38: James Hennins 36; Buckingham; Prince Edward; Cooper; John EPPES; Buckingham; M.A. Hennins 26; buckingham; Prince Edward; James CRATE; Buckingham; Alpheus Hennins 6, Betty Hennins 4, Sarah Hennins 3; 25 Dec 1854

46/1: Clinton Goode 38; Cumberland; Prince Edward; Laborer; Dar GOODE; Cumberland; Dolly Goode 36; cumberland; Prince Edward; Sal HARRINGER; Richmond; William Goode 14, Phillip Goode 7; 1 Jan 1850

46/3: Albert Green 46; Prince Edward; Prince Edward; Laborer; Charles PRICE; Prince Edward; Cicily Green 44; Prince Edward; Prince Edward; George BELL; Prince Edward; Sarah Green 14, David Green 12, Isaac Green 10; 1 Jan 1822

46/6: Sanders Street 50; Purrenberg (Pearisburg, Giles Co?); Prince Edward; Laborer; Dr. TERRY; Prince Edward; Martha Street 30; Prince Edward; Prince Edward; Charles PRICE; Prince Edward; Willis Street 9, Mumford Street 4, John Street 2, Sandy Street infant; 25 Dec 1854

46/10: George Booker 54; Cumberland; Prince Edward; Lborer; Charles E. PRICE; Prince Edward; Eda Booker 60; Prince Edward; Prince Edward; William BEUFORD; Prince Edward; Ø; 20 Aug 1864

46/11: Charles White 42; Charlotte; Prince Edward; Laborer; Pat JACKSON; Farmville; Susan White 29; Prince Edward; Prince Edward; Bennett MORE; Prince Edward; Emily White 9, Elsey White 6, Mary White 4, John White 2; 5 Apr 1855

46/15: Isaac Flagg 48; charlotte; Prince Edward; Laborer; Pat JACKSON; Farmville; Charlotte Flagg 40; buckingham; Prince Edward; Pat JACKSON; Prince Edward; William Armstead Flagg 20, Linwood Flagg 17, Lucy Ann Flagg 11, Esther Flagg 9, Nicholas Flagg 5; 15 Oct 1844

46/20: Essex Clark 36; Prince Edward; Prince Edward; Laborer; Phebe CLARK; Prince Edward; Amelia Clark 34; Prince Edward; Prince Edward; William ANDERSON; Prince Edward; Matilda Clark 4; 12 Aug 1860

46/21: Sam P. Walker 44; Cumberland; Prince Edward; Laborer; Mrs. M. ALLEN; Prince Edward; Sally Walker 48; Prince Edward; Prince Edward; Mrs. Polly FUQUA; Prince Edward; Ø; 25 Dec 1864

46/22: William W. Boles 28; Buckingham; Prince Edward; Laborer; Mrs. B. BOWLES; Prince Edward; Amanda L. BOLES 19; buckingham; Prince Edward; P.A. FORBES; Buckingham; Lucinda Bowels 3, Martha J. Bowles 1; 26 Dec 1861

46/24: Cupid Coles 36; Prince Edward; Prince Edward; Laborer; Mrs. Polly VENABLE; Prince Edward; Caroline Coles 36; Prince Edward; Prince Edward; Born Free; Ø; Samuel Coles 3; 1 Jan 1863

46/25: William Ritchie 60; Prince Edward; Prince Edward; Shoemaker; John W. REDD; Prince Edward; Maria T. Ritchie 62; Prince Edward; Prince Edward; Lewis SKIDMORE; Charlotte; robert ritchie 16, William Ritchie 10; 25 Dec 1836

46/27: Jerry Alms 56; Prince Edward; Prince Edward; Laborer; Mrs. P. ALMS; Prince Edward; Sallie Alms 60; Prince Edward; Prince Edward; Albert REDD; Prince Edward; Ø; 25 Dec 1864

46/28: James Beuford; Goochland; Prince Edward; Laborer; B.L. BEUFORD; Prince Edward; Cila Beufordd 48; Prince Edward; Prince Edward; B.L. BINFORD; Prince Edward; Henry beuford 16, Nancy Beuford 10; 25 Dec 1848

46/30: Henry Woodson 32; Prince Edward; Prince Edward; Laborer; Mrs. N. WOODSON; Prince Edward; Mary Woodson 26; Prince Edward; Prince Edward; Born Free; Ø; Ø; 15 Mar 1863

46/31: Henry Scott 46; Prince Edward; Prince Edward; Laborer; James L. LIGAN; Prince Edward; Caroline Scott 40; Prince Edward; Prince Edward; James M. WOOTTEN; Prince Edward; Susan Scott 16, Jenny Scott 9, Thomas Scott 4; 25 Dec 1846

46/34: George Moseley 29; Prince Edward; Prince Edward; Laborer; Alex WEST; Prince Edward; Mayde Moseley 36; Amelia; Prince Edward; Alex WEST; Prince Edward; Ø; 1 Jan 1861

46/35: Lincoln Carrington 69; Amelia; Prince Edward; Carpenter; Robert KELTRO; Bedford; Sukey Carrington 50; Prince Edward; Prince Edward; John LOVINE; Bedford; Ø; 25 Dec 1846

46/36: William Green 28; Charlotte; Prince Edward; Shoemaker; Charles CRAWLEY; Prince Edward; Martha Green 24; Prince Edward; Prince Edward; Thomas TREADWAY; Prince Edward; Mackey Green 4, Thomas Green 2; 30 Aug 1861

46/38: Sam Eppes 24; Prince George; Prince Edward; Laborer; Thomas PROCTOR; Petersburg; Sarah Eppes 22; Charlotte; Prince Edward; Thomas PROCTOR; Petersburg; Ø; 10 Mar 1865

46/39:Silas Anderson 24; buckingham; Prince Edward; Laborer; B. GILLS; Buckingham; Ella Anderson 21; Prince Edward; Prince Edward; George R. DAVIS; Prince Edward; Ø; 12 Aug 1865

Table 20 Richmond County

Register of Children of Colored Persons whose Parents Ceased to Cohabit which the Father Recognizes to be His

(pg/line; child/age; pob; res; last owner/res; f/res, f/age; f/last owner/res; m/age; m/res, m/last owner; f name)

1/1: Mary Catharine Bowzer 14; Warsaw, Richmond; Warsaw; Richard JEFFRIES; Glebe Farm; Warsaw; 40; Thomas JONES; Warsaw; Jane Bowzer 35; Washington, D.C.; Thomas WALKER; Tappahannock, Essex; Junius Bowzier

1/2: William Thomas Bowzier 9; Richmond; Warsaw; Richard JEFFRIES; Glebe Farm; Warsaw; 40; Thomas JONES; Warsaw; Jane Bowzer 35; Washington, D.C.; Thomas WALKER; Tappahannock, Essex; Junius Bowzier

1/3: Ellen Norah Bowzier 12; Richmond; Not Known; Sold in Richmond during the war, 1864; Not Known; Warsaw; 40; Thomas JONES; Warsaw; Jane Bowzer 35; Washington, D.C.; Thomas WALKER; Tappahannock, Essex; Junius Bowzier

1/4: Mariah Bowzier 6; Richmond; Washington, D.C.; Thomas WALKER; Tappahannock; Warsaw; 40; Thomas JONES; Warsaw; Jane Bowzer 35; Washington, D.C.; Thomas WALKER; Tappahannock, Essex; Junius Bowzier

1/5: John Robert Solomon Soil 8; Farnun (Farnham?) Church, Richmond; Richmond; Free; Ø; Richmond; Mrs. George CRUTCHER; Farnun (Farnham?) Church; Hannah Soil 43; Richmond; Free

1/6: Charles Hannibal Solomon Soil 8; Farnun (Farnham?) Church, Richmond; Richmond; Free; Ø; Richmond; Mrs. George CRUTCHER; Farnun (Farnham?) Church; Hannah Soil 43; Richmond; Free

1/7: Lucinda Solomon Soil 5; Farnun (Farnham?) Church, Richmond; Richmond; Free; Ø; Richmond; Mrs. George CRUTCHER; Farnun (Farnham?) Church; Hannah Soil 43; Richmond; Free

1/8: Henry Lee Solomon Soil 4; Farnun (Farnham?) Church, Richmond; Richmond; Free; Ø; Richmond; Mrs. George CRUTCHER; Farnun (Farnham?) Church; Hannah Soil 43; Richmond; Free

1/9: Rolla Lee 16; Lancaster; Richmond; Henry BISCOE; Farnun (Farnham?)Church, Richmond; Richmond; 45; W.W. DOUGLAS; Warsaw, Richmond; Elsie Lee 36; Dead; Henry BISCOE; Ø; Jessie Lee

1/10: Samuel Lee 14; Lancaster; Richmond; Henry BISCOE; Farnun (Farnham?)Church, Richmond; Richmond; 45; W.W. DOUGLAS; Warsaw, Richmond; Elsie Lee 36; Dead; Henry BISCOE; Ø; Jessie Lee

1/11: Fleet Clummer Lee 12; Lancaster; Richmond; Henry BISCOE; Farnun (Farnham?)Church; Richmond; 45; W.W. DOUGLAS; Warsaw, Richmond; Elsie Lee 36; Dead; Henry BISCOE; Ø; Jessie Lee

1/12: Moses Diggs 15; Northumberland; Richmond; Mary BLACKWELL; Fairfield, Northumberland; Richmond; 47; William HARDIN; Dead; Sally Diggs 30; Dead; Sarah WINSLEAD?; Northumberland; Nelson Diggs

1/13: Mariah Diggs 14; Northumberland; Richmond; Mary BLACKWELL; Fairfield, Northumberland; Richmond; 47; William HARDIN; Dead; Sally Diggs 30; Dead; Sarah WINSLEAD?; Northumberland; Nelson Diggs

1/14: Juliett Campbell 13; Richmond; Richmond; Betsy H. LINDEN; Baltimore, Maryland; Richmond; 48; Eugene FICKLAND; Spotsylvania; Mary Campbell 23; Dead; Mrs. LINDEN; Baltimore, Maryland; Richard Campbell

1/15: Richard ___ Campbell 11; Richmond; Richmond; Betsy H. LINDEN; Baltimore, Maryland; Richmond; 48; Eugene FICKLAND; Spotsylvania; Mary Campbell 23; Dead; Mrs. LINDEN; Baltimore, Maryland; Richard Campbell

1/16: George Henry Campbell 9; Richmond; Richmond; Betsy H. LINDEN; Baltimore, Maryland; Richmond; 48; Eugene FICKLAND; Spotsylvania; Mary Campbell 23; Dead; Mrs. LINDEN; Baltimore, Maryland; Richard Campbell

1/17: Nancy Godard 23; Richmond; King George; Mrs. James MORRIS; Cherry Hill, Richmond; Richmond; 48; John MITCHELL; Dead; Richmond; Peggy Goddard 20; Dead; Mrs. James MORRIS; Cherry Hill, Richmond; Samuel Godard

1/18: Mahalia Godard 22; Richmond; Richmond; Mrs. Ealsie MORRIS; Dead; Richmond; 48; John MITCHELL; Dead; Richmond; Peggy Goddard 20; Dead; Mrs. Ealsie MORRIS; Cherry Hill, Richmond; Samuel Godard

1/19: Sally Godard 19; Richmond; Richmond; Mrs. Ealsie MORRIS; Dead; Richmond; 48; John MITCHELL; Dead; Richmond; Peggy Goddard 20; Dead; Mrs. Ealsie MORRIS; Cherry Hill, Richmond; Samuel Godard

1/20: Samuel Godard 18; Richmond; Richmond; Mrs. Ealsie MORRIS; Dead; Richmond; 48; John MITCHELL; Dead; Richmond; Peggy Goddard 20; Dead; Mrs. Ealsie MORRIS; Cherry Hill, Richmond; Samuel Godard

1/21: Peter Godard 10; Richmond; Richmond; William MITCHELL; Richmond; Richmond; 48; John MITCHELL; Dead; Richmond; Peggy Goddard 20; Dead; Mrs. Ealsie MORRIS; Cherry Hill, Richmond; Samuel Godard

1/22: Aaron Gibson 19; Augusta; Augusta; William GAMBELL; Augusta; Richmond; 60; Dr. WELFORD; Richmond; Patsie Gibson 50; Augusta; William GAMBELL; Augusta; Randall Gibson

1/23: John Henry Gibson 13; Augusta; Augusta; William GAMBELL; Augusta; Richmond; 60; Dr. WELFORD; Richmond; Patsie Gibson 50; Augusta; William GAMBELL; Augusta; Randall Gibson

1/24: Margaret Gibson 11; Augusta; Augusta; William GAMBELL; Augusta; Richmond; 60; Dr. WELFORD; Richmond; Patsie Gibson 50; Augusta; William GAMBELL; Augusta; Randall Gibson

1/25: Archie Gibson 9; Augusta; Augusta; William GAMBELL; Augusta; Richmond; 60; Dr. WELFORD; Richmond; Patsie Gibson 50; Augusta; William GAMBELL; Augusta; Randall Gibson

1/26: Harriet Lewis 13; Richmond; Richmond; Robert LARNKIN; Richmond; 36; John LARNKIN; Richmond; Evaline Smith 30; Richmond; Theopolis WRIGHT; Ø; Martin Lewis

1/27: Anna Bailey 2; Richmond; Richmond; Moses SELF; Richmond; Richmond; 30; Redman PERCEL; Richmond; Ann Johnson 30; Richmond; Moses SELF; Richmond; Stephen Bailey

1/28: William Henry Mathews 12; Richmond; Richmond; Free Born; Ø; Richmond; 43; Arthur BEARNARD; Richmond; Lizzie Mathews 20; Dead; Free Born; Ø; William Mathews

1/29: Burta Mathews 7; Richmond; Essex; William BENAM; Essex; Richmond; 43; Arthur BEARNARD; Richmond; Betsey Rob 21; Essex; Absom GOLDMAN; Essex; William Mathews

1/30: John Henry Canada 26; Richmond; In the U.S. Army; Lucy BRANHAM; Richmond; Richmond; 48; Lucy BRANHAM; Richmond; Betsey Canada 41; Was sold in New Orleans; Ø; Richmond; Adam Canada

1/31: Malicia Ann Adkins 5; Richmond; Richmond; Free Born; Ø; Richmond; 35; Thomas BARRACKS; Richmond; Hannah Jones 24; Richmond; Free Born; Ø; Nelson Adkins

1/32: Am__a Veney 27; Richmond; Richmond; Free Born; Ø; Richmond; 55; Jerry FREE; Richmond; Charlott Veney 50; Northumberland; Free Born; Ø; Jerry Veney

1/33: Mary Veney 25; Richmond; Richmond; Free Born; Ø; Richmond; 55; Jerry FREE; Richmond; Charlott Veney 50; Northumberland; Free Born; Ø; Jerry Veney

1/34: Judy Veney 23; Richmond; Richmond; Free Born; Ø; Richmond; 55; Jerry FREE; Richmond; Charlott Veney 50; Northumberland; Free Born; Ø; Jerry Veney

1/35: Maria Jane Veney 22; Richmond; Richmond; Free Born; Ø; Richmond; 55; Jerry FREE; Richmond; Charlott Veney 50; Northumberland; Free Born; Ø; Jerry Veney

2/1: John Lomill 8; Richmond; Richmond; Free; Ø; Richmond; 40; Solomon G.A. CRUTCHER; Richmond; Hannah Veney 30; Richmond; Free; Ø; Solomon Lomill

2/2: Charles Lomill 7; Richmond; Richmond; Free; Ø; Richmond; 40; Solomon G.A. CRUTCHER; Richmond; Hannah Veney 30; Richmond; Free; Ø; Solomon Lomill

2/3: Lucinda Lomill 5; Richmond; Richmond; Free; Ø; Richmond; 40; Solomon G.A. CRUTCHER; Richmond; Hannah Veney 30; Richmond; Free; Ø; Solomon Lomill

2/4: Henry L. Lomill 3; Richmond; Richmond; Free; Ø; Richmond; 40; Solomon G.A. CRUTCHER; Richmond; Hannah Veney 30; Richmond; Free; Ø; Solomon Lomill

2/5: Mary Atkins 11; Richmond; Richmond; Free; Ø; Richmond; 35; Born Free; Ø; Mariah Veney; Dead; Ø; Ø; Thornton Atkins

2/6: Martha Liverpool 28; Richmond; Richmond; Lucy BROKENBORO; Warsaw, Richmond; Richmond; 44; William BROCKENBORO; Richmond; Elsie Liverpool; Richmond; Lucy BROCKENBORO; Warsaw, Richmond; John Liverpool

2/7: Stewart Liverpool 18; Essex; Not Known; John A. PARKER; Tappahannock, Essex; Richmond; 44; William BROCKENBORO; Richmond; Elizabeth Liverpool; Dead; John A. PARKER; Tappahannock, Essex; John Liverpool

2/8: Robert Boyd 12; Richmond; Richmond; James MONTGOMERY; Richmond; Richmond; 47; Lucy BROCKENBORO; Richmond; Lucy Boyd; Dead; William Van NESS; Ø; Jerry Boyd

2/10: Julia Ann Campbell 13; Richmond; Richmond; Betsey CLINDIN; Baltimore, Maryland; Richmond; 48; Eugene FICKLAND; Fairfax; Mary Campbell 24; Dead; Betsey CLINDIN; Ø; Richard Campbell

2/11: Rachael Anna Campbell 9; Richmond; Richmond; Betsey CLINDIN; Baltimore, Maryland; Richmond; 48; Eugene FICKLAND; Fairfax; Mary Campbell 24; Dead; Betsey CLINDIN; Ø; Richard Campbell

137

2/12: George Henry Campbell 7; Richmond; Richmond; Betsey CLINDIN; Baltimore, Maryland; Richmond; 48; Eugene FICKLAND; Fairfax; Mary Campbell 24; Dead; Betsey CLINDIN; Ø; Richard Campbell

2/13: Martha Ann Skelton? 4; Richmond; Richmond; Free born; Ø; Richmond; 43; James MARTLY; Richmond; Sarah Skelton? 24; Dead; Free Born; Ø; Major Skelton?

2/14: Cornelia Veney 18; Richmond; Richmond; Free Born; Ø; Richmond; 49; Born Free; Ø; Rachael Veney 38; Dead; Free Born; Ø; James Veney

2/15: Margarett Veney 15; Richmond; Richmond; Free Born; Ø; Richmond; 49; Born Free; Ø; Rachael Veney 38; Dead; Free Born; Ø; James Veney

2/16: Autrin? Webb 26; Richmond; Not Known; Harry SAUNDERS; Richmond; Richmond; 60; Lucy FLEET; Richmond; Fannie Webb; Sold out; Harry SANDERS; Richmond; Ned Webb

2/17: Alexander Webb 20; Richmond; Not Known; Harry SAUNDERS; Richmond; Richmond; 60; Lucy FLEET; Richmond; Fannie Webb; Sold out; Harry SANDERS; Richmond; Ned Webb

2/18: __rola Ellen Fields 14; Richmond; Maryland; Benjamin MIDDLETON; Richmond; Richmond; 47; James C. MARTLY; Richmond; Judy A. Webb 35; St. Mary's Co. Maryland; Benjamin MIDDLETON; Richmond; Hezakiah Fields

2/19: Eliza Jane 8; Richmond; Richmond; Walter DOUGLAS; Richmond; Richmond; 34; Len? CRUMP; Richmond City; Judy Rich 25; Richmond; Walter DOUGLAS; Ø; Joseph Newton

2/20: Mary Robinson 13; Richmond; Richmond; Free; Ø; Richmond; 35; E.F. LAMOINE; Richmond; Mary Robinson 30; Richmond; Free; Ø; Charles Robinson

2/21: Francis Holmes 14; Richmond; Richmond; William INGRAHAM; Richmond; Richmond; 41; Lucy C. BRANHAM; Richmond; Luisa Holmes 40; Richmond; Mrs. Mary INGRAHAM; Ø; James Holmes

2/22: Richard Wright 16; Middlesex; Richmond; John HUNDERLY; Essex; Richmond; 55; Thomas WRIGHT; Essex; Anna Wright 50; Essex; John HUNDERLY; Essex; Benjamin Wright

2/23: Ordessa Wright 15; Middlesex; Richmond; John HUNDERLY; Essex; Richmond; 55; Thomas WRIGHT; Essex; Anna Wright 50; Essex; John HUNDERLY; Essex; Benjamin Wright

2/24: Arthur R. Ball 12; Essex; Washington City; Free Born; Ø; Richmond; 42; Born Free; Ø; Frances Ball 41; Washington City; Born Free; Ø; James H. Ball

2/25: Mary Louisa Ball 10; Essex; Washington City; Free Born; Ø; Richmond; 42; Born Free; Ø; Frances Ball 41; Washington City; Born Free; Ø; James H. Ball

2/26: William T. Ball 6; Essex; Washington City; Free Born; Ø; Richmond; 42; Born Free; Ø; Frances Ball 41; Washington City; Born Free; Ø; James H. Ball

2/27: William Cox 15; Goochland; Goochland; John ALLEN; Goochland; Richmond; 45; Slave; Dr. WALKER; Goochland; Marria Prosey 35; Dead; John ALLEN; Goochland; Mat Cox

Adline Cox 12; Goochland; Goochland; John ALLEN; Goochland; Richmond; 45; Slave; Dr. Walker; Goochland; Marria Prosey 35; Dead; John ALLEN; Goochland; Mat Cox

2/28: Betsey Moore 26; Richmond; Alabama; Henry TAYLOE; Richmond; Richmond; 49; Henry TAYLOE; Richmond; Jennie Moore 37; Dead; Henry TAYLOE; Richmond; Ruffin Moore

2/29: _o__is Moore 17; Richmond; Baltimore, Maryland; Henry TAYLOE; Richmond; Richmond; 49; Henry TAYLOE; Richmond; Jennie Moore 37; Dead; Henry TAYLOE; Richmond; Ruffin Moore

2/30: Louisa Moore 19; Richmond; Alabama; Henry TAYLOE; Richmond; Richmond; 49; Henry TAYLOE; Richmond; Jennie Moore 37; Dead; Henry TAYLOE; Richmond; Ruffin Moore

2/31: Caroline (Moore) 22; Richmond; Alabama; Henry TAYLOE; Richmond; Richmond; 49; Henry TAYLOE; Richmond; Jennie Moore 37; Dead; Henry TAYLOE; Richmond; Ruffin Moore

2/32: Joseph Veney 8; Richmond; Richmond; Free; Ø; Richmond; 30; Free; Ø; Judy Veney 26; Richmond; Ø; Ø; Clayborn Veney

2/33: Willie C. Johnson 6; Richmond; Richmond; Free; Ø; Richmond; 27; Free; Ø; Mary S. Johnson 19; Dead; Ø; Ø; Lieutenant Johnson

2/34: Ann M. (Johnson) 4; Richmond; Richmond; Free; Ø; Richmond; 27; Free; Ø; Mary S. Johnson 19; Dead; Ø; Ø; Lieutenant Johnson

2/35: Estella Kelsick 10; Richmond; Richmond; John PAYTON; Richmond; Richmond; 30; John BELFIELD; Richmond; Lucy Redman 24; Westmoreland; Richmond; Moses Kelsick

2/36: William Kelsick 7; Richmond; Richmond; John PAYTON; Richmond; Richmond; 30; John BELFIELD; Richmond; Lucy Redman 24; Westmoreland; Richmond; Moses Kelsick

Table 21 Richmond County

Register of Colored Persons cohabiting together as Husband and Wife

(pg/line; h/age; pob; h/res; occ; h/last owner/res; w/age; pob; w/res; w/last owner/res; m/age; children/ages; date cohabitation)

1/1: John Barber 70; Petersburg; Richmond; Farmer; Thomas JONES; Warsaw, Richmond; Mary Lomax 30; Richmond; Richmond; Sydney JEFFERES; Warsaw; Andrew Barber 14, James Barber 12, Thomas Barber 10, Mary Jane 6, Charles 3, Lucy 2; 1851

1/2: Elijah Campbell 64; Richmond; Richmond; Farmer; Mrs. Oscar YERBY; Warsaw, Richmond; Mary Davenport 30; Richmond; Richmond; Washington; Richmond; Ealsie 11, Dasie 9, Elijah 5, Isaac 3 ½, James 1; 1854

1/3: Bartlett Macham 63; Middlesex; Winsor, Richmond; Farmer; Dorsey FICKLAND; Lancaster; Patsy Johnson 18; Lancaster; Richmond; George CRITCHER; Richmond; Lucy Ann 22, Zackery 18, Judy 18, Riff 13, William 11, Bartlett 5, Mary 24; 1836

1/4: William Wood 24; Richmond; Richmond; Farmer; Jerry WEBB; Richmond; Martha Palmer 23; Richmond; Richmond; Lucy L. FLUT; Richmond; Clorana 9, Robert 7; 1853

1/5: Daniel J. Veney 52; Richmond; Richmond; Farmer; Jerry WEBB; Richmond; Hannah Verney 43; Richmond; Richmond; Ø; Ø; Ø; 1864

1/6: George Parker 45; Richmond; Richmond; Farmer; Mrs. Thomas LYELL; Richmond; Ellen Bailey 35; Richmond; Richmond; William MIDLETON; Chestnut Level, Westmoreland; Ø; 1860

1/7: John Veney 29; Richmond; Richmond; Miller Free; Ø; Julia Ann rich 30; Richmond; Richmond; Free; Ø; James Rich 13, Walton Rich 7, Andrew Veney 5, Joseph Veney 2; 1860

1/8: William Spence 29; Richmond; Richmond; Farmer; Free; Ø; Laura Banks 16; Richmond; Richmond; albert YERBY; Willow Grove, Richmond; Lucy Spence 3, William Henry Spence 3 mos; 1862

1/9: Samuel Corbin 53; Richmond; Richmond; Farmer; James DICKERSON; Richmond; Lucy Rich 36; Richmond; Richmond; Free; Ø; Catharine 25, Henrietta 21, Louisa 16, Mary Ellen 8, Randolph 6, Harriett 5, Leah 4; 1840

1/10: Leroy Ougham 47; Richmond; Richmond; Farmer; James DICKERSON; Richmond; Mary Baylor 37; King George; Richmond; James DICKERSON; Richmond; Lucy Ellen 3, Matis 2, Jefferson 1; 1846

1/11: William Dunaway 45; Richmond; Richmond; Farmer; Kenner CRAWLEY; Richmond; Jennie Soil 36; Richmond; Richmond; William PITTS; Richmond; Isabella; 18, George 15, Arthur 10, Mary Ann 1; 1847

1/12: Aaron Taylor 57; Richmond; Richmond; Farmer; Noel T. BOLOSTON; Richmond; Judiah Hilliards 60; Westmoreland; Richmond; John NADON; Westmoreland; Ø; 1846

1/13: George Thompson 58; Westmoreland; Richmond; Farmer; William PORTER; Dead; Margarett 45; Richmond; Richmond; Mrs. Francis BURINULT; Not Known; Ø; 1850

1/14: Cyrus Norris 36; Richmond; Richmond; Farmer; W.W. DOUGLAS; Warsaw, Richmond; Sinia Robinson 30; Fauquier; Richmond; Oscar YEARBY; Dead; Louisa 10, Junius 7, Anna 3, Famice 1; 1855

1/15: Harry Webster 67; Lancaster; Richmond; Farmer; Eppie NORRIS; Lancaster; Eliza Weaver 66; Lancaster; Richmond; W.W. DOUGLAS; Warsaw, Richmond; Henry Wilson Webster 40, Polly Baels (married) 30; 1825

1/16: Jessie Lee 45; Richmond; Richmond; Farmer; W.W. DOUGLAS; Warsaw, Richmond; Mary Robinson 25; Fauquier; Richmond; Oscar YEARLEY; Dead; Elsie 5, James 2; 1860

1/17: Nelson Diggss 44; Northumberland; Richmond; Farmer; William HARDIN; Dead; Mary Ann Drake 25; Richmond; Richmond; Lucy OLDERSON; Farnham Church, Richmond; Nelly 5, Elmonia 6 mos; 1860

1/18: Burgess Williams 52; Richmond; Richmond; Farmer; Richard HIPKINS; Essex; Ann Jackson 30; Richmond; Richmond; Mrs. Oscar YERBY; Farnham Church, Richmond; Daniel Williams 26, Alfred Williams 18; 1838

1/19: Washington Carl 35; Northumberland; Richmond; Farmer; Daniel GARLAND; Richmond; Peggy Jackson 27; Richmond; Richmond; Hamilton THRIFT; Farnham Church, Richmond; Ellar Jane 11, Alice Elizabeth 8, William Oliver 5, Catharine 3; 1854

1/20: David Veney 55; Richmond; Richmond; Farmerp Free; Ø; Judy Veney 49; Richmond; Richmond; Free; Ø; Lewis 30, John 25, David 21, Elias 18, Joseph 15, Catharine 20, Humphrey 13, Griffin 12; 1828

1/21: George Weldon 24; Richmond; Richmond; Farmer; Free; Ø; Pressie Thompson 23; Richmond; Richmond; Free; Ø; Ø; 1864

1/22: Richard Campbell 48; Richmond; Richmond; Farmer; Eugene FICKLAND; Spotsylvania; Mary Boler 38; Lancaster; Richmond; Dorsey FICKLAND; Lancaster; rose 3, Harriett 1 1/2; 1860

1/23: George Newton 35; Richmond; Richmond; Farmer; Isaac CARRINGTON; Charlotte; Larinda Plummer 26; Richmond; Richmond; Richard LYELL; Richmond; Ø; 1852

1/24: Soloman Sanders 40; Richmond; Richmond; Farmer; John MITCHELL; Dead; Maria Levet 30; Richmond; Richmond; Arthur BARNARD; Richmond; Cloracy 14,m Elizabet 11, Soloman 9, John James 4, days, Edmund 8, Robert 6, Charles 4; 1851

1/25: Ka,es Samders 40; Richmond; Richmond; Farmer; John MITCHELL; Dead; Ann Palmer 35; Richmond; Richmond; Free; Ø; Lucinda 15, John James 13, Mary 11, James Nelson 10, Austin 8, Joseph 5 mos; 1850

1/26: Thomas Gibson 46; Richmond; Richmond; Farmer; John MITCHELL; Dead; Cina Newton 28; Richmond; Richmond; John MITCHELL; Dead; Soloman 12, Thomas 6, John 3, Lucy 1; 1852

1/27: Daniel Thompson 48; Richmond; Richmond; Farmer; Free; Ø; Hannah Newsome 48; Richmond; Richmond; Free; Ø; Virginia 17, Moses 13, Lucy 12, Prissy 6; 1848

1/28: William Winters 44; Westmoreland; Richmond; Farmer; Dr. W.H. FAIRFAX; Westmoreland; Becky Robinson 42; Essex; Richmond; Dr. W.H. FAIRFAX; Westmoreland; Humphry 12; 1852

1/29: Richard Truman 45; Richmond; Richmond; Farmer; John MITCHELL; Dead; Eliza Tucker 50; Richmond; Richmond; Free; Ø; Ø; 1830

1/30: Samuel Godard 48; Richmond; Richmond; Farmer; John MITCHELL; Dead; Sarah Laws 30; Richmond; Richmond; John MITCHELL; Dead; Adam 4; 1859

1/31: James Gordon 48; Richmond; Richmond; Farmer; John C. MITCHELL; Dead, Richmond; Mary Cox 37; Richmond; Richmond; Robert MITCHELL; Richmond; Martha 20, Alexander 18, William Gordon 16, Thomas 14, Celia 8; 1844

1/32: Cprme;ois Cpx 42' Richmond; Richmond; Far,er' Rpbert <OTCJE::' Richmond; Catjarome Tucks 38; Richmond; Richmond; robert MITCHELL; Richmond; Elizabeth 13, Mary 11, Travis 10, William 6, Laura 5, Robert & Peter, twins 1; 1852

1/33: Frank Spurlock 35; Henrico; Richmond; Farmer; Dr. WELLFORD; Sabine Hall, Richmond; Mariah Smith 28; Richmond; Richmond; robert MITCHELL; Richmond; Lucy Lewis 6, Augstin 3, Francis Ellen 1; 1858

1/34: Randall Gibson 60; Goochland; Richmond; Farmer; Dr. WELFORD; Sabine Hall, Richmond; Frances Maiden 39; Richmond; Richmond; Free; Ø; Ø; 1852

1/35: Martin Lewis 36; Westmoreland; Richmond; Farmer; John LAMKIN; Richmond; Lucy wiggins 25; Lancaster; Richmond; John LAMKIN; Richmond; Alfred 11, Millie 10, William 8, Moses 5, Jack 2; 1854

1/36: Stephen Bailey 23; Richmond; Richmond; Farmer; redman PERCEL; Richmond; Mariah Johnson 24; Richmond; Richmond; Moses SELF; Richmond; Laura 1; 1865

1/37: Joseph Scisson 41; Richmond; Richmond; Farmer; Free Born; Ø; Elizabeth Thompson 50; Westmoreland; Richmond; Free Born; Ø; Ø; 1849

1/38: Henry Henderson 42; Westmoreland; Richmond; Farmer; Mrs. Ann TAYLOR; Richmond; Lidia Veney 53; Richmond; Richmond; Free Born; Ø; Mary Frances 13; 1849

1/39: Peter Landon 69; Richmond; Richmond; Farmer; John MITCHELL; Richmond; Sophie Young 50; Richmond; Richmond; John MITCHELL; Richmond; Ø; 1844

2/1: William Mathews 43; Richmond; Richmond; Farmer; Arthur BEARNARD; Richmond; Easter Baylor 22; Richmond; Richmond; Dr. WELFORD; Sabine Hall, Richmond; Walter 6, Willie Ann 3, Bettie 5 mos; 1859

2/2: George Dandridge 49; Essex; Richmond; Farmer; William BANEM; Essex; Becky Holmes 35; Essex; Richmond; William BANEM; Essex; Edward 26, Alfred 25, Judy 22, Robert 18, Margrett 19, Georgeanna 8; 1837

2/3: Adam Canada 48; Richmond; Richmond; Farmer; Mrs. Lucy BRANHAM; Richmond; Becky Smith 25; Richmond; Richmond; Mrs. Lucy BRANHAM; Richmond; Simon 6, Eliza Ann 4, Georgeanna 2, Adam Canada 5 mos; 1859

2/4: Natt Garner 44; Westmoreland; Richmond; Farmer; Daniel ATWELL; Port Royal, Caroline; Abie Johnson 27; Richmond; Richmond; Daniel GARLAND; Richmond; Ø; 1856

~~Olmstead Jackson 44, Lancaster~~

2/5: Nelson Adkins 35; Richmond; Richmond; Farmer; Thomas BARRICKS; Richmond; Fannie Elms 35; Richmond; Richmond; Mrs. Lucy FLEET; Richmond; Laura Moore 13 mos; 1862

2/6: William Thompson 30; Richmond; Richmond; Farmer; Free Born; Ø; Ellen Holmes 25; Middlesex; Richmond; James BROWN; Richmond; James Henry 3; 1861

2/7: Daniel Johnson 23; Richmond; Richmond; Farmer; William MISCALL; Richmond; Lucy Conway 25; Nottoway; Richmond; Joseph WELLS; Dinwiddie; Ø; 1865

2/8: George Currie 40; Essex; Richmond; Farmer; William B__MAN; Essex; Frances Paine 30; Richmond; Richmond; Arthur BURNETT; Richmond; Virgina 12, Diana 9, Lucy 7, James 5, George 3; 1853

2/9: Cyrus Washington 60; Westmoreland; Richmond; Farmer; Juila GIBSON; Richmond; Peggy Godard 58; Richmond; Richmond; Julia GIBSON; Richmond; Becky 40; Adam 38; Henrietta 35, Lucy 28, Celia 26, Margarett 23, Easter 19, Elsie 15, Bell 12; 1825

~~Cen___ Gaines? 38; Westmoreland~~

2/10: Lewis Wadkins 36; Richmond; Richmond; Farmer; Henry LATHAM; Dead; Hannah Newton 25; Richmond; Richmond; Thomas SANDERS; Dead; Charles 6 mos; 1862

2/11: William Paris 33; Richmond; Richmond; Farmer; Henry HARWOOD; Richmond; Lucella Cox 30; Richmond; Richmond; Free Born; Ø; Matilda Ann 8, Ezekell 9 mos; 1857

2/12: Cornelius Ward 37; Richmond; Richmond; Farmer; Henry TAYLOR; Richmond; Mary Veney 28; Richmond; Richmond; Edward SANDERS; Richmond; Eliza 7; 1857

2/13: William Harrod 55; Richmond; Richmond; Farmer; Daniel GARLAND, Jr.; Richmond; Marth Ball 40; Richmond; Richmond; Free Born; Ø; Judy 5; 1853

2/14: William Napier 27; Richmond; Richmond; Farmer; Edward S. SANDERS; Richmond; Agnes Newton 25; Richmond; Richmond; William MAHUNDER?; Richmond; Lorinda 10, Emanuel 6, Julia 4, Rachel 3; 1862

2/15: Daniel Wheeler 19; Richmond; Richmond; Farmer; Olmsted BELFIELD; Richmond; Harriett Williams 26; Richmond; Richmond; John BROCKENBORO; Richmond; Austin 5, Lavinia 1; 1858

2/16: George Thomas 39; Richmond; Richmond; Carpenter; Henry TAYLOR; Richmond; Nancy Johnson 30; Westmoreland; Richmond; William R. HALL; Westmorland; John Henry 16, Thomas 12, George 10, Richard 4, Arthur 3, Julius 2; 1848

2/17: Henry Currey 50; Richmond; Richmond; Farmer; Mrs. Lucy FLEET; Richmond; Mary Smith 50; Richmond; Richmond; Mrs. Lucy FLEET; Richmond; Ø; 1846

2/18: Robert Jackson 47; Richmond; Richmond; Farmer; Free Born; Ø; Polley Bundy 46; Essex; Richmond; Free Born; Ø; Sophia 14, George Henry 12; 1852

2/19: Virgil Amos 24; Wilmington, No. Carolina; Richmond; Farmer; Rufus AMOS; Halifax; Martha Frances 20; Halifax; Richmond; Rufus AMOS; Halifax; Ø; 1843

2/20: Robert J. Gaston 28; Northumberland; Richmond; Farmer; William CORMON; Richmond; Lucy Green 25; Caroline; Richmond; Sanford R____S; Richmond; George Andrew 3, Dora 10 mos; 1862

2/21: Charles Johnson 45; Lancaster; Richmond; Farmer; A. DUNAWAY; Richmond; Rachel Page 38; Richmond; Richmond; George CRITCHER; Richmond; Hannah 15, Julius 13, Thomas 10, Charles 9, Armistead 18, ___ 6; 1845

2/22: James Jackson 50; Westmoreland; Richmond; Farmer; Matilda MIDDLETON; Richmond; Hannah Jenkins 45; Richmond; Richmond; Free; Ø; Ø; 1851

2/23: Aaron Fitchugh? 61; King George; Richmond; Farmer; Sidney LANE; Richmond; Lucinda Wood 60; Richmond; Richmond; Sidney LANE; Richmond; Peter 19; 1836

2/24: Sofford Godard 53; Richmond; Richmond; Farmer; John C. MITCHELL; Richmond; Amanda Beverly? 38; Caroline; Richmond; Henry HARROD?; Richmond; Emily 21, Daniel 18, Jesse 17, Stafford 15, Harrison 10, Andrew 8, Shadric 7, Peter; 1846

2/25: Daniel Foushee 35; King William; Richmond; Farmer; Dr. MIDDLETON; Richmond; Lucy Lorrill? 25; Richmond; Richmond; William PITTS; Richmond; Frank 13, Nellie 9, Henry 6, Sarah 2; 1852

2/26: ~~Jerry Venie 55; Richmond~~; Richmond; Farmer; Free; Ø; ~~Charlotte Vaney~~, Maria Atwell? 18; Ø; Ø; Thomas SHERMAN; Richmond; Ø; 186_

2/27: John Thompson 37; Richmond; Richmond; Farmer; Free; Ø; Eliza Veney 40; Richmond; Richmond; Free; Ø; Ø; 1836

2/28: Lewis Jones 40; Essex; Richmond; Farmer; William ENGLISH; Richmond; Ellen Diggs 26; Richmond; Richmond; Thomas ENGLISH; Richmond; Emily 8, Dolly 6, Milli__ 3; 1853

2/29: Bundy Rich 42; Richmond; Richmond; Farmer; Free; Ø; Mary Lewis 41; Lancaster; Richmond;; Free; Ø; Sarah 16, David 14, William 12, Milford 16, Beverly 7, Elizabeth 4, Anna 1; 1849

2/30: Thomas G. Thomas 54; Richmond; Richmond; Farmer; Henry TAYLOR; Richmond; Ann Palmer 46; Richmond; Richmond; Henry TAYLOR; Richmond; Ø; 1843

2/31: Elijah Williams 48; Richmond; Richmond; Farmer; Robert HOPKINS; Essex; Ellen Russ 28; Richmond; Richmond; Mary CHINA; Richmond; Harriett 6, Mary 3; 1860

2/32: Samuel Cl_ton 49; Richmond; Richmond; Farmer; Mary CHINA; Richmond; Henrietta Corbin 19; Richmond; Richmond; Free; Ø; Matilda 3, George Henry 4 mos; 1863

2/33: Gabriel? Adkins 60; Richmond; Richmond; Farmer; Mrs. BURNETT; Hanover; Fannie Castor 30; Richmond; Richmond; Robert HOPKINS; Richmond; Lydia 12, Susana 6, Lea 5, Georganna 4, Fannie 2 mos; 1854

2/34: Thomas Page 34; Richmond; Richmond; Farmer; George CUTCHER; Richmond; Sally Carter? 25; Richmond; Richmond; Henry LANDEN?; Richmond; William? 6, Thomas 3, John H. 1 mo?; 1856

2/35: Washington Veney 51; Richmond; Richmond; Farmer; Free; Ø; Fannie Jackson 36; Richmond; Richmond; Free; Ø; William? 21, Henry 16, Martha 15, Joseph 14, Cathrine 10, Washington 8, Becky 6, Prissa 3; 1844

2/36: Edward Carter 53; Northumberland; Richmond; Farmer; James LAMKIN; Richmond; Lucy Lamkin 52; Lancaster; Richmond; James LAMKIN; Richmond; Charles 12, Mason 9, Allen 21, Betsey 21; 1845

2/37: George Laws 38; Richmond City; Richmond; Farmer; J.C. MITCHELL; Richmond; Judy Gordon 38; Richmond City; Richmond; William MITCHELL; Richmond City; Daniel 15, Eliza 12, Gordon 9, George 6, Beckey 4; 1849

2/38: Henry Rich 45; Richmond City; Richmond; Farmer; Free; Ø; Peggy Maiden 40; Richmond City; Richmond; J.W. BELLFIELD; Richmond; Sidney 15, William? 13, Harriet 9, W__ 8, Anna 5, Clayborne 3, Fannie 1; 1849

2/39: Tasker Cupid 40; Richmond City; Richmond; Farmer; Richard BELLFIELD; Richmond; Laura Maiden 37; Richmond; Richmond; J.W. BELLFIELD; Richmond; Mildred 16, Cesetina? 14, Laura 12, Margarett 7, Archer 41, Hannah 1; 1849

3/1: Solomon Veney 28; Richmond; Richmond; Farmer; Free Born; Ø; Becky Thompson 27; Richmond; Richmond; Free Born; Ø; Ø; 1863

3/2: Thomas Barnes 52; Richmond; Richmond; Farmer; Richard BELLFIELD; Richmond; Chamie Denton; Richmond; Dead; William TAYLOR; Mt. Airy, Richmond; Cinga 9, Joseph 8, Erius 3; 1853

3/3: Gowen Corbin 32; Richmond; Richmond; Farmer; Benjamin TUCKER; Richmond; Catharine Corbin 25; Richmond; Richmond; Born Free; Ø; William Henry 4, Gowen C. 2; 1860

3/4: Simon Henderson 29; Richmond; Richmond; Farmer; Olmstead WELFORD; Richmond; Amanda Lathrup 28; Washington, No. Carolina; Richmond; John CORVINCE; Dansville; Ø; 1863

3/5: Henry Date 64; Richmond; Richmond; Farmer; Robert CARTER; Richmond; Cris Hughes 65; Richmond; Richmond; Robert CARTER; Richmond; Thomas Date 37; 1829

3/6: Joseph Blair 27; Richmond; Richmond; Farmer; Carter WELFORD; Richmond; Fannie More 27; Richmond; Richmond; Carter WELFORD; Richmond; Auther 1; 1865

3/7: William Jackson 62; Richmond; Richmond; Farmer; Born Free; Ø; Alsie Henry 50; Westmoreland; Richmond; Born Free; Ø; 1862

3/8: Benjamin Wright 55; Essex; Richmond; Farmer; Thomas WRIGHT; Essex; Emma Williams 30; Richmond; Richmond; William A. WRIGHT; Essex, Dead; Sarah Ann 2; 1861

3/9: Anderson Scott 60; King & Queen; Richmond; Farmer; William Alfred WRIGHT; Dead; Fannie Taylor 70; King & Queen; Richmond; William A. WRIGHT; Dead; Ø; 1836

3/10: Obadiah Robinson 30; King & Queen; Richmond; Farmer; Edward WARE; Essex; Harriett Jenkins 26; Richmond; Richmond; Free Born; Ø; Ø; 1865

3/11: Glasgo Newton 60; Westmoreland; Richmond; Farmer; Elizabeth PORTER; Fairfax; Ellen Smith 40; Westmoreland; Richmond; William PORTER; Dead; Matilda 15, Isabella 14, James Henry 11, Hannah 5; 1850

3/12: Charles Sykes 34; Sampson Co., No. Carolina; Richmond; Farmer; Henssil CLARK; Richmond; Easter Williams 40; Richmond; Richmond; Col. CARTER; Dead; Ø; 1866

3/13: John Moore 45; Richmond; Richmond; Farmer; William TAYLOR; Richmond; Julia Ward 25; Richmond; Richmond; Henry TAYLOR; Richmond; Ø; 1864

3/14: James Ball 42; Westmoreland; Richmond; Farmer; Born Free; Ø; Evalina Moore 35; Richmond; Richmond; Henry TAYLOR; Richmond; Virginia 3; 1862

3/15: William Miles 60; Richmond; Richmond; Farmer; John BROCKENBORO; Richmond; Alsie Johnson 60; Mathews; Richmond; Lucy BROCKENBORO; Richmond; Ø; 1836

3/16: Daniel Street 53; Richmond; Richmond; Farmer; John BROCKENBORO; Richmond; Sopha Bray 59; Richmond; Richmond; Edward BROCKENBORO; Dead; Ø; 1846

3/17: Goen Corbin 60; Richmond; Richmond; Farmer; Lucy FLEET; Richmond; Rose Brown 40; King William; Richmond; Lucy FLEET; Richmond; Henry 40, Harriett 36, John 30, Robert 25, Octavio 20, Mary 18, William 15, Thomas 12, Laura? 6; 1826

3/18: George Newton 35; Richmond; Richmond; Farmer; Isaac C. CARRINGTON; Charlotte; Lorinda Plummer 26; Richmond; Richmond; Richard LYELL; Richmond; Ø; 1854

3/19: Griffin Rich 67; Richmond; Richmond; Farmer; Free Born; Ø; Jane Cox 40; Richmond; Richmond; John C. MICHELL; Richmond; Thomas 26, Mary 23, Peter 21, William 20, Emma 14, Kindsey? 11, Frank 3; 1825

3/20: Peter Garrett 37; King & Queen; Richmond; Farmer; George W. DILLERT; Essex; Betsey Roy 36; Essex; Richmond; Oscar YEARBY; Dead; Mary 13, George 12, Sofrona 10, Polly 7, Banam 1; 1849

3/21: John Carter 35; Richmond; Richmond; Oysterman; Harry SAUNDERS; Richmond; Ellen Waddy; 20; Richmond; Richmond; Peter RICE; Richmond; Lattie 6, Tanna 5, Emma 1; 1856

3/22: John Willis 30; Essex; Richmond; Farmer; William BENNAM; Essex; Margarett Holmes 30; Essex; Richmond; William BENNAM; Essex; Ø; 1863

3/23: Benjamin Lewis 38; Richmond; Richmond; Farmer; Richard LYELL; Richmond; Mariah Bailey 30; Richmond; Richmond; Henry LYELL; Richmond; Laura Virginia Betts 8, John Dandridge 13, Mary Elizabeth 10, Jennie 15, Lucy 12, Susan 17, Daniel; 1850

3/24: Davis Sarrell 60; Richmond; Richmond; Farmer; William PITTS; Richmond; Ellen Conelly 32; Richmond; Richmond; William PITTS; Richmond; Ø; 1836?

3/25: Daniel Veney 47; Richmond; Richmond; Farmer; Born Free; Ø; Virginia Jones 23; Richmond; Richmond; William PORTER; Dead; Frances Ann 15, Harriett Elizabeth; 1864

3/26: Humphrey Veney 56; Richmond; Richmond; Farmer; Born Free; Ø; Betsey Rich 52; Richmond; Richmond; Born Free; Ø; Griffin 36, Jeremiah 30, Major 23, Emaline 28; 1834

3/27: Jessie Hackett 37; Westmoreland; Richmond; Miller; Elizabeth HARRISON; Westmoreland; Jane Henderson 35; Northumberland; Richmond; Born Free; Ø; Rosella 14, Josephine 11, Luellyn 5, Martha 4, John 18 mos; 1845

3/28: David Smith 53; Richmond; Richmond; Carpenter; Daniel PORTER; Westmoreland; Elsie Booden 43; Richmond; Richmond; Daniel PORTER; Dead; Joshua 14, Moses 13, Elrias? 12, Edward 4, Mary 3, 1846

3/29: Robert Rich 60; Richmond; Richmond; Farmer; Free Born; Ø; Betsey Johnson 30; Richmond; Richmond; Free Born; Ø; Ø; 1864

3/30: George Eatman 61; Richmond; Richmond; Farmer; Henry TAYLOR; Richmond; Winnie Moore 47; Richmond; Richmond; Henry TAYLOR; Richmond; Sarah 24, Horace 21, Ruffin 15, Judy 13, Marcus 9, John 4; 1847

3/31: Jasper Wright 24; Lancaster; Richmond; Farmer; Hemp_l CLARK; Richmond; Julia Brooks 23; Richmond; Richmond; Walter BROKENBORO; Richmond; Henry 1; 1865

3/32: Cornelius Locus? 42; Richmond; Richmond; Farmer; Robert CARTER; Dead; Rebecca Willis 45; Richmond; Richmond; Robert CARTER; Dead; Betsey Ann 2; 1854

3/33: Matt Cox 45; Cumberland; Richmond; Farmer; Doctor WALKER; Goochland; Sarah Newton 25; Richmond; Richmond; Robert CARTER; Dead; Washington 7 mos; 1862

3/34: Thomas Clay 60; Pittsylvania; Richmond; Farmer; John FURGERSON; Pittsylvania; Matilda Newton 20; Richmond; Richmond; Robert CARTER; Dead; William 2; 1863

3/35: Leroy Beech 23; Richmond; Richmond; Farmer; Free Born; Ø; Ann Fulet 27; Richmond; Richmond; Thomas HOWARD; Richmond; Ø; 1861

3/36: Jerry Middleton 55; Northumberland; Richmond; Carpenter; Thomas ALEXANDER; Northumberland; Lavina Gilmore 51; Richmond; Richmond; William John JUBEE; Richmond; Willie 23, James 21, Jerry 16; 1838

3/37: Jacob Wright 56; Richmond; Richmond; Farmer; Carter WELFRD; Richmond; Lucilla Willis 52; Richmond; Richmond; Carter WELFORD; Richmond; Ø; 1830

3/38: Joseph Thompson 30; Richmond; Richmond; Farmer; Free Born; Ø; Arretta Hudson? 26; Richmond; Richmond; Betsey PORTER; Richmond; Warren 19, Arthur 8, William 6, Henry 1; 1852

3/39: Richard Armstrong 52; Richmond; Richmond; Farmer; William CARRY?; Westmoreland; Milley Bailey 50; Westmoreland; Richmond; Joseph MOON; Northumberland; W_ Ann 28, James 27, Bett A.? 18, Mary 17, Susan 13; 1837

4/1: Cyrus Gillis 40; Spotsylvania; Richmond; Farmer; Arthur BERNARD; Richmond; Judy Muse 30; Richmond; Richmond; Arthur BEARNARD; Richmond; Salley 13, Susan 11, John 10, Newton 8, Silas 6, Peter 4, William 1; 1854

4/2: Charles Clayton 35; Richmond; Richmond; Farmer; Arthur BERNARD; Richmond; Polley David 28; Richmond; Richmond; Arthur BEARNARD; Richmond; Thomas 9, Isiah 8, Warner 4, Josiah 2; 1856

4/3: George Jackson 38; Richmond; Richmond; Farmer; N.T. BOLLISTON; Richmond; Jane Scott 28; Richmond; Richmond; Arthur BEARNARD; Richmond; Henry 8, Emma 4; 1856

4/4: Austin Wheeler 60; Richmond; Richmond; Dining Room Servant; William F. BROCKENBORO; Richmond; Lucinda Barrett 53; Richmond; Richmond; Carter WELFORD; Richmond; Julia 33, Katy 32, Daniel 25, Lavenia 25; 1832

4/5: Ruffin Moore 49; Prince William; Richmond; Farmer; Henry TAYLOR; Richmond; Sarah Winston 48; Richmond; Richmond; Carter WELFORD; Richmond; Sarah 3; 1860

4/6: Charles Patrick 25; York; Richmond; Farmer; Edmund WINN; York; Alsie Hill 19; Richmond; Richmond; Carter WELFORD; Richmond; Ø; 1866

4/7: George Shackleford 30; Richmond; Richmond; Laborer; Rohn SHACKLEFORD; Richmond; Mariah Gaskin 26; Northumberland; Northumberland; William BOOTH; Northumberland; Betty Alice 1, Walter 9, Lucy Jane 7, Ocha 4; 1856

4/8: George Robinson 43; Westmoreland; Richmond; Oysterman; Warner H. BANK; Lancaster; Martha Clark 28; Northumberland; Richmond; F. BARNES; Northumberland; Julia Ann 7, Margarett 6, Louisa? 3, John 1

4/9: Mose Blue 31; Richmond; Richmond; Laborer; Free; Ø; Betsey Newton 31; Richmond; Richmond; Ø; Ø; Nancy Ann 11, Mary Jane Hestra 8, John B. Mitchel 7, Lidia Ann 3

4/10: Joseph Bla__ 61; Richmond; Richmond; Laborer; Caroline CLARK; Richmond; Agnes Moore 31; Richmond; Richmond; Caroline CLARK; Richmond; Malinda 16

~~Willie C. Johnson 6; Richmond; Richmond; Farmer; Born Free; Ø~~

4/12: Mortimore Maden 28; Richmond; Richmond; Farmer; Born Free; Ø; Eliza Hall 20; Richmond; Richmond; John BROKENBROUGH; Richmond; Caroline 7; 1863

4/13: William A. Ball 27; Richmond; Richmond; Farmer; Born Free; Ø; Susan Henry 25; Richmond; Richmond; Born Free; Ø; Buckanna 9, Mary A. 5, William A.A. 13 mos; 1860

4/14: Thomas Davis 60; Richmond; Richmond; Farmer; Benedict CRABB; Westmoreland; Judah Taylor 30; Westmoreland; Richmond; Richard MOXLEY; Westmoreland; Elizabeth 21, Thomas 15, Joseph 13, Susan 13, Francis 11, Milton 7, Geeson? 4; 1856

4/15: Stephen Brooks 45; Essex; Richmond; Laborer; John W. DISHMAN; Richmond; Mahala Gordon 21; Richmond; Richmond; William MORRIS; Richmond; Ø; Aug 1864

4/16: Peter Henry 70; King & Queen; Richmond; Farmer; Henry HOWARD; Richmond; Ellen Smith 48; Richmond; Richmond; Mrs. Mary H. MITCHELL; Richmond; Peter 3, Easter 16, Anderson 12, Lucy E. 10, Alice 6; 1846

4/17: Payne Davis 49; Richmond; Richmond; Farmer; William K. MORRIS; Richmond; Martha A. Coats 22; Appomattox; Richmond; William K. MORRIS; Richmond; Leroy 6, Henry 3, Joseph 2; 1860

4/18: Louis Davis 33; King George; Richmond; Farmer; William K. MORRIS; Richmond; Mary Mitchell 23; King George; Richmond; William K. MORRIS; Richmond; Caroline 12, James 8, Charles 5, Moses 3; 1861

4/19: Harry Lee 60; Richmond; Richmond; Farmer; William E. HILL; Richmond; Jennie Atkins 58; Richmond; Richmond; Mrs. Mary BRANNUM; Richmond; Laurence 18, Mariah 10, Elizabeth 7; 1847

4/20: Robert Lewis 38; Richmond; Richmond; Farmer; William F. BROCKENBRAGH; Richmond; Ratha Smith 43; Richmond; Richmond; W.T. BROCKENBRAGH; Richmond

4/21: William Burle 51; Westmoreland; Richmond; Farmer; Born Free; Ø; Ellen Ball 50; Westmoreland; Richmond; Born Free; Ø; Isadora 5, Maria _. 21, George 15, Thomas 14, Arcissa/Areissa 9; 1842

4/22: Lucius Lewis 22; Northumberland; Richmond; Farmer; Syrus HOO_L; Richmond; Frances? Snyder 21; Richmond; Richmond; Albert YERBY; Richmond; Charles Lewis 3; 1862

Dennis Johnson 2 ; Westmoreland; Richmond; Laborer; William O'Mohandrith?; Alexandria; Polly Johnson 60; Westmoreland; 1812

4/23: Juby Urgham 73; Richmond; Richmond; Farmer; W.W. RAINES; Richmond; Lucy Williams 80; Richmond; Richmond; W.W. RAINES; Richmond

4/24: Nathaniel Carter 55; Prince William; Richmond; Farmer; William G.? WARE; Fluvanna; Frances Hanus? 50; Richmond; Richmond; Born Free; Ø; Charles 21, Nathaniel 18; 1836

4/25: Joseph Gaskins 31; Richmond; Richmond; Carpenter; Thomas LITTERAL; Washington City; Harriett Henderson 28; Richmond; Richmond; Alexander BRYANT; Richmond; Mary Jane 7, Josephine 4, Richard 3, Pegg 2 mos; 1858

4/26: Oliver Tolls 40; Northumberland; Richmond; Farmer; James LAMPKIN; Richmond; Cresa Wares; Westmoreland; Dead; Joseph CLARK; Northumberland; Martha 17, Caroline 15, Emily 12, Lucinda 8, A__dia 6, Cornelia 5; Cora; 1841

4/27: Elijah Yerby 46; Richmond; Richmond; Farmer; Albert YERBY; Richmond; Winnie Madin 30; Richmond; Richmond; Mrs. Gray? FLEET; Richmond; Augusta 8; 1853

4/28: Jessie Veney 38; Richmond; Richmond; Farmer; Born Free; Ø; Philitia Jones 36; Westmoreland; Richmond; Born Free; Ø; Henry 3, Hannah A. 2 days, Sarah J. 13?, Mack J. 7, Camile 5; 1854

4/29: William Brown 41; Richmond; Richmond; Farmer; Mrs. Mary BRANNUM; Dead; Susan Martin 31; Richmond; Richmond; Joseph WALLACE; Richmond; Catharine 14; 1849

4/30: Ch__s N. Johnson 61; Westmoreland; Richmond; Farmer; Born Free; Ø; Ann Lewis 47; Westmoreland; Richmond; Born Free; Ø; Andrew L. 15, Sarah 12, Fred K.N. 10, Robert D. 8, William A. 25, Thomas S. 23, James E. 21, Mary E. 18; 1839

4/31: Nacio Glasgo 41; Richmond; Richmond; House Servant; Carter WELFORD; Richmond; Julia Wheeler 33; Richmond; Richmond; Carter WELFORD; Richmond; Mary Bubeula? 8, James Henry 3, Landon 10, Lucinda 2 mos

4/32: Thomas Rich 26; Richmond; Richmond; Farmer; Born Free; Ø; Judah Norris 29; Richmond; Richmond; Dr. William DOUGLAS; Richmond; Henry 15, Eliza 10, Fannie 5; 1863

4/33: William Wood 34; Richmond; Richmond; Farmer; Jerry WEBB; Richmond; Martha Palmer 32; Richmond; Richmond; Edward FLEET; Richmond; Clarence 9, Robert 8, William 2 mos; 1849

4/34: William Lewis 34; Northumberland; Richmond; Oysterman; Mrs. Rebecca SCOTT; Richmond; Elizabeth Carter 26; Lancaster; Richmond; Littleton MITCHELL; Richmond; Charles 15, Roberta 14, Wesley 13, Louisa 6, Emma 4; 1836

4/35: Peter Newton? 26; Richmond; Richmond; Farmer; Free Born; Ø; Eliza Joan Hackett 23; Westmoreland; Richmond; Free Born; Ø; Harriett, Elijah 3, John 1; 1862

4/36: N._eanilton 41; Richmond; Richmond; Farmer; Free Born; Ø; Mary Newton 36; Richmond; Richmond; Free Born; Ø; Eliza Ann 15, Josephus? 12, Henrietta 9, Isabella 6, Betsey 2; 1851

4/37: Peter Jenkins 35; Richmond; Richmond; Farmer; Free Born; Ø; Haney Thompson 36; Richmond; Richmond; Free Born; Ø; Harry 14, 1849

4/38: Daniel Jenkins 39; Richmond; Richmond; Farmer; Free Born; Ø; Mary Thompson 37; Richmond; Richmond; Free Born; Ø; John 10, Nancy 7, Anna 1; 1855

Table 22: Roanoke County, VA

Register of Children of Colored Persons whose Parents had ceased to cohabit which the Father recognizes to be his

(pg/line; child/age; pob; res; last owner; res; f res; f age, f/last owner; res; m/age; m/res, m/last owner; res; f name)

1/1: David Bruce 27; Henrico; Roanoke; D.S. REED; Roanoke; Roanoke; 47; D.S. REED; Roanoke; Crecey; Dead; D.S. REED; Roanoke; Billy Bruce

1/2: Aleck Bruce 25; Henrico; Roanoke; D.S. REED; Roanoke; Roanoke; 47; D.S. REED; Roanoke; Crecey; Dead; D.S. REED; Roanoke; Billy Bruce

1/3: Marshall Bruce 23; Henrico; Roanoke; D.S. REED; Roanoke; Roanoke; 47; D.S. REED; Roanoke; Crecey; Dead; D.S. REED; Roanoke; Billy Bruce

1/4: Susan Bruce 21; Henrico; Roanoke; D.S. REED; Roanoke; Roanoke; 47; D.S. REED; Roanoke; Crecey; Dead; D.S. REED; Roanoke; Billy Bruce

1/5: Betty Bruce 19; Henrico; Roanoke; D.S. REED; Roanoke; Roanoke; 47; D.S. REED; Roanoke; Crecey; Dead; D.S. REED; Roanoke; Billy Bruce

1/6: Richard Bruce 17; Henrico; Roanoke; D.S. REED; Roanoke; Roanoke; 47; D.S. REED; Roanoke; Crecey; Dead; D.S. REED; Roanoke; Billy Bruce

1/7: Napoleon Bruce 14; Henrico; Roanoke; D.S. REED; Roanoke; Roanoke; 47; D.S. REED; Roanoke; Crecey; Dead; D.S. REED; Roanoke; Billy Bruce

1/8: Ben Bruce 12; Henrico; Roanoke; D.S. REED; Roanoke; Roanoke; 47; D.S. REED; Roanoke; Crecey; Dead; D.S. REED; Roanoke; Billy Bruce

1/9: ~~Horace Langhorne 12;~~ Roanoke; Roanoke; F. SORRELL; Ø; Roanoke; Ø; Ø; Roanoke; Ø; Ø; D.S. REED

1/10: Henry Langhorne 5; Roanoke; Roanoke; F. SORRELL; Roanoke; Roanoke; 28; F. SORRELL; Roanoke; Martha; Dead; W. WATTS; Roanoke; George Langhorne

1/11: Mary Jeffers 13; Roanoke; Roanoke; C. BANDY; Roanoke; Roanoke; 30; William KEFAUVER; Roanoke; Judy; Dead; C. BANDY; Roanoke; James Jeffers

1/12: Greene Jeffers 12; Roanoke; Roanoke; C. BANDY; Roanoke; Roanoke; 30; William KEFAUVER; Roanoke; Judy; Dead; C. BANDY; Roanoke; James Jeffers

1/13: Rosetta Jeffers 8 Roanoke; Roanoke; C. BANDY; Roanoke; Roanoke; 30; William KEFAUVER; Roanoke; Judy; Dead; C. BANDY; Roanoke; James Jeffers

1/14: Ellen Jeffers 15; Roanoke; Roanoke; Jim PERSINGER; Roanoke; Roanoke; 45; Jacob PERSINGER; Roanoke; Vina; Dead; Jim PERSINGER; Roanoke; Albert Jeffers

1/15: Amanda Jeffers 7; Roanoke; Roanoke; Jacob PERSINGER; Roanoke; Roanoke; 45; Jacob PERSINGER; Roanoke; Vina; Dead; Jim PERSINGER; Roanoke; Albert Jeffers

1/16: Washington Jeffers 19; Roanoke; Roanoke; William PERSINGER; Roanoke; Roanoke; 45; Jacob PERSINGER; Roanoke; Vina; Dead; Jim PERSINGER; Roanoke; Albert Jeffers

1/17: Stephen Monroe 14; Roanoke; Roanoke; N. BURRILL; Roanoke; Roanoke; 45; N. BURRILL; Roanoke; Molly; Dead; N. BURRILL; Roanoke; Henry Monroe

1/18: Isabella Monroe 12; Roanoke; Roanoke; N. BURRILL; Roanoke; Roanoke; 45; N. BURRILL; Roanoke; Molly; Dead; N. BURRILL; Roanoke; Henry Monroe

1/19: Ellen Geary 9; Roanoke; Roanoke; John NEFF; Roanoke; Roanoke; 41; Jacob TROUT; Roanoke; Lucy; Dead; J. RIBBLE; Roanoke; Robert Geary

1/20: Betty G. Geary 5; Roanoke; Roanoke; J. MILLER; Roanoke; Roanoke; 41; Jacob TROUT; Roanoke; Harriet; Dead; M. MILLER; Roanoke; Robert Geary

1/21: Minerva Journot 8; Roanoke; Roanoke; D.S. REED; Roanoke; Roanoke; 38; Matilda OLIVER; Roanoke; Sethe; Dead; D.S. REED; Roanoke; Patrick Journot

1/22: Susan Journot 6; Roanoke; Roanoke; D.S. REED; Roanoke; Roanoke; 38; Matilda OLIVER; Roanoke; Sethe; Dead; D.S. REED; Roanoke; Patrick Journot

1/23: Sam Marshal 21; Botetourt; Roanoke; Frances WALTON; Roanoke; Roanoke; 49; D. SHANKS; Roanoke; Charlotte; Dead; Mrs. CRUSE; Botetourt; Edmund Marshal

1/24: Dave Marshal 19; Botetourt; Roanoke; Frances WALTON; Roanoke; Roanoke; 49; D. SHANKS; Roanoke; Charlotte; Dead; Mrs. CRUSE; Botetourt; Edmund Marshal

1/25: Ann Marshal 20; Botetourt; Roanoke; William COUCH; Botetourt; Roanoke; 49; D. SHANKS; Roanoke; Charlotte; Dead; Mrs. CRUSE; Botetourt; Edmund Marshal

1/26: Patsey Marshal 16; Botetourt; Roanoke; Frances WALTON; Roanoke; Roanoke; 49; D. SHANKS; Roanoke; Charlotte; Dead; Mrs. CRUSE; Botetourt; Edmund Marshal

1/27: Harriet Washington 8; Botetourt; Roanoke; R. THAXTON; Roanoke; Roanoke; 31; Nancy CHAPMAN; Roanoke; Lucinda; Dead; R. THAXTON; Botetourt; Randall Washington

1/28: John H. Washington 6; Roanoke; Roanoke; R. THAXTON; Roanoke; Roanoke; 31; Nancy CHAPMAN; Roanoke; Lucinda; Dead; R. THAXTON; Roanoke; Randall Washington

1/29: Margaret Otey; Roanoke; Roanoke; Peggy VINYARD; Roanoke; Roanoke; 39; William B. PRESTON; Roanoke; Ann; Roanoke; Peggy VINYARD; Roanoke; Omstead Otey

1/30: Laura Otey 8; Roanoke; Roanoke; Peggy VINYARD; Roanoke; Roanoke; 39; William B. PRESTON; Roanoke; Ann; Roanoke; Peggy VINYARD; Roanoke; Omstead Otey

1/31: Mit Otey 3; Roanoke; Roanoke; Peggy VINYARD; Roanoke; Roanoke; 39; William B. PRESTON; Roanoke; Ann; Roanoke; Peggy VINYARD; Roanoke; Omstead Otey

1/32: Charles Otey 2; Roanoke; Roanoke; Peggy VINYARD; Roanoke; Roanoke; 39; William B. PRESTON; Roanoke; Ann; Roanoke; Peggy VINYARD; Roanoke; Omstead Otey

1/33: Sarah Otey 5; Roanoke; Roanoke; Peggy VINYARD; Roanoke; Roanoke; 39; William B. PRESTON; Roanoke; Ann; Roanoke; Peggy VINYARD; Roanoke; Omstead Otey

1/34: Louisa Wade 8; Bedford; Botetourt; William A. WADE; Bedford; Roanoke; 36; William A. WADE; Bedford; Eliza; Dead; W.A. WADE; Bedford; Phil Wade

2/1: James H. Davis 2; Lynchburg; Washington; Richard WADE; Lynchburg; Roanoke; 24; S.B. ZIMMERMAN; Baltimore, Maryland; Margaret 20; Bristol, Tennessee; Richard WADE; Lynchburg; R.P. Davis

2/2: Monroe Whitlock 6; Roanoke; Roanoke; William HATCHER; Roanoke; Roanoke; 51; William JOHNSON; Roanoke; Ann; Dead; William HATCHER; Roanoke; Titus Whitlock

2/3: Randall Whitlock 4; Roanoke; Roanoke; William HATCHER; Roanoke; Roanoke; 51; William JOHNSON; Roanoke; Ann; Dead; William HATCHER; Roanoke; Titus Whitlock

2/4: Phoebe Ann Banks 17; Bedford; Roanoke; G.B. BOARD; Roanoke; Roanoke; 38; William A. STAPLES; Bedford; Lucinda; Dead; R. THAXTON; Roanoke; Isaac Banks

2/5: Ellen Banks 15; Franklin; Roanoke; G.B. BOARD; Roanoke; Roanoke; 38; William A. STAPLES; Bedford; Lucinda; Dead; R. THAXTON; Roanoke; Isaac Banks

2/6: Tom Banks 14; Bedford; Roanoke; R. THAXTON; Roanoke; Roanoke; 38; William A. STAPLES; Bedford; Lucinda; Dead; R. THAXTON; Roanoke; Isaac Banks

2/7: Thornton Homes 21; Roanoke; Roanoke; Ira JETER; Roanoke; Roanoke; 57; F. SORRELL; Roanoke; Peggy; Roanoke; Ira JETER; Roanoke; Hector Homes

2/8: Moses Owens 17; Roanoke; Roanoke; J.H. SMITH; Roanoke; Roanoke; 46; J.H. SMITH; Roanoke; Nancy; Dead; J.H. SMITH; Roanoke; Stepney Owens

2/9: Columbus Banks 19; Roanoke; Roanoke; Sally MILLER; Roanoke; Roanoke; 42; Sperral F. SIMMONS; Roanoke; Harriet; Dead; J. MILLER; Roanoke; Warner Banks

2/10: Ann Banks 18; Roanoke; Roanoke; Sally MILLER; Roanoke; Roanoke; 42; Sperral F. SIMMONS; Roanoke; Harriet; Dead; J. MILLER; Roanoke; Warner Banks

2/11: Ellen Banks 16; Roanoke; Roanoke; K. KAIZER; Roanoke; Roanoke; 42; Sperral F. SIMMONS; Roanoke; Harriet; Dead; J. MILLER; Roanoke; Warner Banks

2/12: James Banks 14; Roanoke; Roanoke; J. MILLER; Roanoke; Roanoke; 42; Sperral F. SIMMONS; Roanoke; Harriet; Dead; J. MILLER; Roanoke; Warner Banks

2/13: Peyton Banks 10; Roanoke; Roanoke; Susan MILLER; Roanoke; Roanoke; 42; Sperral F. SIMMONS; Roanoke; Harriet; Dead; J. MILLER; Roanoke; Warner Banks

2/14: Henry Chalmerns/Chalmems 19; Botetourt; Roanoke; M. MOORMAN; Roanoke; Roanoke; 55; J.H. SMITH; Roanoke; Malinda; Roanoke; William WATTS; Roanoke; William Chalmerns/Chalmems

2/15: Sally Chalmerns/Chalmems 18; Roanoke; Lynchburg; M. MOORMAN; Roanoke; Roanoke; 55; J.H. SMITH; Roanoke; Malinda; Roanoke; William WATTS; Roanoke; William Chalmerns/Chalmems

2/16: Rosa L. Chalmerns/Chalmems 9; Botetourt; Roanoke; M. MOORMAN; Roanoke; Roanoke; 55; J.H. SMITH; Roanoke; Malinda; Roanoke; William WATTS; Roanoke; William Chalmerns/Chalmems

2/17: James E. Beale 21; Roanoke; Bedford; G.W. CARR; Roanoke; Roanoke; 49; William ROBINSON; Roanoke; Mary; Roanoke; William WATTS; Roanoke; London Beale

2/18: Sally Beale 18; Roanoke; Roanoke; J.P. HOLCOMB; Roanoke; Roanoke; 49; William ROBINSON; Roanoke; Mary; Roanoke; William WATTS; Roanoke; London Beale

2/19: Mary Beale 15; Roanoke; Roanoke; William ROBINSON; Roanoke; Roanoke; 49; William ROBINSON; Roanoke; Mary; Roanoke; William WATTS; Roanoke; London Beale

2/20: John Beale 12; Roanoke; Roanoke; William ROBINSON; Roanoke; Roanoke; 49; William ROBINSON; Roanoke; Mary; Roanoke; William WATTS; Roanoke; London Beale

2/21: Martha A. Beale 8; Roanoke; Roanoke; William ROBINSON; Roanoke; Roanoke; 49; William ROBINSON; Roanoke; Mary; Roanoke; William WATTS; Roanoke; London Beale

2/22: Moses Spurlock 18; Roanoke; Roanoke; T. EVANS; Roanoke; Roanoke; 44; T. EVANS; Roanoke; Matilda; Ø; Ø; Ø; Ø; Almstead Spurlock

2/23: Betsey Cuff 17; Roanoke; Bedford; Fannie PETTY; Roanoke; Roanoke; 52; Free; Ø; Lucinda; Dead; John GRIFFIN; Roanoke; Henry? Cuff

2/24: Martha J. Brown 13; Roanoke; Roanoke; William B. PRESTON; Roanoke; Roanoke; 60; A. REED; Roanoke; Lucinda; Roanoke; William B. PRESTON; Roanoke; Thomas Brown

2/25: Eli Hackley 13; Amherst; Roanoke; H. HANSBOROUGH; Roanoke; Roanoke; 36; H. HANSBOROUGH; Roanoke; Mimy; Dead; H. HANSBOURGH; John Hackley

2/26: Fanny Hackley 11; Amherst; Roanoke; H. HANSBOROUGH; Roanoke; Roanoke; 36; H. HANSBOROUGH; Roanoke; Mimy; Dead; H. HANSBOURGH; John Hackley

2/27: Maria Hackley 9; Amherst; Roanoke; H. HANSBOROUGH; Roanoke; Roanoke; 36; H. HANSBOROUGH; Roanoke; Mimy; Dead; H. HANSBOURGH; John Hackley

2/28: Sam Hackley 6; Roanoke; Roanoke; H. HANSBOROUGH; Roanoke; Roanoke; 36; H. HANSBOROUGH; Roanoke; Mimy; Dead; H. HANSBOURGH; John Hackley

2/29: George Lewis 17; Roanoke; Roanoke; Nancy CHAPMAN; Roanoke; Roanoke; 64; G.G. HARTMAN; Roanoke; Sally; Franklin; Nancy CHAPMAN; Roanoke; Ned Lewis

2/30: Becky Marshal 23; Botetourt; Roanoke; G.P. TAYLOE; Roanoke; Roanoke; 64; George P. TAYLOE; Roanoke; Phamy; Dead; G.P. TAYLOE; Roanoke; Frank Marshal

2/31: Ailsy Marshal 17; Roanoke; Roanoke; G.P. TAYLOE; Roanoke; Roanoke; 64; George P. TAYLOE; Roanoke; Phamy; Dead; G.P. TAYLOE; Roanoke; Frank Marshal

2/32: Thornton Marshal 15; Roanoke; Roanoke; G.P. TAYLOE; Roanoke; Roanoke; 64; George P. TAYLOE; Roanoke; Phamy; Dead; G.P. TAYLOE; Roanoke; Frank Marshal

2/33: ~~Wesley~~ Marshal 4; Roanoke; Roanoke; G.P. TAYLOE; Roanoke; Roanoke; 64; George P. TAYLOE; Roanoke; Phamy; Dead; G.P. TAYLOE; Roanoke; Frank Marshal

2/34: Lucy Gilbert 17; Roanoke; Roanoke; G.P. TAYLOE; Roanoke; Roanoke; George P. TAYLOE; Roanoke; Cina; Dead; G.P. TAYLOE; Roanoke; John Gilbert

3/1: George Hunt 25; Henrico; Roanoke; D.S. REED; Roanoke; Roanoke 53; D.S. REED; Roanoke; Elsie; Dead; D.S. REED; Roanoke; Solomon Hunt

3/2: Royal Hunt 23; Henrico; Roanoke; D.S. REED; Roanoke; Roanoke 53; D.S. REED; Roanoke; Elsie; Dead; D.S. REED; Roanoke; Solomon Hunt

3/3: Parthena Hunt 20; Henrico; Roanoke; D.S. REED; Roanoke; Roanoke 53; D.S. REED; Roanoke; Elsie; Dead; D.S. REED; Roanoke; Solomon Hunt

3/4: Minna Hunt 18; Henrico; Roanoke; D.S. REED; Roanoke; Roanoke 53; D.S. REED; Roanoke; Elsie; Dead; D.S. REED; Roanoke; Solomon Hunt

3/5: Brandon Hunt 18; Henrico; Roanoke; D.S. REED; Roanoke; Roanoke 53; D.S. REED; Roanoke; Elsie; Dead; D.S. REED; Roanoke; Solomon Hunt

3/6: Nelly Hunt 16; Henrico; Roanoke; D.S. REED; Roanoke; Roanoke 53; D.S. REED; Roanoke; Elsie; Dead; D.S. REED; Roanoke; Solomon Hunt

3/7: Pompey Hunt 14; Henrico; Roanoke; D.S. REED; Roanoke; Roanoke 53; D.S. REED; Roanoke; Elsie; Dead; D.S. REED; Roanoke; Solomon Hunt

3/8: Doctor Hunt 11; Roanoke; Roanoke; D.S. REED; Roanoke; Roanoke 53; D.S. REED; Roanoke; Elsie; Dead; D.S. REED; Roanoke; Solomon Hunt

3/9: Fanny White 15; Franklin; Roanoke; J. KEFAUVER; Floyd; Roanoke; Charles ROTTER; Franklin; Emily

3/10: William White 13

3/11: Harriet White 6

3/12: Sarah White 12; Franklin; Roanoke; J. KEFAUVER; Floyd; Roanoke; Charles ROTTER; Franklin

3/13: Maria Wurts 30; Roanoke; Roanoke; James PERSINGER; Roanoke; Roanoke; 66; James PERSINGER; Roanoke; Linda; Dead; J. McCRANDER; Roanoke; Frank Wurts

3/14: Charles Wurts 23; Roanoke; Roanoke; James PERSINGER; Roanoke; Roanoke; 66; James PERSINGER; Roanoke; Linda; Dead; J. McCRANDER; Roanoke; Frank Wurts

3/15: Julia Ann Taylor 20; Franklin; Franklin; Ed POWELL; Franklin; Roanoke; 44; Isam FERGUSON; Roanoke; Sarah J. Dead; E. POWELL; Farnklin; Jordan TAYLOR

3/16: Abraham Taylor 18; Ø; Ø; Ed POWELL; Franklin; Ø; Ø; Ø; Ø; Sarah J.

3/17: Louisa Taylor 17; Ø; Roanoke; Ed POWELL; Franklin; Ø; Ø; Ø; Ø; Sarah J.

3/18: Fannie Taylor 16; Ø; Roanoke; Ed POWELL; Franklin; Ø; Ø; Ø; Ø; Sarah J.

3/19: Bettie Taylor 11; Ø; ROANOKE; Ed POWELL; Franklin; Ø; Ø; Ø; Ø; Sarah J.; Ø; E. POWELL; Franklin

3/20: Marsella Taylor 10; Ø; Franklin; Armstead BURRILL; Franklin; Ø; Ø; Ø; Ø; Harriet; Dead; Armstead BURRILL; Franklin

3/21: Josephine Taylor 9; Ø; Franklin; Armstead BURRILL; Franklin; Ø; Ø; Ø; Ø; Harriet; Ø; Armstead BURRILL; Franklin

3/22: Silas Taylor 5; Franklin; Roanoke; Ed POWELL; Franklin; Roanoke; 44; Isam FERGUSON; Roanoke; Sarah J. Dead; E. POWELL; Franklin; Jordan Taylor

4/1: Harriet Blaney 45; Roanoke; Missouri; Ø; Ø; Roanoke; 74; Jacob SPESSARD; Roanoke; Nancy; Dead; N. SPESSARD; Roanoke

4/2: Alfred Blaney 43; Roanoke; Roanoke; E. THOMAS; Roanoke; Ø; Ø; Ø; Ø; Ø; Ø; Ø; Ø; Richard Blaney

4/3: James Blaney 41; Roanoke; Roanoke; E. THOMAS; Roanoke; Ø; Ø; Ø; Ø; Ø; Ø; Ø; Ø; Richard Blaney

4/4: Elias Blaney 39; Roanoke; Tennessee

4/5: Susan Blaney 37; Roanoke

4/6: John Blaney 35; Roanoke

4/7: Samuel Blaney 33; Roanoke; Ohio

4/8: Ann Blaney 31; Roanoke; Roanoke; Betsy EVANS; Roanoke; Ø; Ø; Ø; Ø; Ø; Ø; Ø; Ø; Richard Blaney

4/9: Eliza Blaney 29; Roanoke

4/10: Floyd Blaney 18; Craig; Botetourt; Ann M. SPESSARD; Roanoke; Ø; Ø; Ø; Ø; Ø; Ø; Ø; Ø; Richard Blaney

4/11: Joe Blaney 27; Roanoke; Montgomery; Emily BRANCH; Montgomery; Roanoke; Ø; Ø; Ø; Ø; Ø; Ø; Ø; Richard Blaney

4/12: Mary E. Wilson 10; Roanoke; Roanoke; Free; Ø; Roanoke; 38; Free; Ø; Susan; Ø; Free; Ø; Cary Wilson

165

4/13: Alfred Blaney 20; Roanoke; Roanoke; S. PHILLIPS; Roanoke; Roanoke; 39; E. THOMAS; Roanoke; Hannah; Dead; S. PHILLIPS; Roanoke; James BLANEY

4/14: James Blaney 17; Ø; Roanoke; S. PHILLIPS; Roanoke

4/15: Nancy Blaney 16; Ø; Botetourt; J. HAMMOND; Botetourt; Ø; Ø; Ø; Ø; Hannah

4/16: Myron Blaney 15; Ø; Bedford; D. NEIWINGER; Bedford; Ø; Ø; Ø; Ø; Ø ; Hannah

4/17: Darius Blaney 12; Ø; Roanoke; P. LEESON; Betetourt

4/18: Robert Blaney 8; Ø; Roanoke; J. GOODWIN; Ø; Roanoke; 39; Ø; Ø; Ø; Ø; Ø; Ø; James Blaney

4/19: ~~illy Blaney 13; Roanoke; Roanoke; Betsy EVANS; Ø; Roanoke~~

4/20: Thomas Page 2; Botetourt; Botetourt; Rolin LEE; Botetourt; Roanoke; 28; J.S. THOMAS; Caroline; Martha Ann 24; Botetourt; Rolin SEE; Botetourt; Walter Page

Table 23: Roanoke County, VA

Register of Colored Persons Cohabiting Together as Husband and Wife

(pg/line; f/age; pob; res; last owner; res; occ; w/age, res; last owner; res; child/age; date cohabitation)

1/1: Peter Anderson 60; Middlesex; Roanoke; Farmer; George P. TAYLOE; Roanoke; Rebecca Byers; Ø; Roanoke; George P. TAYLOE; Roanoke; Ø; Jan 1837

1/2: Willis Raford 45; Bath; Roanoke; Farmer; B. TINSLEY; Roanoke; Malinda Banks 31; Roanoke; Roanoke; J. McCLENNAHAN; Roanoke; Clayborne 6, Sherman 10 mos; Aug 1859

1/3: Dandridge Harris 30; Nelson; Roanoke; Farmer; Susan HARDING; Roanoke; Abby Hornes 36; Roanoke; Roanoke; J. RICHARDSON; Roanoke; Ø; July 1860

1/4: Edmund Johnson 30; Roanoke; Roanoke; Farmer; Charles OLIVER; Roanoke; Amanda Crocket 25; Roanoke; Roanoke; J.H. SMITH; Roanoke; Billy 2, Mary 11, Lee 12, Betty 5; Jan 1853

1/5: Ephraim Banks 38; Fauquier; Roanoke; Farmer; William OATS; Roanoke; Melvina Hughs 24; Culpeper; Roanoke; William OATS; Roanoke; Matilda 3, Ephraim 7 mos; Apr 1858

1/6: Aldridge Carter 28; Fauquier; Roanoke; Farmer; H. HANSBOROUGH; Roanoke; Martha Banks 31; Fauquier; Roanoke; H. HANSBOROUGH; Roanoke; Adelaide 12, Lisby 9, Wesley 5; Aug 1853

1/7: Richmond Crony; Halifax; Roanoke; Farmer; William MOULTON; Botetourt; Sarah Bryan; Charlotte; Roanoke; W. VINYARD; Roanoke; Dick 26

1/8: Frank Simmons 28; Franklin; Roanoke; Farmer; Julina SIMMONS; Franklin; Mary E. Poindexter 26; Franklin; Roanoke; C. POINDEXTER; Franklin; Sally 3, William 11 mos; June 1862

1/9: Oliver Burrill 45; Franklin; Roanoke; Farmer; J.H. BURRILL; Franklin; Maria Harper 49; Ø; Roanoke; J. HARPER; Franklin; Ø; Nov 1852

1/10: Peter Harden 45; Nelson; Roanoke; Farmer; J.B. HARDING; Roanoke; Harriet Lewis 25; Roanoke; Roanoke; Nancy CHAPMAN; Roanoke; John 3, Sally 2, Charles 7, Ned 6, Mary L. 5; June 1858

1/11: Samuel Oliver 39; Roanoke; Roanoke; Farmer; Matilda OLIVER; Roanoke; Ann Hafe? 38; Lynchburg; Roanoke; J.B. LANE; Bedford; Minerva 5, Charles 19, Thomas 17, Julius 7; Dec 1846

1/12: Henry Duckwiler 32; Roanoke; Roanoke; Blacksmith; G.B. BOARD; Roanoke; Charlotte Turk 30; Roanoke; Roanoke; J.B.C. LOGAN; Roanoke; John H. 3, Fanny 9, Nelly 7, Mary 5; 7 Feb 1857

1/13: Andy Green 55; Roanoke; Roanoke; Farmer; J.H. GRIFFIN; Roanoke; Amanda Duckwiler 30; Roanoke; Roanoke; B. DEYERLE; Roanoke; Fanny 4, Greene 3, Anna 3 mos; Mar 1856

1/14: Abednego Taylor 38; Roanoke; Roanoke; Farmer; W. MUSE; Roanoke; Louisa Cofer 35; Roanoke; Roanoke; T. LUNSFORD; Roanoke; Lola 10, Morris 7, Stephen 16, Lawson 14; Dec 1850

1/15: William Turner 29; Albemarle; Roanoke; Farmer; J. HALL; Montgomery; Sarah Taylor 23; Albemarle; Roanoke; John BARNES; Montgomery; Walter G. 18 mos; Mar 1864

1/16: William Owens 40; Roanoke; Roanoke; Farmer; Charles THOMAS; Roanoke; Sally Taylor 23; Roanoke; Roanoke; J. HALL; Montgomery; Nancy 5, Rachel 3, William 12 mos; Jan 1860

1/17: Israel Owens 38; Roanoke; Roanoke; Farmer; Charles THOMAS; Roanoke; Mary Taylor 41; Roanoke; Roanoke; Jane KENT; Roanoke; Joe 13; 22 Feb 1853

1/18: Aleck Dow 26; Roanoke; Roanoke; Farmer; Jane KENT; Roanoke; Amanda Smith 28; Floyd; Roanoke; J. GORDON; Montgomery; Maria 6 mos; Feb 1865

1/19: Lewis Worrell 25; Southampton; Roanoke; Farmer; M. PITZER; Roanoke; Kitty Skipper 21; Roanoke; Roanoke; J. PITZER; Roanoke; Dan 2, Emmeline 15 mos; Dec 1862

1/20: Harvey Keen 58; Botetourt; Roanoke; Blacksmith; T. LANGHORN; Botetourt; Priscilla King 46; Roanoke; Roanoke; T. LANGHORN; Botetourt; Louisa 18, Rosa 14, Catharine 9, Elijah 24, George 20, Mary 19

1/21: Nelson Anderson 48; Bath; Roanoke; Farmer; B.T. TINSLEY; Roanoke; Lucinda Banks 48; Bedford; Roanoke; Catharine REED; Botetourt; Margaret 9, Marth 7, Betsey A. 14, James A. 13, Rachel 11; Mar 1851

1/22: John Banks; Botetourt; Roanoke; Farmer; S.?F. SIMMONS; Roanoke; Sarah; Roanoke; Roanoke; A. GREENWOOD; Montgomery

1/23: Albert Steward 48; Wythe; Roanoke; Farmer; J. ALIFF; Roanoke; Suban/Susan? Sanders 48; Franklin; Roanoke; Free; Ø; And. J. 19, B.P. 17, Paterson 25, William 23; Dec 1840

1/24: Baldwin Simms 38; Roanoke; Roanoke; Mason; J. DEYERLE; Roanoke; Fannie Goldstone 40; Franklin; Roanoke; J. DEYERLE; Roanoke; J.E. 9; Mar 1856

1/25: Jerry Vinyard 26; Augusta; Roanoke; Farmer; D. COMER; Augusta; Lucy Hill 37; Augusta; Roanoke; J.A. PATTERSON; Augusta; Ø; May 1860

1/26: Almstead Queman 53; Fauquier; Roanoke; Farmer; George MILLER; Roanoke; Nancy Mokens 50; Roanoke; Roanoke; George MILLER; Roanoke; Charles 13, Winnie 11, Archie 8

1/27: Lewis Spurlock 33; Roanoke; Roanoke; Farmer; C. BURRILL; Roanoke; Betsey Simms 26; Roanoke; Roanoke; C. BURRILL; Roanoke; Molly 3, Harry 6 mos, Laura 8, Joe 5; 22 Feb 1856

1/28: Shelby Banks 34; Roanoke; Roanoke; Farmer; Fannie HARVEY; Roanoke; Fannie Irving 28; Bedford; Roanoke; A. SANDERS; Roanoke; Rosella 9, Ed 2; Dec 1855

1/29: Samuel Kershaw 45; Camden Co., So. Carolina; Roanoke; Carpenter; W.? POWERS; Roanoke; Mary Smith 40; Ø; Roanoke; W.? POWERS; Roanoke; Cyrus 13, Mary 4, James M. 18, Sallie 16, Matilda 15; 1847

1/30: Aaron Yerby 41; Lancaster; Roanoke; Farmer; J. TROUT; Roanoke; Nancy Raford 32; Ø; Roanoke; J. TROUT; Roanoke; Leslie 9, Emmeline 3, Nancy 1; Jan 1853

1/31: Tom Claytor 31; Roanoke; Roanoke; Farmer; G.P. TAYLOE; Roanoke; Mary German 27; Botetourt; Roanoke; G.P. TAYLOE; Roanoke; William 2, Anne 11, Sam 6, Lina 4; 1 May 1854

1/32: E. Calloway 33; Bedford; Roanoke; Farmer; William WATTS; Roanoke; Jennette Nickolas? 23; Roanoke; Roanoke; William WATTS; Roanoke; Ø; Dec 1860

1/33: Peter Jeffers 31; Roanoke; Roanoke; Farmer; R. KEGGY; Roanoke; Lucy Campbell 24; Roanoke; Roanoke; E. McCLENNAHAN; Roanoke; Ella 8, Alice 1, Sally 6, Maria 4; Apr 1859

1/34: A. Watkins 47; Albemarle; Roanoke; Farmer; B. PITZER; Roanoke; Harriet Anderson 35; Roanoke; Roanoke; B. PITZER; Roanoke; Matilda 23, Adaline 11; Dec 1842

1/35: Kit Anderson 38; Botetourt; Roanoke; Farmer; G.P. TAYLOE; Roanoke; Judy Williams 27; Botetourt; Roanoke; G.P. TAYLOE; Roanoke; Daniel 7, Maria 15 mos; 1853

1/36: Sawney Glandres? 29; Roanoke; Roanoke; Farmer; N. BURRILL; Roanoke; America Braxton 22; Roanoke; Roanoke; N. BURRILL; Roanoke; Jinnie C., John 1 mo; Feb 1863

1/37: Moses Johnson 32; Halifax; Roanoke; Farmer; D.S. REED; Roanoke; Lucy J. ANDERSON 31; Roanoke; Roanoke; Matilda OLIVER; Roanoke; Ø; Mar 1858

1/38: Patrick Journot 38; Roanoke; Roanoke; Farmer; Matilda OLIVER; Roanoke; Ailsy Patterson 24; Roanoke; Roanoke; James KENT; Roanoke; Abe L. 1; 25 Dec 1864

1/39: John Williams; Ø; Roanoke; Farmer; G.C. LANGHORN; Botetourt; Lucy James; Ø; Roanoke; N. WIRT; Roanoke

2/1: Dennis Carr 43; Halifax; Roanoke; Farmer; D.S. REED; Roanoke; Emmeline Goggins 27; Roanoke; Roanoke; C. LUNSFORD; Roanoke; William 4, Henry 3, Henrietta 1, Jack 11, Lelia 9, Laura 7; 1854

2/2: Randal Bently 26; Roanoke; Roanoke; Farmer; F. SORRELL; Roanoke; Missouri Smith 21; Ø; Roanoke; F. SORRELL; Roanoke; Charlotte 3, Ishanal 17 mos; Sept 1861

2/3: George Leftridge 44; Roanoke; Roanoke; Farmer; J. PERSINGER; Roanoke; Patsey Gish 35; Roanoke; Roanoke; G.R. GISH; Roanoke; Loyal 2, Taylor 1, Eliza, John H. 17, Charles 15, George 6, James 4; Mar 1844

2/4: Caesar Steptoe 45; Bedford; Roanoke; Farmer; J.H. SMITH; Roanoke; Laura Kently 40; Botetourt; Roanoke; G.W. CARR; Roanoke; Louisa 9, George 8, Wilson 5, Oliver 3, Jim 17, Lavinia 14, Lidia 10; Dec 1846

2/5: Caesar Dennis 57; Bedford; Roanoke; Farmer; William B. PRESTON; Roanoke; Hannah Hurt 40; Bedford; Roanoke; William B. PRESTON; Roanoke; Sally 12, Elisha 10, John 8, Cora 6, Blanche 5, And. J. 21, Perry 17, Jim 14, Taylor 13, Tom 3

2/6: Pascal Neal 38; Roanoke; Roanoke; Farmer; Charles OLIVER; Roanoke; Grace Sanders _5; Roanoke; Roanoke; William WATTS; Roanoke; Robinson 5, Dolly 3, Preston 1; Dec 1858

2/7: Miles Robinson 61; Amelia; Roanoke; Farmer; William M. PEYTON; Roanoke; Winnie Williams 25; Botetourt; Roanoke; George TAYLOE; Roanoke; Ø; Mar 1847

2/8: Isam Huntly 38; Campbell; Roanoke; Saddler; William NOFSINGER; Roanoke; Rose Fry 34; Bath; Roanoke; William NOFSINGER: Roanoke; Henry 12, Isam 8; Dec 1850

2/9: J. Martin 27; Roanoke; Roanoke; Farmer; B. TINSLEY; Roanoke; Silla Edwards 30; Roanoke; Roanoke; George P. TAYLOE; Roanoke; Ella 1; 15 July 1862

2/10: J. Crocket 33; Botetourt; Roanoke; Farmer; J.H. SMITH; Roanoke; Nancy Pate 26; Roanoke; Roanoke; William WATTS; Roanoke; Susan 8, Asa 5; Apr 1858

2/11: J. Whales 55; Ø; Roanoke; Farmer; William WATTS; Roanoke; Polly Scott 45; Roanoke; Roanoke; William WATTS; Roanoke; Linda 12, Aleck 9, Harry 17, Gallinus 15; Nov 1848

2/12: A. Brown 25; Culpeper; Roanoke; Farmer; Lucy BROWN; Culpeper; Martha Richardson 23; Roanoke; Roanoke; J.H. SMITH; Roanoke; Ø; Dec 1865

2/13: E. Allen 61; Ø; Roanoke; Farmer; J. RICHARDSON; Roanoke; Judy Toliver 52; Botetourt; Roanoke; J. RICHARDSON; Roanoke; Margaret 18, Malinda 11, Aug 1836

2/14: N. Ashbury 43; Bedford; Roanoke; Shoemaker; J. ASHBURY; Roanoke; Ann Stratton 27; Ø; Roanoke; J. EDMONDS; Roanoke; Granville 5; Oct 1859

2/15: A. Neal 35; Roanoke; Roanoke; Farmer; J. KENT; Roanoke; Sukey Mingel 25; Botetourt; Roanoke; K. LANGHORN; Botetourt; Doshy 1, Ben 11, Sally 7, Joe 5, Bob 3; 15 May 1854

2/16: William Lawson 56; Roanoke; Roanoke; Farmer; Joel STOVER; Roanoke; Peggy Taylor; Ø; Roanoke; J. STOVER; Roanoke; Greene 24, Jim 20, John 17, Nat 32, Milly 30, Henry 26; 11 May 1833

2/17: And. Washington 32; Roanoke; Roanoke; Farmer; N. CHAPMAN; Roanoke; A_ma Logan 27; Hawkins Co., Tennessee; Roanoke; George HARTMAN; Roanoke; Ø; Feb 1865

2/18: Harry Martin 56; Alleghany; Roanoke; Farmer; M. PITZER; Roanoke; Sally Lewis 53; Montgomery; Roanoke; N. CHAPMAN; Roanoke; Ø; 1862

2/19: Jim Washington 47; Roanoke; Roanoke; Farmer; N. BURRILL; Roanoke; Maria 42; Botetourt; Roanoke; J.H. GRIFFIN; Roanoke; Ann 18; 1847

2/20: Tom Banks 46; Roanoke; Roanoke; Farmer; N. BURRILL; Roanoke; Celia 40; Roanoke; Roanoke; N. BURRILL; Roanoke; Agnes 12, Dick 9, Suckey 7, Sally 1, Margaret 18, Tom 16, Netty 14; 1847

2/21: Dan Johnson 36; Roanoke; Roanoke; Farmer; N. BURRILL; Roanoke; Nancy Watson 30; Roanoke; Roanoke; N. BURRILL; Roanoke; Ø; 1858

2/22: William Braxton 34; Roanoke; Roanoke; Farmer; N. BURRILL; Roanoke; Julia Moore 30; Surry; Roanoke; James A. WILLIAMS; Roanoke; Ned 12, Henry 8; 1853

2/23: Shirley Spurlock 31; Roanoke; Roanoke; Farmer; N. BURRILL; Roanoke; Grace Moker 29; Roanoke; Roanoke; N. BURRILL; Roanoke; Eliza 6 mos, Gilliam 7, Dick 5, Nat 3; 1858

2/24: William Simons 23; Roanoke; Roanoke; Farmer; N. BURRILL; Roanoke; Eliza Banks 20; Roanoke; Roanoke; N. BURRILL; Roanoke; Sukey 1; 1862

2/25: Pat Brickey 30; Roanoke; Roanoke; Farmer; Sam PHILLIPS; Roanoke; Kate Savage 23; Roanoke; Roanoke; William WATTS; Roanoke; Ø; 1865

2/26: Stephen Lock 44; Lancaster; Roanoke; Farmer; T.R. MUSE; Roanoke; Winny? Carter 38; Roanoke; Roanoke; E.R. MUSE; Roanoke; William 6, Ellen 4, Margaret 1, James 17, Charles 15, Ann 12; 1848

2/27: Sam German 59; Prince William; Roanoke; Farmer; G.P. TAYLOE; Roanoke; Judy Anderson 43; Bedford; Botetourt; Kitty LANGHORN; Botetourt; ~~Mary~~; 1833

2/28: Sam Morris 36; Roanoke; Roanoke; Farmer; J.C. MILLER; Roanoke; Lucy A. Langhorn 30; Roanoke; Roanoke; J.C. MILLER; Roanoke; Sally 8, Bob 5, Becky 3, Richard L. 15, William S. 13, Tilla 9; 1851

2/29: Daniel Ball 52; Nelson; Roanoke; Carpenter; J.B. HARDING; Roanoke; Ellen Banks 42; Roanoke; Roanoke; Asa HOLLINS; Franklin; Ø; Nov 1860

2/30: Ross Clark 32; Spotsylvania; Roanoke; Farmer; M.B. LOYD; Pulaski; Lucy Jenkins 44; Roanoke; Roanoke; F. RORER; Pulaski; Ø; Nov 1863

2/31: Edward Burke 68; Roanoke; Roanoke; Farmer; William WALTON; Roanoke; Maria Anderson 65; New London; Roanoke; William WALTON; Roanoke; Shelton 27, Morgan 22, Christianna 30, Jacob 45, Madison 40, Charles 30; Dec 1818

2/32: Titus Johnson 24; Roanoke; Roanoke; Farmer; N. BURRILL; Roanoke; Sally Hickman 19; Hanover; Roanoke; C. BURRILL; Roanoke; John 18 mos; Feb 1863

2/33: Phillip Watkins 35; Campbell; Roanoke; Blacksmith; J.W. HURT; Roanoke; Jane Parish 55; Roanoke; Roanoke; D. SHANKS; Roanoke; Ø; 24 Dec 1861

2/34: William Barnett 22; Roanoke; Roanoke; Farmer; J. PRITCHARD; Roanoke; Amanda 19, Franklin; Roanoke; J.D. HORN; Franklin; Charles 17 mos; 1864

2/35: Frazer Pitzer 36; Roanoke; Roanoke; Farmer; J. PITZER; Roanoke; Seely Deyerle 27; Roanoke; Roanoke; B. DEYERLE; Roanoke; Chant 8, Joe 8, Nat 6, Ellen 4; Oct 1855

2/36: Peter Abingdon 28; Henry; Roanoke; Farmer; Joe PENN; Henry; Lucinda Cobb 21; Patrick; Roanoke; John COBB; Patrick; Bob 2; 25 Dec 1863

2/37: Joe Glasgow; Richmond; Roanoke; Carpenter; G.P. TAYLOE; Roanoke; Lucy Gilbert 42; Botetourt; Roanoke; G.P. TAYLOE; Roanoke; John 15, Becky 14, Nancy 12?, Collins 6, Lucy 4, Caroline 26, Mary 25, Sarah 23, Joe 21; 4 July 1839

2/38: George Gilbert 57; Prince William; Roanoke; Carpenter; G.P. TAYLOE; Roanoke; Caroline Wooden 51; Montgomery; Roanoke; J. LANGHORN; Montgomery; Albert 14, Dick 12, Joe 11; Jan 1850

2/39: Lee Davis 36; Amherst; Roanoke; Carpenter; E. TERRY; Roanoke; Maria Jeffers 26; Roanoke; Roanoke; William PEYTON; Albemarle; Richard 4, Lee 18 mos; Jan 1861

3/1: William Lee 27; Roanoke; Roanoke; Farmer; John EVANS; Roanoke; Sally Brown 23; Ø; Roanoke; Colin BASS; Roanoke; Andy 1; 25 Dec 1864

3/2: Wyatt Rose 27; Bedford; Roanoke; Farmer; William BILBROOK; Bedford; Ellen Goggins 23; Forrest Co. (Mississippi?); Roanoke; C.?C. Oatey; Bedford; Ø; June 1865

3/3: Andrew Wimbush 26; Roanoke; Roanoke; Farmer; A. REED; Roanoke; Mary Lew 31; Albemarle; Roanoke; H. HANSBOROUGH; Roanoke; Ø; June 1860

3/4: Anthony Lawson 24; Roanoke; Roanoke; Farmer; C. CAMPBELL; Roanoke; Rose Fleming 23; Roanoke; Roanoke; William ROBINSON; Roanoke; Ø; 6 Aug 1864

3/5: Washington Hardy 50; Roanoke; Roanoke; Farmer; A. JAMES; Roanoke; Judy Cook 44; Roanoke; Roanoke; William WOODSON; Roanoke; Royal 10, Henry 7, Warrick 4, Ann 24, Mike 20, George 18; Aug 1836

3/6: George Anderson 60; Bath; Roanoke; Farmer; William M. PEYTON; Albemarle; Laura A. Rooki_ 49; Mecklenburg; Roanoke; Matilda OLIVER; Roanoke; Catharine 18, George 17, Henrietta 26, Lucy 35, Joe 31, Rachel 22; 10 June 1830

3/7: J.H. McGeorge 37; Franklin; Roanoke; Farmer; William WOOD; Franklin; Rachel Reynolds 40; Botetourt; Roanoke; D. BOONE; Roanoke; Harvey E. 8, Letitia 1; Mar 1857

3/8: Greene Johnson 34; Bedford; Roanoke; Farmer; Free; Ø; Caroline Jeter 22; Bedford; Roanoke; J. JETER; Roanoke; Ø; July 1864

3/9: Burrill Woods; Pittsylvania; Roanoke; Farmer; Arm WOODS; Franklin; Lucy Preston; Franklin; Roanoke; F. PRESTON; Franklin; Nancy 12, Sam 2, Rachel 15, Eliza 14, Ann 13; 1843

3/10: Lewis Fleming 30; Roanoke; Roanoke; Farmer; William WATTS; Roanoke; Mary J. Lawson 26; Roanoke; Roanoke; C. CAMPBELL; Roanoke; Mary 2, Anthony 6 mos, Littleton 6, Ned 5; 25 Dec 1857

3/11: Tom Oliver 31; Roanoke; Roanoke; House Servant; C. OLIVER; Roanoke; Rhoda Dandridge 21; Roanoke; Roanoke; B. TINSLEY; Roanoke; Mary 4 mos; 25 Dec 1864

3/12: Tom Jeffers; Bedford; Roanoke; Farmer; I.? SINCLAIR; Bedford; Susy Ball; Roanoke; William WATTS; Roanoke; Ailsy 17, Blanche 13, Caroline 9, Wesley 21, Julianna 20, Allen 18; 1842

3/13: Adam Betts; Bedford; Roanoke; Farmer; J. McCLENNAHAN; Roanoke; Chloe Oliver; Nottoway; Roanoke; Matilda OLIVER; Roanoke; Lewis 53

3/14: Sam Snyder 50; Roanoke; Roanoke; Farmer; Lucy CARVIN; Roanoke; Sarah Cavel 40; Ø; Roanoke; Napoleon CAVEL; Kanawha; Mary E. 3, Samuel 11 mos; June 1862

3/15: Albert Levisey 48; Franklin; Roanoke; Blacksmith; Arm LEVISEY; Franklin; Silla Heald 46; Franklin; Roanoke; William WADE; Franklin; Sophy 7, Jincy 3, Lewis 20, Jinnie? 16, Edmund 10; 1843

3/16: Randall Washington 31; Roanoke; Roanoke; Farmer; Nancy CHAPMAN; Roanoke; Matilda Watkins 23; Roanoke; Roanoke; B. PITZER; Roanoke; Hannah 8, John H. 6; Sept 1860

3/17: Lewis Dangerfield 44; Shenandoah; Roanoke; Farmer; William OUTS; Roanoke; Malinda Hackley 42; Madison; Roanoke; William OUTS; Roanoke; John 11, Ben 9, Newton 15, Maria 14, Jim 12; Sept 1850

3/18: Clayborne Archer 25; Roanoke; Roanoke; Farmer; Matilda OLIVER; Roanoke; Jinnie Rosser 20; Roanoke; Roanoke; T. EVANS; Roanoke; Jackson 3, Thomas 2; 1 Mar 1862

3/19: Joseph King 34; Halifax; Roanoke; Farmer; Dan TROUT; Roanoke; Angeline Lee 28; Roanoke; Roanoke; Dan TROUT; Roanoke; Martha 7, Emma 6, Alice 3, Jim 8, Andy 11, William 10; Oct 1854

3/20: Edward Beale 33; Roanoke; Roanoke; Farmer; S. GREENWOOD; Roanoke; Prudence Fowler 27; Roanoke; Roanoke; Jacob PERSINGER; Roanoke; Rufus 8; Dec 1857

3/21: Billy Brown 68; Roanoke; Roanoke; Farmer; Lucy JOHNSON; Roanoke; Fannie Kane 69; Roanoke; Roanoke; John JOHNSON; Roanoke; Ø; Mar 1821

3/22: Wash. Vaughan 26; King William; Roanoke; Farmer; Betsey COOK; King William; Fannie Cley 27; Madison; Roanoke; Tom ALL; Loudoun; Sally A. 2, July 1862

3/23: Henry Langhorn 33; Roanoke; Roanoke; Mason; D. DEYERLE; Roanoke; Caroline Morson 26; Rockbridge; Roanoke; D. DEYERLE; Roanoke; Chap 5, Dan 8 mos, Sam 7, _annie 6; Sept 1858

3/24: George Morton; Roanoke; Roanoke; Farmer; J. RICHARDSON; Roanoke; Ailsey Allen; Roanoke; Roanoke; J. RICHARDSON; Roanoke; Emma - Milly 6, Thomas 6 mos; Aug 1858

3/25: William Winger 41; Amelia; Roanoke; Farmer; A. DETON; Roanoke; Margaret Washington 33; Montgomery; Roanoke; Nancy CHAPMAN; Roanoke; Israel 15; 25 Dec 1848

3/26: William Washington 23; Montgomery; Roanoke; Farmer; Nancy CHAPMAN; Roanoke; Amelia Clark 40; Amelia; Roanoke; A. DETON; Roanoke; Ø; July 1856

3/27: Peter Tolivar 43; Augusta; Roanoke; Farmer; S. HUBBARD; Roanoke; Melvina Dow 31; Roanoke; Roanoke; S. HUBBARD; Roanoke; Jim 6, Andy 3, Rachel 8 mos, Harriet A. 10, Josephus 8; Oct 1853

3/28: Patrick Reed 59; Charlotte; Roanoke; Farmer; D.S. REED; Roanoke; Polly Powell 45; Halifax; Roanoke; D.S. REED; Roanoke; Clementina 6, James 4, Silas 2, Moses 14, Paulina 10, Eliza 8; June 1851

3/29: James Bratton 55; Montgomery; Roanoke; Farmer; Jane KENT; Roanoke; Emma Early 45; Roanoke; Roanoke; Jane KENT; Roanoke; Jimmie 6, Charles? 4, Ann 16, Edmund 12; 8 Dec 1848

3/30: Solomon Hunt 53; Halifax; Roanoke; Farmer; D.S. REED; Roanoke; Annika Smith 43; Halifax; Roanoke; D.S. REED; Roanoke; Israel 7 mos, Taylor 5, Ann 4, Mary 2; Dec 1858

S/31: Hartley Johnson 78; Mecklenburg; Roanoke; Farmer; G. GISH; Roanoke; Jinnie Oliver; Gloucester; Roanoke; Matilda OLIVER; Roanoke; Edmund 36, Betsy Ann 38

3/32: Ned Thompson 30; Bedford; Roanoke; Farmer; G. TURNER; Roanoke; Margaret Sanders 18; Roanoke; Roanoke; Free; Ø; ~~Bashe~~, Susie 3, Martha 5, 1860

3/33: Tom Whiddon 30; Bedford; Roanoke; Farmer; G. TURNER; Roanoke; Kate Jimmerson?; Franklin; Roanoke; Mrs. ARTHUR; Franklin; Molly 3; 1861

3/34: Caesar Lomax 58; Orange; Roanoke; Farmer; J. EARNEST; Roanoke; Rebecca Chapman 46; Fauquier; Roanoke; J. ERNEST; Roanoke; Caesar 7, Lettie 4, Margaret 21, Hillard 11, Eliza 9; 1841

3/35: Billy Hicks 39; Roanoke; Roanoke; Farmer; R.P. JONES; Montgomery; Winnie Pate; Roanoke; Roanoke; J. McCLENNAHAN; Roanoke; Edmund 15, Mary 7, Henry 18, Jerry 17; 1847

3/36: Lewis Calloway 24

3/37: Washington Anderson; Roanoke; Roanoke; Farmer; A. WHITE; Roanoke; Agnes Monroe 47; Roanoke; Roanoke; N. BURRILL; Roanoke; Delia 11; 29 Sept 1850

3/38: David Lawton 55; Roanoke; Roanoke; Farmer; Jane LEWIS; Roanoke; Maria Banks 45; Roanoke; Roanoke; J. SMITH; Roanoke; Ellen 20, John T. 16, Maria 13, Milly 26, Greene 24, Clay & Freeland 23; 1839

3/39: Peter Wyatt; Dinwiddie; Roanoke; Farmer; B. TINSLEY; Roanoke; Lucinda 60; Bedford; Roanoke; B. TINSLEY; Roanoke; Ø; Sept 1853

4/1: Moses Shovey 29; Roanoke; Roanoke; Farmer; Free; Ø; Martha Wilkison 22; Henrico; Roanoke; B. TINSLEY; Roanoke; Ellen 4, John D. 2 mos; Sept 1860

4/2: Thomas J. Frog; Montgomery; Roanoke; Farmer; Jane KENT; Roanoke; Adaline Fields 27; Greenbrier Co., (W. Virginia); Roanoke; Sarah HANNAH; Roanoke; Ø; Dec 1857

4/3: Patterson Stewart 25; Roanoke; Roanoke; Farmer; Free; Ø; E.J. Banks 22; Roanoke; Roanoke; Free; Ø; James Washington 2; 25 Dec 1861

4/4: Willis Skinner 54; Edenton, No. Carolina; Roanoke; Farmer; J.R. ANDERSON; Henrico; Dinah 50; Ø; Roanoke; J. LIGINAUGER; Botetourt; Ø; 25 Dec 1865

4/5: H.C. Scruggs; Roanoke; Roanoke; Farmer; Smith PETTY; Roanoke; Emmeline Cuff; Franklin; Roanoke; Free; Ø; Missouri E. 2; Aug 1862

4/6: Mat Beven 25; Roanoke; Roanoke; Farmer; William WATTS; Roanoke; Ellen Sanders 22; Roanoke; Roanoke; William WATTS; Roanoke; Mary 4 mos; Mar 1865

4/7: Simon Smith 36; Halifax; Roanoke; Farmer; D.S. REED; Roanoke; Louisa Carrington 36; Halifax; Roanoke; D.S. REED; Roanoke; Prince 7, Allen 3, Kent 14, Laura 9, Kittie 11; May 1851

4/8: Omstead White; Franklin; Roanoke; Farmer; Charles POTTER; Franklin; Emily Keefauver 35; Franklin; Roanoke; Julia KEEFAUVER; Floyd; Sarah 12, Harriet 6, Fannie 15, William 13; Dec 1850

4/9: Henry Chambers 26; Franklin; Roanoke; Farmer; William CHAMBERS; Franklin; Maria Webster 26; Franklin; Roanoke; Polly SIMMONS; Roanoke; Mary E.C.; 1860

4/10: Robert Webster; Franklin; Roanoke; Farmer; Mark PREDUE; Franklin; Nancy Lurnsey; Franklin; Roanoke; Polly SIMMONS; Roanoke; Maria, Mary, Bob & John, Frank, Ned, Jane, Josiah

4/11: Ferry Hudson 47; Nottoway; Roanoke; House Servant; Charles OLIVER; Roanoke; Mary Wilkison 48; Hanover; Roanoke; Charles OLIVER; Roanoke; Prentice 9, Mary 7, Antoinette 18, Kate 12; Aug 1846

4/12: Doctor Johnson 27; Franklin; Roanoke; Farmer; Stephen PRESTON; Franklin; Catharine Brooks 29; Franklin; Roanoke; Andrew BROOKS; Franklin; Ø; Mar 1861

4/13: John Guy 58; Ø; Roanoke; Farmer; Free; Ø; Eliza Rafle? 45; Augusta; Roanoke; William W.T. PEYTON; Albemarle; Nancy, Rhoda; 1836

4/14: Anderson Plate_ 49; Franklin; Roanoke; Farmer; J.S. HALE; Franklin; Milly Thompson 25; Roanoke; J.S. HALE; Franklin; Ø; 1841

4/15: Aleck Duckwiler 30; Montgomery; Roanoke; Farmer; G.B. BOARD; Roanoke; Nancy Lewis 27; Roanoke; Roanoke; Lewis ZIRCLE; Roanoke; Lucy 3, Jane 9, Laura 8, Mary 6; Mar 1856

4/16: Albert Oliver __; Roanoke; Roanoke; Farmer; Matilda OLIVER; Roanoke; Amanda Taylor 24; Roanoke; Roanoke; Susan THRASHER; Roanoke; Sally 3?, Charles 3, Martha 2 mos; Sept 1860

4/17: Daniel Phelps 51; Franklin; Roanoke; Farmer; Mary PHELPS; Franklin; Sarah Banks 49; Franklin; Roanoke; Robert HARVEY; Roanoke; Claiborne 15, Harston 14, Harriet 9, Taswell 27, Sam 21, Charity 16; June 1837

4/18: John Harper 51; Nottoway; Roanoke; Farmer; James C. HARPER; Franklin; Charlotte Smith 47; Franklin; Roanoke; S__ SMITH; Franklin; Fanny, Judy, Rhoda?, Rosabelle, Abigal, Ann 24, Nancy?, Adaline?, Eliza J., Betsey, William; May 1837

4/19: William Leftridge 40; Bedford; Roanoke; Farmer; Edna GLEASON; Roanoke; Jinnie Williams 22; Roanoke; Roanoke; George P. TAYLOE; Roanoke; Sarah F. 8 mos; 25 Dec 1860

4/20: Abraham Snyder 50; Roanoke; Roanoke; Farmer; Henry SNYDER; Roanoke; Laura A. Johnston 20; Nottoway; Roanoke; Xo__ HUDSON; Roanoke; Milly 5 mos; May 1865

4/21: Pompey Hopson; Henrico; Roanoke; Farmer; Curtis EVES; Tennessee; Julia Johnson 20; Amelia; Roanoke; James KAISER; Bedford; Fannie 6 mos; Oct 1863

4/22: Anderson Pullen 35; Craig; Roanoke; Farmer; Lethe GIBBONS; Craig; Caroline McKeever 30; Craig; Roanoke; Robert WILEY?; Craig; Ø; Jan 1855

4/23: Phil Wade 36; Bedford; Roanoke; Farmer; William A. WADE; Bedford; Judy Lee 43; Bedford; Roanoke; Henry ADAMS; Bedford; Ø; Dec 1862

5/1: George Preston 60; Bedford; Roanoke; Farmer; William B. PRESTON; Roanoke; Phillis Crawley 50; Bedford; Roanoke; William B. PRESTON; Roanoke; Mary, Charlotte, Wesley, Bob, Laura, Daniel 18, Martha 30, Jane, Sally, Matilda, Frances

5/2: Pleasant Preston 42; Bedford; Roanoke; Farmer; E. McCLENNAHAN; Roanoke; Sarah Ball 38; Roanoke; Roanoke; E. McCLENNAHAN; Roanoke; Ø; Mar 1857

5/3: Aaron Snyder 41; Roanoke; Roanoke; Farmer; J. VINYARD; Roanoke; Nelly Reed 26; Ø; Roanoke; William MOULTON; Botetourt; Ø; Mar 1857

5/4: Frank Hackley 35; Culpeper; Roanoke; Farmer; William OUTS; Roanoke; Betty Edmundson 33; Botetourt; Roanoke; C. HOUSMAN; Botetourt; Cinderella 4; 25 Dec 1860

5/5: Mat McGeorge 50; Bedford; Roanoke; Farmer; Susan THRASHER; Roanoke; Lucy Adams 30; Bedford; Roanoke; G._. ADAMS; Bedford; Frank 12, Ann E. 2, Charley 8 mos, John 14, Sally 15, Harvey 13; Jan 1850

5/6: Charles Banks 53; Roanoke; Roanoke; Farmer; E. McCLENNAHAN; Roanoke; Nancy Pate 47; Roanoke; Roanoke; James McCLENNAHAN; Roanoke; Shelton 19, Stewart 17, Betsy 15, Jacob 11, Ellen 9, Malinda 30, Joanna 24, Nancy 23; Nov 1835

5/7: John Hardy 44; Bedford; Roanoke; Farmer; ?. ASBY; Roanoke; Emmeline Boone 44; Franklin; Roanoke; ?. ASHY; Roanoke; Jackson 4, Joseph 4 mos; Dec 1860

5/8: Albert Cosby 32; Roanoke; Roanoke; Farmer; Jane LEWIS; Roanoke; Maria E. Baily 32; Roanoke; Roanoke; T. TOSH; Roanoke; Emma 15; 1850

5/9: Tom Davis 25; Kanawha Co; Roanoke; Farmer; G.W. CARR; Roanoke; Rhoda Burks 23; Roanoke; Roanoke; G.W. CARR; Roanoke; Josephine 2; June 1852

5/10: Jerry Micklass? 38; Roanoke; Roanoke; Blacksmith; William WATTS; Roanoke; Milly Moulton; Roanoke; Roanoke; E. McCLENNAHAN; Roanoke; Ø; Mar 1849

5/11: William Watkins 36; Botetourt; Roanoke; Blacksmith; William MOFSINGER; Roanoke; Sophy Wright 38; Franklin; Roanoke; J.H. SMITH; Roanoke; William 10, Lewis 7, Price 5; Sept 1859

5/12: Ishmael Sims 76; Botetourt; Roanoke; Farmer; William WATTS; Roanoke; Mary Lewis 45; Campbell; Roanoke; William WATTS; Roanoke; Lewis 10, Mary 8, William 5 mos, Ben 19, Virginia 17, Laura A. 16, Baldwin 13; Jan 1847

5/13: J. Anderson; Campbell; Roanoke; Farmer; A. WHITE; Roanoke; Sarah Fields; Roanoke; Roanoke; J. DYERLE; Roanoke; Aggy 42, Lewis 32, Harriet 29

5/14: Wilson Burks 44; Botetourt; Roanoke; Farmer; William P. HOLCOMB; Roanoke; Katy Lewis; Campbell; Roanoke; William P. HOLCOMB; Roanoke; Ed 5; May 1853

5/15: Jack K. Finley 46; Rockbridge; Roanoke; Farmer; William WATTS; Roanoke; Milly Balldaw 35; Rockbridge; Roanoke; Samuel G.? BURKS; Roanoke; Lewis 15, Martha 13, Susan 2; May 1849

5/16: Harry Ridout 39; Roanoke; Roanoke; Carpenter; William WATTS; Roanoke; Jennie Hardy 27; Franklin; Roanoke; J. BANDY; Roanoke; Birney 11; May 1853

5/17: Jack Sanders 31; Bedford; Roanoke; Farmer; J. GOGGINS; Bedford; Marinda Burks 26; Botetourt; Roanoke; J.A. SMITH; Roanoke; John J.A. 7, Amelia S. 5; May 1857

5/18: Edmund Johnson 37; Roanoke; Roanoke; House Servant; Matilda OLIVER; Roanoke; Katey Jackson 40; Henrico; Roanoke; D.S. REED; Roanoke; Betsey A. 3, Elvira 3 mos; Jan 1849

5/19: John Archer 35; Roanoke; Roanoke; Farmer; Matilda OLIVER; Roanoke; Mary Allen 25; Roanoke; Roanoke; J.? RICHARDSON; Roanoke; Wesley 7, John G. 5; Sept 1858

5/20: Marshal Bruce 23; Henrico; Roanoke; Farmer; D.S. REED; Roanoke; Rachel Anderson 23; Roanoke; Roanoke; Matilda OLIVER; Roanoke; Carter 3; 1863

5/21: James Goldstone 36; Roanoke; Roanoke; Farmer; T. EVANS; Roanoke; Susan Archer 28; Roanoke; Roanoke; T. EVANS; Roanoke; Indiana 1, Charles 6, Jeff D. 5, Mary 3; Jan 1856

5/22: Lewis Hackley 27; Culpeper; Roanoke; Farmer; William OUTS; Roanoke; Eliza Reynolds 23; Botetourt; Roanoke; Sam WOODS; Roanoke; William 7, Alfred 3, Charles 6 mos; 1858

5/23: Winston Mead 37; Bedford; Roanoke; Farmer; Cornelia MEAD; Bedford; Cindrella Hopson 26; Powhatan; Roanoke; William TERRY; Bedford; John R. 7, Horace 3; Oct 1858

5/24: Joe Williams 65; Bedford; Roanoke; Farmer; Ben WILKS; Bedford; Jane McCLENNAHAN 54; Roanoke; Roanoke; Ø; Ø; Ø; Apr 1865

5/25: Dan Watkins 54; Campbell; Roanoke; Farmer; Margaret JOHNSON; Roanoke; Maria Richards 52; Roanoke; Roanoke; Nancy WHITE; Roanoke; Ann 24, Taylor 14; Mar 1838

5/26: William Beverly 29; Botetourt; Roanoke; Farmer; Gordon KENT; Wythe; Patience McCary 26; Roanoke; Roanoke; F. SORRELL; Roanoke; Eliza A. 4, James T. 2, William 9 mos; Nov 1859

5/27: Preston Burrell 38; Roanoke; Roanoke; Farmer; William WATTS; Roanoke; Phillis Sanders 29; Roanoke; Roanoke; William WATTS; Roanoke; Ø; Mar 1855

5/28: Patterson Evans 40; Botetourt; Roanoke; Farmer; James HOLCOMB; Bedford; Rose Johnson 35; Roanoke; Roanoke; James HOLCOMB; Bedford; James 6, Letty 4, Lee 2, Booker 14, Jeff 12, Laura 10, Silla 8; May 1850

5/29: John Franklin 48; Prince Edward; Roanoke; Shoemaker; F. JAMES; Roanoke; Laura Thiers 45; Charlotte; Roanoke; William DENNIS; Roanoke; Mary 10, Allen 5, Silva 16, John H. 15, Betty 12; Dec. 1848

5/30: Richard Jeffers 74; Nottoway; Roanoke; Miller; E. OLIVER; Roanoke; Betsey Foster 64; Bath; Roanoke; William M. PEYTON; Albemarle; Peter 39, Maria 28; Nov 1835

5/31: Henry Langhorn 36; Campbell; Roanoke; House Servant; William WATTS; Roanoke; Jane Preston 31; Bedford; Roanoke; E. McCLENNAHAN; Roanoke; Henry 11 mos, Charles 9, Betty 7, Sarah 4; Mar 1854

5/32: Ab. Carrington 34; Halifax; Roanoke; Farmer; Betsey REED; Roanoke; Susan Phillips 37; Halifax; Roanoke; Betsey REED; Roanoke; Betsey 7, Theodore 3, Anna S. 7 mos, Alice 14, Ida 12, Sam 8; 1851

5/33: George Hawkins 44; Botetourt; Roanoke; Farmer; G.W. CARR; Roanoke; Louisa Goldstone 24; Roanoke; Roanoke; G.W. CARR; Roanoke; Charles 4, Mary 3; Jan 1861

5/34: George Phillips 85; Halifax; Roanoke; Farmer; D.S. REED; Roanoke; Susan Primus 61; Carlotte; Roanoke; D.S. REED; Roanoke; Betsey 36, Jane 31, Phinneas 29, William 47, Amanda 45, Susan 33; Sept 1818

5/35: Aaron Tayloe 44; Botetourt; Roanoke; Farmer; F.R. MUSE; Roanoke; Jane Watkins 34; Halifax; Roanoke; J. HARTLEY; Roanoke; Ellen S. 5, Rose Ann 3; June 1860

5/36: Edmund Carter 35; Botetourt; Roanoke; Farmer; F.R. MUSE; Roanoke; Harriet 44; Ø; Roanoke; T.R. MUSE; Roanoke; Joseph 7, Frances 5, Lewis 3, Silas 13, Dennis 11, Emily 9

5/37: Josiah Rafer 41; Bath; Roanoke; Blacksmith; B. TINSLEY; Roanoke; Ellen Ammons 38; Montgomery; Roanoke; B. TINSLEY; Roanoke; Ø; Dec 1845

5/38: Lewis Booker 68; Roanoke; Roanoke; Farmer; William WATTS; Roanoke; Louisa Kently 52; Roanoke; Roanoke; William WATTS; Roanoke; Kently 18, Harriet 8; Jan 1843

5/39: George Liftrich 40; Bedford; Roanoke; Laborer; Dolly LIFTRICH; Lynchburg; Fanny Fox 25; Ø; Roanoke; J.H. SMITH; Roanoke; William 4 mos; May 1864

6/1: Robert P. Davis 24; Botetourt; Roanoke; Preacher; S.B. ZIMMERMAN; Baltimore, Maryland; Mary Connor 18; Pulaski; Roanoke; Elizabeth KENT; Pulaski; Ø; 19 Feb 1866

6/2: Elijah Anderson 45; Roanoke; Roanoke; Woodcutter; Alex WHITE; Roanoke; Phillis Taylor 32; Roanoke; Roanoke; Maria LEWIS; Roanoke; Edward 16, Shedrick 5, Sarah 4, Aleck 2, Lucinda 1; 25 Dec 1849

6/3: William Curtis 23; Henry; Roanoke; Laborer; Free; Ø; Clara Curtis 25; Roanoke; Roanoke; John JOHNSON; Roanoke; Fannie 6 mos; Oct 1864

6/4: Dennis Hopkins 40; Caroline; Roanoke; Laborer; Daniel HOGUE; Montgomery; Mary Willis 29; Roanoke; Roanoke; John TROUT; Roanoke; Ø; 1851

6/5: Ferdinand Banks 53; Roanoke; Roanoke; Carpenter; Robert HARVEY; Roanoke; Silva Miner; Roanoke; Roanoke; Mike TROUT; Roanoke; Josephus 17, Martha 16, Emma 15, John 14, Maria 5, Edward 22, Charles 20, Cynthia 19, Ellen 18; 1843

6/6: John Webster 42; Montgomery; Roanoke; Blacksmith; David SHANKS; Roanoke; Ellen Matthews 22; Roanoke; Roanoke; William HATCHER; Roanoke; Julia 2; Jan 1863

6/7: Tom Toliver 25; Franklin; Roanoke; Carpenter; John TOLIVER; Franklin; Cynthia Noel 22; Franklin; Roanoke; Charles NOEL; Franklin; John 5 mos; Dec 1862

6/8: Ned Taylor 48; Montgomery; Roanoke; Farmer; Henry CHAPMAN; Roanoke; Sarah Barlow 38; Bedford; Roanoke; G. ADAMS; Bedford; John H. 9, Edward 3; Sept 1855

6/9: Isaac Banks 38; Bedford; Roanoke; Farmer; William A. STAPLES; Bedford; Jane Johnson 32; Montgomery; Roanoke; John SMITH; Roanoke; Ø; 25 Dec 1860

6/10: William Dandridge; Ø; Roanoke; Gardner; Ira JETER; Roanoke; Clarkie Berry; Amelia; Roanoke; Armstead NEAL; Roanoke; Maria 17, Violet 16, Washington 30, Sam 20, Ann 19; 1830

6/11: Hector Homes 57; Roanoke; Roanoke; Farmer; F. SORRELL; Roanoke; Eve Johnson 52; Roanoke; Roanoke; C.R. CAMPBELL; Roanoke; Ø; Jan 1852

6/12: John Jewett 30; Albemarle; Roanoke; Farmer; Mrs. McKEY; Lynchburg; Hannah Homes 40; Albemarle; Roanoke; G.W. CARR; Roanoke; David 17, John 15, Mary 12, Peter 9, William & James 6, Phil 26, Albert 22, Jacob 20, Anne 18; July 1838

6/13: Henry Cuff 52; Franklin; Roanoke; Farmer; Free; Ø; Jane Nelson 50; Botetourt; Roanoke; Free; Ø; Ø; Jan 1859

6/14: William Chevalier 45; Montgomery; Roanoke; Farmer; Free; Ø; Pelina Cain 30; Roanoke; Roanoke; W. POWERS; Roanoke; Elizabeth 8, Fannie 4, Mary 1, Simon 16, Charles 13, Lewis 10; 1846

6/15: Stepney Owens 46; Bedford; Roanoke; Farmer; John H. SMITH; Roanoke; Martha Preston 31; Bedford; Roanoke; T. LUNSFORD; Roanoke; Charles 8, Nancy 5, Jane 14, George 12, Washington 10; May 1851

6/16: Stephen Kinney; Rockingham; Roanoke; Farmer; Albert REED; Roanoke; Amanda Ferris/Fearis; 48; Prince Edward; Roanoke; A. REED; Roanoke; Sam B. 15, John D. 14, Harriet 27, Margaret 19, Caroline 17; 1838

6/17: Ed Curtis 47; Charlotte; Roanoke; Farmer; David REED; Roanoke; Eliza Cank 45; Halifax; Roanoke; David REED; Roanoke; Lucy J. 11, Betty 9, Caroline 7, Hunter 17, Walter 15, Taylor 13; Mar 1841

6/18: William Chambers 55; Bedford; Roanoke; Farmer; J.H. SMITH; Roanoke; Clary Fleming 28; Franklin; Roanoke; J. __UT; Roanoke; Adaline 5, ___ 3, Martha 1; Mar 1859

6/19: Reuben Hicks 43; Roanoke; Roanoke; Farmer; D.R. MONTAGUE; Montgomery; Isabella Bracket 38; Roanoke; Roanoke; C. PETITT; Roanoke; Thornton, Maria 10, Patience 6, Harriet 4, Seely 2, Jimmie 21, Mary 16, Edward 14, Ailsy 13; 25 Dec 1844

6/20: William A. Fisher 26; Fauquier; Roanoke; Blacksmith; Moses BOOTH; Franklin; Maria F. Beard 26; Franklin; Roanoke; J. BEARD; Franklin; A_ Ann? 7, Gille Francis 5, Francis? J. 3; 30 April 1858

6/21: Charles Lewis 43; Roanoke; Roanoke; Farmer; F. RORER; Pulaski; Henrietta Goloon? 30; Roanoke; Roanoke; F. RORER; Pulaski; Rosetta 3, Nathaniel 3 mos, James 12, John 8, Nelson 6; 1853

6/22: Bob Coleman; Prince Edward; Roanoke; Blacksmith; F. WHORLEY; Bedford; Elva 55; Bedford; Roanoke; J. SMITH; Roanoke

6/23: Granville Roberts 53; Roanoke; Roanoke; Shoemaker; P. WOODRUFF; Montgomery; Marion Fleming 49; Roanoke; Roanoke; Elizabeth McCLENNAHAN; Roanoke; Granville 9, Juilus 23, Maria 15, Evelina 13; 8 May 1840

6/24: Tom Wright 51; Bedford; Roanoke; Farmer; J.C. KAIZER; Bedford Delia Gish 45; Roanoke; Roanoke; I.? BRUFF; Botetourt; Charley 15, Sellers 13, Norman 11, Mary 6, Nancy 23, Jimmie 19, Osborn 17; Sept 1837

6/25: Jeff Pankey 66; Prince Edward; Roanoke; Farmer; J.C. MILLER; Roanoke; Tilla 58; Prince Edward; Roanoke; Betsey SHIREY?; Roanoke; Ø; 1836

6/26: Almsted Spurlock 41; Roanoke; Roanoke; Carpenter; T. EVANS; Roanoke; Mary Morris 29; Roanoke; Roanoke; Fannie FARLEY; Roanoke; Ga_illa 7, Morgan 3, Lucy A. 16, Caroline 12, Nannie 8; Mar 1848

6/27: David Hannah 45; Roanoke; Roanoke; Farmer; William WATTS; Roanoke; Becky Lewis 38; Campbell; Roanoke; William WATTS; Roanoke; Lydia 8, Samuel 5, Watson 20, Lettie 15, Cornelius 13

6/28: London Beale

6/29: Bob Johnson 46; Roanoke; Roanoke; Farmer; F. SORRELL; Roanoke; Nancy Johnson 38; Campbell; Roanoke; F. SORRELL; Roanoke; Moses 5; 15 Feb 1858

6/30: John Richardson 35; Roanoke; Roanoke; Farmer; W.H. KYLE; Roanoke; Martha Freelon 32; Campbell; Roanoke; T. SINCLAIR; Roanoke; Ø; Dec 1862

6/31: Reuben Johnson; Bedford; Roanoke; Farmer; Mary C. OATEY; Bedford; Kitty 43; Bedford; Roanoke; Mary C. OATEY; Bedford; Lucy 9, Rittie (Kittie?) 5, Robert 4, Matilda 17, Pelina 14, Julia 8; 1846

6/32: Spencer Jones 28; Lunenburg; Roanoke; Farmer; C. CARTER; Nottoway; Henrietta Anderson 23; Roanoke; Roanoke; C. CARTER; Nottoway; Laura 6, Lizzie 4, George 1; Apr 1857

6/33: Jackson Hurst 30; Halifax; Roanoke; House Servant; B. SIMS; Roanoke; Rebecca Power; Halifax; Roanoke; B. SIMS; Roanoke; Lawrence 8, Luther 4, Georgianne 2; Dec 1857

6/34: Essex Noel 65; Bedford; Roanoke; Carpenter; P. BUFORD; Bedford; Martha Lowry; Ø; Roanoke; P. BUFORD; Bedford; Priscilla 13, Nelson 11, Essex 7, William 18, Ludy E. 17, Lucinda 15; Mar 1846

6/35: Samuel Moulton 34; Fluvanna; Roanoke; Shoemaker; F. JAMES; Roanoke; Harriet 37; Roanoke; Roanoke; F. JAMES; Roanoke; Ø; 1856

6/36: Abraham Teale 37; Henry

6/37: Paul Carrington 30; Halifax; Roanoke; Farmer; D. REED; Roanoke; Silvia Bruce 26; Roanoke; Roanoke; Matilda OLIVER; Roanoke; Dilsy 18 mos, Milly 1 mo; 1860

6/38: Peter Brooks 49; Charlotte; Roanoke; Farmer; A. REED; Roanoke; Elizabeth Fearis 40; Prince Edward; Roanoke; A. REED; Roanoke; Virginia 12, Alice? 8, Nannie 5, Daniel 3, Alberta 1, Patrick 23, Rachel 22, Louisa 15, Milton 13; 1842

6/39: George Ross 52; Lynchburg; Roanoke; Farmer; D. DAVIS; Roanoke; Susan 40; Franklin; Roanoke; J. GLEASON; Roanoke; Ø; Aug 1865

7/1: Alfred Blaney 43; Roanoke; Roanoke; Farmer; E. THOMAS; Roanoke; Lucy Tosh 36; Roanoke; Roanoke; William WOODS; Roanoke; Amanda 9, Mary 8, James 6, Lucy 3, George 6 mos, Charles 18, John 16, Henry 14, Nancy 13; 1847

7/2: Charles Malaga 25; Kanawha; Roanoke; Farmer; R. PHILLIPS; Roanoke; Macy Qualls 32; Bedford; Roanoke; R. PHILLIPS; Roanoke; Ø; Feb 1860

7/3: Griffin Mitchel 36; Roanoke; Roanoke; Farmer; William WOODS; Roanoke; Maria Sims 24; Albemarle; Roanoke; David BRAND; Roanoke; David 3, William F. 1; Dec 1861

7/4: Nelson Archer 35; Roanoke; Roanoke; Farmer; Matilda OLIVER; Roanoke; Martha Claiborne 23; Norfolk; Roanoke; H. HANSBOROUGH; Roanoke; Hugh 3, Becky 1; Jan 1862

7/5: Tom Priest 30; Fauquier; Roanoke; Farmer; Phelin DOTHERD; Chase City (Mecklenburg?); Elizabeth Smith 23; Botetourt; Roanoke; Prissy McDONALD; Botetourt; Wilanna 2; May 1863

7/6: Stephen Bently 53; Roanoke; Roanoke; Farmer; Betsey EVANS; Roanoke; Charlotte Ridout 52; Roanoke; Roanoke; Frank SORRELL; Roanoke; Granville 26, Henrietta 22, Mary E. 31, Edmund 28; Dec 1836

7/7: Cary Wilson 38; Bedford; Roanoke; Farmer; Free; Ø; Patsey Nelson 32; Roanoke; Roanoke; Free; Ø; Ø; June 1859

7/8: James Blany 39; Roanoke; Roanoke; Farmer; E. THOMAS; Roanoke; Fluentine Johnson 23; Bedford; Roanoke; David BARNETT; Roanoke; Rose 6, Mary 3; 1859

7/9: Lewis Goldstone 65; Botetourt; Roanoke; Farmer; Thomas TOSH; Roanoke; Judy Leftridge 66; Bedford; Roanoke; Powell HUFF; Roanoke; Ø; 1827

7/10: Archer Williams 34; Dinwiddie; Roanoke; Farmer; Ben FERRIS; Botetourt; Anna 29; Dinwiddie; Roanoke; Ben FERRIS; Botetourt; John 3, Stevers 1 mo; 1859

7/11: John Campbell 28; Roanoke; Roanoke; Farmer; William REYNOLDS; Roanoke; Eliza Wilson 28; Roanoke; Roanoke; Elizabeth SMITH; Roanoke; Martha J. 6, James E. 5, Ella 1; Feb 1857

7/12: Philip Clark; Prince Edward; Roanoke; Farmer; Ben FERRIS; Botetourt; Mary Napper; Roanoke; Roanoke; Ben FERRIS; Botetourt; Ø; Aug 1859

7/13: George Washington 29; Rappahannock; Roanoke; Farmer; James McCONKEY; Roanoke; Emmeline Smith 26; Roanoke; Roanoke; James McCONKEY; Roanoke; Sarah 7, Mary 3; June 1857

7/14: Joe Simms 23; Albemarle; Roanoke; Farmer; Dan BRAND; Roanoke; Ann Blaney 31; Roanoke; Roanoke; Betsey EVANS; Roanoke; ~~Milly 13~~; Sept 1863

7/15: Joseph Campbell 31; Roanoke; Roanoke; Farmer; Charles BARNET; Roanoke; Martha T_vrine 28; Roanoke; Roanoke; J. GOODWIN; Roanoke; Ø; Sept 1858

7/16: Jesse Gray 56; Botetourt; Roanoke; Farmer; James HANNAH; Botetourt; Jane Wallace; Augusta; Roanoke; Alex GIBSON; Botetourt; Harriet J., Margaret, Maria, Mary S. 27, Moses W. 25, Andrew; Jan 1836

7/17: Nathan Mars 36; Montgomery; Roanoke; Farmer; Free; Ø; Peggy Bracken 45; Botetourt; Roanoke; Ira JETER; Roanoke; Ø; Aug 1860

7/18: Philip Campbell 33; Roanoke; Roanoke; Farmer; John GARST; Roanoke; Elizabeth Hopkins 23; Roanoke; Roanoke; John GARST; Roanoke; Maria C. 3, George 6 mos; Aug 1862

7/19: Peyton Randolph 40; Bath; Roanoke; Farmer; Edward LANGHORNE; Campbell; Sarah Burrell 28?; Roanoke; Roanoke; John DABNY; Roanoke; William 16, Lucy 15, Peyton 14, Henry 13, Susan 11, George 10, Macellis 7, Mary A. 8; 26 Dec 1848

7/20: Sander Henry 25; Franklin; Roanoke; Farmer; Free Born; Ø; Ø; Elizabeth McGuire 30; Roanoke; Roanoke; Free Born; Ø; Ø; Nov 1864

7/21: William Adams 26; Amherst; Roanoke; Barber; George W. WARRICK; Lynchburg; Sarah Crawford 24; Chesterfield; Roanoke; Nancy CRAWFORD; Lynchburg; Wallace 6, Realia 1; Feb 1857

7/22: Charles Lovely 47; Roanoke; Roanoke; Blacksmith; H. EDMUNDSON; Roanoke; Lucy Radford 46; Bedford; Roanoke; Joseph CAMPBELL; Roanoke; George 17, Kate 9; 7 Feb 1847

189

Table 24: Scott County, VA

Register of Colored Persons cohabiting together as Husband and Wife

(pg/line; h/age; pob; res; occ; last owner/res; w/age; pob; w/res; last owner/res; child/age; date of cohabatation)

1/1: Charles McConnell 48; Ø; Scott; Farmer; A.B. McCONNELL; Scott; Hannah 48; Scott; Scott; J. RAYNY; Scott; Jane 19, Thomas 11, Robert 8, Roxanna 2; 19 Nov 1846

1/2: Willis Salling 45; No. Carolina; Scott; Farmer; George W. SALLING; Nancy 50; Russell; Scott; Free; Ø; Rosa Ellen 21, Charlotte 14; 1842

1/3: Anthony Cane 46; No. Carolina; Farmer; Henry CANE; Scott; Fannie 46; Russell; Scott; Free; Ø; Henry 22, Harry 18, Delia 18, William 15, Jim 12, Robert 9, Tilda 7; Dec 1843

1/4: Amos Turner 50; Bedford; Scott; Tanner; Jacob GISH; Botetourt; Nancy 40; ; Scott; Jim DINGUS; Scott; Rebecca 23, William 22, Judy 17, Andy 16, Sam 14, Frances 13, Maria 8, Angeline 6

1/5: Abraham Carter 26; Cumberland; Scott; Blacksmith; Henry S. CAIN; Scott; S_arny 21; Giles; Scott; R.R. SHELTON; Scott; Victoria 3; 1861

1/6: Sam Dykes 67; Fairfax; Scott; Farmer; James DYKES; Scott; Elizabeth 55; Tennessee; Scott; J. DYKES; Scott; Easter 26, Smith 18, Nath 14, Jeff 17, Lige 28; Dave 26, Selah 21, Rebecca 30, John 21, George 25, Ailsey 24

1/7: Jake Bnater 46; Scott; Scott; Farmer; John OWENS; Nicey 40; Scott; Scott; Thomas Quilan; Scott; Mary 19, Hulda 16, William 12, Ellender 10, James E. 8, Amy 3; 6 June 1847

1/8: James Sales 65; Essex; Scott; Henry CAIN; Scott; Louisa 40; Ø; Scott; Henry CAIN; Scott; Campbell 16; 1849

1/9: Lewis Bradford 22; No. Carolina; Scott; James HENDERSON; Scott; Ann 19; Mercer; Scott; James HENDERSON; Scott; Charley 1 ½; Dec 1863

1/10: Levi Wood 54; Scott; Scott; Farmer; James WOOD; Scott; Jane 33; Hawkins, Tennessee; Scott; J. DRAPER; Scott; ~~Addie 8, Elizabeth 2~~; Mar 1866

1/11: Reddick Cain 45; Southampton; Scott; Farmer; Henry CAIN; Scott; Selah 26; Scott; Scott; J.O. WOODS; Scott; Aleck 6, Jackson 3; 1858

1/12: Charles Brawn 50; Ø; Scott; J.R. BEANNER; Scott; Selina 52; Ø; Scott; J.O. WOODS; Scott; Matilda 19, Peggy 14, Creed 8, Thomas 7, Amy 6, Susan 13

1/13: George Wilson 40; Russell; Scott; Wesley BECKLEY; Scott; Sarah E. 32; Russell; Scott; Wesley BECKLEY; Scott; Caroline 13, Fannie 11, Louiza 7, Mary 4, James 1; 1850

INDEX

139; Lucy, 96; M.J., 94; Maj.
R., 37; Mrs. N., 112; R., 37;
Syrus, 47, 121
ALLMAN, 83
Alms: Lewis, 98; Nancy, 98
ALMS: Alice, 92; Patsy, 100;
Walter, 98
Amanda, 4, 17, 25, 30, 32, 174,
183, 188
Amanda J., 4
Amelia, 18
Amelia A., 26
Amelia S., 182
America, 20
AMES: Alice, 40, 58
Amherst, 23
Amisity, 26
Ammons: Ellen, 184
Amos: Virgil, 147
AMOS: Edmond J., 25; Edward
J., 18, 22; Elizabeth, 15;
James, 57; Rufus, 147
Amy, 191, 192
And: Hannah, 56
And. J., 169, 171
Anderson, 7, 20, 32, 154; Alice,
76; Ben, 76; Benjamin, 8;
Billy, 76; Charley, 76;
Daniel, 56; Elijah, 97, 184;
Eliza, 119; Elizabeth, 1;
Emma, 119; George, 175;
Griffin, 41, 108; Harriet, 170;
Henrietta, 187; J., 181;
Jenny, 76; Jimmy, 76; John,
83; Judy, 173; Kit, 170;
Louisa, 14; Lucinda, 56, 83;
Madison, 41; Maria, 29, 173;
Mary, 63; Mary A., 43;
Moses, 115; N., 119; Nancy,
76; Nelly, 76; Nelson, 169;
Parthena, 56; Parthenia, 100;
Pat, 48; Peter, 8, 167; Pierce,
119; Priscila, 56; Quintanna,

108; Rachel, 7, 182; Robert,
119; Sallie, 48; Scylla, 97;
Somerville, 100; Spencer, 63;
Thomas, 56; Washington,
178; William, 56
ANDERSON: C., 44, 74, 115,
119, 121; F., 53; George, 1,
41, 108; George W., 23, 30;
H., 56; J.R., 178; Jonas, 19;
Leach, 48; Lucy J., 170;
Martha, 74; Mrs. K., 67;
R.C., 38, 62, 77, 87; S., 119;
T., 44, 119; William, 61
Andrew, 5, 8, 17, 22, 26, 30,
83, 147, 189
Andrew J., 18
Andrew L., 155
Andy, 174, 176, 177, 191
Angeline, 31, 191
Ann, 1, 6, 14, 16, 22, 27, 159,
160, 172, 173, 175, 177, 179,
182, 185, 191; Eliza, 92
Ann B., 4
Ann E., 21, 180
Ann Jane, 82
Anna, 15, 148, 156, 168, 188
Anna S., 183
Anne, 84, 170, 185
Anne B., 24
Anne E., 25
ANSON: Charles, 96
Anthony, 175; Fanny, 23;
Mark, 18
Antoinette, 179
Aplen: Eliza, 9
APLEN: Nancy, 9
Apson: Robert, 32
Archer, 149; Clayborne, 176;
John, 182; Nelson, 188;
Susan, 182
Archie, 169
Arcissa/Areissa, 154
Arminta, 7

Armistead, 147
Armstead: Ann, 61; Clem, 114;
  Cornelia, 61; Ella, 97;
  Goliah, 110; Hezakiah, 97;
  Ida, 97; J., 110; Jeff, 110;
  Jenny, 110; John, 61, 114;
  Julia, 114; Leroy, 97;
  Mildred, 97; Page, 114;
  Robertta, 97; Susan, 61;
  Thomas, 97; William, 92, 97
ARMSTEAD: John, 109, 110,
  113, 114; John H., 65; Mrs.
  C., 71; W., 119; William, 44
Armstrong: Edward, 19;
  Rachel, 25; Richard, 152
Arnold: Elsee, 32
Arthur, 146, 152
ARTHUR: Mrs., 177
Asa, 171
ASBY: ?., 181
Ashbury: N., 172
ASHBURY: J., 172
Atkins: Jane, 107; Jennie, 154;
  Mary, 137; Sterling, 107;
  Thornton, 137
ATKINS: Miss J., 107
Atwell: Maria, 147
ATWELL: Daniel, 145
AUGIN: John, 77
Augusta, 155
Austin, 146; Buck, 39; C.
  Francis, 48; Hannah, 48;
  Henry, 39; Henry F., 48;
  Mary L., 48; Rhoda A., 20;
  Robert, 22; Sarah Jane, 48;
  Spencer B., 48; William, 48
Auther, 149
Ayres: Betty, 79; Decker, 79;
  Hannah, 79; Powell, 79;
  Thomas, 79
B.P., 169
B__MAN: William, 145

Badley: Charles, 85;
  Emrick/Eunick, 85; H.L., 85;
  Lizzie, 85; Lucy J., 85; Sally,
  85; William D., 85
Bagby: David, 97; Louisa, 97
Bagley: Edward, 110; Elvira,
  110; Griffin, 110; Louisa,
  110; Lucy, 110; Mary J., 110
BAGLEY: Mrs. M.S., 110
Bai_: Samuel, 16
Bailey: Anna, 136; Lizzie, 126;
  Lucy J., 104; Mariah, 151;
  Milley, 152; Sam, 104;
  Stephen, 136; William, 126
BAILEY: John, 104
Baily: Maria E., 181; Monroe,
  9; Richard, 19
Baker: __nas, 11; Betsey, 44;
  Claiborne, 49; Cora, 119;
  David, 54; Ed, 54; Francis,
  44; Frederick, 54; Germon, 2;
  Ida, 54; John, 54; Judy, 54;
  Lucy, 54; Mariah W., 49;
  Mary, 54; Milly, 49;
  Pleasant, 44, 119; Rose, 54;
  Sarah E., 54; Thomas, 54;
  Violet, 54
BAKER: Allen, 53; Eliza, 53,
  54; Mrs. E., 53, 54
Baldwin, 181
BALDWIN: Albert, 60; C., 33;
  S., 53
Ball: Arthur R., 139; Daniel,
  173; Ellen, 154; Frances,
  139; James, 150; James H.,
  139; Marth, 146; Mary
  Louisa, 139; Sarah, 180;
  Susy, 175; William A., 154
Balldaw: Milly, 181
Banam, 150
BANDY: C., 158; J., 182
BANEM: William, 145
BANK: Warner H., 153

195

Banks: Ann, 161; Charles, 181;
Columbus, 161; E.J., 178;
Eliza, 173; Ellen, 160, 161,
173; Ephraim, 167;
Ferdinand, 184; Isaac, 160,
185; James, 161; John, 169;
Lucinda, 169; Malinda, 167;
Maria, 178; Martha, 167;
Norbern, 5; Peyton, 161;
Phoebe Ann, 160; Sarah,
179; Shelby, 169; Thomas,
19; Tom, 160, 172; Warner,
161
Banner: Mary, 108; William,
108
Barbason: Salinda, 4
Barber: Franklin, 18
Barbery, 82
BARDMAN: Edward, 115
Barkes: Charlotte, 10
Barlett: Mary J., 95
Barlow: Sarah, 185
Barnes: Thomas, 149
BARNES: F., 153; John, 168
BARNET: Charles, 189;
Thomas M., 11
Barnett: Julia, 29; William, 174
BARNETT: Charles, 14, 18;
Charles H., 4; Charles T., 12;
David, 28, 188; Edward, 16;
James, 12, 27; John, 27; John
D., 13; Samuel, 27
BARRACKS: Thomas, 136
Barrett: Angeline, 7; Biddie, 7;
Crockett, 21; Josephine, 7;
Lucinda, 153
BARRETT: William, 65
BARRICKS: Thomas, 145
Bartlett: A.L., 95; Augustus, 67;
Ben, 60; Betsy, 95;
Caledonia, 95; Catherine, 60,
67; Ella, 60; Emily, 67;
Ennis, 67; Fred, 60; George,

60, 95; Henry, 95; James, 60,
67; James W., 95; Jane, 60,
123; Jenny, 60; John, 95;
Joseph, 123; Mamranth J.,
95; Margaret, 60; Maria, 67;
Mary, 60; Paul, 60; Rhoda,
95; Samuel, 60; Simuel, 95;
William, 67; Woodson, 60
~~Bashe~~, 177
BASS: Colin, 174; Collin, 22
Baste: Alex, 117; Ella, 117
Bates: Alex, 83; Anderson M.,
100; David, 100; Elvira, 83,
100; Jane V., 100; Letty E.,
100; Nancy, 66, 100;
Travann, 100; William, 66
BATTLE: Dr., 108
Batton: Eliza, 3
Batts/Botts: Clara, 74; Richard,
74
Baulden: Amanda, 49; Betsey,
85; Edward, 49; Elsey, 49;
Emaline, 85; Hannah, 85;
M.A., 49; Madison, 49;
Mary, 49; Peter, 85; Pitt, 49;
Sam, 85; Samuel, 85;
Sterling, 49
Baxter: Daniel, 87; John, 87;
Lucy, 87; Osborne, 87;
Rachel, 87
BAYERS: Sheffield, 3
Baylor: Easter, 145
BEACH: William, 85
Beale: Edward, 176; James E.,
161; John, 162; London, 161,
187; Martha A., 162; Mary,
162; Sally, 161
Bean: Moses, 31
BEAN: John, 30
BEANNER: J.R., 192
Beard: Maria F., 186
BEARD: J., 186

BEARNARD: Arthur, 136, 145, 153
Beasley: Elvira, 63; John T., 63; Thompson, 63
BEASLEY: D.A., 106; Jack, 63, 64
BEATTEY: William, 91
Beavers: Jemimah, 3
Beckey, 148
BECKLEY: Wesley, 192
Becky, 146, 148, 173, 174, 188
Bedford: Albert, 120; Joseph, 120; Louisa, 120; Lucinda, 120; Rebecca, 120
Bee: Martha, 59; Robert, 59; Samuel, 59; Willie, 59
Beech: Leroy, 152
BELCHUS: Ben, 110
BELFIELD: John, 140; Olmsted, 146
Bell, 146; Allen, 124; Anderson, 126; Baker, 126; Biddy, 124; Booker, 109; Charles, 30, 126; Cynthna, 124; Delia, 126; Easter, 109; Frank, 126; Henry, 124; Julia, 124; Martha, 126; Mary, 126; Mitchell, 126; Molly, 38; Sylvia, 126; William, 114, 124
BELL: Adam, 126; David, 83; G.W., 124; George, 109; George W., 52; J.B., 124; James, 52; John B., 124; Mary, 121; Thomas, 38, 109, 117; William, 103
BELLFIELD: J.W., 148; Richard, 149
Ben, 172, 176, 181
BENAM: William, 136
Bench: Hack, 104; Isham, 104; Martha, 85; Phillis, 104; Sam, 85; Thomas, 85

BENCH: Elisha, 85, 104; William, 36
Benjamin, 13
BENNAM: William, 151
BENNET: Garner, 17; Harrison, 17
Bentley: America, 98; Jane, 98; Julia, 98; Scipio, 98
Bently: Randal, 170; Stephen, 188
Berkeley: A., 119; Bruce, 91; Early, 91; Edward, 91; Eliza, 119; Elizabeth, 119; Emma, 91; L., 119; Laura, 34; Lydia, 117; Margaret, 91; Monroe, 119; Patrick, 34; Patsey, 34; Peyton, 34, 117; Phebe, 34; Saul, 91; Sophy, 34; Stephen, 34
BERKELEY: Dr., 48, 84, 111
BERNARD: Arthur, 152
BERNET: Henry, 10
Berry: Clarkie, 185
BERRY: James, 111
Bertha, 30
Bessie, 5
Betsey, 148, 156, 179, 183
Betsey A., 169, 182
Betsey Ann, 152
Betsy, 181
Betsy Ann, 177
Bett A., 152
Bettie, 31, 145
Betts: Adam, 175; Laura Virginia, 151
Betty, 82, 167, 183, 185
Betty Alice, 153
BEUFORD: William, 95; William E., 63
Beven: Mat, 178
Beverly, 148; Amanda, 147; Elizabeth, 4; Mattison, 4; William, 182

BILBROOK: William, 174
Billy, 167
BIRCHFIELD: Abraham, 3;
   John, 2, 3
Birney, 182
BISCOE: Henry, 134
Bla__: Joseph, 153
Black: Addoway, 26; Eliza, 24;
   Mills, 8
BLACK: Harvey, 9; John, 22
BLACKWELL: Mary, 134
Blair: Joseph, 149
BLAKE: Demas, 75
Blanche, 171, 175
Bland: C., 73; Charity, 107; Ed,
   107; Ellen, 73; Ellis, 73;
   William, 73
Blaney: —illy, 166; Alfred, 165,
   166, 188; Ann, 165, 189;
   Darius, 166; Elias, 165;
   Eliza, 165; Floyd, 165;
   Harriet, 165; James, 165,
   166; Joe, 165; John, 165;
   Joseph, 18; Myron, 166;
   Nancy, 166; Richard, 165;
   Robert, 166; Samuel, 165;
   Susan, 165
BLANEY: James, 166
BLANTON: Charles, 68; Dr.,
   89; James, 71; Mrs. E., 127;
   Mrs. N.E., 78; Nancy, 78, 84;
   Thomas, 93, 107; W., 78
Blany: James, 188
Blue: Alice L., 60; H. Ann, 60;
   Mose, 153; Noah H., 60;
   Thomas F., 60
Bluens: Reuben, 17, 24
Blunt: Lucy A., 105; Thomas,
   105
Bnater: Jake, 191
BOARD: G.B., 160, 168, 179
Bob, 172, 173, 174, 179, 180
Boles: Henry, 14

Bolling: Aggie, 110; Joseph,
   110; Lucy, 85; Martha, 85;
   Patrick, 85; Phebe, 85; Pitt,
   85; Spencer, 110; Sterling, 85
BOLLING: P., 113; Phil, 57;
   William, 72
BOLLISTON: N.T., 153
BONDURANT: J., 43; John,
   43, 90, 108; S., 86; Sam, 86
Booden: Elsie, 151
Booker, 183; Agnes, 96; Alice,
   96; Allen, 105; Amanda, 118;
   Amelia, 45; Amy, 38;
   Benjamin, 44; Betsey, 44;
   Betty, 96; Beverly, 62;
   Branch, 56; Carlether, 61;
   Carlethn, 61; Cora Ann, 126;
   Crecy, 112; Daniel, 107;
   Edward, 45; Edwin, 44;
   Eliza, 75; Ellen, 111, 118;
   Fanny, 45, 77; Hampton, 93;
   Henry, 108, 115; Hercules,
   58; Isabella, 115; Israel, 38;
   J., 123; Jacob, 96; James, 77;
   Jane, 123; John, 44; Joseph,
   75; Judy, 44; Lewis, 112,
   115, 184; Lizzie, 111;
   Louisa, 61, 111; Lucy, 96;
   Major, 44, 119; Maria, 58;
   Martha, 112; Martha A., 118;
   Mary, 56, 93, 107, 119; Mary
   Ann, 77; Melinda, 105, 108;
   Molly, 38, 111; Moses, 96;
   Ned, 126; Nicholas, 96;
   Otilla, 108; Page, 45; Patsy,
   38; Peter, 61; Powell, 108;
   Rachel, 62; Richard, 96, 105;
   Robert, 118; Sarah, 96;
   Sayler, 111; Vina, 115;
   William H., 62; Willie, 112
BOOKER: George, 90; J.M.,
   123; Jenny, 73; Mrs. A., 72;

Mrs. C., 75; Nancy, 69; William, 98

Boon: Archer, 13

Boone: Emmeline, 181; Louisa, 10

BOONE: D., 175

BOOTH: Moses, 186; William, 153

Bosley: Shepperd, 36

Boswell: Maria, 18; Mary, 103; Sarah, 36; Shepherd, 103

Bouser: Lucy, 32

BOWLER: Lerod, 10

Bowman: Laura, 41

BOWYER: Charles, 28

Bowzer: Jane, 133; Mary Catharine, 133

Bowzier: Ellen Norah, 133; Junius, 133; Mariah, 133; William Thomas, 133

Boyd: Harriet, 16; Jerry, 137; Lucy, 137; Robert, 137; Susan, 9

BOYD: John H., 57

BOYER: Charles, 13

Bracken: Peggy, 189

Bracket: Isabella, 186; James, 32

Bradford: Lewis, 191

Bradley: Emily, 61; George, 61; Isiah, 61; James, 61; Jenny, 61; Martha, 61; Samuel, 61; Sarah, 61

BRADLEY: William, 109

BRADSHAW: Mrs., 41; Mrs. L., 105; Mrs. M., 101, 102, 107; Mrs. P., 101, 117; Mrs. S., 108; Samuel, 58; William, 79

Bragg: Parhena/Zarehena, 6; Sarah, 26

Braggs: Griffin, 82; Mary A., 82

Branch: Alice, 61; Anderson, 105; Ann, 107; Archy, 40; Ben, 127; Betty, 105; Beverly, 41, 61, 107; Branch, 45; Caroline, 104; Cary, 93; Cassandra, 58; Catherine, 41, 52; Chaney, 52; Creed, 58; Davy, 45; Edward, 81; Edwin, 113; Eliza, 61, 105; Elizabeth, 86; Elsy, 87; Elvira, 105; Fanny, 61; Francis, 107; Harriet, 97; Henry, 40, 58; Isaac, 127; Jacob, 127; Jiggem, 45; Joel, 36, 86; John, 113; John R., 107; Lilly, 127; Lucella, 45; Lucy, 45, 127; M. Ann, 58; M. Cath, 58; Maria, 58; Mary, 45, 107, 113; Math, 58; Milly, 127; Nancy, 81, 93; Pat, 86; Patty, 36, 104; Paula, 110; Peter, 105, 110; Polly, 61; Richard, 52, 81, 97; Robert, 81, 104; Ruth, 107; Sally, 73; Samuel, 73; Sarah, 58; Shadrack, 87; Sydney, 81; Tazewell, 97; Washington, 58; William E., 81

BRANCH: Emily, 165; J.T., 92, 94, 106; John F., 105

Brand: Emma, 13

BRAND: Dan, 189; David, 188

BRANHAM: Lucy, 136, 145; Lucy C., 138

BRANNUM: Mary, 154, 155

BRANSON: H.L., 80

Bratten: John, 30

Bratton: James, 177; Julia, 14

Brawn: Charles, 192

Braxton: America, 170; Carter, 70; E. Jane, 70; Pleasant, 70; William, 172

Bray: Sopha, 150
BRENT: Janah, 38; Jonah, 38;
   Josiah, 64
Brickey: Pat, 173
Bridewell: Aaron, 87; Alex, 87;
   Annes, 87; Harriet, 87;
   Henry, 87; Jacob, 87; John,
   87; Patsy, 87; Peter, 87
BRIDEWELL: Addison, 94; J.,
   87; William, 87
BRIDWELL: Joseph, 73
Brier: Betsey, 84; Henry, 84
Briggs: Lewis, 31
BROCKENBORO: Edward,
   150; John, 146, 150; Lucy,
   150; William, 137; William
   F., 153
BROCKENBRAGH: W.T.,
   154; William F., 154
BROKENBORO: Lucy, 137;
   Walter, 152
BROKENBROUGH: John, 153
Brooks: __ge, 12; Adaline, 9,
   15; Catharine, 179; Gibson,
   15; Julia, 152; Margaret A.,
   23; Martha, 12; Peter, 187;
   Phil, 97; Stephen, 154
BROOKS: Andrew, 179
Brown: _oshua, 23; _wis, 24;
   A., 171; Abbe, 69; Abram,
   56, 69; Albert, 56, 103;
   Alice, 87, 117; Amanda, 11;
   Anderson, 63; Ann, 12;
   Barnet, 7; Bethe, 87; Betsy,
   112; Betty, 67, 117; Billy,
   176; Caroline, 97; Clem, 44;
   Dandridge, 1; Daniel, 106;
   Eden, 24; Edward, 23, 112;
   Edwin, 87; Eliza, 69, 103,
   117; Elizabeth, 67; Elvira,
   94; Emma, 67; Fannie, 16;
   Fanny, 63, 103, 121; Frances,
   69; Frank, 122; George P.,

51; Glasscow, 117; Grace A.,
   106; Hamilton, 7; Harriet, 69,
   122; Harrison, 44; Hattie, 69;
   Henry, 69, 117; Isaac, 94;
   Jack, 117; James, 121; Jeff,
   51; Jenny, 94; Joseph, 106,
   117, 122; Julia A., 94; Julia
   Ann, 106; Keziah, 67;
   Lavinia, 87; Lewis, 69; Lilla,
   113; Limby, 117; Louis, 67;
   Louisa, 112; Lousani, 122;
   Lucinda, 15; Lucy, 117;
   Marenda, 30; Marg, 117;
   Maria, 1, 121; Marshal, 56,
   94; Martha, 121; Martha J.,
   162; Mary, 37, 117, 121;
   Nancy, 117; Nannie, 67;
   Nicey, 56; Oscar, 97; Philice,
   27; Robert, 97; Rosa, 87;
   Rose, 69, 150; Sally, 174;
   Samuel, 28; Sarah, 4;
   Staunton, 97; Stephan, 69;
   Stephen, 69, 97, 121; Stokes,
   56, 87, 97; Sukey, 97; Susan,
   87; Thomas, 29, 67, 103,
   112, 113, 162; Walter, 117;
   Washington, 113; Webster,
   87; William, 67, 69, 155;
   Wyatt, 117
BROWN: Crockett, 7; Daniel,
   12; Henry, 17; James, 17,
   145; Lucy, 171; S.D., 122;
   Thomas, 18
Bruce: Aleck, 157; Betty, 157;
   Billy, 157; Bruce, 157;
   Daniel, 83; David, 157; Jane,
   83; Marshal, 182; Marshall,
   157; Napoleon, 157; Richard,
   157; Silvia, 187; Susan, 157
BRUCE: Charles, 76; E., 74;
   Samuel, 111, 115
BRUFF: I., 186
BRUFFY: William, 26

200

Bryan: Sarah, 167
BRYANT: Alexander, 155
Buchanan, 26
Buckanna, 154
BUDD: Henry, 90
BUFINGTON: Henry, 3
Buford, 7; Emeline, 21
BUFORD: P., 187
Bundy: Polley, 147
BURGESS: John, 27
Burk: Rachel, 5
BURK: Nancy, 15
Burke: Agnes, 98; Drusilla, 98;
    Edward, 173; Horace, 98
BURKE: Benjamin, 98
Burks: David, 21; Elizabeth, 10;
    Margaret, 31; Marinda, 182;
    Rhoda, 181; Wilson, 181
BURKS: Samuel G., 181
Burle: William, 154
BURNETT: Arthur, 145; Mrs.,
    148
Burrell: Abbet, 71; Agnes, 111;
    Albert, 111; Caroline, 71;
    Isaac, 111; Jane, 111;
    Jeremiah, 15; Preston, 183;
    Sarah, 189
Burrill: Oliver, 167
BURRILL: Armstead, 165; C.,
    169, 173; J.H.; 167; N., 158,
    170, 172, 173, 178
BURROWS: William, 27
Burton: C., 43; Cath, 118; Cora,
    118; Joseph, 20; Lucy, 86;
    Milly, 86; Rachel, 86;
    Richard, 118; Samuel, 86;
    Sarah C., 86; Susan, 86;
    William, 7; Willie, 118
Bush: James Mattison, 28
BUSH: Griffin, 28; Griffith D.,
    7
BUSTON: William, 6
BUSTRE: William, 3

Butler: Carrie, 109; Gaston,
    109; George, 52; Matilda, 84;
    Milly, 52; Nace, 52; Nathan,
    84; Sarah J., 109; Sukey, 52;
    Susan, 109; Sydney, 109;
    Uriah S., 22; William, 109
Byassy: Andrew, 88; Ashley,
    88; Betty, 42; Clem, 42, 88;
    Dodson, 88; Eliza, 42; Elvira,
    88; Emily, 42; Pinkey, 42;
    Puss, 88; Summer, 88
Byers: Rebecca, 167
C__TE: J., 63
Cabell: C__h, 39; Charlotte, 39;
    Eda Ann, 38; Gilbert, 39;
    Grace, 39; Harriet, 39;
    Isabell, 65; Landon, 39;
    Nick, 62, 65; Patrick, 39;
    Phebe, 38; Sam, 62; Sinai, 62
Caesar, 177
Cager Monroe, 4
Cain: Pelina, 185; Reddick, 192
CAIN: Henry, 191, 192; Henry
    S., 191
CALAHAN: George, 10
CALDWELL: Thomas, 114
Caleb, 29
CALHOUN: Dr., 123; Drury,
    103
CALLAHAN: Edmond H., 30
Calloway: E., 170; Fanny, 28;
    Lewis, 177
Caloway: William, 15
CALOWAY: James, 11, 13
Calvin, 11; Ersie, 10
CAMDEN: Isaac, 110
Camile, 155
CAMP: Andrew J., 18
Campbell, 191; Charlotta I., 25;
    Eliza, 4; Elizabeth, 15;
    George Henry, 134, 138;
    John, 16, 188; Joseph, 189;
    Josephine, 5; Julia Ann, 137;

201

Juliett, 134; Laticia, 6; Lucy, 170; Mary, 134, 137; Peter, 28; Philip, 189; Rachael Anna, 137; Richard, 134, 137; Sarah, 1; William, 5

CAMPBELL: C., 174, 175; C.R., 185; Joseph, 189

Canada: Adam, 136, 145; Betsey, 136; John Henry, 136

Cane: Anthony, 191

CANE: Henry, 191

Cango: Fanny, 103; Peyton, 103

Cank: Eliza, 185

CANNAHAN: William M., 31

Cardwell: Andrew, 51; Jacob, 51; Jeff, 51; Lina, 51; Mack, 51; Stonewall, 51

Carey: David, 5; Fannie, 3

Caroline, 7, 10, 11, 18, 23, 27, 32, 79, 153, 154, 155, 174, 175, 185, 186, 192

CARPER: Russell, 2

Carr: Dennis, 170; James, 4; Mary, 4, 8

CARR: G.W., 161, 171, 181, 183, 185

Carrie, 3

Carrington: Ab., 183; Abram, 52; Archy, 52; Celia, 52; Clem, 52; George W., 52; John, 52; Louisa, 178; Martha, 52; Mary J., 52; Paul, 187; Rachel C., 52; Randal W., 52; Thomas G., 52

CARRINGTON: Alex, 97; Dr., 76, 80; Dr. W., 37; Dr. William, 57; Isaac C., 150; Mrs. B., 115; William, 35, 105, 117

CARRY: William, 152

Carter, 9, 182; _ist_l, 54; Abraham, 10, 191; Aldridge,

167; America, 54; Amos, 64; Anderson, 4; Ann, 113; Betsey, 85; Bettie, 96; Burrell, 54; Charlota, 3; Edmund, 183; Edward, 148; Elizabeth, 156; Fanny, 54; Jhas., 54; John, 151; Katie, 96; Louisa, 85; Lucy, 11; Mary, 68; Nathaniel, 155; Olivia, 54; Patience, 113; Patrick, 96; Rachel, 64; Sally, 148; Sarah, 96, 113; Sarah J., 6; Sena, 85; William, 68; Wilson, 85; Winny, 173; York, 113

CARTER: C., 187; Col., 150; Elizabeth, 4; Frank, 45, 70; Richard, 48; Robert, 149, 152; Sam, 47; Samuel, 51, 113

CARVIN: Lucy, 175

CARY: L., 86; Mrs. J., 121; William H., 50

Casey: Benjamin, 52; Betsey, 52; Daniel, 52; Gaskill, 52; Jenny, 52

Castor: Fannie, 148

Caswell, 14, 30

Catharine, 19, 23, 155, 168, 175

Catherine, 3, 8, 82

Cathrine, 148

Cavel: Amanda, 112; Robert, 112; Sarah, 175; Wash, 112; William, 112

CAVEL: Napoleon, 175

Cecelia, 19

Cecelia A., 5

Celia, 146, 172

Cesar, 6

Cesetina, 149

Chafin: John, 55; Mary, 55

Chalmerns/Chalmems: Henry, 161; Rosa L., 161; Sally, 161; William, 161
Chambers: Dennis, 76; Hal, 77; Hannah, 77; Henderson, 76; Henry, 179; Joseph, 76; Lesser, 76; Margaret, 76; Rachel, 76; Sally, 76; William, 186; William F., 77
CHAMBERS: Allen, 90; Dr., 76; Mrs. M., 86, 110; Mrs. William, 121; Pat, 76; Patsey, 82; William, 179
Champ, 16
Chancellor: Washington, 21
Chant, 174
Chap, 176
Chapman: Rebecca, 177
CHAPMAN: Henry, 185; N., 172; Nancy, 159, 162, 168, 176
CHAPPELL: Dr., 64; W.H., 112; William, 115
Charity, 179
Charles, 3, 5, 6, 10, 16, 23, 27, 29, 32, 146, 147, 148, 154, 155, 156, 168, 169, 171, 173, 174, 177, 179, 182, 183, 184, 185, 188
Charles B., 28
Charles C., 14
Charles E., 9, 13, 21
Charles H., 28
Charles L., 3, 20
Charles Lewis, 154
Charles M., 9
Charles T., 18
Charles W., 12
Charley, 180, 186, 191
Charlotta, 9
Charlotte, 44, 120, 159, 170, 180, 191; Charlotte, 98
Charlton: Jane, 25

CHARLTON: Samuel, 12; William B., 2
Cheatham: Daniel, 56; John, 56; Lewis, 56; Minnie, 56
CHEATHAM: B., 56
Cheese: ___, 21
Chester, 20; Julia, 32; Milly Ann, 71; Peyton, 71; Robert, 71; Susan, 71
Chevalier: William, 185
CHILDERS: Alf, 101
CHILDREE: Thomas, 17, 23; William, 23
Childs: Anderson, 50; Booker, 50; Mary, 50
CHINA: Mary, 148
Christian, 83
CHRISTIAN: Abraham, 12; Edward, 7; Robert, 12; Thomas, 7
Christianna, 173
CHRISTMAN: Gorden, 31
CHUBB__: R., 52
CHUMMY: Bard, 74; R., 74; Ramsom, 58; Ransom, 40; Sam, 104; William, 55
Cina, 163
Cinderella, 180
Cinga, 149
Cl_ton: Samuel, 148
Claiborne, 179; Martha, 188
Clara, 5, 80
Clarence, 156
Clark: Alpheus, 125; Amelia, 177; Anderson, 86; Ann, 102, 114; Ann Maria, 125; Archy, 103; Asa, 103; Charity, 10; Columbus, 125; Dennis, 57; Edward, 69; Edwin, 125; Elizabeth, 125; Emma, 114; Faith, 125; Frederick, 26; George, 7; James, 125; Jane, 103; John, 86; Judy, 86;

Lewis, 125; Lydia, 98; M.L.,
114; Martha, 125, 153; Mary,
69; Mary J., 86; Mary S.,
102; Minerva, 57; Molly,
102; Patrick, 70; Patrick H.,
86; Philip, 189; Robert, 8,
125; Ross, 173; Sallie, 57;
Sally, 103; Simon, 114;
Sophy, 70; Taylor, 86;
Thomas, 98; William, 22,
102; William T., 86
CLARK: Caroline, 153; Dr.,
103; Ed, 80, 105; H.A., 70;
Harmen, 70; Hemp_l, 152;
Henssil, 150; Joseph, 155;
Martha, 91; Michael, 28;
Mrs. Benjamin, 71, 125; Mrs.
M., 105; Mrs. P., 57, 62;
Mrs. Phebe, 69; Ogden J., 69;
S.T., 86; Sam L., 86; Samuel,
77; Thomas, 71, 102
CLARK & LIGAN, 76
CLARKSTON: John M., 102
Clary, 14
Clay, 6, 178; Henry, 52;
Rachel, 52; Thomas, 152
CLAYBORN: George W., 66
Clayborne, 148, 167
Clayton: Charles, 153
Claytor: Tom, 170
Clementina, 177
CLEMENTS: William, 61
Clemms: Alex, 73; Betty, 73;
C., 73
Cley: Fannie, 176
CLINDIN: Betsey, 137
CLOYD: Elizabeth, 31;
Gorden, 22; Gordon, 13, 14;
James, 20
Coats: Martha A., 154
Cobb: Agnes, 44; Benjamin, 44,
78; Eliza, 78; Francis, 44;
Huston, 44; James A., 44;

Jeta, 78; Lucinda, 174;
Melinda, 44
COBB: John, 174
COCHRAN: J., 53; P., 85
COCK: William A., 70, 115
Cofer: Louisa, 168
Cole: Ada, 68; Easther, 34;
Eliza, 68; Emma, 68; Henry,
34; Phineas, 68; Virgie, 68
Coleman: Agnes, 99;
Archambald, 18, 27; Beverly,
111; Bob, 186; Buck, 99;
Collin, 99; Daniel, 99; F.,
111; Frank, 111; Louisa, 111;
Mary, 29, 32, 111; Paul, 99;
Polly, 111; Rose, 111; Sarah,
8; Silas, 99; Susan, 49; Tenie,
25; Thomas, 49
COLEMAN: C., 78; Edward P.,
94; James, 60; White, 6, 31
Coles: Melinda, 75; Moses, 75
Collins, 174
COMER: D., 169
COMPTON: John, 7
Conelly: Ellen, 151
Connor: Mary, 184
Conway: Lucy, 145
Cook: Cornelius, 95; Drucilla,
95; Fanny, 95; Henry, 33;
Judy, 175; Samuel, 95;
Sarah, 33
COOK: Betsey, 176; Blair, 9
COOPER: John, 3
Cora, 155, 171
Corbin: Catharine, 149; Goen,
150; Gowen, 149; Henrietta,
148
Corcoran: Harriett, 53; Harvey,
53; Robert, 53; William, 53
CORMON: William, 147
Cornelia, 3, 155
Cornelia C., 56
Cornelius, 14, 186

CORVINCE: John, 149
Cosby: Albert, 181
Couch: Mary, 35
COUCH: John, 35, 103;
    Johnathan, 35; William, 159
County: Albemarle, 4, 9, 12, 13,
    15, 20, 22, 27, 28, 29, 49, 51,
    64, 111, 119, 168, 170, 174,
    175, 179, 183, 185, 188, 189;
    Alexandria, 155; Alleghany,
    172; Amelia, 4, 13, 30, 37,
    40, 53, 56, 58, 64, 67, 74, 75,
    83, 88, 89, 91, 93, 96, 101,
    105, 106, 107, 108, 111, 122,
    123, 124, 171, 176, 180, 185;
    Amherst, 15, 18, 21, 32, 39,
    62, 73, 109, 162, 174, 189;
    Appomattox, 4, 28, 29, 54,
    61, 62, 67, 74, 75, 79, 84, 86,
    91, 108, 109, 112, 154;
    Augusta, 1, 16, 24, 26, 29,
    135, 169, 177, 179, 189;
    Bath, 3, 7, 167, 169, 171,
    175, 183, 189; Bedford, 1, 2,
    3, 4, 5, 7, 8, 11, 15, 21, 23,
    24, 25, 27, 28, 31, 32, 47, 49,
    52, 54, 91, 100, 123, 124,
    160, 161, 166, 168, 169, 170,
    171, 172, 173, 174, 175, 177,
    178, 180, 182, 183, 184, 185,
    186, 187, 188, 191; Beteourt,
    24; Bland, 7, 23; Botetourt,
    4, 11, 13, 20, 21, 29, 30, 159,
    161, 163, 165, 166, 167, 168,
    169, 170, 171, 172, 173, 174,
    175, 178, 180, 181, 182, 183,
    184, 185, 186, 188, 189, 191;
    Brunswick, 75, 77, 87, 98,
    108, 111, 125; Buchanan, 8;
    Buckingham, 1, 4, 19, 23, 28,
    34, 38, 39, 41, 44, 51, 55, 56,
    57, 59, 60, 61, 62, 63, 64, 66,
    67, 68, 69, 71, 73, 74, 75, 76,

78, 79, 80, 82, 83, 91, 94, 95,
96, 107, 109, 112, 113, 115,
118, 120, 122, 127;
    Campbell, 1, 2, 3, 4, 6, 7, 8,
10, 14, 18, 22, 24, 27, 29, 30,
32, 41, 75, 95, 110, 113, 115,
171, 173, 181, 182, 183, 186;
    Caroline, 5, 8, 16, 18, 27,
101, 145, 166, 184; Charles
City, 12, 82; Charlotte, 13,
20, 31, 33, 35, 46, 47, 48, 49,
51, 52, 53, 54, 55, 56, 57, 61,
62, 63, 64, 65, 66, 67, 69, 71,
74, 75, 76, 77, 81, 82, 83, 84,
90, 91, 93, 94, 95, 96, 97, 98,
100, 104, 108, 110, 111, 113,
114, 116, 117, 118, 119, 122,
123, 126, 167, 177, 183, 185,
187; Chesterfield, 18, 30, 58,
189; County, 13; Craig, 165,
180; Culpeper, 2, 167, 171,
180, 182; Cumberland, 3, 8,
13, 14, 16, 33, 34, 38, 42, 43,
44, 45, 48, 50, 52, 55, 56, 57,
58, 61, 64, 65, 66, 68, 70, 71,
72, 73, 74, 75, 76, 78, 79, 80,
83, 84, 89, 91, 92, 94, 95, 96,
98, 100, 102, 104, 105, 107,
109, 111, 113, 114, 116, 117,
118, 119, 121, 123, 125,
126,152, 191; Dinwiddie, 40,
79, 100, 145, 178, 188;
    Essex, 133, 136, 137, 139,
145, 147, 148, 149, 150, 151,
154, 191; Fairfax, 137, 150,
191; Fauquier, 15, 19, 167,
169, 177, 186, 188; Floyd, 2,
9, 11, 13, 19, 23, 24, 26, 29,
30, 164, 168, 178; Fluvanna,
93, 155, 187; Franklin, 1, 3,
4, 7, 11, 12, 13, 16, 17, 19,
28, 29, 160, 164, 167, 173,
174, 175, 177, 179, 181, 184,

7, 11, 12, 13, 14, 20, 28, 169, 182; York, 153
Cousin: Henry, 33; Washington, 33
Cox: Adline, 139; Amy, 31; Jacob S., 26; Jane, 150; Jeff, 117; Lina, 34, 117; Lucella, 146; Mary, 28; Mat, 139; Matt, 152; Mattison, 1; Nannie, 117; Napoleon, 34; Queen, 34; Wash, 117; Washington, 34; William, 139; William W., 34
COX: George, 1, 40, 63; Mary, 34, 117; Matthew, 40; Polly, 68; William, 1, 29
CRABB: Benedict, 154
Craig, 28
CRAIG: John, 22
CRATE: H., 105; John V., 122; Joseph, 41, 109; Thomas, 41
CRATICK: Edward, 2, 5
Crawford: Abraham, 11; Ann, 22; Daniel, 22; Sarah, 189
CRAWFORD: Nancy, 189
Crawley: A., 85; Africa, 90; Alex, 37; Armstead, 49; Charles, 37; Eda, 98; Emily, 49; Jaime, 98; James, 90; Jenny, 43, 90; Katy, 85; Martha, 98; Phillis, 46, 180; Robert, 98; Sally, 37; Sarah, 98; Solomon, 46, 98
CRAWLEY: Alex, 37, 46, 49, 50, 85; Alex B., 98; Edward, 98; James, 94
Creasey, 79
Crecey, 157
Creed, 192
CRITCHER: George, 147
Crocket: Amanda, 167; J., 171
Crockett, 6, 23; Hugh, 20
CROCKETT: Hugh, 12, 21, 30

Crony: Richmond, 167
CROWDER: Marshal, 125
Crowley: Stephen, 90
CRUMP: Charles A., 59; Len, 138
CRUSE: Mrs., 159
CRUTCHER: Mrs. George, 133; Solomon G.A., 137
CUAD: Col. T.H.T., 112
Cuff: Betsey, 162; Emmeline, 178; Henry, 162, 185
Cummins: Austin, 116; Ellis, 116; Hannah, 116; Martha, 116; Milly, 116; Pat, 116; Patrick, 116
Cunningham: Ed, 112; Edward, 42; Frances, 42; Frank, 42; Letty A., 112; William, 42
CUNNINGHAM: J., 85
Cupid: Tasker, 149
CURRAN: George W., 30; James, 28; Wadda, 26; Wadde, 6, 7
Currey: Henry, 146
Currie: George, 145
Curtis: Caroline, 20; Clara, 184; Ed, 185; Mary, 1; Matilda, 2; Spencer, 2; William, 184
CURTIS: Benjamin, 2
CUTCHER: George, 148
Cynthia, 22, 26, 184
Cyrus, 169

Dabney: Lucy, 9
DABNY: John, 189
DALBY: John, 79; John A., 109
Dallas: George, 90; Mary, 90; Robert, 90
Dan, 168, 176
DANCE: Parson, 121

Dandridge: George, 145; John, 151; Lucy, 16; Margaret, 4; Rhoda, 175; William, 185
Dangerfield: Lewis, 176
DANGERFIELD: Ann E., 10, 11, 21
Daniel, 6, 11, 19, 25, 66, 83, 147, 148, 151, 153, 170, 180, 187; Elizabeth, 100; James, 100; John, 100; Martha, 17, 77; Sally, 77, 100; Samuel, 100; Shad, 77; Spencer, 100
DANIEL: Charles, 56; G.W., 38, 64, 74, 76, 84, 97, 119; George W., 60, 66, 68, 96, 118; John, 93; R.P., 100; S.W., 72
Date: Henry, 149; Thomas, 149
Dave, 191
Davenport: Archy, 54; Fanny, 54; Margaret, 52; Peter, 52; Rachel, 52
DAVENPORT: S.B., 54; Samuel B., 52
David, 4, 8, 13, 21, 23, 24, 25, 30, 148, 185, 188; Polley, 153
Davis: Alfred, 21; James H., 160; Julia, 5; Lee, 174; Louis, 154; Payne, 154; R.P., 160; Robert P., 184; Thomas, 154; Tom, 181
DAVIS: D., 187; E.H., 91; Erastus, 65; George R., 61; Henry, 94; Mrs. N., 63; N., 67; Thomas, 48; William, 1, 3, 20, 21
Dawson: Alexander, 6; Cooper, 68; Robert, 68; William, 68
Day: Albert, 16; Emma, 21; John, 25; Josiah, 20
Dazzle: Mary, 46
Dean, 20; Frank, 13; Martha, 3

Deaton: Caleb, 21
Deem: Booker, 65; Eliza, 65; George, 65; James, 65; Judy, 65; Lucy, 65; William, 65
DeJARNETTE, 81
Delia, 82, 178, 191
DELWEILER: Joseph, 10
Dennis, 183; Caesar, 171; Caroline, 71; Douglass, 93; Harriet, 93; Robert, 71; Samuel, 71
DENNIS: William, 183; William H., 119
Denton: Chamie, 149
Depha, 82
DETON: A., 176
Deyerle: Seely, 174
DEYERLE: B., 168, 174; D., 176; J., 169
DIALLY: Walter, 25
Diana, 145
Dick, 167, 172, 174
DICKERSON: Robert, 60
Dickinson: Benjamin, 124; Betty, 124; Dinah, 124; Henry, 124; James, 124; Jordan, 124; Juliet, 124; Junius, 124; Landvina, 124
DICKINSON: Asa, 49, 93; Dr., 55
Diggs: Ellen, 147; George, 68; Mariah, 134; Martha, 68; Moses, 134; Nelson, 134; Sally, 134
Dill: Benjamin, 6; Joseph, 9; Thomas, 9
Dillan: Peyton, 53
DILLERT: George W., 150
Dillon: Branch, 53; Nancy, 53; Violet, 53
DILLON: Dr., 108; Dr. A., 116; Dr. Alex, 98; John, 53, 55, 77, 78

Dilsey, 18
Dilsy, 187
Dinah, 84, 178
DINGUS: Jim, 191
DISHMAN: John W., 154
Dobbins: Floyd, 26
DOBBINS: Samuel, 24;
    William, 8, 26
Doctor, 82
Dodson: Aaron, 55; Betsey
    Ann, 55; Frank, 55; Judith,
    55; Mary J., 55; Robert L.,
    55; Spencer, 55; Stanhope,
    55
DOLBY: John, 66
Dolly, 84, 147, 171
Dora, 147
Doretha, 24
Doshy, 172
DOTHERD: Phelin, 188
DOUGHTERTY: David, 28
DOUGLAS: Dr. William, 156;
    W.W., 134; Walter, 138
Douglas G., 29
Douglass, 83
Dow: Aleck, 168; Melvina, 177
DRAPER: J., 192
DRUIN: Samuel, 68; Weaver,
    83
Drusilla, 26
Duckwiler: Aleck, 179;
    Amanda, 168; Henry, 168
DUDLEY: Isaac, 20, 23; Sarah,
    11
Duinin: Cleia, 79; Emma, 79;
    Henry, 79; Mary, 79;
    William, 79
Duke: Nancy, 19
DUNAWAY: A., 147
DUNCAN: Harriet, 81
DUNNINGTON: William, 61,
    68, 93, 95, 114
Dupuy: Lewis, 100; Lydia, 100

DUPUY: ?, 123; Asa, 34; Dr.
    James, 52; Emily, 99;
    George, 99; James, 86; John,
    73, 75, 79, 83, 96; Joseph,
    100; Mrs., 85; Mrs. Asa, 117;
    Mrs. E., 104; Mrs. P., 52
DUVALL: Robert, 97
DYE: John, 5
DYERLE: J., 181
Dykes: Rola, 21; Sam, 191
DYKES: J., 191; James, 191

EARHEART: Adam, 29, 30;
    George, 30, 31, 32
Early: Charles, 50; Emma, 177;
    Sarah, 50
EARNEST: J., 177
Ease: Jacob, 4
Easter, 6, 7, 146, 154, 191
Eatman: George, 151
Ed, 169, 181
Eda, 82
Edie, 11
Edmands: Ed, 122; Frank, 122;
    Joseph, 122; Julia, 122;
    Louis, 122; Mack, 122;
    Richard, 122; Sallie, 122;
    Violet, 122
Edmond, 7
Edmonds: Cath, 90; John H., 90
EDMONDS: E., 90; Eda, 46; J.,
    172
Edmonia, 4, 83
Edmonson: __ham, 11;
    Alexander, 26; Arminia, 17;
    Caswell, 14; Lewis, 14;
    Malinda, 22
EDMONSON: David, 22, 25;
    Henry, 9, 25; Maria, 14;
    Mary, 27; Sarah, 30
Edmund, 176, 177, 188
Edmunds: Catherine, 42

EDMUNDS: Ed, 78, 88, 125; J.F., 114
Edmundson: Betty, 180
EDMUNDSON: H., 189
Edward, 4, 11, 24, 31, 82, 145, 151, 184, 185, 186
EDWARD: John, 98
Edward P., 9
Edwards: John, 96; Silla, 171
EDWARDS: E., 42; Jenny, 98; Milton, 111
Eggleston: Kit, 76; Martha Jane, 76; Violet, 76; William Henry, 76
Elam: Jenesta, 112; William, 112
ELAM: Joel, 112; John O., 112; William P., 73
Eldred, 31
Elfine, 25
Elijah, 156, 168
Elisha, 171
Eliza, 5, 7, 9, 11, 16, 24, 26, 146, 148, 156, 160, 171, 172, 175, 177
Eliza A., 182
Eliza Ann, 145, 156
Eliza F., 28
Eliza J., 179
Eliza Jane, 138
Eliza M., 12, 19
Elizabeth, 8, 11, 15, 16, 22, 24, 25, 148, 154, 185, 191, 192
Elkin: James, 53; Matilda, 53
ELKIN: C., 53, 60
Ella, 36, 170, 171, 188
Ellen, 2, 3, 5, 12, 15, 16, 18, 24, 29, 30, 48, 69, 83, 173, 174, 178, 181, 184
Ellen A., 28
Ellen S., 5, 183
Ellender, 191

ELLERTON: F., 91; William, 104
Ellie, 13
ELLINGTON: P.A., 58
Elliott: Albert, 54; Amanda, 40; Daniel, 40, 106; Fanny, 54; Felix, 54; Floyd, 106; Henrietta, 106; Julia, 54; Mary, 54; Nancy, 54; Peter, 54; Sarah, 54, 106; William, 54
ELLIOTT: Allan, 54; Lill, 49; William, 98; Willis, 40, 106
Ellis: Celina, 66; Edward, 70; Elizabeth, 66; Ellis, 66; Emma, 70; John, 70; Julia, 70; Margaret, 66; Mary, 33, 70, 120; Rosetta, 66; William, 120; Zach, 66
Ellison: David, 118; Nan, 118; William D., 118
Elms: Fannie, 145
Elrias, 151
Elsie, 19, 146, 163
Elva, 15, 186
ELVIN: William, 66
Elvira, 13, 182
Elworth, 84
Ely: Charles, 79; Tabby, 79
ELY: J.B., 72, 117; James B., 56, 79, 91; Joseph B., 109
Emaline, 151
Emanuel, 146
Emeline, 1, 23, 80
Emeline G., 19
Emiline, 11, 12
Emily, 9, 11, 22, 83, 147, 155, 164, 183
Emily I., 20
Emily T., 17
Emma, 2, 32, 84, 150, 151, 153, 156, 176, 181, 184
Emma J., 4

Emmeline, 168, 169
Engle: Harriet, 20
ENGLES: Agnes, 2
ENGLISH: Thomas, 147;
    William, 147
Ephraim, 167
Eppes: Ba_tanna, 116; Edward,
    116; Jacob, 95; Louisa Ann,
    95; Margaret, 116; Phillip,
    57; Robert, 57; Sallie, 40;
    Sally, 57; Virginia, 95;
    Washington, 57
EPPES: Eliza, 83; Isaac, 40;
    J__ W., 67; Mrs. M.B., 78
Erius, 149
ESKRIDGE: Alex P., 30;
    Alexander, 5, 6, 7, 8
Essex, 187
Ester, 6
Ethel, 14
ETHERIDGE: William, 109
Eunice, 29
Euzitta, 24
Evans: Ada, 75; Amanda, 72;
    Amy, 72; Cabell, 96;
    Cornelia, 56; Douglass, 105;
    Edward, 96; Eliza, 56, 112;
    Elizabeth, 113; Harley, 112;
    Herod, 35; Isham, 37, 56;
    James, 72; Jessee, 75; John,
    112; Marg, 105; Margaret,
    62; Melinda, 75; Nancy, 62;
    Palmer, 56; Patterson, 183;
    Polly, 112; Robert, 62;
    Rosetta, 96; Sally, 37; Sarah,
    56, 72; Thornton, 113;
    William D., 62
EVANS: Betsey, 188, 189;
    Betsy, 165, 166; E., 77;
    Edward, 29; James, 17, 110;
    John, 122, 174; T., 162, 176,
    182, 186; William, 67, 75
Evelina, 186

EVES: Curtis, 180
Eviline, 10
Ewing: Doctor, 50; Emma, 50;
    J.T., 93; Jane, 50; Joseph, 93;
    Joseph A., 93; Martha, 50;
    Patrick, 50; Pattie, 93;
    Spencer, 50; Susan, 50
EWING: Thomas, 49, 50, 93,
    101
Ezekell, 146

Fairfax: _ewis, 23
FALSE: Matt, 89
Fannie, 148, 156, 178, 180,
    184, 185, 191, 192
Fanny, 3, 22, 23, 25, 32, 168,
    179
Farley: Daniel, 104; James,
    104; Oliver, 104; Pa__lia,
    104; Polly, 104
FARLEY: B.A., 58; Fannie,
    186; Joseph, 102; S.F., 106;
    T., 101
FARRELL: Mrs. M., 47
FASE: S., 119
Faulkes: Branch, 64; Louisa, 64
FAULKES: Mrs. M., 64
FAULKNER: Alex, 47
FAWLER: M., 49
Fawlkes: ___ M., 106; Albert,
    106; Harry T., 106; Laura A.,
    106
FAWLKES: George, 51; Mrs.
    B., 50; Mrs. E., 105
Fayette, 84
Fearis: Elizabeth, 187
Feather: Fanny, 4
FEATHER: William, 4
Felix, 58
Fennall: Ida, 28
FERGUSON: Alexander, 11;
    George, 10; Isam, 164
FERRIS: Ben, 188, 189

211

Ferris/Fearis: Amanda, 185
FICKLAND: Eugene, 134, 137
Fields: __rola Ellen, 138;
    Adaline, 178; Ferry, 8;
    Hezakiah, 138; Sarah, 181
Finley: Jack K., 181; Ruth, 7
Finney: Phebe, 16
Fippen: Martha, 40
FIPS: Frank, 28
Fisher: Charlotta, 10; Eliza, 31;
    William A., 186
Fitchugh: Aaron, 147
FITZGERALD: _.W., 48
Flagens: Dilcy, 18
FLEET: Edward, 156; Lucy,
    138, 145, 146, 150; Mrs.
    Gray, 155
Fleming: Clary, 186; Lewis,
    175; Marion, 186; Rose, 174
Flemming, 6
Flemmings: Anacha, 24
FLETCHER, 39
FLIGER: Eli, 24
FLIGGER: Ann, 3; Eli, 8
Flippen: Pernilla, 41
FLIPPEN: Benjamin, 40, 41;
    J.L., 122; Sarah, 41, 107
FLIPPIN: James, 68
Flora, 13, 28, 83
Florence, 22
Floyd, 9, 11, 23, 24
Floyd H., 14
Follis: Amanda, 23
Folse: Jacob, 104
Foltz: Jane, 19; Millie, 17
FOLTZ: Henry, 3, 9, 10, 17, 18,
    20, 25
FORBES: Cal, 39; Mrs. E., 63
Ford: Alfred, 110; Ann, 110;
    Samuel, 27
FORD: Hez., 97
Fordice: Squire, 3
Forest: Daniel, 89; Hannah, 89

Forge: Margaret, 6
Forrow: Gabel, 3
Fortner: __rles, 24; George, 5;
    Lewis, 31; Mitchell, 3; Sarah,
    26
FORTNER: William, 26
Foster: Anderson, 50; Ann, 50;
    Anne, 109; Archer, 116;
    Benjamin, 116; Betsey, 183;
    Booker, 50, 94, 103;
    Callahan, 94; Ed, 94; Emma,
    50; Gelina, 116; Henrietta,
    94; Henry, 41; James, 103;
    Joseph, 109; Judy, 116;
    Mariah, 94; Martha, 94, 103;
    Mary, 109; Mary F., 103;
    Nulty, 50; Perlinna, 50;
    Richard, 109; Robert, 116;
    Samuel B., 50; Sarah, 50;
    Thomas, 50
FOSTER: James, 50, 51; John,
    60, 69, 87, 88, 98, 104, 105,
    125; Peter, 98
Fountain: Clem, 65; Jane, 65;
    Maria, 65; Richard, 65
Foushee: Daniel, 147
Fowler: Albert, 114; Austin,
    114; Calvin, 81; Edmund, 81;
    Eliza, 114; Ellen, 81; Fanny,
    81; Henry A., 104; James,
    81; M. Louisa, 104; Nellie, 3;
    Prudence, 176; Samuel, 81;
    William, 104
FOWLER: Mrs. M., 104;
    Pleasant, 80, 81, 114
FOWLKES: Mrs. H., 56; Mrs.
    P., 64, 121
Fox: Cyrus, 78; Docia A., 78;
    Fanny, 184; Fanny Jane, 78
Fraction: Easter Jane, 14; Ellen,
    13; John, 13; Nancy A., 17;
    Othello, 4

Fralan: Asher, 48; Beverly, 48; Daniel, 48; Frances, 48; John D., 48; Nancy, 48

Frances, 11, 13, 180, 183, 191; Martha, 147

Frances Ann, 151

Francis, 17, 154

Francis J., 186

Frank, 13, 28, 147, 150, 179, 180

Franklin: John, 183

FRANKLIN: Lucy B., 28

Fred K.N., 155

Frederick, 82

FREE: Jerry, 136

Freeland, 178

Freeler: Nancy, 109; Robert, 109

Freelon: Martha, 187

FRETWELL: William, 37, 67

Frinnell: Asa, 48; Rhoda, 48

FRIZZELL: Wesley, 30

Frog: Thomas J., 178

Frow: Julia, 7

Fry: Rose, 171

Fulet: Ann, 152

Fuller: Ann, 73; Henry, 73; Jane, 73; Lucy, 73; Patience, 73; Pryor, 73; William, 73

Fulse: Henrietta, 104; William, 104

FULSE: Ridley, 95

FULTZ: Henry, 28

Fuqua: Davy C., 116; Lucy, 116; Patsey, 116; William, 116

FUQUA: Stephen, 38, 64

FURGERSON: John, 152

G__ns: Harvey, 31

Ga_illa, 186

Gabel, 6

Gaines: Adam, 94; Albert Thomas, 114; ~~Cen__~~, 146; Clarissa, 114; Collins, 114; Henry, 54; Jane, 94; R. Ann, 54; Rachel, 54; Richard, 54, 114; Sukey, 54; Susan, 114; Thomas, 114; Zach, 54

Gaiter: Patza, 27

Gallinus, 171

GAMBELL: William, 135

GAMFFREY: George, 110

GARDER: James, 2

GARDNER: Charles, 24; John, 9; Thomas, 93

Garitson: Lucy, 14

GARLAND: Daniel, 145

GARLAND, Jr.: Daniel, 146

Garner: Natt, 145

GARNET: William, 11

GARNETT: James, 10; Thomas H., 62

Garrett: Peter, 150

GARST: John, 189

Gaskin: Mariah, 153

Gaskins: Joseph, 155

Gaston: Robert J., 147

GAULIN: John B., 97

GAUPHIN: George, 126

Geary: Betty G., 158; Ellen, 158; Robert, 158

Gee: Fanny, 125; Jenny, 125; Rhoda, 125; Robert, 125

Geeson, 154

General Warren, 17

Georganna, 148

George, 4, 6, 12, 14, 18, 22, 23, 24, 84, 145, 146, 148, 150, 154, 168, 171, 175, 185, 187, 188, 189, 191

George A., 13, 20

George Andrew, 147

George D., 31

George Henry, 147, 148

George M., 3
George W., 3, 20, 30
Georgeanna, 145
Georgianne, 187
German: Mary, 170; Sam, 173
Germinia, 10
Gertrude, 82
GETTS: Watt, 94
GIBBONS: Lethe, 180
Gibbs: Abram, 85; Ann, 85;
    Lawrence, 30; Queen, 85
GIBBS: Miles, 124
Gibson: Aaron, 135; Archie,
    135; John Henry, 135;
    Margaret, 135; Patsie, 135;
    Randall, 135
GIBSON: Alex, 189; Hugh, 16;
    Julia, 146
Gilber__: Charlotta, 20
Gilbert, 3, 7, 15; George, 174;
    John, 163; Lucy, 163, 174
Giles, 12, 13, 31; Edmund, 67;
    Lavinia, 67
Gilham: James A., 41; Mary,
    40; Sarah, 40; William, 40
GILHAM: G., 54; German, 54;
    James N., 52
GILLAM: Isham, 55, 65
Gille Francis, 186
GILLESPIE: Joseph, 122;
    Joseph R., 107
Gillham: Ann, 106; Charles R.,
    106; Jack B., 106; Joseph L.,
    106; Paschal, 106; Reuben,
    106; Sarah, 106; William H.,
    106
GILLHAM: Edward, 107
Gilliam, 172
Gillis: Cyrus, 152
~~Gills: Wilson~~, 89
GILLS: Archy, 63; ~~Miles~~, 89
GILMER: George, 11, 13, 22
Gilmore: Lavina, 152

GILMORE: George, 9
Gish: Delia, 186; Patsey, 171
GISH: G., 177; G.R., 171;
    Jacob, 191
Givens: Samuel, 29
Glandres: Sawney, 170
Glasgo: Nacio, 155
Glasgow: Joe, 174
GLASSAN: Marcus, 117
Glasville: Lewis, 18
GLEASON: Edna, 180; J., 187
Gleeves: Sampson, 20
Glenn: Booker, 57; Dolly, 57;
    Isaac, 7
GLENN: Dr., 94; James, 118;
    Peyton, 113
Glieves/Gliever: Granville H.,
    20
Glosper: Asley, 19
GLOVER: Sam, 65
Godard: Mahalia, 135; Nancy,
    135; Peggy, 146; Peter, 135;
    Sally, 135; Samuel, 135;
    Sofford, 147
Goddard: Peggy, 135
GOFFREY: Joseph, 75
Goggins: Ellen, 174; Emmeline,
    170
GOGGINS: J., 182
GOLDMAN: Absom, 136
Goldston: Margaret, 20
Goldstone: Fannie, 169; James,
    182; Lewis, 188; Louisa, 183
Goloon: Henrietta, 186
Good: Augustus, 111; Bettie,
    111; Eliza, 111; Elvira, 111;
    Henry, 111; Jessie, 111;
    John, 111; Louisa, 111;
    Martha, 111; Robert, 111;
    Sarah, 111; Scipton, 17
GOOD: John, 7
Goode: Aleck, 69; Betsey, 69;
    Betty, 80; Caroline, 80;

214

Hancock: Margaret, 6
Hanlon: Nash, 99; Rhoda, 99;
  Stephen, 99
HANLON: Miss F., 99
Hannah, 22, 23, 84, 147, 149,
  150, 166, 176, 191; Aaron,
  118; Ann, 118; Claiborne,
  108; David, 186; James, 118;
  John H., 118; Letcher, 118;
  Lizzie, 108; Thomas, 118
HANNAH: James, 189; Sarah,
  178; William, 118; William
  M., 108
Hannah A., 155
HANSBOROUGH: H., 162,
  167, 174, 188
Hanus: Frances, 155
HAR__: Nathaniel, 9
Hardee: Frances, 8; Jefferson,
  12
Harden: Peter, 168
HARDIN: William, 134
HARDING: J.B., 168, 173;
  Susan, 167
HARDWAY: William, 111
Hardy: Jennie, 182; John, 181;
  Washington, 175
HARDY: G., 36; George, 36,
  126; Joseph, 102
HARLEY: James B., 16
HARMER: Catharine, 2
Harper: Anderson, 58;
  Catherine, 58; John, 179;
  Maria, 167
HARPER: G., 49, 111; J., 167;
  James C., 179; Mrs., 60;
  Newton, 91; Sallie, 61;
  Sarah, 58
Harriet, 15, 17, 21, 23, 28, 82,
  148, 158, 161, 178, 179, 181,
  183, 184, 185, 186, 187
Harriet A., 177
Harriet J., 189

Harriet R., 9
Harriet V., 6
Harriett, 148, 150, 156
Harriett Elizabeth, 151
Harris: Dandridge, 167; Ed, 95;
  Joseph, 95; Lucy, 95; Matt,
  95; Richard, 21; Sarah, 28
HARRIS: John, 113
Harrison, 22, 147; Aggy, 75;
  H., 75; Henrietta, 75; Jenny,
  75
HARRISON: B., 34; Elizabeth,
  151
Harrod: William, 146
HARROD: Henry, 147
Harry, 7, 156, 169, 171, 191
Harston, 179; Epperson, 1
HARSTON: Elizabeth, 1
HART: Barnet, 109
HARTLEY: J., 183
HARTMAN: G.G., 162;
  George, 172
Harvey, 7, 180; Agnes, 73;
  Albert, 121; Alice, 54;
  Anthony, 53; Betsey, 53;
  Buddy, 73; Christian, 53;
  Clem, 54, 73; Eliza, 115,
  121; James, 10, 54; Jane, 54;
  Jenny, 54; Julius, 115; Kit,
  75; Lee, 75; Lingus, 53;
  Lizzie, 54; Lucy, 73; M., 73;
  Martha, 121; Mary, 121;
  Mattie, 73; Nathan, 73;
  Peggy, 53; Phineus, 121;
  Puss, 73; Rachel, 115;
  Robert, 115; Samuel, 121;
  Sarah, 54, 75; Sterling, 73;
  Susan, 115; Taylor, 121;
  Warsham, 121
HARVEY: Charles C., 53;
  Fannie, 169; Jerusha, 83;
  Johann, 121; Nathan, 47;

Nathaniel, 5, 17, 20; Robert, 179, 184; Thomas, 54
Harvey E., 175
Harwah/Harmah: Claiborne, 108
HARWAH/HARMAH: William M., 108
HARWOOD: Henry, 146
Haskins: Guil, 60; John, 60, 120; John H., 110; Judah, 110; Mary, 60; Melinda, 120; Mose, 60; Phil, 60; Robert, 110
Hatcher: Frances P., 14
HATCHER: William, 160, 184
HATCHETT: W., 92; William, 92
Hawkins: General, 23; George, 183; Lewis, 29
HAWKS: Lee, 100
Hayden: Samuel, 28
Hays: Calvin, 76; Nancy, 76
Headen: Minnis, 3
HEADEN: Elizabeth, 3
Heald: Silla, 176
Henderson, 16; Harriett, 155; Jane, 151; John, 29; Lucinda, 22; Martha, 16; Millie Ann, 5; Simon, 149
HENDERSON: Amanda, 16; Francis, 11; Frank, 14; Giles, 16; Giles J., 19; James, 191; Jonas, 14; William, 4
Hendrick: Eliza, 19; George, 68; Mary, 68; Mary A., 68
Henrietta, 1, 12, 14, 32, 146, 156, 170, 175, 188
Henry, 4, 5, 6, 13, 14, 17, 24, 26, 27, 28, 82, 147, 148, 150, 152, 153, 154, 155, 156, 170, 171, 172, 175, 177, 183, 188, 189, 191; Alsie, 149; Anderson, 74; Dora, 66;

Edmonia, 66; Elvira, 92; Henry, 66; Isabella, 92; Jacob, 13; Lucinda, 74; Martha, 74; Missouri, 74; Pat, 92; Patrick, 66, 74; Peter, 154; Rosetta, 66; Samuel, 66; Sander, 189; Susan, 154; Thomas, 66
Henry C., 25
Henry Thomas, 2
Hergens: Alfred, 31
Herrietta, 3
Hestra: Mary Jane, 153
Hickman: James, 14; Jeremiah, 22; Sally, 173
Hicks: Alex, 111; Andrew, 22; Billy, 177; Celia, 111; Daniel, 78, 118; Dennis, 111; Henry, 78; Isabel, 34, 118; Lilybeth, 78; Maria, 78; Reuben, 186; Susan, 111
HICKS: Thomas, 54
HICKSON: Betsy, 96; Dr. Thomas, 83
Hill: Alsie, 153; Bitty, 62; J_v_, 62; Joanna, 62; Lucy, 169; Lucy J., 47; Martha, 74; Mary E., 47; Wesley Hill, 47; William, 74
HILL: Mrs., 51; William E., 154
Hillard, 177
HILLARD: J.B., 76
Hilton: Agnes, 62; Betty, 62; Calvin, 62; Hampton, 62; Henry, 62; Pelina, 62; Peyton, 62
Hines: Clark, 108; Lucy, 108; Mary A., 108; Palina, 108; Samuel, 108; Tuta, 108
HINES: Joseph, 71, 108; Joshua, 123
Hinton: Sally, 62; William, 62

217

Hiram, 27
Hitson: Julia, 21
HOBBS: Albert, 100
Hobson: Frances, 66; James,
66; Siras, 3
HOBSON: Augustus, 2; C., 73;
Mary, 74
Hogans: Isaac, 3
HOGE: Daniel, 5, 8, 16, 27;
Daniel H., 18, 29; Jame, 4;
James, 5, 14; James H., 18;
William, 8, 23
HOGUE: Daniel, 184
HOLBEE: Robert, 5
Holcomb: Ella, 97; James, 97
HOLCOMB: J.P., 161; James,
183; William P., 181
HOLIBY: George, 25
HOLLIDAY: Ann, 116; Robert,
69
HOLLINS: Asa, 173
Holly: Malinda E., 2
Holmes: Becky, 145; Ellen,
145; Francis, 138; James,
138; Jenny, 37; Luisa, 138;
Margarett, 151; Sally, 36
Holms: Nancy, 31
Homes: Hannah, 185; Hector,
160, 185; Thornton, 160
HOO_L: Syrus, 154
Hopkins: Alexander, 12;
Andrew, 16; Daniel, 31;
Dennis, 184; Elizabeth, 189;
Moses, 12
HOPKINS: Robert, 148
HOPPER: Gabriel, 64
Hopson: Cindrella, 182;
Pompey, 180
Horace, 151, 182; Alex, 37;
Betsey, 72; Ella, 72; Johnny,
72; Margaret, 79; Nat, 79;
Patty, 79; Randal, 72; Sally,
74; Sam, 37, 72, 74, 79;

Susan, 72; Willie, 74; Wyatt,
79
HORN: J.D., 174
HORNBERGER: Hiram, 6, 10
Hornes: Abby, 167
Hosburn: _eorge, 24
HOUSMAN: C., 180
Howard: Amanda, 122;
Beverly, 122; Harriet, 122;
Howard, 29; Millie, 24;
Sarah, 122; Sydney, 122
HOWARD: Henry, 154; Ira, 24,
29; Thomas, 152
HOWE: John D., 7, 8
Hoyl, 19
Hu_de: Catharine, 18
HUBBARD: E.W., 113; P., 86;
S., 177
Hudson: Alice, 67; Arretta, 152;
Betty, 67; Branch, 67; Ella,
67; Ferry, 179; Frank, 67;
Henry, 67; J__ H., 67; Julia,
67; Louisa, 67
HUDSON: Xo__, 180
HUFF: James, 5; Powell, 188
Hugh, 16, 188
Hugh F., 9
Hughes: Cris, 149; Rebecca, 1
HUGHES: John P., 64
Hughs: Melvina, 167
Hulda, 191
Hulda Ann, 26
Humphrey, 3
HUNDERLY: John, 139
Hunley: Ellis, 79; Harriet, 79;
John, 79; Remus, 79
HUNLEY: Charles, 46
Hunt: Brandon, 163; Doctor,
164; George, 163; Minna,
163; Nelly, 164; Parthena,
163; Pompey, 164; Royal,
163; Solomon, 163, 177

Jeff, 183, 191
Jeff D., 182
Jeffers: Albert, 158; Amanda, 158; Ellen, 158; Greene, 158; James, 158; Lucy, 11; Maria, 174; Mary, 158; Peter, 170; Richard, 183; Rosetta, 158; Tom, 175; Washington, 158
Jefferson: Ange, 122; Charlotte, 53; Frances, 64; Newman, 38; Sarah, 38; Thomas, 38, 53, 64, 122
Jeffeson: Teressa, 23
Jeffries: Abby, 50; Beverly, 90; Car., 117; Doctor, 117; Eliza, 90; Fanny, 50; James, 51; Mary A., 51; Sarah, 117; Syndey, 50
JEFFRIES: Ed, 50; Luther, 51; Miss M., 52; Richard, 133
JEFFRIES/JEFFINS: Jack, 111
Jemison: Joseph, 8
Jenilla, 36
Jenison: Catharine, 19
Jenkins: Daniel, 156; Hannah, 147; Harriet, 149; Joseph, 116; Lewis, 27; Lucy, 173; Peter, 156; Suckey, 116
JENKINS: James D., 48; John, 55
Jennie, 2, 13, 151
Jennings: Hariet, 31
JENNINGS: Sa_, 125
Jenny, 83
Jeremiah, 22, 151
Jerry, 14, 82, 152, 177
Jesse, 147
Jeter: Alice, 47; Beverly, 106; Caroline, 175; Clara, 104; George D., 106; Gilman, 104; Henry, 104; John, 104; Linsey, 104; Mariah, 106;

Melinda, 106; Robert, 104; Sydney, 47; William, 47
JETER: Ira, 160, 185, 189; J., 175; Peyton, 107
Jewett: John, 185
Jim, 171, 172, 176, 177, 191
Jimmerson: Kate, 177
Jimmie, 177, 186
Jincy, 176
Jinnie, 176
Jinnie C., 170
Joanna, 181
Joe, 168, 169, 172, 174, 175
John, 4, 5, 6, 7, 8, 12, 13, 15, 16, 18, 19, 20, 23, 24, 32, 83, 150, 151, 152, 153, 156, 168, 170, 171, 172, 173, 174, 176, 179, 180, 184, 185, 186, 188, 191
John A., 19, 27
John D., 178, 185
John G., 182
John H., 3, 11, 30, 148, 171, 176, 183, 185
John Henry, 146
John J.A., 182
John P., 7
John R., 182
John T., 4, 178
John W., 8
Johns: Albert, 78; Amelia, 78; America, 78; Armstead, 78; Betsy, 123; Cilia, 37; Martha, 78; Nice, 123; Patrick, 78; William, 123
JOHNS: Ann, 76; James, 37; Joel, 97, 118; Monroe, 116; William, 122
Johnson, 23; Abie, 145; Absalom, 30; Albert, 2; Alfred, 30; Alsie, 150; Amanda, 83; America, 56; Anan, 85; Angeline, 5; Ann,

136; Ann M., 140; Ann T., 88; Archer, 99; Betsey, 151; Betsy, 79; Betty, 115; Bob, 187; Booker, 92; Carrington, 115; Ch__s N., 155; Charles, 56, 88, 147; Cl.em, 55; Clarissa, 88; Dan, 172; Daniel, 85, 109, 145; ~~Dennis~~, 155; Diana, 41, 109; Docia, 99; Doctor, 179; E. Jane, 58; Eddie, 88; Edmund, 79, 167, 182; Edward, 85; Eliza, 85; Elizabeth, 5, 101; Elvira, 99; Eve, 185; Fanny, 13; Felix, 8; Filice, 2; Florida, 99; Fluentine, 188; Frances, 122; Giles, 29; Greene, 175; Hannah, 18; Hartley, 177; Henry, 10; Isaac, 58; Isham, 99, 101; Israel, 40; Jacob, 99; James, 13; Jane, 92, 185; Jefferson, 18; Jenny, 72; Jerry, 55; John, 59, 85, 115; Julia, 57, 180; Julius, 99; Katie, 72; Lanta, 91; Lewis, 53; Lieutenant, 140; Louisa, 115; Lucy, 55, 91; Luke, 56; M.A., 55; Maria, 99; Marshal, 99; Martha, 85; Mary, 10, 24, 29, 56, 59, 85, 92, 115; Mary S., 140; Mary V., 88; Matt, 83; Millie, 30; Moses, 170; Nancy, 83, 146, 187; Nelson, 115; Oscar, 19; Pat, 72; Patsey, 91; Peter, 55; Plina, 27; ~~Polly~~, 155; Reuben, 187; Rose, 12, 183; Salle, 91; Sally, 92; Scipio, 122; Spencer, 16; Susan, 53; Titus, 173; Virginia, 25; Walker, 57; William, 24, 40, 41, 55, 83; Willie C., 140, 153; Willis, 91

JOHNSON: John, 176, 184; Lucy, 176; Margaret, 182; S.S., 116; Sylvanius, 57; William, 16, 19, 24, 29, 160
Johnston: Laura A., 180
Jones: __niel, 24; Abraham, 27; Alice, 80; Alpheus, 80; Ann, 23, 46, 88; Arabella, 71; Archer, 80; Benjamin, 88; Beverley, 126; Caroline, 88; Charles, 28; Clementine, 9; Daniel, 1; David G., 45; Dicey, 41; Effert, 92; Eliza, 23; Elizabeth, 31; Ellis, 88; Elvira, 106; Emma, 71; Evan, 88; Fanny, 27; Frank, 96; G.H.L., 106; George, 45, 126; Hannah, 136; Harrison, 28; Irene, 80; Jack, 80; James, 28; Jane, 96; Joseph, 22; Josephine, 92; Lewis, 147; Lucy, 31; Maria, 45; Martha, 11, 96, 126; Mary, 1, 92; Monroe, 80; Nancy, 8; Parthenia, 126; Philitia, 155; Richard, 17, 31; Robert, 6; Rosa, 96; Sally, 37, 38; Samuel, 71; Spencer, 187; Susan, 80; Thomas, 45, 88; Victoria J., 107; Virginia, 151; William, 6, 16, 26, 41, 96, 107
JONES: Frances, 32; Isabella, 27; J.N., 63; John, 12; Katy, 40; Louis, 82; Lynch, 28; M. Katy, 106; R.P., 177; Richard P., 8, 23; Thomas, 133; William, 37, 38, 41, 63, 113; William B., 37, 38, 80
Jones/Janes: Margaret, 127; Nannie, 127
JONES/JANES: William, 127
Jordan: Michael, 27

JORDAN: Mrs. E., 104
Joseph, 7, 9, 13, 18, 20, 25, 28, 82, 148, 149, 154, 181, 183
Joseph W., 21
Josephine, 13, 27, 84, 151, 155, 181
Josephus, 156, 177, 184
Joshua, 151
Josiah, 20, 153, 179
Journot: Minerva, 159; Patrick, 159, 170; Susan, 159
JUBEE: William John, 152
Judy, 145, 146, 151, 158, 179, 191
Juilus, 186
Julia, 6, 7, 22, 26, 27, 32, 100, 146, 153, 184, 187
Julia A., 8
Julia Ann, 153
Julianna, 175
Julius, 146, 147, 168

KAISER: James, 180
KAIZER: J.C., 186; K., 161
Kane: Fannie, 176
Kate, 2, 179, 189
Kate C., 31
Kate E., 5
Katy, 153
Kee: _n_as, 24
Keefauver: Emily, 178
KEEFAUVER: Julia, 178
Keen: Harvey, 168
KEFAUVER: J., 164; William, 158
KEGGY: R., 170
KEISTER: Jacob, 15
Kelsick: Estella, 140; Moses, 140; William, 140
Kennedy: Leticia, 29
KENNEDY: Giles, 29
Kent, 3, 178; Mary, 11; Rebecca, 11

KENT: Ann, 16; Elizabeth, 3, 184; Gordon, 14, 182; Hugh, 19, 23; J., 172; Jacob, 14; James, 4, 14, 15, 17, 29, 170; James R., 12, 22; Jane, 168, 177, 178; Joseph, 30
Kently, 184; Laura, 171; Louisa, 184
KERBY: James W., 3; Stephen, 24
Kershaw: Samuel, 169
Kindsey, 150
King: Chloe, 38; Daniel, 57; Hampton, 57; Harrison, 4; Jane, 38; Joseph, 176; Katy, 57; Lewis, 57; Nancy, 16; Paul, 57; Priscilla, 168; Scylla, 57; Washington, 57
Kinney: Betsey, 115; Ellen, 115; Harriet, 115; Ida, 115; Reuben, 115; Stephen, 185
Kittie, 178
Kitty, 187
Knight: Chaney, 116; David, 20; Jack, 116; James, 59
KNIGHT: John H., 73, 82, 85, 112, 118, 124
Knuckles: Eliza, 102; H., 102; Laura, 102
KOWADDIN/ROWADDIN: J.A., 116
Kyle: Edie, 12; Hannah E., 30
KYLE: Jeremiah, 24; W.H., 187
Kyles: John, 120; Lucy, 120; Mary, 120; Matilda, 120; Nelson, 120; William, 11

L. Norvell, 16
Lacey: Betsey, 119; Daniel, 119; Robert, 47, 119
LACEY: Dr. H., 52; Dr. J., 47
Lacy: Harriet, 47

222

Leroy, 154
Leslie, 169
Lestre: John, 15; Martha A., 24
Letitia, 175
Lettie, 22, 177, 186
Letty, 183
Levi, 32
Levisey: Albert, 176
LEVISEY: Arm, 176
Lew: Mary, 174
Lewellen, 20
Lewis, 5, 6, 17, 175, 176, 181,
    183, 185; Allen, 6; Ann, 155;
    Becky, 186; Benjamin, 151;
    Betty, 101; C__cia, 9;
    Charles, 186; David, 101;
    George, 162; Harriet, 136,
    168; Henry, 10; John, 26;
    Katy, 181; Lucius, 154;
    Maria, 19; Martin, 136;
    Mary, 30, 148, 181; Nancy,
    179; Ned, 162; Robert, 154;
    Sally, 172; William, 15, 156
LEWIS: Jane, 178, 181; Maria,
    184
Liberia, 34
Lidia, 171
Lidia Ann, 153
Lidia J., 15
Liftrich: George, 184
LIFTRICH: Dolly, 184
Ligan: Benjamin, 108; Betsey,
    46; Cara, 41; Celina, 125;
    Martha, 125; Patrick, 108;
    Solomon, 46, 125; Sukey,
    108; William, 46
LIGAN: A., 35, 105; B., 127;
    J.L., 80; James, 79, 103, 114,
    117; James D., 45, 78, 96;
    James L., 91; James T., 44;
    Joseph, 41, 78; Joseph D.,
    127; Joseph L., 108, 126;
    Joseph S., 108; Louisa, 76,

78, 105, 126; Mrs. Ag, 46,
    125; Mrs. Lou, 58; P., 76
Lige, 191
Liggens: Major, 18
LIGINAUGER: J., 178
Lina, 170
Linda, 5, 164, 171
LINDEN: Betsy H., 134
Lindsay: Mary, 77; Patty, 77;
    Peter, 77
Lipscomb: Betsey, 83; Elisha,
    83; Mary Ann, 93; O., 93;
    William, 93
LIPSCOMB: F., 66; Paschal,
    108
LIPSCOME: Robert, 22; Robert
    I., 17; Robert K., 17; Robert
    R., 3
Lipscone: Rosanna, 24
LIPSCONE: Robert, 20, 24
Lisby, 167
LITTERAL: Thomas, 155
Littleton, 175
Liverpool: Elizabeth, 137;
    Elsie, 137; John, 137;
    Martha, 137; Stewart, 137;
    William, 32
Lizzie, 117, 187
Lock: Stephen, 173
Locke: Nannie, 118
Locket: Amanda, 118; Andrew,
    118; Asa, 118; Ellen, 118;
    Elvira, 118; Harriet, 118;
    Lucy, 118; Rate, 118;
    Stephen, 118; William, 118
LOCKET: Legget, 71
LOCKET/LUCKET: Ed, 106
LOCKETT: J.T., 56
Locus: Cornelius, 152
Logan: A_ma, 172; Amy, 79;
    Betty, 77; Ed, 119; Edmund,
    79; George, 77; Jessee, 77;
    Judah, 119; Julia, 77

224

Margaret A., 14
Margaret J., 8
Margarett, 146, 149, 153
Margrett, 145
Maria, 18, 23, 26, 30, 154, 168, 170, 172, 176, 178, 179, 183, 184, 185, 186, 189, 191
Maria C., 189
Maria J., 4
Maria Jane, 2
Mariah, 154
Mariah L., 5
Marie, 11
Mars: Nathan, 189
Marshal: Ailsy, 163; Ann, 159; Becky, 163; Cornelia, 93; Dave, 159; Edmund, 159; Emmanuel, 93; Frank, 163; George, 110; Jacob, 68; James, 68; Jane, 68; John, 68; Lockie, 110; Patsey, 159; Salina, 93; Sam, 159; Susan, 110; Thornton, 163; Wesley, 163; William, 110
MARSHAL: B., 60; R., 55; Richard, 108
Marth, 169
Martha, 14, 22, 148, 151, 155, 158, 176, 177, 179, 180, 181, 184, 186
Martha A., 28
Martha Ann, 166
Martha J., 188
Martha S., 3
Martin, 32; Harry, 172; J., 171; Susan, 155
MARTIN: Joseph, 112; William, 7
MARTLY: James, 138; James C., 138
Mary, 4, 5, 7, 11, 12, 15, 16, 23, 24, 25, 26, 27, 32, 82, 148, 150, 151, 152, 161, 167, 168,

169, 173, 174, 175, 177, 178, 179, 180, 181, 182, 183, 185, 186, 188, 189, 191, 192
Mary A., 27, 154, 189
Mary Bubeula, 155
Mary C., 9
Mary E., 17, 19, 20, 22, 25, 155, 175, 188
Mary E.C., 179
Mary Elizabeth, 151
Mary F., 17, 21, 26
Mary J., 4, 17
Mary Jane, 155
Mary L., 19, 168
Mary Lucy, 10
Mary N., 7
Mary P., 29
Mary R., 5
Mary S., 6, 189
Mason, 148; Frances, 57; G.H., 57; Robert L., 57
Mathews: Burta, 136; Lizzie, 136; William, 145; William Henry, 136
MATHEWS: John P., 20
Matilda, 19, 27, 148, 150, 162, 167, 169, 170, 180, 187, 192
Matilda A., 28
Matilda Ann, 146
MATLEY: Nat, 91
Matt, 83
MATTAN__: Dr., 48
Matthews: Betty, 84; Edward, 84; Ellen, 184
MATTHEWS: N., 60
Mattley: Adolphus, 106; Starry, 106
MATTLEY: Mrs. B.A., 54
Mays: Pleasant, 17
Mazarine, 26
Maze: Samuel, 18
McCall: Abner, 110; Adelaide, 110; Anderson, 37; Andrew,

110; Boyd, 110; Charlotte, 110; John, 110; Judy F., 110; Lilly, 110; Mary, 110; Sally, 110; William, 37

McCary: Patience, 182

McClellan, 5

McCLENNAHAN: E., 170, 180, 181, 183; Elizabeth, 186; J., 167, 175, 177; James, 181; Jane, 182

McCONKEY: James, 189

McConnell: Charles, 191

McCONNELL: A.B., 191

McCORCKLE: Arthur, 23

McCRANDER: J., 164

McCray: Dilsey, 18

McCUE: Fannie, 30

McDaniel: Hampton, 23

McDANIEL: Floyd, 14

McDONALD: Floyd, 15, 22; John, 16; Prissy, 188

McGee: Mary, 26

McGEE: J.B., 100

McGeorge: J.H., 175; Mat, 180

McGhee: Archy B., 70; Caesar, 70; Edward, 70; James, 70; Judy, 70; Maria, 70; Mary, 70; Sally, 70

McGHEE: N.B., 114; Samuel, 99; William, 70, 81, 103; William H., 118

McGLASSAN: I., 120

McGLEASAN: J., 33

McGuire: Elizabeth, 189

McKeever: Caroline, 180

McKEY: Mrs., 185

McKINNEY: Adam, 56

McKORKLE: Arthur, 2

McNaughton: Walter, 22

McNorton: Frank, 9; Orville, 14; Taylor, 9

McNULT: James, 66, 67, 76; Joseph, 115

McQua: Robert, 5

McSLOCUM: M., 75

Mead: Winston, 182

MEAD: Cornelia, 182

MEADOW: John, 64

Melton: James, 3

Melvin: floyd, 31

Melvina, 26

Melvine: Eveline, 19; Silas, 12

MEREDITH: R., 113

Merritt: Arnold, 1; Jane, 7

METLAINER: Dr., 100

Mi__ie, 92

MICHAUX: Jessee, 53; Mrs., 51, 90

MICHELL: John C., 150

Micklass: Jerry, 181

Mickle: Amanda, 113; Cephas, 111; John, 111, 113; Maria, 111; Milly, 113; Moses, 113; Silas, 113

Middleton: Jerry, 152; Mary, 15

MIDDLETON: Benjamin, 138; Dr., 147; Matilda, 147

Mike, 175

Mildred, 9, 149

Miles: Abram, 72; Joseph, 64; Lydia, 72; Martha, 64; Pleasant, 64; William, 150

Milford, 148

Miller, 45; Aaron, 92; Adeline, 46; Alice, 59, 122; Alpheus, 93; Amanda, 92, 93; Amelia, 93; Anderson, 55, 60; Armstead, 60, 101; Benjamin, 100; Betsey, 89; Betsy Ann, 71; Bettey, 59; Branch, 89; Buck, 39; Caroline, 122; Carrie, 89; Catherine, 45; Charity, 60, 89; David, 46, 125; Ed, 101; Edwin, 59; Eliza, 45, 89, 92, 124; Ellen, 46; Emily, 89;

Emma, 59, 71; Felix, 71; Floyd, 92; Francis, 45; Fred, 60; George, 35, 55, 74, 89, 122; Giles, 93; Harriet, 45, 92, 101; Harry, 122; Henry, 39, 92, 101; Herbert, 45, 124; James, 44; Jenny, 89; Jeter, 60; Laura A., 101; Lewis, 93; Lizzie, 45, 92; Louis, 100; Louisa, 46, 89, 101; Lucinda, 55; Lucy, 39, 122; Lucy B., 101; Margaret A., 93; Maria, 92; Martha, 55, 92, 100; Martha J., 122; Mary, 100; Matt, 89; Mattie, 89; Matty, 122; Milly, 59; Missouri, 55; Molly, 92; Nannie, 92; Pack, 100; Patrick, 55; Paulina, 93; Phillis, 125; Richard, 89, 122; Robert, 93; Rose C., 74; Rosetta, 55; Sallie, 39; Sally Ann, 125; Sam, 60; Samuel, 101; Sydney, 92; Taylor, 59; Vina, 92; William, 89; Willie J., 92

MILLER: A.P., 100; B.T., 71; Charles, 7; Charles H., 19; E.F., 60; Ed, 45, 61, 88, 89, 124; Edward, 92; Elizabeth, 24; Geles. A., 59; George, 169; J., 158, 161; J.C., 173, 186; James, 17, 23; James T., 17; John, 1, 8; M., 158; Mary, 58; Peter, 100; R.A., 89, 92; Richard, 35, 45, 92, 124, 125; Richard A., 122; Robert, 25; Sally, 161; Susan, 161

Milli__, 147

Millie, 6, 7, 10, 30, 70

Millie C., 19

Mills: Ann, 32; Gordon, 8

MILLS: Giles, 107; Jack, 67

Milly, 172, 176, 178, 180, 187, 189

Milton, 154, 187; Amelia, 27

Milton H., 25

Mimy, 162

Miner: Silva, 184

Minerva, 11, 13, 168

Mingel: Sukey, 172

Minna, 84

Minnis, 3; Charles, 75; David, 75; Henry, 75; Katy, 75; Nathan, 75; Peter, 75; Robert, 75

MISCALL: William, 145

Missouri E., 178

Mitchel: Griffin, 188; John B., 153

Mitchell: Anna, 56; Mary, 154; Pat, 86; Robert, 86; William, 56

MITCHELL: J.C., 148; John, 135; John C., 147; Littleton, 156; Mary H., 154; Samuel, 86; Thomas, 27; William, 135, 148

MOFSINGER: William, 181

Mokens: Nancy, 169

Moker: Grace, 172

Mollie, 17, 20

Molly, 158, 169, 177

Momen: Catharine, 27

MOMEN: William H., 27

Monroe: Agnes, 178; Cager, 4; Henry, 158; Isabella, 158; Stephen, 158

Montague: Syrena, 9

MONTAGUE: D.R., 186; Daniel, 1; Rice D., 3, 5, 6, 26, 31; William, 26, 30

Montgomery, 23, 169

MONTGOMERY: James, 137

Moon: __nk, 11

MOON: Joseph, 152

Moore: _o__is, 139; Agnes,
153; Betsey, 139; Caroline,
139; Evalina, 150; Jennie,
139; John, 150; Julia, 172;
Laura, 145; Louisa, 139;
Ruffin, 139, 153; Winnie,
151
MOORE: Mary, 9
MOORMAN: M., 161
More: Fannie, 149
Morgan, 173, 186; ___, 25;
Aaron, 30; Abram, 50; Alice,
50; Crecia Ann, 20; Eliza,
102; Ella, 101; Hannah, 103;
Henry, 103; Indiana, 102;
Jane, 50; Mac, 103; Mary
Frances, 3; Molly, 103; Nick,
103; Patrick, 50; Peter, 17;
Robert, 102; Sallie, 102;
Susan, 50; Sydney, 101;
Thomas, 101
MORGAN: Richard, 30
Morgana: Phebe, 101
Morning: Anthony, 81; Bettey,
81
MORNING: Billy, 81
Morris, 168; Betty, 67; Corine,
67; Cornelia, 66; Harriet, 25;
Isaac, 67; Joseph, 66; Laura,
67; Lucy, 28; Mary, 66, 186;
Nelly, 66; Sam, 173;
Thomas, 16
MORRIS: Ealsie, 135; Mrs.
James, 135; William, 154;
William K., 154
Morris A., 14
Morrison: Matilda, 2; Thomas,
27; Washington, 26
MORRISON: Margaret, 3
MORROW: Joseph, 90
MORSE: B., 95
Morson: Caroline, 176

Morton: Archy, 118; Armstead,
35; Cooper, 120; Elizabeth,
118; Fayette, 35; George,
176; James, 118; Maria, 120;
Susan, 105; William, 35, 105
MORTON: Anne, 58; Charles,
34, 48, 67, 118; Dr. W.S., 65;
Dr. William S., 96; Eliza A.,
79; Hugh, 87; J.W., 65; Jane,
72, 99; Mrs. E., 116; Mrs.
Jacob, 116; T.L., 84; Thomas
L., 115; William, 104;
William S., 58
Moseby: Ed, 76; Jenny, 76
Moseley: Amelia, 112; Ben, 64;
Cuff, 112; Jane, 64; Judy, 64;
Maria, 64
Mosely: Catharine, 18
Moses, 6, 10, 19, 24, 151, 154,
177, 187
Moses W., 189
MOSING: E.W., 106
MOSTON: Hugh, 62
MOTLEY: Henry, 59; Mrs. B.,
105; Mrs. M., 93, 102
Mottley: Harriet, 74; M.J., 74;
Madison, 74
MOTTLEY: Mr., 74; Mrs. M.,
41, 106, 110
Moulten: Nelson, 25
Moulton: Maria, 18; Milly, 181;
Samuel, 187
MOULTON: Robert A., 13;
William, 167, 180
MOXLEY: Richard, 154
MUNDY: William, 70, 115
Munford: Bing/Burg, 78;
Harriet, 78; John Henry, 78;
Landaina, 78; Martha, 78;
Wiley, 78
Muse: Judy, 152
MUSE: E.R., 173; F.R., 183;
T.R., 173, 183; W., 168

Myers: Rosanna, 16

Nancy, 4, 7, 8, 15, 18, 21, 24,
  30, 31, 82, 156, 161, 165,
  168, 169, 174, 175, 179, 181,
  185, 186, 188, 191
Nancy Ann, 153
Nancy K., 22
Nancy R., 9
Nannie, 84, 186, 187
Napier: William, 146
Napper: Mary, 189
Nash: David, 80; Fann, 80;
  Harry, 80; Lizzie, 80; Polly,
  80
Nat, 172, 174
Nath, 191
Nathaniel, 15, 18, 155, 186
Naylor: Amy, 51; Maria, 51;
  Melvin, 51; Nelson, 51
Neal: A., 172; Abbie, 70;
  Camilla, 70; Catherine, 70;
  Cornelius, 70; E. Ann, 70;
  Edward, 70; Emma, 66;
  Judith, 70; Lee, 70; Martha,
  66; Mary, 66; Pascal, 171;
  Peggy, 70; Peter, 70; Vans,
  70; William H., 66
NEAL: Armstead, 185
NEAVES: William, 125
Ned, 168, 172, 175, 179
Neeten: Sarah J., 21
NEFF: John, 158
NEIWINGER: D., 166
Nellie, 19, 147
Nelly, 168
Nelson, 6, 186, 187; Jane, 185;
  Joseph, 27; Lucinda, 69;
  Patsey, 188; Richard, 69;
  Rosetta, 69; William, 69
Netty, 172
Nevison: Ann, 72; M., 72

Newton, 152, 176; Agnes, 146;
  Betsey, 153; George, 150;
  Glasgo, 150; Hannah, 146;
  Joseph, 138; Mary, 156;
  Matilda, 152; Peter, 156;
  Sarah, 152
Nicey, 191
Nichols: Granville, 28
Nickolas: Jennette, 170
Niece: Mary, 3
NOBLE: Sydney, 106; Thomas,
  83; Thomas M., 118
Noel: Cynthia, 184; Essex, 187
NOEL: Charles, 184
Noell: Emeline, 28
NOFSINGER: William, 171
Norah, 82
Norman, 186
NORMEN: Berin, 16
Norrill: Allen, 25
Norris: Judah, 156
Norvell, 20
Norwell: Fannie, 29
Nowlen: Peter, 9

O__TOW: Jim, 91
~~O'Mohandrith: William~~, 155
Oatey: C.C., 174
OATEY: Mary C., 187
OATS: William, 167
OBERLEY: Jacob, 47
OBERTON/OVERTON: J.M.,
  44; Johnathan, 44
Ocha, 153
Octavio, 150
Odes: Catharine, 3
Ogle: Susan, 30
Olie Frances, 19
Oliver, 171; Albert, 179; Allen,
  92; Andrew, 22; Anthony,
  92; Chloe, 175; Jim, 92;
  Jinnie, 177; Julia, 92; Lill,

231

Patrick, 21, 82, 84, 187;
  Charles, 153
Patterson: Ailsy, 170; Brice, 59;
  Claiborne, 73; Eliza, 109;
  Julia, 73; Louis, 73; Lucinda,
  59; Michael, 109; Molly, 73;
  R., 73; Sophia, 59; Stephen,
  59
PATTERSON: J.A., 169
Pattie, 84
Pattison: Albert, 12
Paul, 74
Paulett: George, 41, 122; Milly,
  122; Robert, 41; V_etta A.,
  41
PAULETT: R., 74; R.S., 41,
  122
Paulina, 177
Pay_y: John, 78; Milly, 78;
  Puss, 78
Payne: Robert, 18
PAYNE: John, 30
PAYTON: Howard, 14; John,
  140
Pearman: Ellen, 30
Peck: Charles, 11; Martha, 16
PECK: Charles, 11; Charles D.,
  32; William, 16, 27
Pegg, 155
Peggy, 160, 192
Pegrain: Baker, 36; Ellen, 36;
  Jack, 36
Pegram: Celia, 77; Jack, 87;
  Jemina, 87; John, 87; Milly,
  87; Willis, 77
Pelina, 187
Penalton: Nicey, 32
Pend__: Maria, 24
PENN: Joe, 174
Pennick: Martha A., 114;
  Thomas, 114
Pepper: Eliza, 23

PEPPER: Jesse, 21; John, 13;
  William R., 28
PERCEL: Redman, 136
PERGUSON: Dan, 84
Perkins: Isaac, 86; Jackson, 86;
  James, 86; Susan, 86;
  William, 86
Perkinson: Anthony, 87;
  Benjamin, 84; Patience, 84;
  R., 87; Sallie, 84; Tena, 84;
  Thomas, 84
PERKINSON: Mrs. S., 47; R.,
  87; T.E., 107; Thomas, 56
Permelia, 6
Perry, 171; Eliza A., 22
PERSINGER: J., 171; Jacob,
  158, 176; James, 164; Jim,
  158; William, 158
Peter, 3, 17, 23, 147, 150, 152,
  154, 183, 185
PETERMAN: Jane, 16; John,
  25
Peters: ?, 121; Abbey, 43;
  Abram, 121; Adolphus, 121;
  Ann, 119; Ben, 43;
  Benjamin, 119; John, 121;
  Lucy, 43; Patrick, 121;
  Sallie, 121
PETERS: Dr., 67, 72, 74, 82,
  84, 90, 120, 121
PETERSON: Dr. Benjamin, 96
PETITT: C., 186
Pettis: Maria, 36
PETTIS: J.F., 36; John L., 36
PETTY: Fannie, 162; Smith,
  178
Peyton, 189
PEYTON: William, 174, 175,
  183; William M., 171;
  William W.T., 179
Phamy, 163

Pheasant: James, 65; John, 65; Lavinia, 65; Mary, 65; Robert D., 65; William c., 65
Phelps: Daniel, 179
PHELPS: Mary, 179
Phil, 185
Philice, 13
Philice A., 11
Phillips: ___, 9; Alice, 40; Caroline, 58; George, 183; James, 40, 58; Joseph, 40; Lewis, 23; Lurana, 26; Mahala, 40; Mary J., 40; Nannie, 40; Susan, 183
PHILLIPS: James, 58; Joseph, 40, 74, 88, 101, 102; Mrs. V., 108; R., 188; S., 166; Sam, 173
Phillis, 83
Phinneas, 183
Pickett: Agnes, 83; George, 83
PIERCE: Crockett, 2
Pierre, 20
PIERSON: James, 95
PIGG: James, 53
Pigot: Caroline, 40
Pincher: Byrd, 71; Ed, 71; Hannah, 71; Nannie, 71; Phil, 71; Wallace, 71
PINNACK: Frank, 109
PITTS: William, 147, 151
Pitzer: Frazer, 174
PITZER: B., 170, 176; J., 168, 174; M., 168, 172
Plate_: Anderson, 179
PLUME: George, 72; William, 68
Plummer: Lorinda, 150
Pocahontas, 7
Poindexter: Mary E., 167
POINDEXTER: C., 167; G., 36; George, 103; T., 41; Thomas, 107

Pollard: Curtis, 63; Lucy, 38, 63
POLLARD: T., 103; Thomas S., 63
Polly, 150
Pondexter: William, 10
PORTER: Betsey, 152; Daniel, 151; Elizabeth, 150; William, 67, 84, 150, 151
POTTER: Charles, 178
Powell: Catherine, 75; Isham, 75; James, 82; Jenny, 75; Mary, 82; Nancy, 75; Nelson, 75; Polly, 177; Terry, 46
POWELL: E., 164; Ed, 164; Thomas, 46, 82
Power: Rebecca, 187
POWERS: W., 169, 185
PREDUE: Mark, 179
Prentice, 179
Preston, 18, 83, 171; George, 180; Jane, 183; Jeremiah, 5; Lucy, 175; Martha, 185; Pleasant, 180; Thomas, 2
PRESTON: Anna, 2; Balard, 10; Ballard, 4, 13; F., 175; James, 4, 14; Robert, 4, 13; Sarah, 10; Sarah A., 9; Stephen, 179; Walter, 10, 21; William B., 14, 19, 159, 162, 171, 180
PRETTELL: William, 110
Price, 181; Emmanuel, 65; Hercules, 90; John, 65; Milly, 90; Nancy, 11; Sarah, 65; Susan, 65; Wyatt, 12
PRICE: C.A., 114; James, 64; John, 97; Nathan, 55; Pleasant, 11; R.W., 66, 77; William D., 56
Pride: Catherine, 119; Clem, 119; Dica, 101; Fanny, 119; James, 119; Joseph, 119; Mary E., 119; William, 101

Nelson, 89; Peyton, 64; Polly
S., 50; Rose, 47; Samuel, 50;
Susan, 89; Watt, 64; Watts,
64; William, 89
REDD: Albert, 64, 86; Ed, 50;
F.D., 50; Frank, 49, 87, 103,
125; George, 48, 112; Hiram,
50; J.T., 50; J.W., 51; John,
48; John W., 37, 51, 100,
112; Lee, 51; Louann, 49;
Miss C.H., 50; Mrs. F., 89;
Numan, 64; R. Lee, 100; T.,
50; Truman, 47, 49, 50, 51,
121
Redman: Lucy, 140
Reed: Adolphus, 58; Anne, 125;
Benjamin, 99; Clem, 84;
Elizabeth, 80; Ellen, 8, 80;
Emily, 58; Henry, 80; Isaac,
82; Isham, 99; Jack, 80;
James, 58; Jane, 58; Janius,
58; John, 125; Lancaster,
125; Lewis, 99; Louisa, 82,
84, 98; Lulu, 58; Meyers, 58;
Nancy, 80; Nelly, 180;
Nelson, 58; Nic, 99; Nick,
99; Patrick, 177; Paul, 98;
Peter, 58; Philip, 58; Rhoda,
125; Richard, 98; Samuel,
58; Sarah, 80; Stephen, 80;
Sukey, 99; Sydney, 58
REED: A., 162, 174, 185, 187;
Albert, 185; Betsey, 183;
Catharine, 169; Charles, 88;
Clem, 65, 68; D., 187; D.S.,
157, 159, 163, 170, 177, 178,
182, 183; David, 185; Lina,
95; Louisa, 96
Rees: Isaac, 14
Rennsalaes: Margaret, 37;
Nannie, 38; Rhoda, 63; Tom,
63; Van, 37, 63
Reuben, 10, 15, 24

Reynolds: Amanda, 13; Eliza,
182; Rachel, 175
REYNOLDS: Charles, 11;
William, 188
Rhoda, 5, 22, 179
Rhoda E., 4
RIBBLE: J., 158
Rice: Annie, 91; Betty, 59;
Edmund, 91; Elila, 53; Eliza,
36; Elizabeth, 91; Harriet, 85;
Jenny, 85; John, 59; Lucy
Jane, 53; Maguhate, 53;
Mary, 59; Mary E., 91;
Purdence, 59; Richmond, 91;
Simon, 16; Washington, 53;
William, 36; William J., 85
RICE: Ann, 113; Col. J., 33;
Ed, 71; Frank, 51; Jeff, 122;
John, 47; Mrs. J., 47; Mrs.
M., 53; Peter, 151; William,
63, 68, 101; William J., 36,
85; William L., 73; William
T., 59
Rich: Betsey, 151; Bundy, 148;
Griffin, 150; Henry, 148;
Judy, 138; Robert, 151;
Thomas, 156
Richard, 5, 6, 24, 25, 26, 146,
155, 174
Richard L., 173
Richards: Maria, 182
RICHARDS: Matt, 46
Richardson: Betty, 88; Emma,
88; H., 88; John, 187; Judy,
88; Katy, 110; Len, 110;
Louisa, 55; Maithat, 55;
Margaret, 55; Martha, 171;
Nancy, 55; Nannie, 88;
Norman, 55; Sallie, 55; Sam,
88; Samuel, 55; Thomas, 88
RICHARDSON: Capt. H., 117;
H., 44, 66, 79, 119; J., 167,
172, 176, 182

RICHIE: Watt, 107
Rideout: Docia, 71; Nathan, 71
Ridout: Charlotte, 188; Harry,
    182
RIGGEN: John J., 47
Rilla, 30
Ripper: Hannah, 8
RIPPLE: Henry, 16
Rittie, 187
Rob: Betsey, 136
Robert, 4, 5, 7, 8, 9, 14, 15, 22,
    32, 83, 145, 150, 156, 187,
    191
Robert D., 6, 155
Roberta, 156
Roberts: Granville, 186; Mary,
    29
ROBERTS: T.W., 84
Roberts Wiley: James, 107;
    Jane, 107
Robertson: Robert H., 12
Robinson, 171; Allen, 67; C.,
    33; Celia, 33, 67; Charles,
    138; Elizabeth, 31; Elvira,
    120; George, 153; H., 33;
    Joseph, 6; L., 33, 120; Lina,
    33; Mary, 138; Miles, 171;
    Nancy, 33; Obadiah, 149;
    Peter, 33, 120; Pleasant, 120;
    R., 33; Sukey, 33
ROBINSON: C., 107; Ed, 67;
    Florintine, 28, 31; William,
    162, 174
RODGAS: John, 103
RODGERS: B., 45; B.R., 122
Rogas: Mary P., 103
ROGERS: B.I., 88; B.J., 46;
    B.R., 89
Rojas: Cale__n, 103
Rola, 21
Rollins: Armsted, 26; Maria,
    28; Ruth, 29
RONALD: Charles, 18

Rooki_: Laura A., 175
RORER: F., 173, 186
RORER/ROVER, 28
Rosa, 168
Rosa Bella, 25
Rosa Ellen, 191
Rosabelle, 179
Rosanna, 18, 22
Rose, 21, 25, 188; Eliza, 26;
    Wyatt, 174
Rose Ann, 183
Rosella, 151, 169
Rosetta, 19, 186
Ross: David, 119; Eliza, 64;
    Emily, 20; George, 187;
    James, 57; Jeremy, 57; John,
    64; Letitia, 119; Margaret,
    119; Maria, 22; Mary, 64;
    Mary Ann, 119; Rosina, 57
ROSS: Ferdinand, 11
Rosser: Jinnie, 176
ROTTER: Charles, 164
ROWADDIN/KOWADDIN:
    J.A., 116
ROWER: Ferdinard, 10
Rowlett: Ann, 81; Catherine,
    82; Delia, 82; Easter, 89; Ed,
    81; Ella, 69; Ester, 42;
    Henry, 80; Jacob, 80; James,
    81; Jane, 80; Mary, 80;
    Nancy, 80, 82; Patty, 81;
    Richard, 82; Sarah, 80; Tara,
    80; Thornton, 69
ROWLETT: B., 99, 114; L., 89;
    Mary, 81; Mrs. P., 71;
    Patsey, 71; Thomas, 80, 82;
    Thomas O., 82; William B.,
    82
Roxanna, 191
Roy: Betsey, 150
Royal, 175
RUDD: Buck, 94
Ruffin, 151

236

Pattie, 59; Patty, 58; Polly,
171; Randal, 72; Richard, 78;
Robert, 58, 100; Sally, 67;
Spencer, 126; Susan, 64;
Sylvia, 42; Thomas, 67; Tim,
55; Violet A., 126; William,
51, 63, 114; Willie, 96
SCOTT: B.S., 98; Baker, 34,
117; Ben, 117; Beverly, 63,
71, 110, 116; Charles, 111;
Edmund, 70; Edward B., 71;
George, 43; George O., 113;
J.A., 72; James, 43; Jane,
125; John A., 90, 117; Mrs.
M.J., 64; Mrs. P. Ligan, 69;
R.W., 101; Rebecca, 156;
Richard, 42, 114; S.B., 42;
Sam B., 70, 81; Samuel, 124;
Samuel B., 89; T.E., 73;
W.F., 51, 123; William F., 52
Scruggs: H.C., 178
SEAY: Austin, 13
See: Martha, 123; Syrus, 123
Seely, 186
Sefted: Booker, 7
Selah, 191, 192
SELF: Moses, 136
Selina, 192
Sellers, 186
Sephas: Dicia, 13
Serena, 3
Sermon: George, 6
Sethe, 159
Shackleford: George, 153
SHACKLEFORD: Rohn, 153
SHACKLETON: H., 95;
Thomas, 81
Shadric, 147
SHANKLEY: Joseph K., 31
SHANKLIN: Joseph, 32
SHANKS: D., 159, 173; David,
21, 184
SHANNON: Thomas, 12, 20

Shavers: Rebeca, 14
Shaw: Patty, 39
SHAW: Martha A., 7; R.B.,
119; William, 39, 62
Shedrick, 184; David, 102;
Edward, 102; John Thomas,
102; Lucy, 102; S.E., 102;
Sarah E., 102; Thomas, 102;
William, 102
Sheffy: Lewis, 30
Sheler: Roxanna, 26
Shelton, 173, 181
SHELTON: R.R., 191
SHEPHERD: _., 56; S., 57, 110
Sheridan, 12
Sherman, 167; __ille, 4
SHERMAN: Julia Ann, 11;
Thomas, 147
Shideler: Andy, 81; Eliza, 81;
Mary, 81; Paschal, 81;
Tampa, 81
Shields: __milton, 29
SHIELDS: A., 33; Hamilton, 5;
James, 1
Shiptan, 6
SHIREY: Betsey, 186
Short: Albert, 95; Amelia, 95;
Amy F., 95; Anna, 95;
Edney, 95; James, 95; Mary,
95; Sally, 95; Sydney, 95;
William, 95
Shovey: Moses, 178
SHUFFLEBARGER: Jacob, 7
Sidney, 8, 23, 148
SIGMOND: Joseph, 1
Silas, 152, 177, 183
Silla, 183
Silva, 183
Silvestus, 4
Silvian, 18
Simmes: John H., 106; Martha,
106; Reuben, 106
Simmons: Frank, 167

STOKES: Betty, 82; Col. H., 87; Collins, 70; H., 36, 42, 77, 84, 90, 103; H.E., 77; Hamilton, 82; Hamlin, 81; Henry, 69, 77, 88, 125; Jarman, 81; R., 42, 50; Richard, 42, 46, 49, 88, 95, 125; Susan, 81, 82
Stone: Anderson, 15
STONE: James, 15, 21; Musgrove, 31; William, 18, 26, 31; William A., 6
STONER: John, 11
STOVER: J., 172; Joel, 172
Strang: Rob, 74; Sarah, 74
Stratton: __ny, 10; Ann, 172; Carter, 65; David, 65; Lucy, 65; Martha, 65; Mary, 65; Thomas, 65
Street: Daniel, 150; William D., 7
Stuart, 8; benjamin W., 1; Samuel, 25
SUBLETT: William, 25
SUBLICK: Edward B., 104
Suckey, 172
Sukey, 173
Summons: James, 11
Susan, 21, 23, 151, 152, 154, 165, 171, 181, 183, 187, 189, 192
Susana, 148
Susanna, 11
Susie, 177
Swater: Aaron, 73; Anne S., 73; Fanny, 73; Louisa, 73
SWEAT___: Sarah, 29
SWEET: Harry, 108
Sydney, 84
Sykes: Charles, 150
Symms: Elvira, 102; George, 102; Hannah, 102

T_vrine: Martha, 189
Talliaffero: Willie, 11
TALLIAFFERO: Sarah, 11
Tandy J., 27
Tanna, 151
Tap: Aggie, 48
Taswell, 179
TATLY: T.T., 77
Tayloe: Aaron, 183
TAYLOE: G.P., 163, 170, 173, 174; George, 171; George P., 163, 167, 171, 180; Henry, 139
Taylor, 17, 18, 27, 171, 177, 182, 185; Abednego, 168; Abraham, 164; Abram, 61; Amanda, 179; Andrew, 20; Betsey, 61; Bettie, 165; Caroline, 25; Charles, 17, 30, 96; Charlotta, 18; Charlotte, 12; Elizabeth, 10; Emma, 10; Ephraim, 61; Fannie, 149, 164; Frances, 30; Hannah, 20; Henry, 63; Josephine, 165; Judah, 154; Julia A., 61; Julia Ann, 164; Louisa, 164; Margaret, 61; Margaret J., 27; Marsella, 165; Martha, 83; Mary, 13, 96, 168; Mary E., 63; Nancy H., 63; Ned, 185; Parthenia, 96; Patsey, 96; Peggy, 172; Phillis, 184; Priscilla A., 17; Richard, 31, 96; Robert, 61, 63, 96; Robert W., 63; Sally, 168; Sampson, 83; Sarah, 168; Silas, 165; Susan, 96; Winnie, 63
TAYLOR: Creed, 7; H.P., 42, 112; Henry, 21, 146, 148, 150, 151, 153; Jordan, 164; Margaret, 6; Margaret B., 27; Mary, 7, 8, 16; William, 24,

241

31, 149, 150; William R., 121
Teale: Abraham, 187
Teressa G., 27
Terry: Nancy, 46
TERRY: Dr., 55; E., 174; William, 182
Thadeous, 17
Thaxton: Violet, 43; Wilson, 43
THAXTON: Dr., 65, 68, 97; Dr. W.H., 97; H., 43, 91; R., 159, 160; Rosa, 96
THEAD: Col. T.H., 112
Theodore, 66, 183
Thiers: Laura, 183
Thomas, 5, 15, 21, 146, 147, 148, 150, 153, 154, 168, 176, 191, 192; Catherine, 34; Edwin, 103; George, 146; Harriet, 88; Jenny, 35; John, 88; Julia, 34; Katy, 103; Martha, 35; Patty, 88; Reuben, 103; Robert, 35; Ruben, 35; Ruth, 88; Thomas G., 148; Wilson, 88
THOMAS: Charles, 21, 168; David, 20; E,, 188; E., 165, 166, 188; Giles, 4, 32; J.S., 166; James, 20, 21; Montgomery, 30; William, 9, 15
Thomas A., 3
Thomas R., 8
Thomas S., 28, 155
Thompson: Ann, 3; Becky, 149; Catherine, 124; Chaney, 2; Ella, 124; H.B., 57; Haney, 156; Isabella, 124; Jenny, 124; John, 124, 147; Joseph, 152; Lewis, 124; M.E., 57; Mary, 156; Milly, 179; Ned, 177; Page, 124; Rhoda, 12;

Robert, 20; Susan, 124; William, 145
THOMPSON: J.R., 73
Thornton, 186
THORNTON: Mr. P., 53; William, 53; William L., 96, 97
THRASHER: Susan, 179, 180
Thweatt: Ann, 109; Archy, 97; David, 97; Eda, 124; Ellen, 97; George, 97; Henry, 51, 109, 124; Lucy J., 109; Patsey, 109; Titus, 97
THWEATT: H., 37, 74, 79
Tibbs: Joshua, 107; Louisa, 107; Phulding, 107
Tilda, 191
Tilla, 173, 186
Tinsley: Mary, 8
TINSLEY: B., 167, 171, 175, 178, 184; B.T., 169; Benjamin, 28
Tobias, 9
TODD: J., 37
Toler: __anuel, 24
Tolivar: Peter, 177
Toliver: Judy, 172; Tom, 184
TOLIVER: John, 184
Tollowell: John, 11
Tolls: Oliver, 155
Tom, 171, 172
Top: Benjamin, 48; Jack, 48; Jackson, 48; Lucy, 48; Selpha, 48
Tosh: Lucy, 188
TOSH: T., 181; Thomas, 188
TOTTY: Mrs. __ny, 71
TREADWAY: Thomas, 64, 96, 112
Trent: Daman, 68; Easter, 68; Fanny, 60; James, 60; Julia, 68; Margaret, 68; Sally, 68

243

Waddell: James, 43; Maria, 43; Milly, 43
Waddy: Ellen, 151
Wade: ___, 32; America, 107; Andrew J., 51; Charles A., 105; Claiborne, 107; Daniel, 105; Hampton, 51; Joseph, 107; Louisa, 160; Phil, 160, 180; Relay, 107; Sarah, 51; Susan, 35, 105; Sydney, 107; William, 107
WADE: Charles, 57, 58, 87; David, 1, 9, 16; Hamilton, 5; Henry, 2; Henry C., 26; John, 9; John J., 1, 2, 6; Mary, 3, 5, 24, 25, 31; Millie, 5; Richard, 160; Susan, 1; Susanna, 2, 20; William, 2, 176; William A., 160, 180
Wadkins: Lewis, 146
WAGLE: Boston, 24
Wagner: Wesley, 8
Walker: Alfred, 2; Doctor, 127; Dr., 54; Elizah, 54; John, 54; Joseph, 69; Judy, 69; Lizzie, 38; Maria, 64; Marshal, 38, 64; Philip, 31; Sarah, 127; Stephen, 26; Tina, 54
WALKER: Dr., 139, 152; Thomas, 133
WALKINS/WATKINS: Frank, 69; Henry, 69
WALL: E.G., 120; Floyd, 12; Parris, 14
Walla, 7
Wallace, 189; Jane, 189
WALLACE: Joseph, 155
WALLHALL: Mary T., 17
WALLTHAN: Thomas, 2
WALLTHRAL: Thomas, 28
Walter, 5, 8, 145, 153, 185
Walter G., 168
WALTHAL: Joseph, 104

WALTHALL: James, 106
Walton: Henry C., 80; Jack, 102; Julia, 80; Leana, 80; Lucius, 80; M.A., 102; Martha, 80; Mary, 80; Mary E., 102; Nat, 80; Thomas, 80
WALTON: Frances, 159; Mrs., 82; William, 80, 126, 173
Wang__: Matilda, 6
WANHAM: B.J., 48; Mrs. M.A., 57
Ward: Cronelius, 146; Eliza, 120; James, 127; Joseph, 120; Josephine, 127; Julia, 150; Julia Ann, 127; M.E., 127; Mary, 120; Mary M., 120; Nathan, 120; Sarah, 127; William, 127; Willie Ann, 127
WARD: Baker, 120
WARDIN: William, 67
WARE: Edward, 149; William G., 155
Wares: Cresa, 155
WARHAM: Maj., 87
Warnack: Frances, 36
WARNACK: Archy, 36; John, 36; L.D., 36
Warner, 153
Warren, 152; Aleck, 71; Rachel, 71; Richard, 71
WARREN: H.E., 57, 65, 108
Warrick, 175; Eliza Ann, 21
WARRICK: George W., 189
WARSHAM: Branch, 111; Mrs. M., 119
Washington, 14, 32, 109, 148, 152, 185; And., 172; Carnie, 63; Cook, 115; Cyrus, 146; Daniel, 114; Eliza, 94; Elizabeth, 57; Gallon, 40; Gen, 94; George, 35, 40, 63, 87, 109, 115, 189; Georgiana,

244

115; Harriet, 159; Henry, 5,
115; J.B., 109; James, 87,
178; Jane, 31, 94, 109; Jeff,
94; Jim, 172; John, 57, 114;
John H., 159; Joseph, 109;
Lucy, 94; Lucy A., 63;
Margaret, 176; Martha, 94;
Mary, 114; Meschack, 57;
Nancy, 87, 115; Randall,
159, 176; Robert, 114; Sally,
114; Sally Ann, 35; Sarah,
115; Tamar, 115; William,
177; Zachariah, 114

Watkins: A., 170; Amy, 70;
Anderson, 77; Archer Scott,
70; Booker, 70; Calloway,
113; Clem, 37; Dan, 182;
Edmund, 79; Eura, 79;
Frances, 75; George, 79; H.,
75; Harriet, 82; Henry, 68,
82; Jackson, 77; Jane, 183;
Jane S., 113; Jenny, 79; John,
51, 72; Joseph, 117; Julia, 72;
Laurey, 37; Lina, 51; Louisa,
113; Lucy, 79; Martha, 72,
117; Mary, 70, 72; Matilda,
176; Nancy, 70; Patty, 68;
Peter, 51; Phillip, 173; Polly,
77; Rolla, 113; Sarah, 79;
Scott Archer, 70; Thomas,
37; William, 181

WATKINS: Dr. H., 51; F., 73,
103, 117; F.N., 36, 72, 87;
Frank, 69, 80; H., 49; H.E.,
56, 66, 77, 79, 85, 95, 97,
115; Lee, 117; Mr., 49; Mrs.
A., 47, 85, 87; R.H., 56; T.S.,
113; William, 110

Watson, 186; __lby, 48; Adam,
48; Africa, 123; Agnes, 99;
Albert, 123; Alex, 123;
Berry, 48; Betty, 48; Caesar,
97; Catherine, 86; Cordella,

124; Edward, 124; Elsey, 52;
Emma, 90; Fannie, 90;
George, 99; Hatty, 123; J.B.,
86; James, 52; Jennie Ann,
90; John A., 90; John M.,
123; Judah, 90; Julia, 123;
Laura, 86; Lesea, 47; Lythia
Jane, 2; Martha, 48; Mary,
123; Milly, 123; Nancy, 37,
172; Patrick, 124; Paul, 90;
Porter, 86; Robert, 17; Sally,
97; Sarah, 124; Sawney, 86;
Spencer, 47; Stokes, 90;
Timothy, 86; Whes_y, 123;
William, 124

WATSON: A., 48; Amelia, 37;
Daniel, 90; Egbert, 4, 8, 15;
James, 48; James A., 58;
John, 34; Joseph, 98, 99, 102;
Mrs., 49; Mrs. A., 48;
Parmela, 37; Samuel, 47, 48,
123, 124

Watts: Mary Jane, 2

WATTS: William, 161, 170,
171, 173, 175, 178, 181, 183,
184, 186

Weathers: Charlotte, 27

Weaver: Aaron, 105; Becky,
105; Francis, 105; Henry M.,
105; Julia A., 105; Maria,
105; Pat, 105

WEAVER: Tarn, 105; William,
60, 69, 78, 101, 105

Webb: Alexander, 138; Autrin,
138; Fannie, 138; Judy A.,
138; Ned, 138

WEBB: Jerry, 156

Webber: C., 118; Judy, 118

Webster: Ellen, 2; John, 184;
Maria, 179; Robert, 179;
Sarah, 30

WEED: Charles, 77

WELFORD: Carter, 149, 153, 155; Dr., 135, 145; Olmstead, 149

WELFRD: Carter, 152

WELLS: Joseph, 145

Wesley, 156, 167, 175, 180, 182; John, 49; Lucy Jane, 49

West: Betty, 116; Champion, 116; Hal, 116; Nat, 116; Sally, 116

WEST: Alex, 70; Alex B., 83; Ann, 65; J.W., 120; John W., 120

Wha___: ___, 16

Whales: J., 171

Wheeler: Austin, 153; Birdie, 91; Charles, 91; Daniel, 146; Julia, 155; Lydia, 91; Robert, 91

WHEELER: Mrs., 66; Sam, 61, 75, 94; Samuel, 91

Whiddon: Tom, 177

White: Betty, 123; Branch, 124; Daniel, 8; David, 123; Fanny, 164; Harriet, 164; Hopson, 61; Isaac, 61; Martha, 77; Milly, 124; Myra, 77; Omstead, 178; Robert, 61; Sam, 77; Sarah, 164; Susan, 61; William, 164

WHITE: A., 178, 181; Alex, 184; Archambald, 29; Archbald, 15; Isaac, 20; Lucy, 77; Nancy, 182

WHITEHEAD: James, 51, 53; Joseph, 98, 111, 124; Mrs. M., 78; W., 55

Whitlock: Monroe, 160; Randall, 160; Titus, 160

Whitting: Lewis, 12

WHITTING: William, 12

WHORLEY: F., 186

WHORTON: Gabel, 15

WICK: Joseph D., 69

Wilanna, 188

Wilbern: Robert, 7

Wilburn: William, 3

WILBURN: H., 64; Thomas, 114; William, 64, 79

Wiley: Betty, 107; Fernando, 107; Isabella, 107; James Robert, 41; Jane, 41; Mary C., 107; Sallie, 107; William, 41

WILEY: Robert, 180

Wilhelmina, 27

Wilkerson: John, 29

Wilkison: Martha, 178; Mary, 179

WILKS: Ben, 182

Willa, 26

William, 3, 4, 6, 7, 9, 11, 16, 17, 24, 26, 27, 29, 30, 32, 82, 83, 136, 148, 150, 152, 156, 167, 168, 169, 170, 173, 176, 178, 179, 181, 182, 183, 184, 185, 187, 189, 191

William A., 30, 155

William A.A., 154

William D., 27

William F., 188

William G., 5

William H., 15

William Henry, 149

William J., 1

William M., 10

William N., 19

William P., 7

William R., 9, 10

William S., 173

William W., 24, 31

Williams: Agnes, 67; Albert, 63; Almeta, 14; Almira, 125; Anderson, 46, 125; Archer, 188; Charles, 10, 125; Dan, 35; Daniel, 103; David, 11;

Dicey, 46; Easter, 150;
Educia, 125; Elijah, 148;
Ellen, 103; Emma, 149;
Frances, 26; George, 14;
Griffin, 46; H., 67; Harriet,
146; Isaac, 125; James E., 63;
Jinnie, 180; Joe, 182; John,
170; Joseph, 102; Judy, 170;
Julia, 63, 102, 125; Lee, 102;
Lucy, 103, 155; Mary, 125;
Mary J., 103; Moses, 125;
Nancy, 5; Nicholas, 125;
Peter, 18; Susan, 103; Taylor,
125; Washington, 125;
Winnie, 171
WILLIAMS: James, 39, 62;
James A., 172; Jeff, 75;
Joseph, 65, 75, 116, 118; R.,
111
Williamson: ?., 73; Agnes, 20;
Mary, 73; Susan, 15
Willie, 152
Willie Ann, 145
Willis, 49; Anne, 98; Betsy, 98;
Betty, 98; Celia, 98; Ellen,
98; George, 98; John, 151;
Littleton, 98; Louisa, 98;
Lucilla, 152; Mary, 184;
Milly, 98; Rebecca, 152;
Richard, 2; Sterling, 98
WILLIS: Christopher H., 26
WILMER: George, 9, 11
WILSEY: Martha, 96; Mrs. M.,
120; Mrs. W., 33
Wilson, 171; Benjamin, 31;
Cary, 165, 188; Clem, 43;
Eliza, 188; George, 192;
Mary E., 165; Osborn, 2
WILSON: Ann, 74; B.A., 56,
116; Ben, 38, 72, 93;
Benjamin, 38, 61; John R.,
69; Miles, 23; Miss F., 108;
Mrs. B., 61; Nat, 94, 124; S.,

61; Thomas, 2; W., 59;
Zediah, 14
Wimbush: Andrew, 174
Winfer: Nancy, 14
Winger: William, 176
WINGLE: Edward, 106
Winn: Rose S., 38; Sevian, 38
WINN: Edmund, 153; Priscilla,
19
Winnie, 169
WINSLEAD: Sarah, 134
Winston: Ann, 80; Benjamin,
80; Indiana, 64; John, 38, 64;
Robert, 64; Sarah, 38, 153
WINSTON: Ann, 80
WIRT: N., 170
Wise: Samuel, 42
Wiser: _enry, 24
Witt: Elvira, 102, 111; Peter,
102, 111
WITT: B., 92; Daniel, 61, 106;
E.B., 102; Ed, 45; Edward
B., 111
Womack: Barkas, 121; Jerry,
121; L., 121; Melinda, 91;
Polly, 91; Robert, 91; Violet,
91
WOMACK: A.W., 63; Archy,
53, 111; B.F., 54; D., 79;
D.F., 52, 54, 55; David, 63,
77, 126; E., 126; E.L., 52;
Egbert, 83; John, 86; Joseph,
108; L.D., 86; Mary C., 82;
Mrs. M.C., 71, 83; N., 93;
Polly, 97; T.F., 40; Thomas,
40, 84; Thomas F., 83;
William, 72, 77, 104, 113;
William A., 54; William D.,
123; William L., 111
Wood: Jeff, 66; Levi, 192;
Lucinda, 147; Nancy, 66;
William, 156

247

WOOD: B., 33; Baber, 33; Dr.
H., 115; Frank, 99; James,
192; Marg., 92; Mary, 73;
Miss C.A., 49; Thomas, 3;
Thomas D., 2; William, 175;
William T., 66
Wooden: Caroline, 174
WOODEN: William T., 21
WOODFIN: Mrs. A., 72
Woodfock: Sarah H., 8
WOODRUFF: P., 186; Wilson,
84
Woods: Burrill, 175; Isham, 66
WOODS: Arm, 175; Edmund,
56; J.O., 192; James D., 95;
Mrs. Charles, 67; Sam, 182;
William, 188
Woodson: Agnes, 94; Amanda,
94; Becky, 114; Betsey, 53;
Betsy, 48; Charles, 94, 114;
Daniel, 108; Fanny, 114;
Henry, 94; Isham, 48; James,
53; Loudon, 94; Louisa, 108;
Richard, 94; Sarah, 94;
Tampa, 114; Wilson, 108
WOODSON: Betty, 65; Mrs.
N., 77; Richard, 48, 49, 53;
William, 51, 175
WOOLDRIDGE: Abraham, 30
WOOLWINE: A.S., 2
Wootten: Armstead, 56; Caesar,
70; Calvin, 62; Camilla, 62;
Daniel, 81; Dennis, 58;
Doctor W., 35; Eda, 62;
Emily, 34; Emley, 81;
Fannie, 81; Harriet, 99;
Harry, 38; Isa, 99; Jack, 38,
81; James, 81; Jane, 99, 123;
John, 62; Josephus, 123;
Katy, 35; Martha, 62;
Matilda, 35, 81, 99; May, 62;
Mayat, 56; Millie, 81;
Nathan, 99; Nelly, 58;
Nelson, 62; Pathe, 56;
Richard, 123; Robert, 35;
Rose, 62; Sarah, 58; Spencer,
35; Susan, 56; Vina, 70;
William, 62
WOOTTEN: Dr. L.T., 56; F.J.,
122; F.T., 34, 35, 62, 103,
104, 105, 122; Frank, 62; H.,
34, 35, 38, 63, 70, 80, 81;
James, 44, 78; S.H., 95, 99;
Taylor, 56, 91; Thomas, 92;
W.F., 118; W.T., 58; William
L., 93; William T., 103
Worrell: Lewis, 168
WORSHAM: B.J., 77, 116;
E.L., 79; William, 100
Wright: Allen, 17; Anna, 139;
Benjamin, 139, 149;
Caroline, 17; Jacob, 152;
Jasper, 152; Louisa, 5;
Nathaniel, 17; Ordessa, 139;
Richard, 139; Sophy, 181;
Tom, 186
WRIGHT: F.B., 83; G.B., 79;
Theopolis, 136; Thomas,
139, 149; William A., 149;
William Alfred, 149
Wurts: Charles, 164; Frank,
164; Maria, 164
Wyatt: Peter, 178
WYATT: R., 54
WYGLE: John, 43
Wynn: Armstead, 100
Wynne: Maria, 100

Yearant: Fanny, 18
YEARBY: Oscar, 150
Yerby: Aaron, 169; Elijah, 155
YERBY: Albert, 154, 155
YORKER: William, 70
Young: Andrew, 19; William,
46

Heritage Books by the author:

Some Slaves of Fauquier County, Virginia
Volume I: Will Books 1–10, 1759–1829
Volume II: Will Books 11–20, 1829–1847
Volume III: Will Books 21–31, 1847–1869
Volume IV: Master Index, Will Books 1–31,
1759–1869

Some Slaves of Prince William County, Virginia,
Partial Will Books, 1734–1872

Some Slaves of Rappahannock County, Virginia,
Will Books A to D, 1833–1865 and
Old Rappahannock County, Virginia,
Will Books 1 and 2, 1664–1682

Some Slaves of Virginia, 1674–1894:
Lost Records Localities Digital Collection
of the Library of Virginia

Some Slaves of Virginia:
The Cohabitation Registers of 27 February 1866 from the
Lost Records Localities Digital Collection of the Library of Virginia

Volume I: Augusta County, Buckingham County, Caroline County,
Culpeper County, Floyd County

Volume II: Fluvanna County, Goochland County, Hanover County,
Henry County, Lunenburg County

Volume III: Montgomery County, Prince Edward County, Richmond
County, Roanoke County, Scott County

Volume IV: Smyth County, Surry County, Warren County, Washington
County, Westmoreland County, Wythe County

Volume V: Master Index

CPSIA information can be obtained
at www.ICGtesting.com
Printed in the USA
BVHW041253240222
630015BV00014B/119

9 780788 434082